A MANUAL
FOR
DISCIPLESHIP

# YOUTH AFLAME

## WINKIE PRATNEY

# BETHANY HOUSE PUBLISHERS
MINNEAPOLIS, MINNESOTA 55438
A Division of Bethany Fellowship, Inc.

*Youth Aflame*
Winkie Pratney
Revised Edition, 1983

Library of Congress Catalog Card Number 82-74507

ISBN 0-87123-659-1

Published by Bethany House Publishers
A Division of Bethany Fellowship, Inc.
6820 Auto Club Road, Minneapolis, Minnesota 55438

Printed in the United States of America

## THE AUTHOR

WINKIE PRATNEY, originally from New Zealand, now makes his home in Texas and is a recognized speaker and teacher on college campuses, youth retreats, rallies and Jesus festivals in the U.S. and abroad.

His other books published by Bethany House Publishers are *Doorways to Discipleship, A Handbook for Followers of Jesus,* and *The Nature and Character of God.*

*Truth is never original . . .*
it is *discovered*, not *invented.*


I did not "write" this book; I did not "invent" its ideas
and principles. My work has been that of a scientist,
collecting from and examining hundreds of sources for what
God REALLY said from His Word. I have read *books* and the
*Bible*; studied *messages* and *methods*, weighed *movements*
and *men*, searching for the meaning and principles of true
discipleship. It has taken seven years to compile, but
*centuries* to write. "*YOUTH AFLAME*" is really the product
of *many* great men of God who have prayed, studied,
worked and restudied to sift from Scripture the essentials of
practical Christianity.

I am greatly indebted to the writings of that grand old
giant of revival and evangelism whose works have perhaps
been more instrumental than any other in "reviving revival"
around the world — *Charles Grandison Finney*. Under his
ministry over 80 percent of his converts stayed true to God!
His understanding of soul-winning and Christian living were
truly taught of heaven, proved by a life and ministry in some
people's opinion without parallel since the days of the
apostles. *Finney* had a vital message often restated in this
manual which we shall do well to take heed of in these
terrible days of great backsliding and apostasy. Youth needs
to rediscover his message of God's moral government in the
age that could be stamped with irrationality, anarchy and
lawlessness.

Much blessing has been gained from modern-day saintly
thinkers of diverse backgrounds, like *A.W. Tozer, Watchman
Nee, C.S. Lewis* and *Francis Schaeffer*; from men like *George
Verwer*, whose passion for world evangelism has burned
through the world; *Bill Gothard*, whose counselling materials
in youth conflicts is without equal; from the sermons and
messages of a thousand forgotten saints whose names have
died to memory but whose truth from the living Word still
flames on. My thanks to the men of *Youth For Christ
International* for the privilege of studying under their youth
specialists; to *David* and *Don Wilkerson* for first-hand
experience in big-city gang problems; and for all who gave me
insight in sacrificial living for God in a century of careless
materialism. The crying need and urgency of the hour has

put this material into print without usual acknowledgements in most cases; let those who have in some way contributed to this book thank God for His revelation and join in prayer that these truths will be spread far and wide to the glory of Christ.

My gratitude to those who helped give me insight to areas that needed expansion in this final edition; those who made the *first* edition possible, like *Graham Braddock*, whose talented pen formed many of the illustrations, and *Paul Annan*; to *Faeona*, my wife and my *parents*, whose constructive criticism and care kept me on the job when the going was tough; to my *Nana and Pop* who helped put a dream into print; and to *Loren Cunningham*, my brother beloved, director of the fiery vision of *Youth With A Mission* for his inspiration, and his friends *Harry Conn* and *Gordon Olsen* who provided Scripture research and manuscript suggestions. A very *special* thanks also to the young people I know and love, whose sincerity was a challenge to give them something they could give back to God — a life on fire for His glory.

Lastly, but really first, to the *Lord Jesus* "by Whom the world is crucified unto me and I to the world" Who gave me back life from the power of the grave and Whose tender, careful hand I have felt on mine in penning this present for our Father. To His Name be all the glory.

*WPratney (Phil. 1:21)*

**WINKIE PRATNEY (1967)**
Manurewa, New Zealand

## THE CAUSE
### Why Is A Manual Like This Needed?

It is evident to the discerning Christian that undercurrents of deep uneasiness are washing beneath the waters of Christendom today. *Confusion, complacency* and *compromise* mark the average congregation. Evangelical churches are rocking from the challenges of *rationalism,* the *occult,* and the *mass media* that has suddenly exposed the young to a "global village" of other faiths. Never before has the Bride of Christ been faced with so much stress within and without.

It is with concern for an end-time work of God that this manual has been formulated. *Why* have we become so complacent? What fresh emphasis does the church need to prepare for the vast upheavals she is beginning to face?

Early believers looked with joy to the return of the Master. Today, we know the time is even more "close at hand." They used this truth to generate a converting compassion driving out to reach the lost masses. But we have often made it an excuse for complacency.

*Persecution* was the womb of the early church. Born in the power of the Holy Spirit and the challenge of secular religion co-operating with the political powers of the day, it thrived under bitter opposition. In an environment of tension and danger, the men God used to represent Christ to the world bore a faith that flamed. Stand beside them in the record, the Scriptures that set our pattern. They pray because they must. They give because they love. They speak, for they cannot be silent.

The dark angel of complacency has reaped a deadly harvest. *Spiritual desolation* has followed rampant materialism. We are open to the flood of the Enemy. And whenever the pleas of God for His church to return to their "first love" have been shrugged off or rejected, *judgment* has always struck. It has been so in history. It will be so again, unless we do something NOW.

What *are* the needs of this hour? Faced with the most momentous time in history, blood-bought believers must crystalize problems and provide an answer to this hour of

7

our greatest challenge. We need help that is Scriptural, adaptable, adequate and highly practical. Above all, we need it NOW.

We can learn much from what has gone before. Vital revivals have often come from a re-evaluation of the work and the Word of God. Scripture has the plan, the pattern and the program. Its application has often been scoffed at, criticised or violently opposed. But it has injected new life whenever dared into the veins of shrivelled, dying orthodoxy.

*YOUTH AFLAME* is written for a *future* need fast becoming *present*.

It is directed to half the world who are in search of a goal, a leader and a cause to give their lives to . . . the Youth of Century 21.

It is intended to provide answers for reaching the un-churched and untouched.

It is geared for the confused and the complacent.

It is given with the prayer that God will use it to grip young people with a cause and a vision that will drive them out to shake their world for the Lord Jesus Christ.

A vision of — *YOUTH AFLAME!*

## OPERATION Y.A.

*"YOUTH AFLAME"* has a *triple-pointed presentation* for maximum effect in its introduction into a group willing to become disciples.

It is —

1. *A New Testament MESSAGE* of all the basic practical principles and concepts of true discipleship that can be translated into a life philosophy for every Christian that will be grounded in God Himself.

2. *A New Testament METHOD* of introducing disciple-ship, based on the training pattern laid down in Scripture by

8

the Lord Jesus Himself in training and teaching His own disciples. Any leader planning to use this program may follow the seven phases of *"YOUTH AFLAME"* introducing new material in its chronological order for maximum effect in training youth.

3. *A New Testament STRATEGY* of teaching, that summarises the basic plans of instruction and communication the Master followed in implanting the concepts of discipleship in the lives of His followers.

Teach the *message* of *"YOUTH AFLAME"* in the phasing order of its *methodology* and use as a rule of guidance the *strategy* of teaching the program. Any group that has a willingness to learn and work for God will discover a new dimension in power and witness if they are willing to so use this manual. Each time a group reaches *Phase 7*, a *new* group for training can then be contacted, and a nucleus from those of the first young people share all they have learned under Christ, beginning another cycle of discipleship at *Phase 1*.

---

## PROGRAMME

---

**JUDE**
  Understanding and vision discovered by Philosophy of Discipleship

**JUDAS**
  Salvation discovered by Analysis of True Conversion

**BARTHOLOMEW**
  Heart Purity discovered by Consecration of Life

**MATTHEW**
  Humility and clear conscience discovered by Confession and Restitution

**JAMES (LESS)**
  Self-acceptance discovered by Philosophy of Body Ministry

**THOMAS**
  Faith discovered by Truth and study of Scripture

**JOHN**
Love Unity discovered by Forgiveness and Reproof

**PHILLIP**
Guidance discovered by Yielding of the Will

**SIMON ZEALOT**
Hunger for God discovered by Prayer and Fasting

**ANDREW**
Communication discovered by Methodology of Witness

**JAMES**
Stability and Faithfulness discovered by Identification with Christ

**PETER**
Power of the Holy Spirit discovered by Absolute Surrender

---

| PHASING |
|---------|

**PHASE 1**    The *CAUSE — A Cry from the heart*
(Matthew 3:2-3)
The *Dream Of Discipleship*
A World in Vision
DISCIPLE: *Jude*
DIRECTIONS: Meet potential disciples. Sow seeds of a vision. Plan together mass meetings; challenge to bring unsaved.

**PHASE 2**    The *CHALLENGE — A Call to the heart*
(Matthew 4:19)
The *Door to Discipleship*
Challenge to Live
DISCIPLE: *Judas*
DIRECTIONS: Mass meetings. One or a series of gospel outreaches geared for all-out evangelism. Challenge for salvation.

**PHASE 3**    The *COST — A Consecration To God*
(Matthew 10:34-39)
The *Test Of Discipleship*
Disciples In Clay

10

DISCIPLES: *Bartholomew, Matthew*
DIRECTIONS: Meet those deciding for discipleship. Present the steps of consecration and cost. Discover those who are sincere.

**PHASE 4**     The *CAPABILITY — A Cast For God* (Matthew) 5:1-7; 27; Luke 6:12-49)
The *Trial Of Discipleship*     Faith In Action
DISCIPLES: *James the Less, Thomas, John, Phillip*
DIRECTIONS: Study, informal group discussions. Present and practise basic principles of a disciple's life. Analyze situation, make practical application of concepts. Accent free discussion and question-answer sessions. Spend most time possible here.

**PHASE 5**     The *CHARGE — A Capacity for world burden* (Luke 8:1-5; 9:1-6) The *Tools of Discipleship* Building "Go" Into The Gospel
DISCIPLE: *Simon Zealot*
DIRECTIONS: Screen further those trained, selecting group sub-leaders by spending more time with them. Choose on the basis of good grasp of truth, willingness to learn, leadership ability and the direction of the Holy Spirit. Introduce anti-lethargy tools to group.

**PHASE 6**     The *CAMPAIGN — A Commission for world outreach* (Luke 10:1-20)
The *Demonstration Of Discipleship*
Into All The World
DISCIPLES: *Andrew, James Zebedee*
DIRECTIONS: Informal group study sessions; practical demonstration and application of witnessing concepts in area. Prepare for possible repercussion and opposition.

**PHASE 7**     The *COMMANDER — A Comforter for conquest* (Luke 24:46-49)     The *Director of Discipleship*
Enablement Of Witness     DISCIPLE: *Peter*
DIRECTIONS: Intensive prayer, challenge and seeking God for power to extend witness. After this, group divides to multiply, each member forming a nucleus for a new group, repeating Phase 1.

## STRATEGY

### TO REACH A WORLD

Here is a *PERSONAL STRATEGY* for selecting and training a team of disciples using the material and methods of this Manual. Based on the strategy of the Master General Himself, the Lord Jesus Christ, it is a chronological outline of the basic steps in imparting, reproducing and propagating true discipleship.

### 1. *SELECTION* —

Find from the group you have the ones who are honestly WILLING TO *LEARN*. This was the Lord's SINGLE CONDITION demanded of every young man He asked to follow Him — the willingness to "learn of Him" and change basic ways of living for the greater good of God and His Universe. Concentrate on the few who are truly interested; don't waste time on the "know-it-all" or stubbornly self-centred who are not willing to be followers of Jesus (Psalm 119:73; Matthew 11:29).

### 2. *SPEND TIME* —

Give *every moment* of your spare time to these "learners." There is always a cost in imparting a vision; a cost of TIME and much personal PRIVACY. You must be ready to make these sacrifices. Let them live with your life. Gain their confidence by being the kind of person they can confide in (John 1:38-39; Luke 4:42).

### 3. *SET APART* —

There should come a stage in your training where you give them a chance to be "set apart" for the task of world outreach. If God has given you the gift of spiritual leadership under Him, call your team beside you in a step of consecration to Him and the work of the Gospel. They must understand that it will cost them *everything*, perhaps even their lives to do the job (Mark 3:13-14; Mark 8:34-35).

### 4. *SHARE* —

Give to them everything you have BY EXPERIENCE.

12

It is not what you KNOW, but what you PERCEIVE that is important. Teach them the great Truths of Christ that will be their working ideology of discipleship. Make sure they have the basic *principles,* and the *application* will follow naturally. In teaching, use SIMPLICITY, constant REPETITION and LIFE-RELATED ILLUSTRATIONS (John 17:17,19).

5.   SHOW —

Teach by BEING. We learn best by being *shown* how to do it first, then copying the manner or methods. The leader has great responsibility to BE all that he wants to teach. Let those you would lead see you put into practice in your own life those principles you preach. Get them into the practical WITH theoretical (Mark 3:14).

6.   STIPULATE —

*Never* be vague. Outline in *detail* that which is to be done part by part, and assign specific tasks to each member of the team. Give each jobs that they are able to carry out with a maximum of trust in God's help. DELEGATE responsibility (Philippians 4:9).

7.   SUPERVISE —

Watch over your team while they work. Be always available for advice when it is needed. Determine before God to set a standard for righteousness and godliness in your own life that will be a constant challenge to those you seek to train. Your team will be a CARBON COPY of your *own* life. Keep very humble and very teachable yourself before the Lord Jesus. *Encourage* wherever possible; *rebuke* or warn if it becomes necessary, that there will not be looseness and an allowance of sin in your team spirit (Matthew 23:8,11-12; 2 Timothy 4:2; James 5:16).

---

## HOW TO USE THIS BOOK

---

"YOUTH AFLAME" is a *total training concept.* There are many ways to use this book. It may be adapted to a number of different usages, dependent on your need:

1.   AS A NEW CHRISTIAN: "YOUTH AFLAME" will be an invaluable guide to help you grow quickly in your

Christian life. Begin in *"JUDAS"* and read carefully through to the end of *Philip,* and you will learn the basic working principles of being a true child of God. Then, use the *"Symptom Index"* in the back to find particular problems in your life you need help with; look them up under the page "code numbers" listed, and simply do what the section asks you to do for total victory in that area. Take your Bible and *look up all the Scriptures* marked under any section you want to study more. This will help you get a quick understanding of the message of the Word of God.

2. *AS A MINISTER:* This manual will prove exceptionally valuable as a *study guide.* Use the *"Analysis Index"* at the back of *"YOUTH AFLAME"* in order to give you a rough guide to the problems your young people are facing. The index is listed with *two sets of symptoms* under each disciple title. The first lists *negative* signs, the second signs of *development* in that particular area. If you see a preponderance of signs in the first part, you know the problem areas will find answers in *that* part of the manual. If, on the other hand, your group or individual shows signs largely in the second part of that section, you know they have learned some lessons from God in that area. The index can be used as a good *counselling discernment guide* for locating problem areas. The Manual is basically geared to high school groups and up. Fill out areas with your own personal illustrations and studies from Scripture, using the sections as an outline.

3. *For CAMPS and CONFERENCES:* *"YOUTH AFLAME"* will be an invaluable guide for retreats and study camps. *Raise questions* around an area, then use the manual to find guidelines for defining a Christian approach to the problem. For youth camps in a "four-meeting" time-limit, the most valuable subjects will be those under *JUDAS* (salvation), *BARTHOLOMEW* (dating and sex), *JOHN* (bitterness) and *SIMON ZEALOT — PETER* (Christian living and God's power). For longer camps, add *ANDREW* and *PHILIP* to the list.

4. *TRAINING FOR CHRISTIAN REFORMATION:* Bible college, Christian liberal arts college and seminary students will find this manual a challenging and thought-provoking study as an attempt to provide a simple *unified field* of Christian knowledge. Many sections are deliberately limited in content to provoke thought and discussion. Pay particular

attention to *JUDE, JUDAS, PHILIP* and *SIMON ZEALOT;* the discussions grouped under *PETER* and *ANDREW* will also be fresh and stimulate renewed studies in these vital areas. This book is geared to *spiritual revolution,* and requires the vision of young thinkers to devise means of application and training.

---

### FORWARD AND ONWARD!

---

"A program to develop the new Christian is one of the greatest need of the 20th-Century church."

*You hold in your hands such a program.*

*This Manual was born in need.* Everywhere, young people, pastors, evangelists, youth and personal workers are asking "Why can't somebody produce an effective follow-up for training young converts in the major basics of faith?"

I have felt heartbreak in leaving crusades in which scores of sincere young people have given their lives to God; because, from experience, in just a few months many would "fall away". Can we always blame the messenger or his message? Too often the fault was in *LACK OF TRAINING* afterwards. When we try to evangelize, we will reproduce what we already have. Vicious cycles of half-hearted Christians could be arrested by the injection of small groups of victorious young people into each one. We often forget that the Lord Jesus called most of His disciples with just a simple — "Follow Me" — but spent over THREE YEARS afterwards in training them.

*We must emphasise discipleship* — and that demands *thorough* training! Most of our follow-up systems are painfully limited to "tips" on prayer, Bible study and witness; essential, but usually not comprehensive enough to meet life's demands. Any total training concept must be a *synthesis of THREE programs:* (1) A clear, simple *Bible study course* designed to introduce new converts into the basics of the Christian's life; (2) A *spiritual "check-up" manual,* or Christian "first-aid" primer giving Bible prescriptions for spiritual problems; (3) A set of *counselling principles* for both recognizing and dealing with others who come to us for guidance and counsel.

"YOUTH AFLAME" is such a synthesis. I have searched the pages of Scripture and sifted the minds and ministries of some of God's choicest servants, looking for the lowest common denominators of discipleship. "YOUTH AFLAME" is the result of prayer, trial, tears and the guidance of the Holy Spirit of God. Wherever possible, denominational issues and controversies have been avoided; a core is left which almost all of God's children will agree is necessary for spiritual survival and aggressive Christianity. "YOUTH AFLAME" will be useful to all but the stubborn Pharisee, and he who has already solved all his problems in working with young people. Should you differ with any of this material, let there be honest searchings of heart and much grace, that together we may "prove all things" and "hold fast to that which is good". Many of these concepts are God's spiritual secrets, underlying most of His mighty works in history. If you treat this book like a cafeteria, taking what you want and leaving the rest, the very material you *omit* may be the vitamins you most *need*. Dare to try out all *concepts as a whole*.

Many revivals of God's work have resulted from a return to simple New Testament principles outlined here. Read this book RIGHT THROUGH and examine "whether these things be so" under the light of Holy Scripture. You may need to ask yourself some of these questions: (1) Is the method of concept I am using NOW bringing *results* that are glorifying the Lord Jesus Christ? (2) Is this material the result of theory, tradition and guesswork, or is it scriptural, reasonable and eminently practical? (3) Have others used this with the evident blessing of God? (4) Am I WILLING TO TRY IT?

"Read and read again . . . for a little from *God* is better than a great deal from man; what is from man is uncertain, lost and tumbled over and over; but what is from God is as fixed as a nail in a sure place."

— John Bunyan

## A CHALLENGE TO COMMITMENT

*"Is there not a cause?"*

Some 3,000 years ago, a young man asked that question. It is significant for this age that it was both a *YOUNG man* and that he had good reason for asking questions about causes.

*It seems God has a special interest in youth.* Why? Young people have imagination. Youth can capture a vision quickly. And young people dare to believe when they are faced with the impossible. David, Joshua, John and Mary were all youth linked with Omnipotence.

*Exploding population* has thrust young people into importance as never before. Over half the world is young. They are looking for something to believe in, something to live for — something, if need be, to die for. And if Christianity cannot come up with an answer, masses of young people now training to conquer their world WILL.

Our restless, searching world needs *answers* — *real* answers. This bewildered century has deep needs. No longer will blind tradition and form satisfy our incisively questioning generation. The Gospel of the Lord Jesus Christ DOES meet the total man, or it is just another dead religion doomed to be a relic in a scientific age.

*God made a promise to young people.** That promise WILL be fulfilled! As always, it is conditioned. That condition is AVAILABILITY. Call it dedication, total surrender, commitment — what you will; if you are willing, the promise is to you.

*Your life MUST be God-centered.* Thousands of religious young people are discontented with the mediocrity of "existing" their lives. Many young people have already decided to desert what seems to be a sinking ship, unwilling to plow through dead tradition to search for truth. To these, we must bid a sad, but decisive — goodbye. There is no longer room for compromisers or the careless; only a crash program born in the vision and heart of youth sold out to God can reach the masses of unevangelized teenagers and twenties that are today's young world.

This manual is written to *YOU*. It is time we got very real with ourselves and God. Either He does love this world and wants to reach it through YOUR life, or the Gospel is a great lie. Christ either MEANT what He said, or Christianity is a lovely, but impractical dream.

*Much of what you have in your hands may seem radical.* In an age of tradition it may appear so to some. But it is NOT *new.* Much of this has been laid out in method or principle in Scripture before. Only now has it begun to show significance as we have tried all other doors and found they led to disillusion.

So — take this book. Read it. Apply it. *LIVE IT OUT!* The WORLD is in your hands. You may be God's hinge to help turn history (*Joel 2:28).

"Who knowest whether *thou* art come into the Kingdom for such a time as this?"

YOUNG PERSON — *I DARE YOU!*

"The harvest truly is great, but the laboure are few; pray ye therefore the Lord of the Harvest that He would send forth labourers into His vineyard." (Luke 10:2).

# JUDE

## (WHO HAD MANY FACES)

"Jesus knew from the beginning who they were that believed not . . ."

John 6:64

What kind of
disciple are
you?

PHASE: 1 .. *A World In Vision*
SECTION: 1 .. *"D" For Dedication In Relation*
MATERIAL: .. *Discipleship As A Philosophy*

## WELCOME TO THE WORLD OF DISCIPLESHIP!

*You are invited* on a voyage of discovery. You will briefly meet the Twelve in the pages of this book. Each has a message to give you. Perhaps, in these men you will even find YOURSELF — and God's call to life's greatest adventure in Him! Whatever your *real* name is, we will call you *JUDE*. He was a mystery disciple; an unknown person. Possibly you feel the same. What interests us most right now is that he had *more than one name*. Each can give you a key to a disciple's life.

*THADDEUS* was one name. This is not common. You don't meet many *Thaddeuses* around. But *you too*, are uncommon! No matter how little talent or ability you have, you are UNIQUE in God's world. No one else can quite take your place to fill your job in His Kingdom. As little as we do know about *Thaddeus* we are sure of this — JESUS CALLED HIM. To *hear* that call you must be *listening*. You must *obey* it. And you must be willing to *forsake all* and *follow*. Are you in *THADDEUS'* category?

Another name was *LEBBAEUS*. This interesting name means — *"man of the heart."* God is most interested in the supreme center of *your* love. Are you really intent on following Jesus? Then you must fall in love with a Voice and Vision that will carry you along a path of loneliness, of longing, perhaps even death — but a path of gladness. Only the *love of Christ* can reach this rebel world far from God. Do you want the right kind of "heart" for this path? Will you spend TIME? Are you a *Lebbaeus*?

Perhaps you are a *JUDE*. He was chosen for a chapter in God's Book. *Jude* has some talent and an earnest concern for his world. But above all, he was a *servant*. All that *Jude* had and was, he surrendered to the control and direction of Jesus. He gave God his head, his heart and his hands. He lived to please *God first*. I hope you are a *Jude*. If you want

22

to make it in the adventure of discipleship, you will have to *swallow pride* and *renounce all rights* to your own life. You must be willing to be counted an *outcast* in a God-rejecting world. You must be ready to go any place or do anything He asks. It is possibly hardest of all to be a *Jude. Will you?*

How would you define discipleship?

*The last name* is a *warning* to all of us. Our mystery disciple's fourth name was *JUDAS.* We cannot help but be reminded of *Iscariot.* We will say more about him. But we cannot pass this name without looking into our *own* hearts. "Am *I* a *Judas?* Would *I* sell out Christ for power, pleasure, fame or fortune? Is there a thirty, dirty pieces of silver in my life?" (Some have sold out Jesus for less than that!) Our *Judas did* run away when *Iscariot* brought the soldiers to arrest Jesus. But he *came* back to faith, and was honored with the last church letter before John closed the Scriptures. The *other Judas* — the one that could lurk in each of our lives — died a *traitor,* a rotten body swinging in the wind. His money bought only a *graveyard;* his "fame,"the stigma of history's most terrible betrayal.

You are — *DUST* or *DESTINY!*

Sell your birthright to the world, the flesh and the Devil and your future will be dust. But find the place *God* wants you to discover and a door will open to you — your DOORWAY OF DESTINY!

---

## PHILOSOPHIES AFLOOD

---

An IDEA is a SPARK — *a spark that can fire a world.* "As a man thinketh in his heart — so IS he" (Proverbs 23:7). The way you think is the way you will live. We LIVE what we really BELIEVE. There are many philosophies, or ordered ideas for living, in our world. Most have some good points that capture young people's interests. All but ONE have serious weaknesses and dangerous consequences when a life is based on them. "Beware in case any man trick you through philosophy and empty deception, according to the basic principles of the WORLD and not after CHRIST" Paul warned (Colossians 2:8). How much of the world's ideas run your life? It has SIX basic ones:

23

## [1]  FORMALISM

### FAITH IN TRADITION

This is the beginning of the Big Lie, the Satanic start of decay in religious thinking. A Formalist is a person NOT WILLING TO CHANGE the way he does things because it has "always been done this way." He pays too much attention to the past for living now. Men may be commended for trying to keep great memories alive. We can and MUST learn from the past or we repeat its mistakes. But in a world of constant change, the method of yesterday may not work today.

Formalism *denies God's right to change patterns.* The *Pharisees* were the Formalists of Israel in Jesus' day. They clung stubbornly to a false idea of God's love-law, until their traditions actually broke the very commandments they boasted about protecting! Their own rules built on God's simple laws became more and more complex and foolish. Although many Pharisees in Jesus' day *seemed* outwardly moral and upright, Jesus rebuked them very strongly. He called them "whitewashed tombs, broods of snakes, and children of Hell!"

Formalism breeds the most dangerous kinds of religious selfishness disguised as righteousness. Jesus saw through the Pharisee format fronts. He would not behave according to their invented moral standards, but lived by the searching law of Heaven. He exposed them for what they really were! The Pharisees did not truly love *God.* Their "god" had become their own ideas and theories. They had actually broken His first commandment with a maze of their own rules.

Formalism can also involve *RITUAL* — praising or worshipping some earthly thing or being other than God. From jewelled crosses to a crown on a person put on a pedestal, ritual squeezes out true worship. Objects made to AID worship can themselves become worshipped. People all

24

over the world pay tragic homage to wood, stone and metal, hoping these things have special power to meet their needs. The invented multi-headed gods of ancient *Egypt,* the gilded statues in *Rome,* icons in *Athens* and images in *India,* the all-too-human gods of Greek and Roman times, *all* break God's *first* law. His *second* commandment also says "You shall NOT make for Me any graven image" (Deut. 5:8-10). God is too big to put into a picture, too infinite to represent by statues. Nothing in the created Universe could describe or contain Him. *Any* representation is a *mis*-representation. "God is Spirit," the Lord Jesus said, "and they that worship Him must worship Him in Spirit and in truth . . . Blessed are they who have not seen, yet have believed" (John 4:23-24; 20:29; Hebrews 11:1; Exodus 20:4; John 1:18; Colossians 1:15; 1 Timothy 1:17; 6:16).

Why does God prohibit the creation of images in worship of Him?

*People used or blessed of God* can invite the dangers of Formalism. *No* saint, holy person or even angel is to be given the glory that belongs only to God (1 Peter 1:24). It is thus sin against God to "hero-worship" someone He is using. We can pray for them, work and rejoice with them. But if we copy their *mannerisms* instead of their *Master,* we hurt God and often embarrass His servants. Now do not be afraid to *learn* from other men or women of God by studying their ways to solve problems (1 Corinthians 11:1). Remember though, no one in recorded history began a new move of God by pretending to be someone else.

How *grieved* God is when men or women forget Him in their devotion to His friends. God is *jealous* for our loving worship; He will share His glory with no man. Why should we use earthly objects to steal from God what is His alone? (Exodus 34:13-15; Deuteronomy 4:23-24; 5:8-9; 6:15; Isaiah 42:8; John 8:50; Acts 12:23; 1 Corinthians 10:31; Revelation 4:11; 19:10; Acts 17:24-25).

God's MESSAGE must never be changed; it is true and *always* speaks to man. If we are unwilling to change our METHODS or PATTERN, however, we fall into Formalism. We Christians must also give strict attention to our changing cultures, languages and issues, so our preaching of the Gospel will always be framed in fresh ways and understandable terms. We must move with the moving "pillar of fire!" (Exodus 13:21). Men of God like Wesley, Luther, Booth, Finney, and Moody all broke dusty church-ruts and changed

25

Thought:
How foolish
to place
one's hopes
and dreams
upon those
things which
will ultimately
rust, die, and
fade away.

their world; never take *your* patterns from methods that make no mark on history or society. Keep simple and uncluttered.

## [2] MATERIALISM

### FAITH IN THINGS

When people get settled and comfortable, they tend to pay less attention to their *Maker* and more attention to the *things He made.* Even useful or  needed things can take the first place in time and affections that rightfully belong to the Lord. Jesus knew the danger we call Materialism, for His land had many Materialists. When He multiplied by a miracle the loaves and fishes to feed a hungry crowd, people tried by force to make Him their "King of Things" (John 6:13-15).

They wanted a God or leader who would give them anything they liked. They thought that having whatever they wanted would make them happy. But Jesus knew this was not true. Fame or possessions can never in themselves bring happiness. True treasure cannot be bought with gold; the riches that last are the peace, love and joyful faith in Jesus.

"Don't set your love on things below" Jesus told us (John 6:25-36). "Don't hoard up on earth that which can be eaten by insects, corroded by rust or stolen by a thief. Don't worry over what you are going to eat or drink, or what kind of clothes to wear. All those not knowing the care and concern of your Father are like that." The way to happiness and provision is to "seek first God's rule in our life" — His Lordship, guidance and love (Matthew 6:33).

Materialism makes *CREATION,* not the *Creator* the object of devotion. The man who would be Christ's disciple must hold *lightly* to the world and *tightly* to God (Luke 14:33; Colossians 3:2). A disciple of the Lord Jesus is no longer his own. He is "bought with a price" (1 Corinthians 6:19-20).

He does not belong to himself any more. He is a love-slave of the Lord Jesus and a slave has no personal property or rights of his own. If you will OWN Christ, all you own IS Christ's! If your affections drift from *God Himself* to center on some "thing" He gave you to enjoy, He may have to take it away or make you sick of it.

What is the inevitable end of a hedonistic life-style?

"Things" can hurt when they tug for the attention that belongs to God! We can't break free from these feelings unless we are willing to wholly give all we have to Christ. Are you ready to see ALL you have taken away, lost and gone forever from your life and love? This is not easy, but it is a first condition for true discipleship. God does not want any "thing" but YOUR LOVE FOR IT. Materialism cannot live hand in hand with true discipleship (Matthew 13:44-46; Mark 10:28-30).

*Hedonism*, as popularized by Hefner's "Playboy Philosophy," fits in here. The strange thing is that if we seek pleasure *for pleasure's sake*, we will never find it. It is like the proverbial end of the rainbow. The man who tries to *save* his life by living totally to serve himself actually LOSES it because he becomes a slave to his lusts, and pays the penalty of sin (Luke 9:24; 1 Timothy 5:6; Romans 6:16). The *foundation of moral freedom* is self-*love* in the context of self-*denial*; this is *not* a paradox. *Self-love* simply means unselfishly choosing your own highest good; *self-denial* is the willingness to subordinate personal desires to the revealed will of God, whether that implies sacrifice or not. A *by-product* of a holy life is happiness. Man was never meant to live on the level of an animal (Luke 14:26-35; 18:29-30; John 10:10; Ephesians 3:14-21; 2 Corinthians 9:8; 1 Peter 2:11; 4:2).

---

### [3] HUMANISM

---

## FAITH IN MAN

It is good to "believe in man" *if* we mean by this that there is POTENTIAL in people (under God's care) for kindness, good deeds, creativity and obedience. Scripture says man IS wonderful, because he was made in finite, miniature likeness to God Himself. This makes us very *special*; we are very important to Him. The Bible teaches that despite mankind's fall into sin "we being evil, know how to give good gifts to our children" (Luke 11:13). Even wrong cannot wholly destroy our inbuilt admiration of real goodness and purity. We were *made* to live justly and respect right. A man can even live wickedly while looking wistfully at goodness (Romans 7:15-16). No one chooses to be miserable or evil for *its own sake*. This is a first truth of human nature; people were made to dread misery and desire the happiness which God planned as the natural result of holy living.

Humanism's fatal mistake is to confuse *CAPACITY* with *CHOICE*. A man *can* know right and how to do it. From the dawn of moral awakening, however, the whole record of  Scripture and history is that we *chose instead* to do WRONG. Even the seemingly "good" actions of unchanged men and women are done from secret selfishness (like *hope* of self-gain or *fear* of punishment and disapproval). "Too much good in even the worst of us" is not what the Bible says — "All have sinned and come short of the glory of God . . . there is NONE that does good, no, not one" (Romans 3:23,10; 7:18). Sinful people cannot please God with their excuses for rebellion in "good deeds" (Isaiah 64:6; Matthew 7:21-23; Galatians 2:16; 1 Corinthians 13:3).

*A Humanist's answer is not real.* It does not account for the disgusting dictatorship of sin in the human heart. Good FUTURE deeds (even *if* made from the right motives) cannot cancel out bad ones. If wrong has been done, the penalty of God's broken law must be passed. God must be strictly fair. His justice cannot simply excuse, for instance, a murderer on his promise of future behavior. Now *selfishness unchecked would murder* God's Universe. Besides this, ALL sin is a unit; one sin is *just as bad* as another, because at root, *both* are selfish choices to disobey God. Since all sin hurts God and breaks His law, all sin has the *same penalty*. In God's government, the very least punishment He can give is to cut off the sinner from being with people who *do* love God and obey Him. (A sinner would *spoil* Heaven and make it like

Hell.) The Bible calls this penalty DEATH. God does not *want* man to die. Our first parents were told that to foolishly break God's commands would bring this death. They understood, but *still* disobeyed! Sadly enough, each of us follow their influence from the first moment we knew right from wrong. All our world is truly guilty before its grieved Creator (Psalm 14:1-3; Romans 3:9-28).

What is the source of modernism?

*Humanists* try to deny or ignore sin. To justify themselves they may do many "good works." These may *seem* acceptable in the sight of *men*, but God searches the heart and sees our *real* motives. All of our works will be exposed by the light of Heaven. We all know deep inside that "it is appointed unto man once to die, and after death the judgment" (Hebrews 9:27; Acts 17:31). *Psychiatry* can at best EXPOSE the CAUSE of our guilt, leaving *psychology* to make an attempt to help us *live* with it. But none of our studies can REMOVE it. Only the Law-Giver Himself can pardon; only the blood of Christ shed "for the forgiveness of many" can rescue us through God's conditions of our repentance and trust.

---

## [4] MODERNISM

---

### FAITH IN MEN

Modernism grows out of *religious humanism.* A Modernist lives by his feelings like other selfish people, but the desires that seem to move him *most* are the needs of the sick, uneducated, poor and hungry. And who is *not* touched by human need? How *noble* such efforts seem, even when a man merely uses human plight to gratify his selfishness or appease his conscience. What a tragedy that such deeds of giving can be used as *excuses* for not doing the *first* thing God asks of a man; *surrender to Christ.* Although Modernism has 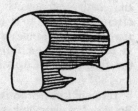 attempted many needed relief and social programs that have been of help to the world, it has helped keep alive a terrible lie, that man can make it on his own.

29

What is the
difference
between true
Christian
social
concern and
humanistic
social
endeavor?

There are *serious flaws* in the good deeds philosophy, besides those mentioned under Humanism. Jesus taught a life of good works not FOR salvation, but *as a natural result* of His own inner *transformation* of our hearts. True Christians do good flowing from the love that is a consecration to the highest good of God and His Universe, in glad service for their Heavenly Father (John 9:4-5). Jesus too, was moved with compassion by human need. But He did *not* come merely to start relief programs. He had the ability to supply food for others. He fed multitudes, BUT always did these miracles within a limit of spiritual response. He wanted to meet the needs of the whole man. In fact, He distrusted those who followed Him for the supply of physical need alone (John 6:26).

The Gospel has built-in power to change society. Society is simply a lot of separate people living together and *no one* can change people like *God*. To alter the living conditions of people is really only a side-issue. The Bible shows us that *changing* conditions alone will not necessarily change the ultimate *choice* of a man or woman's heart. Environment only *influences* our decisions, never *creates* them. We are much more than our food, houses and books. Giving selfish people better homes or nicer food will not transform their natures; they will simply be more refined sinners. If we center our hearts on God, our life will change deeply enough to affect both our living conditions and our world, but simply moving a man's *home* will not move his *heart*.

Can you see that the most *sacrificial* giving is useless for impressing God if done for anything less than His ultimate glory (1 Corinthians 13:3). Involvement in "good works" without showing the fruit of the Spirit (Galatians 5:22-23) is nearly always some kind of attempt to hide from truth and justify sin against God. *Good will* and *popularity* are often important to a Modernist. Much is sacrificed on the altar of peaceful relations with all men. He will usually go out of his way to compromise rather than offend the world by the absolutes of Christian commitment.

Jesus did *not* promise His followers popularity, but *LIFE*. We need to remember that "friendship with the world is enmity with God" (James 4:4; John 15:18-19; 1 John 2:15). Men who *conform* to the world will not *change* it. Early Christians were often hated, despised, and persecuted.

Some were even murdered, but the Gospel spread; "the blood of martyrs is the seed of the church." Ten of the twelve disciples died violently for their Lord. Jesus Himself said, "The world will *hate* you because *I* am not of the world."

In Modernism, *miracles* also are suspect if not "impossible." Forced to deny plain words in the Scriptures that expose and condemn all natural man's selfish actions, the Modernist has to question ALL Scripture that does not agree with his life. The God's Divine Directory becomes a book "written by man" full of "Mistakes." Its plain demands become "Misinterpretations." Modernism joins Satan by asking "Hath God said?" when He very plainly HAS said! (Genesis 3:1). This philosophy tries to take the *supernatural* from *Scripture* and *society*, undermining faith in God and His Word. Here, the Bible is not our absolute guide for life under the light of God's Holy Spirit. A Modernist *rethinks* truth in a way that clouds Christ's clear commands. He makes *darkened reason*, not intelligent trust in the Word of a wise and holy God, his rule. *Subtle changes* in understanding of truth, *double-thinking*, and *silence* on issues that clarify *sin* are all marks of Modernism.

Take for instance, the philosophy of *situation ethics*, an outgrowth of Modernism. Here situations are created that apparently *defy solution* within the direction of *Bible* laws. Fletcher and his followers suggest *rejecting* the laws of God whenever the situation seems to warrant it, replacing them with "love," which means *whatever you want it to mean* in the situation. In almost every case the laws of God are either *falsely defined*, totally *misinterpreted* or *misunderstood* in their content, spirit and application. And in *each* case, God is patently *left out* of the whole show! No one apparently thinks that He can step in and work a *miracle*, like delivering someone or changing around an authority's mind. Situational ethics completely fails to take the direct intervention of God into account because the Modernist does not think He *can* and *will* step in to answer the prayer of faith as He has before (2 Chronicles 32:1-22; Psalm 20:6-7; 18:2-19; 34:4-10; Daniel 3; 6:1-23; Luke 4:29-30).

We cannot just TEACH man to be good. Today's highly educated generation are only smarter sinners. The city killer is no less evil than the jungle head-hunter. Both have selfish hearts, expressed in more or less educated ways. Our

31

conscience needs to be cleared and reawakened; we need forgiveness and cleansing from our past; we need a force inside of us to guard our minds as a *block* to future wrong. We need power to live *above ourselves* and not be a slave to selfishness. God, by the Holy Spirit, can do this. He can point out what man without God cannot see — the "exceeding sinfulness of sin" (Romans 7:13). A pig in a sty cannot tell men what a "clean" home is like. It has a wrong idea of "clean" in the mud. Only God can show us our wrong *and* conquer it. He wins our rebel hearts by His great love then takes up His own home in our lives by His Holy Spirit (Revelation 3:20; Ephesians 3:17).

---

## [5] RATIONALISM

---

### FAITH IN MIND

After denying God's Word and God's rights, it is only a simple step to give up all pretence of religion and deny *God Himself.* Rationalism leaves out God altogether and starts just with *man.* It is a philosophy that tries to find an explanation of man and the Universe without God. A Rationalist prides himself on being a thinker; in trying to deny God, he will usually end up being as foolish in his *conclusions* as he has been in his *premises.*

God made our world and our lives to blend perfectly *only in Him.* A man who turns his back on God has a hard job explaining life! The very *Universe* speaks of God; our own *beings* tell us that we are personal, and ultimately that *we* must have come from Another Person. A Rationalist has big questions to answer; *who* or what is *Man;* how did we get here; why is the Universe the way it is? It is interesting to see the strange answers some people come up with when they do not want to believe God. It takes much more faith to be an *atheist* than a Christian! God has placed *so many signs* of His reality around us that it becomes very hard to keep Him out of our lives. The Rationalist has the worst time of all. He not only has to find non-Christian answers to his questions; he also has to try to live in his answers — *if* he can. And just *nobody* has ever successfully and happily done it.

If God did not make the Rationalist and his world, who or what *did?* Now he cannot say "God" because he wants to be an atheist. He is scared to bring in any kind of person because he knows this will be really admitting there is a God, though he is using some other word. Many Rationalists call instead on their limited knowledge of Science. Very popular is the idea that *time, matter* and *chance* all somehow gave us our complex Universe and life itself. But — time and chance are *not* personal. This leaves him with a frightening result; then *man* is not really a person! Questions like "What am I here for?", "What does life mean?", "Why am I alive?" have *awful* answers — "For no reason at all." "Life means absolutely nothing." "We are here without meaning." "The world and all creatures in it are one giant accident."

What are the consequences of pride in the life of a rationalist?

Besides this, he will have to do a lot of juggling *facts.* Honest scientific study tends to strongly *confirm,* rather than deny, intelligent Creation. One of the biggest problems the Rationalist will lose sleep over is this; how could a world as *big* as ours form life by *accident* when we cannot duplicate even simple forms by *design?* And how could a being as complex as Man develop by chance when there is just NOT ENOUGH *TIME* in the history of the Universe to do it?

Scientists like *Newton, Kepler, Galileo* and *Bacon* had no problems as Christians in developing studies of man and our world. They knew that facts and worship *were* part of the same Reality. Their picture of man (as God's special creation in a very wonderful world) gave us the *basis* of the modern scientific method. But today's non-Christian scientist is in grave trouble. He is not just *living* in a world directed by force laws; he IS part of the machinery of the Universe! He is thus no longer a person, he is merely a highly-developed *machine.* Things like beauty, art, poetry, faith, morality and love must mean absolutely *nothing.* Man without God has feelings that he cannot logically fulfil in his non-Christian system. Here man as we know him is *dead.* Maybe one day one of his own machines will replace him. Death is the *absolute end* of his meaningless existence. A Rationalist pays an awful price for his pride.

Why must
the
rationalist
end up
questioning
even his own
existence?

Without a true picture of the Infinite-Personal God (Who has promised to *show* us what *true* truth really is), the Rationalist runs into still another problem. How can he *know* what is true? Plato said something like this thousands of years ago: "How can you really understand any *part* of something unless you have seen the *whole?*" So — how CAN a finite man be sure of ANYTHING he calls "truth" if he does not know ALL the facts of the Universe? Unless he is *shown* truth by Someone Who *does* know all things (and that is where the Bible begins talking about God), he is unsure of *anything*. When you come to think about it, he cannot even be sure that *he himself* exists!

The Rationalist begins *only* with himself and ends up not even being sure of *that!* He denies being created by a Personal God and ends up only a *machine;* he tries to throw out God and winds up throwing away *himself* as well. Paul shows us in his letter to the Roman Christians that a man who behaves like a Rationalist gets into trouble with sin of all sorts, from sexual immorality to merciless violence. He starts off priding himself as a *thinker* and ends up a *stinker.* He gives up faith, fights off everything God does to love him back, and ends up taking pleasure in those who commit crimes worthy of death. It is no fun being a Rationalist. He loses his *moorings*, his *morals* and maybe even his *mind.* No wonder the Bible says, "The fool has said in his heart — No, God!" (Psalm 14:1; Romans 1:18-22).

## [6] COMMUNISM

### FAITH IN MARX

Communist young people are revolutionaries often deeply dedicated, who are shocked, sickened and very angry with the mess our world is in. They dislike the rich holding power over the poor; the lazy ruler who lives on over-worked subjects. They hate superstition and empty religious tradition being used as a tool to control people. They are ready to be interested in people's needs and to teach others what they believe. They are often willing to sacrifice time, money or even their lives to change society. *Marx* and *Engels* laid the thought groundwork of this philosophy. *Lenin*, who saw his brother killed by despots as a young man, took their ideas and used his group-work genius to mould them into a widespread world power that is devoted to a cause greater than the individual, emphasizing training and discipline. Communism is marching to scientifically remake man.

There are *two kind* of Communism — *PAPER* and *PRACTICAL. Paper* (theoretical) Communism, in its *simplest*

form, proposes to *wipe out selfishness* from society. It is the logical result of rationalism; it is materialistic science based on three non-Christian ideas: (1) There is *no God;* (2) There is nothing in the Universe but *matter in motion* (no spirit, no supernatural, no life after death); and (3) Man is wholly *made what he is* by his surroundings (totally determined by his environment, and more particularly, by his *economic* environment). Communism is a fusion of complex theories of economics and sociology (the mechanics of people). Marx married these studies to a discovery *he* believed was an unchangeable law of history. This "law" had created a series of "class wars" that were leading to Universal Communism. He called his ideas *"dialectical materialism."*

In this Marxist "diamet," every country changes by conflict until it finally ends up Communist. This "diamet" lies behind all the strange and sometimes contradictory steps of Marxist strategy. The true Marxist passionately believes he is working with the stream of history; his every effort simply "speeds up" this law of change. He *believes* in this law like a Christian believes God answers prayer. Accordingly, a Communist thinker studies ways to *create tensions* that cause the society under attack to react in conflict. He believes critical points come when these opposing forces overthrow each other. The resultant *new* force then will bring that society inevitably one step closer to Communism. Engels claimed that *three main ideas* described this process: (1) *Any kind* of *change* signals *progress;* (2) *retreat* is only part of the pattern of *attack* and advance; (3) to destroy *one* existing thing means ultimately the building of a new step towards Communism.

How does
the communist
message
counterfeit
the Christian
message, and
why must the
Christian be
aware of
this?

Do not ask the young Marxist who is bent on destroying an existing order what plans he has for a *new* one. He may not know. But he believes he is working with an unchangeable law; history is on *his* side; out of the ashes, Communism will one day come! All possible means of creating chaos are used, from *absurdity* to *violence*. Sinful man is by nature chaotic and absurd; perhaps this explains some of Marxism's appeal to the frustrated and bitter. The pseudo-intellectual with a chip on his shoulder over what the world has done to him is a prime target. He is already at war with society; it is easy to think of "progress in terms of chaos" feeling like that. *Thousands* of students have already done so. It *does* have a certain violent "appeal."

Such zeal and dedication, sacrifice and loyalty to a cause is to be much admired. The idea of men being given common ownership of means of production and distribution is a good idea; the early Christians did it too (Acts 4:32). But the discerning will see serious, deadly flaws. The first is the RELIGION a Communist makes out of *denying* religion. *Empty superstition,* the "opiate of the people," *needs* to be taken from men and women. It cannot help anyone and only hinders progress. But Christian *reality* must replace that emptiness. An avowed Marxist is also an avowed *atheist.* Science, production, and power are introduced in this system to "replace" God. To Marx, man was nothing more than an animal. Like a dog, he has no spiritual being. A Man was considered "sick" if he could not put God out of his mind. A man called *Pavlov* helped give Lenin a highly developed system of *"brainwash"* to aid in the removal of such "superstition." It involves erasure and re-education of thought. Subtle forms of psychological torture based on drugs, prolonged discomfort, fear, exhaustion and mental confusion are used. This process is very powerful, but not necessarily irresistable. People who, in treatment are too "sick" to be "healed" (therefore useless), are usually exterminated for the "general good." God's *moral law* is suppressed or rejected. Bible absolutes are replaced by careful redefinitions that give the Marxist a completely artificial morality. There is no "right" other than the good of the cause. *History itself* becomes god. Deception and even *murder* can be perfectly "right" in Communist philosophy because *truth is re defined* to mean *anything* that advances world Communism. Thus by definition, a Marxist CANNOT lie or be unjust in the party interests.

People as *unique individuals* are not important here as God considers them. In this system you are only important for what you can *do* in the *group*. A perfect society however *already* exists on earth (based on similar principles) that is without problems of crime or civil disobedience. It is not troubled by the aged, disabled or retarded. And it is not Marxism. This highly efficient, totally productive society is called a *beehive*.

In Marxism, what happens to the person as an *individual*?

Bees have no crime problem because they have no *free choice*; they function programmed like machines under the force law called *instinct*. Unproductive members simply die or are killed; more bees are raised to take their place. All bees are literally *worked to death*; the survival of the fittest rules. No bee is individually important. Each bee's worth is measured only in its contribution to the total hive; on its own it means absolutely *nothing*. Unfortunately this society does not produce poets, artists, inventors or lovers. So who *wants* to live in a beehive?

People want to be accepted in a group, but they also want to be known and loved for their own worth. God loves you *as YOURSELF*. You are more important than any idea; you were important enough for the Lord to die for (John 15:13).

In *PRACTICAL* Marxism, *anything* is legal that gets Marxist results. This theory makes it easier to act selfishly in the name of unselfishness. For instance people can even be directed to needed *violence* in party thought by preaching *"peace"* since by *Marxist definition* "peace" *means* Communist *world conquest*. If on the other hand, only open riot or revolt can change a situation, a Communist will do all in his power to spark and fire that unrest. In practical Communism, which is often very *different* from theory, control can be taken in the name of the *people* when it is actually in the hands of a few *leaders*.

The philosophy of *"take* according to *ability* and *give* according to *need"* requires an *incentive* to prevent loss of initiative. Marxists have developed a basic control system geared to one of the most powerful psychological drives in the world — *FEAR*. There cannot be real confidence and love in such a force system. But true Christianity has the one more powerful control — LOVE. And "perfect love casts out all fear" (1 John 4:18; 2 Timothy 1:7). *Communism* says "I

37

How did
philosophical
atheism
influence
Hegel's
thought?

will put a new coat on every man." *Christ* Jesus says —
"Repent and believe — and I will put a *new man* in every
coat" (2 Corinthians 5:17). God always changes a man's life
in the context of world history. He saves him not only for
*himself* but for his *lost society*. Christ gives men meaning for
their own lives AND their world.

Although Communism copies or counterfeits many Christian METHODS, it preaches an opposing *message*. To think
differently in a Communist system is the worst possible crime.
Men and women must *suspend* all independent thinking and
obey fixed rules of thought and leadership. Only in true
Christian discipleship do people discover that they hold in
their hands the key to their *own*, and their *world's* destiny.
Vital Christianity is a greater social force than Communism
because it is the only system that gives a complete, rational
dynamic for social change *without* destroying the individual.

---

## [7] EXISTENTIALISM

---

### FAITH IN FAITH

Some young people have *given up hope* of finding meaning
in Rationalist logic. Instead they have come to believe that
fact and meaning are *not* part of the *same reality*. The
German philosopher *Hegal* (he gave Marx *his* basic idea for
dialectical materialism) first invented the idea that has really
altered a lot of secular thinking.
He said in effect — "Stop thinking
of cause and effect. Think instead
of *one* fact opposed to *another* fact
and the result *combining* to be a
new fact." Now, I hope I can
explain *how* he got this idea! First,
if there *is* no God, there *are* no
absolutes. So who can say what is
*"true"*? Next, if there are no absolutes, then there really are
no *opposites* either, because opposites come from the
absolute ideas of right and wrong, true and false, etc. Why
then *should* anything really be "opposite" to another thing?
Now he could say that if two things were *opposed*, they also
could be the *same*. If that sounds silly, it *is*. In fact, no one

can prove how two things can be opposed and be the same by using finite *logic*. Hegel hoped some day another person would find out a way to do it. No one *did* because no one really *could*. It took a long time for his idea to catch on, but it did eventually. The generation that grew up believing it is *our* generation.

How did Kierkegaard get around the rationalistic problem that troubled Hegel?

Hegel's idea replaced *conflict* with *combination*. Have you heard about the three blind men who met an elephant? One felt its *tail*, another its *leg*, the third its *ear*. Number one said, "The elephant is like a *snake*." Number two said, "Nuts! The elephant is like a *tree trunk*." Number three said, "You are both insane, the elephant is like a *palm leaf*." The point is they were all *opposed*, but all were also right because they could not see the whole elephant. Hegel tried to use this idea.

Another man called *Soren Kierkegaard* gave Hegel's theory the *missing link* that made it popular. Hegel had tried to use his *mind*, and it had not worked to prove his theory. Kierkegaard didn't *bother*. He said in effect that no one could *ever* do it; proof was not *needed* if you accepted it "by faith."

When Kierkegaard said *that* he opened the door to a way of thinking no one had *ever used before* in the Western Christian world. Here we have a world terrified by the Rationalist explanation that man is a meaningless *machine*. "Facts" (not *Christian* facts, but secular ideas) destroyed the things man found hope in. But instead of returning to *Bible* truth, non-Christians did something different. They simply began to accept the idea that meaning had *nothing to do* with facts. Today thousands of young people think that truth can only be found in *personal experience*. Human happenings are not to be talked about in factual terms of logic. They think the world *has* no meaning *outside themselves*. This way reality can become whatever you *want* it to be; there *is* no reality outside of your own mind. This is the basis of the philosophies of Existentialism.

The existentialist searches for meaning by nonlogical "leaps of faith." These "leaps" may take many forms; the commonest are experiments with *sex*, *drugs*, certain kinds of hard and acid rock *music* and various *Eastern* techniques for achieving mystical experience. Because these searches *are* existential (experience-centered), only the person who *has*

What are
some of the
problems
that befall
the genuine
existentialist?

them can know them. They "do not exist" outside of himself. They do not rest on any factual truth that can be *shown* to be real outside the individual's own being. They are subjective, not objective. They cannot be given to another; they cannot be seen, felt, weighed or measured by someone else; they cannot even be described. This is individuality at its wildest. Here people have *nothing in common at all.* Each man makes up his own world; it is only real if it is real *to him.*

Existentialism cannot really be *defined.* At least it cannot be explained *by the existentialist,* since he does not operate in logical categories; he does not put things into files in his mind. Existentialism takes many forms, all of which are searches that seem to bring some kind of meaning. There is *Jasper's* "final experience," *Heidigger's* "Angst" and *Satre's* "self-authentication by acts of the will." The only thing they have in common is this: all base hope on a *non-rational, non-logical, non-communicable* act or experience. Here we also fit the disciplines of *transcendental meditation* (which involves the use of a *mantra* as a concentration-point around which the problems of life can be left behind and serenity achieved), *zen, yoga,* and other forms of Eastern philosophies and religions which reach for meaning in a non-rational way. What a horrifying secular alternative to find answers and purpose; failure here has often led to *suicide.*

All these ideas may temporarily soothe the mind but cannot clear the conscience. And here is the *horrible end* of existentialism; here is the tragic result of such non-Christian thinking. If it *is* true that modern man can only find meaning by throwing away logic, then *true* meaning ultimately lies in discarding *ALL REASON.* And so? Then *meaning* lies in *MADNESS!* If meaning and mind are opposed, true freedom lies in INSANITY. Temporary thought disconnection by the use of drugs or semi-religious rites involving this leap could be better replaced by *permanent* disconnection of the mind — LOBOTOMY. Yet most young people who begin on this search do not see where their non-rational search is leading — to the *darkness of insanity.* What a choice for secular people; between *thinking* and being a *machine,* or *feeling* deeply, and going *mad!* The terror of these two non-Christian extremes is impossible to adequately describe; it can only be measured in the exploding insanity and suicide rates.

This *same thinking* marks the "new theologies"; they unify also in separating the "truth" of their religious systems from the tests of history and science. Here a "Christian" experience may be "taken by *faith*" WHEN THAT FAITH IS *NOT* BIBLE FAITH, which is never "blind." True faith is founded in the character and promises of God which are *both* open to the tests of history and science, as well as experience.

In your own words, what do you think the Bible means when it says we are to love the Lord with "all our minds"?

Christians often forget a vital command — "You shall love the Lord . . . with all your *MIND.*" God writes His laws on our hearts *and* minds (Hebrews 8:10; 10:10). To combat this thinking, we must discipline our MINDS for God. The early Church understood what they preached. The Gospel was not "magic" for them. To be saved is to come to the "knowledge of truth" and "understand" God's Word (1 Timothy 2:4; Matthew 13:3). Being simple and child like is NOT the same as being stupid and childish. To be a true child of God is to be a *thinking person;* to live in Supreme Intelligence (Acts 17:2; 18:4; 17:17; 18:19; 24:25; 26:25; 28:23). A child of God believes in *facts* and is not afraid of them; he knows *true* facts and *true* premises will always lead closer to the God of Truth. He enjoys the wonder of worship with both his heart and mind. He has facts to back up his experience; he knows *why* he believes. Without facts, men are dangerously open to deception. The danger is this: if faith is based only on your own experience and not able to be verified, how do you know *your* experience with Christ was a true experience with the Christ of the Bible? How could you be sure that it was not just a Christ of your own imagination, or worse, a Satanic *counterfeit?* (Matthew 24:23-24).

Without Bible foundations, men in search of religious experiences are dangerously open to deception. Modern man, reacting against impersonal technology is rapidly moving into a non-Christian mysticism without Bible content. Even the *word* "Jesus" has become an enemy of the *Person* of the Lord Jesus because people can use it to describe a Christ of their own invention that has no relationship to the Living Lord of Scripture and history (2 Corinthians 4:1-4). We can mark this generation with one word — DECEPTION. The Church must open her eyes to see this spirit for what it really is, and to fight it out of all our thinking and teaching.

What basic
human drive
would make
a practicing
existentialist
so open to
demonic
deception
and why?

## [8] SPIRITISM

### FAITH IN FEAR

The last of the philosophies of Hell is *Spiritism.* Existential searches almost always open the door to Spiritism, which is involvement with the occult world of *demonic forces.* This communication with deceiving spirits often follows a person's

 hunger for the supernatural that has not been met by a powerless Churchianity. We expect communion from our Maker. Christianity was never meant to be a blind slavery to an aloof, impersonal God. We were made to know and love our Lord. Since God is a Spirit, true fellowship is not centered on external things, or even in our souls. Fellowship with Christ takes place by *direct communion* in our human spirits. The supernatural "pickups" of intuition and devotion that God built into every man and woman, long to share with Him. But this is the key difference: in the Bible such communion is *always made with our mind fully alert and wakeful.*

Spiritists are men (and even *more* often women) who have been *tricked* by a Satanic counterfeit of Christian communion with God. *Curiosity,* the *death* of a dearly loved friend or relative, the desire for supernatural *power* or reality; all may bring a seeker into contact with others who have knowingly or unknowingly given over their lives, senses and spirits to communication with *impersonating demons.* The Bible is gravely clear in warning of the awful danger of this practice (Leviticus 19:31). God has ruled that we should *only* contact *His* spiritual world under the rulership and guidance of the real Christ of Scripture, cleansed by His blood and in full control of our faculties.

*Outside* these safeguarding limits, a seeking person falls easy prey to the cunning traps of Satan's demonic world. *Deception, insanity* and *spiritual destruction* can result from ignoring commands of God. Satan is the "Prince of lies." He can transform himself into an *"angel of light"* like that seen on many LSD trips. His demonic forces easily imitate the

42

voices of dead loved ones, produce light, movement, sound or even *matter*. Some even stage mock "battles" between themselves: when one "drives away" the other, the Spiritist is convinced his demonic guide is "good."

What are some of the contemporary attempts to control the minds of young people and why must these things be avoided at all cost?

*You* can be attacked if you experiment with *any form* of spiritist device. *Divination techniques* by the I. Ching, Tarot or playing cards often open the doors to deception; *fortune-telling tools* like the *crystal ball, tea-leaves* or *palmistry* are other avenues. Seemingly harmless *astrology* and *horoscopes* are forms of the *same Satanic technique:* to seek guidance (even in "fun") from some other *non-Christian* source outside of the Bible and the guidance of the Holy Spirit. Directly *more* dangerous are experiments with the *ouija* board or *seances;* these techniques can put the unwary in *direct contact* with the forces of Hell. *Any form* of seeking guidance outside of God's methods of direction brings terrible danger and is forbidden *under penalty of DEATH* in the Bible (Exodus 22:18; Leviticus 19:31; 20:27; Genesis 40:8). BEWARE of any technique, game or entertainment that directs you to even *temporarily* give up the *conscious control* of your mind and will! This includes *trancendental meditation*, hard and acid rock *music* exposures at high levels, "entertainment" *hypnosis*, religious *chants* and of course, the use of hallucinogenic *drugs*. At such unguarded moments people can be directly attacked by demons and be invaded or even *possessed* by the agents of Hell. *All* sorcery and occultism is condemned *without reservation* in Scripture (Deuteronomy 18:9-14; Exodus 7:11-12; Leviticus 19:26,31; 20:6,27; 1 Chronicles 10:13-14; 2 Kings 21:5-6; Isaiah 2:6; 8:19; Jeremiah 27:9-10; Zechariah 10:2; Malachi 3:5; Acts 8:9f; 16:16f; Galatians 5:19-21; 2 Timothy 3:8; Revelation 21:8; 22:15).

*The steps* to demonic control usually are: (1) *interest* or *curiosity;* (2) some form of *experimentation* "for fun"; (3) fulfillment of the condition of *mental passivity;* (4) *surprise, pleasure,* or half-scared thrill in discovering some supernatural *reality* in the experiment; (5) *deeper* involvement; deceiving spirit *helps* person in some way to gain their trust and confidence; (6) demonic force tightens control, begins to "hook" the personality of experimenter; (7) *fear* begins; slavery of the will has already developed; (8) *deep* periods of depression; fear as demonic control *increases;* (9) total *possession;* strong *suicide* thoughts; *torment*. Demonic forces

43

Why is
repentance
and faith
necessary
before God
can share His
life with us?

also can attack if the will loses control of the personality in sins connected with *violent emotion* like *hatred, bitterness, sexual lust* or *violence.*

Spiritism is Satan's most *powerful counterfeit* of New Testament Christianity. The miracles done by witchcraft or sorcery deeply appeal to the secular thrill-seekers who will not surrender to the God of the Bible. Scriptures reveal that the last days will bring in a revival of Spiritism (2 Thessalonians 2:1-12; 1 Timothy 4:1; 1 John 4:1-3). Only Christians who pay the price to discard a "form of godliness" (2 Timothy

3:5), can produce the supernatural reality that is motivated and directed by the love of God. Satan can *imitate* miracles but he cannot duplicate *love.* Spiritists often believe they are serving "God," but their god is the *god of this world,* the *Devil* (2 Corinthians 4:4).

Now God doesn't put on *"shows"* to impress people. The things we call *"miracles"* are *common* in Heaven. God's new people will *all* be given the keys to the secrets of His Universe. Learning supernatural powers are *not* the most important thing; what is *really* important is to be the kind of person God can *trust* with His secrets. That is why God puts so much stress on our holy walk in this world. It would be *wrong* for God to share His powers with a selfish person. Think of all the damage they could do to the Universe! Satan's *first temptation* to Eve was to urge them into trying powers they were not yet mature enough to handle. The Devil still captures men by the same suggestion — *"You* shall be *as gods . . ."* (Genesis 3:5). God will never "bribe" men into serving Him. He does not respond to selfish appeals from sinners for power or control over others with forces that ordinary people do not have.

Neither does God use miracles to *"prove"* anything. His *own* reality can already be known from nature's glories and by first truths of human intuition. He does not have to do anything "spooky" to show He is there. Why *should* He give more proof? If men will not obey the light He has *already* given them — increasing their light would only increase their *condemnation.* God works miracles by suspending one of His natural, Universal laws, bringing something to pass that is humanly impossible. He sometimes grants these to *deliver* His servants from danger; to *transport, equip* or enable someone to do work God has called them to. Other times, He may do something supernatural simply to *stir up excitement* in a place among His children so that men might ask "by what power" such things are taking place (Acts 4:7; 12:1-11; 8:39; Matthew 14:24-29; Mark 6:7; 16:17-20). Remember that miracles are not an END, but simply one of a number of God's *MEANS.* To seek God for signs or miracles for their *own* sake is not only *wrong,* but opens up the possibility of Satanic deception (Luke 1:18-22; Matthew 12:39). Yet true Christianity has *always* advanced when the declaration of Truth in the Lord Jesus has been coupled with a demonstration of the power of God.

Quote: "If the infinite-personal God of the Scriptures truly does not exist, then walk with respect upon the grass, for it is higher than you."
Francis Schaeffer

```
┌─────────────────────────────┐
│                             │
│   SUMMARY CHART:            │
│                             │
└─────────────────────────────┘
```

These six basic ideas from Hell define the Enemy's work in men's ideas. Satan's attacks are always geared TO THE MIND. Whenever he is at work, you will see examples of the philosophies we have studied. To sum up, each DENIES —

1.  *FORMALISM — MATERIALISM*
    God's right to *change* people and work *with* them; His right to be *loved* and *worshipped* as *Creator* of all mankind.

2.  *HUMANISM — MODERNISM*
    God's revealed *judgment* of rebellion and sin; His own supernatural powers and error-protected Book.

3.  *RATIONALISM* (ATHEISM)
    God's right to be recognized *at all;* Personal, Infinate, Maker, Ruler and Judge of the whole earth.

4.  *MARXISM* (COMMUNISM)
    God *moves in history* on man's behalf; His value on the individual man, and power to *change society* for the better.

Thought:
The really
terrifying
thing about
sin is that
the great
mass of
mankind is
under its
deception,
and the Bible
leaves no
doubts as to
who their
allegiance is
given over to
(1 John 3:8a).

5. *EXISTENTIALISM*

God's *testable* evidences of truth; the fusion of fact and feeling, reason and meaning in Bible premises of faith.

6. *SPIRITISM* (OCCULT)

God's *safeguards* in His *Word* and in His *Son,* the Lord Jesus; His ultimate right to be worshipped in spirit and truth.

The *first* idea pair cover *RELIGIOUS deceit;* the *second* pair, *ATHEISTIC denials;* and the *last* pair, *OCCULT deception.* This web interconnects the whole world of wickedness. We as Christians must take firm steps to block such thought-attacks from our thinking and speaking. *We will LIVE what we really BELIEVE.* Now, no one arrives at any of these things without *first* ignoring some protection God has made. Each one begins when we reject one of His witnesses to truth. To be free from these false ideas we must stay clean of sin, and live honestly for God. No one can stand before the Great Thinker of the Universe and tell Him that they arrived at this kind of thinking by doing everything He told them to do! ALL men who love these lies are truly "without excuse" (Romans 1:20).

A *religious* man's failure usually begins when he denies God the right to *change him (FORMALISM)* and begins to pay too much attention to the *things* God made *(MATERIALISM).* This kind of sin prompts him to ignore God's warnings and get involved in over exalting people *(HUMANISM).* When next he starts playing with God's Word, he usually ends up arguing away large parts of it *(MODERNISM).* From there he can just strip away all his dead religious trappings and not even call himself a "believer in God" — *(RATIONALISM).* Now he is ready to join in social movements to change mankind *without God,* like *MARXISM.* Since Communism cannot remove his need for the spiritual and the personal, he may move into *EXISTENTIALISM.* This search *outside of logic* (for his missing meaning) then may end with him being enclaved in the madness and darkness of Satan's *occult* world *(SPIRITISM).* Now, here is a prediction. Two extremes like Marxism and Spiritism cannot properly function using people without each other. Possibly forms of both will *unite* as the end of time draws near. SATAN *WILL BE* SERVED. He has drawn millions along these paths of

46

deception and hopelessness that lead to Hell. He clouds consciences, convincing men and women of the "rightness" of their life of lies. He carefully blinds others to God's warning: "There *is* a way that *seems* right to a man, but the END of it are the ways of DEATH" (Proverbs 14:12). Sinful mankind is headed for an irreversible worship of the "god of this world" (John 14:30).

Before you picked up this book, what was *your* definition of discipleship?

## THE PHILOSOPHY OF DISCIPLESHIP

*REAL Christian discipleship* was designed to meet *all* man's needs *without* the fatal flaws of darkened human wisdom. Obeying the Bible and surrendering one's life to God's direction and control reveals the many empty promises of other philosophies and their utter powerlessness to meet the whole man's needs. The church *must* go back to Bible Christianity! *Sinners* can become Christians when CHRISTIANS become CHRISTIAN! It is not easy to be a disciple. Much of what passes for Christianity today is a half-hearted attempt to reconcile the cross-bearing life with comfortable living. We cannot be selfish and saintly too. The world has never been moved by the mildly interested. Unless you are open to the changes of God and live in utter obedience to the Holy Spirit's commands, you may as well close this book *now.* If you want to MOVE your world, you must be prepared to pay the high cost of discipleship! Are you ready to re-examine *your* premises?

*What IS Christianity?* IS it so different from every other religion in the world? Christ's claim is "You shall know the *Truth* and the *Truth shall set you free."* Either the Gospel answers *all* man's basic needs, or Christ is an outright liar. We cannot present Christianity to the world if we are not convinced that the message of good news is the one irrefutable REALITY that can meet every need. What makes the difference?

47

# CHRISTIAN VS. RELIGION

True Christianity is *not* a religion; it is people through Christ *returning to normal*. Religions are *our* substitutes for God; through Christ *God* has substituted for *us!* The Creator put an echo of His nature in our beings; men cannot find real peace apart from Him. We awaken to a frightening and great world in which *we* are only a tiny fragment of personality. Because we learn this, nothing even partly satisfies our spirit that fails to at least point to: (a) *A Person* (or Persons) able to (b) *direct* or *take care* of this awesome Universe. Accordingly, man-made religions assume *three great divisions:* the worship of a *PERSONAL* god, an *INFINITE* god or some kind of non-*Christian combination* of both. We can roughly divide all religions like this:

1. *The PERSONAL-finite god(s)* . . . (*POLYTHEISM*) "The world has *many* gods."

From their earliest recorded rejection of the real God, people have made up substitutes for Him that were *small enough* to fit into their own selfish lives. Men and women have worshipped *Baal, Ashteroth, Ammon* and *Moloch* in *Bablyon, Egypt* and *Assyria; Venus, Jupiter, Zeus* and  *Bacchus* of Greece and Rome were other ideas of a god that was personal but finite. The *East* added some other ideas. The *Hindus,* for instance, have some *330 million* gods. They are all *finite, unsatisfied* and *selfish*. They use each other, and strive for fulfillment, just like the humans who invented them. Although *Zoroastrianism* bears some resemblance to monotheism, it is perhaps more accurately classed under this heading, with its Supreme Being, Ahurha Madza, not very much greater than the opposing "bad" spirit, Agura Mainya. No god small enough for *us* to copy is *big enough* to meet all of our needs. This kind of thinking ends up in the dark religion of *Animism,* where people have to placate an endless number of spirits. This gives Satan's demonic agents plenty to do, and binds whole countries in fear and superstition.

## 2. The Impersonal-INFINITE god . . . (PANTHEISM) — "God *is* everything."

What is the basic premise of pantheism and what is it about this system that is so contrary to biblical Christianity?

Some Eastern people *reacted* to this confusion; they came up with ideas of a god without a face. Such an "impersonal Something" lying at the *root* of both thought and matter is described, for instance, in the *Upanishads*. The ancient multi-headed gods of Egypt supposedly showed facets of an Infinite Deity they could not describe; most Eastern thinking revolves around this picture of God. Their hunger for the Infinite as a source of peace, wisdom and power gave us Pantheism, or, as Francis Shaeffer puts it, *"pan-everything-ism."* Here God is *PART* of creation; He *is* the world, the stars, the Universe, animals — and God is also *Man*. This is another idea that makes Satan happy. It is the same lie he got successfully across to Adam and Eve when they fell into sin. The Bible teaches, on the other hand, that God made a real Universe *outside of Himself.* If *it* fell apart, *He* would not. Man *is* related to God (by creation), but is not *himself* God. He will *always* remain finite even in God's family, but he will always be *personal*.

*Buddha* began a religion. He thought that if he renounced both *desire* and *individuality* (within his own high ethics), he could *abolish suffering*. Life ends rather awfully for a Buddhist however. He will be lost in the "sea of Nirvanah" the *essence* of all *existence*. Buddha's attractive "eightfold path" leads not to life but to *death* — the death of *personality*. Today many of his followers worship at shrines and temples adorned with *his statue;* this is the very *opposite* of his teaching! Men just cannot *live* when they deny person-ality. They will not easily throw away their God-given uniqueness.

*Confucianism* is another attempt a clever Chinese made to guide the life of his people. He *failed* however to banish his followers rightful *anxiety* over their future and the unseen world, because he simply avoided talking about it. *Taoist* temples show yet another failure. Set up on pantheistic lines, they are now mostly homes of *polytheistic* Animism. People prefer *personal demons* to worshipping some "nameless everything." The only thing making this kind of thinking popular with Westerners is the development of *existentialism* with its emphasis on experience without logic. It is a very impractical sort of religion for helping others.

Why is true
social
concern
lacking in
societies that
believe in
reincarnation?

Often used in these systems are the tools of *meditation, yoga disciplines, fasting, drugs* or *special foods* to help achieve "cosmic" — or *"God-consciousness."* Common to most Eastern religions is the Satanic lie of *reincarnation* that gives a person a *reason* to dissolve their own individual personalities and accept demonic attack or madness as reality. Related closely to this is the "Law of Karma," an ultimate extension of the dogma of *inherited morality* and personality, which appeals for its "neat" solution of the problem of evil and suffering. It states that all *life runs in cycles of rebirth.* Each born simply suffers *punishment* for bad behavior or *reward* for good works in the *previous* life. The "fortunate-born" thus have just *cause* for selfrighteousness and no real reason to help lift the social leper. Practically it leads to intense forms of selfishness, pride and unconcern for the miserable, as evidenced in the caste systems of India.

Because we do not *know* everything, we need someone to *show* what is right. And because we have the ability to *choose* right and wrong, we must live *unselfishly* for all to be happy. The only person with a *right* to rule everything is the person who *knows everything* and is *not selfish.* That person is qaulified to be our God and King. He will give us fair laws! We need someone who is *big* enough to guard, protect and sustain us; that someone should be another *person* we can enjoy and share with, a person who could be understood and loved despite his greatness.

3. *PERSONAL-INFINITE . . . (MONOTHEISM)* — Only *One all-powerful* God.

The remaining three major religions are *Islam, Judaism* and multitudes of church groups commonly called "Christian" in Greek Orthodox, Roman Catholic and Protestant forms. They unite in more or less agreeing with the Personal-Infinite God of the Scriptures' description, but they are *still religions* without a *relationship.*

(a) *ISLAM* — knows "no God but *Allah,* and *Mohammed* is His Prophet." The *Koran* is the supreme and final written authority for life; Mohammed, the last of the great prophets. Adam, Abraham, Moses and Jesus are also listed as prophets or holy men who prefigured *his* final arrival to bring the Islamic faith. Islam asks of its faithful: *prayer* (five times a day on call), a day light hour *fast* of one month each year

50

(night reserved for feasting if recovery needed); prohibition of *intoxicants, gambling* and certain *foods;* a *pilgrimage* to Mecca (in person or representation); and repetition of the *creed.* Here Allah is *served,* but hardly *loved; respected,* but not *enjoyed* because He is not really *personal* at heart to the Moslem. The pilgrim of Islam has *no* peace of heart because he can never *know* the outcome of his destiny in this life. He can only hope and pray that he will be found acceptable when his *"good works"* are done in hope of reward. *Allah* is *never* moved; whatever happens to him is the fatalism of what "Allah wills."

(b) *JUDAISM* — in its *vital* form is the foundation of the New Testament revelation of God's sacrificial love for man. From the time of Abraham, God found faithful men who would preserve the truth of His great and loving nature and show the world what it meant to be a follower of the *true* God. Israel remains today as the timepiece of God's calendar for the outcome of history. He has specially marked Israel as *His* land and His people. Although many Israelites *forgot* God, He has found many from the ranks of formal Judaism who have recognized their Messiah and know how to worship the Father in Spirit and truth. Only in the *New* Testament is God's forgiveness and offer of immortality better clarified, while Old Testament blessings are made *present* and extended in many ways to *all* nations.

Thought: If I beat myself 100 times to gain God's favor, how tragic it would be upon arriving in front of heaven's gate to hear God say, "Sorry, you can't come in—I wanted 101."

## FAITH VS. FATALISM

This is where the *message of the Bible* is so different from religions. The God it speaks about is absolutely unique. He is BOTH Infinite AND Personal! *There is no other God like Him.* He is the *only* God who has the qualifications to be our God and to be worshipped as such. If people would honestly study the facts they would see that the Bible God *really deserves* to be loved. It is silly to put other gods before Him. If people serve gods less than *themselves,* they deny their *minds;* if they serve gods *unlike* man, they destroy their own *meaning.* We can say that "god is only an infinite everything," but we will have to keep searching for an answer to our *own*

51

unique personalities. We can on the other hand say "God is personal and little," but we will have to find something else worth worshipping. Others may even *abandon* God, try to use their minds, but feel like *machines* and live in black despair; also, others may abandon God, but try *feeling* instead and start thinking like *idiots*, ending up in madness and death.

No matter *what* lies we think up, the true God will *always be there*, feeling sorry for us. *Face it;* we can only live sanely, rationally, meaningfully and consistently if we worship this God who is both INFINITE and PERSONAL. This God will let us honestly *think* as well as *feel*. He reveals Himself in ways we can study and think as well as in ways that we can love and enjoy.

*The Lord Jesus Christ* is the *central focus* of the Bible. He was no ordinary man. His *birth* split history in two; His *life* and *work* alone makes Him the world's greatest figure. But the thing that really counts is the fact that *His tomb is empty* (Luke 24:5-6). That deserted grave means that *Jesus is alive* — NOW! (Revelation 1:8). A man was asked why he left his religion to be a Christian. He said: "If *you* were walking along a road and saw two leaders and teachers at the fork of  that road — one *dead* and the other *alive* — which one would you ask the way?" And that is the secret of the Gospel. We serve a *living* Christ. He is not some past "static example." He is *actively involved* with our world. The history of all other faiths show blind obedience to unchanging futures and uncaring Gods. But the *God of the Bible* is not like that. He is a MOVING God working with creative mankind in a changing world. And He is neither too small to help us or too impersonal to care.

You can see the *fixed futures* of other faiths. The *Moslem's* God is not personally involved with his follower. Whatever happens was "Allah's will." What does *Allah* care about his choices? A man cannot change Allah's mind. Look at the poor *Buddhist*, with no power to affect his destiny. His ambition is to sink himself into *nothingness*, hoping after countless reincarnations to become part of the great Universal, uncaring stream of Time. Listen to the chanted prayers of the follower of *Rome's* brand of religion; how can *he* know what is true when only the *church* he serves can interpret for him? And how does he *feel* when his "infallible" church *changes* her truths?

What is the ultimte proof of God's care for us?

See the *Marxist* working with his "inevitable law" of history. If his dialectic *fates* him to rule the world, he can hope for happiness even when he feels deep inside he is really heading for Hell. Even some *Christians* think of God as the Great "Fixer," pulling the strings behind everything people do. We are "only puppets" on a gigantic stage called Life that God is amusing Himself with. No wonder Baudelaire said: "If there *is* a God, He is the *Devil.*" And little wonder that some theologians have *given up their reason* in trying to *defend* such a God, saying hopefully, but blindly in the face of evil — "Yet, God *is* good."

Could God possibly *care* for earth's teeming millions; could He even *want* to care? If God *arranged* the contradictions of beauty and ugliness in our lives, if we are only *pawns* on God's giant chessboard of triumph and tragedy, it is hard to help feeling hurt when terrible things happen to our world, no matter how much we trust God. He becomes more and more impersonal and far-off. But is God *REALLY* like that?

*Then Jesus came!* Into our world blazed the light of an amazing revelation. God *cared* for us; He *still* cares. He is concerned about every detail of our lives. The most wonderful revelation of the Bible is the glimpse it gives us of *God's nature.* We see a CONCERNED, FEELING God, not one of indifferent power; One Who is touched with *our* hurt (Hebrews 4:15). We see a God Who is *saddened* by our misery and *grieved* over our insane rebellion.

We even see a God Who is willing to *CHANGE* HIS PLANS when we ask Him! (Psalm 106:40-45; Genesis 18:20-32; Exodus 32:7-14; Jeremiah 18:5-10; 26:3; Joel 2:13; 2 Kings 20:1-7). We see a God Who is so really PERSONAL it makes us *weep* at what has happened to His world and to His heart. We see the REAL God by the Book He has given us — and our wondering souls discover that He is *love!*

But this God made us in the finite, miniature likeness of Himself — able to *choose,* free to do right or wrong. God gave

Charles Finney once said, "Sin is moral insanity." Why do you think Finney made such a statement?

us rules of action, suited to our nature. He set up *moral penalties* to *limit disobedience* that could eventually hurt the rest of His Universe. The Bible shows us that we can make only *one* of two supreme choices; the choice to *serve ourselves* or the choice to put *God first* in our lives and live as a result for the highest good of His Universe.

*All plans* we make in life will depend on which of these choices we make. We are usually left to choose for ourselves.

If we go *wrong*, we cannot ruin *His* goals since He can bring *penalties* on any rebel sinner. These punishments (both *personal*, such as *disharmony* and *guilt*, and *governmental*, such as the *coming judgment* and exclusion from eternal life) act as *limiters* to the amount of damage we can bring on ourselves and our world. God, in loving mercy, longs to *put off* this punishment in the hope that sinners will turn to their Friend Who has always loved them despite their sin.

God rarely uses *force* with His moral creation. But since the *fall*, God has sometimes had to use an *emergency control*. The Bible calls it "hardening the heart." Here he specially *over rules* man's free will in emergencies (Exodus 11:9-10; Deuteronomy 2·25; Joshua 11:20; 1 Kings 22:19-23; Psalm 22:28; 66:7; Proverbs 21:1; Jeremiah 32:27-30; 50:9; Daniel 4:17,32; Zephaniah 3:8; John 7:30; 18:31-32; 19:9-11; Romans 13:1; Revelation 17:17). In such "Will-freezes," God does *not* hold men responsible; His judgments *only* apply to men's free choices. The "will-freeze" is used to *govern* or *fulfill* some of His prophecies. He NEVER decides your choice for *salvation;* your *own* response to His call will determine your eternal destiny. You see, no informed Christian is a *fatalist;* he is both a true *realist* and a happy *optimist.* He can and must be both!

*Men are not a robot race.* We are the "unprogrammed" creation. God has done *all He can* to help save fallen people; now He calls *US* to join the Divine effort! He has *deliberately chosen* to limit Himself to our free response in the carrying out of His will (Ezekiel 3:17-18; 33:7-8; John 17:17-23; Acts 1:8). We can grieve God or make Him *glad* by our lives! Many of the Father's *future* decisions depend on *our own*. This is why *you* must go into all the world and preach the Gospel to every creature. *Christ* does not delay His coming; His *followers* delay it! (Matthew 24:14). God is *right now* extending all the help He can give. The rest is up to YOU. The key to save this generation is in OUR hands! (1 Corinthians 3:9).

What is the one limitation God has to face?

*God is not hindered by time*. He has all eternity to accomplish His will. He is not limited by *resources* — the whole earth is His. He is not hindered by lack of *power* or of *wisdom* or *ability*. He is limited *only* by those He created free who do not serve Him with a perfect heart and a willing mind . . . He is limited by MAN'S DISOBEDIENCE (Psalm 78:41). He wants YOU to help Him carry out His goal (John 20:21).

Will *YOU* become a disciple — a learner — a young person who will obey Him? Will you learn at His nail-scarred feet? Will you put your life completely at His disposal to do as He commands? Will you WORK WITH GOD? Will you rebel or obey? Will you be a FAILURE — or will you CHANGE YOUR WORLD?

*LORD — HERE AM I:*

*SEND —*

● My Sister
● My Brother
● (Someone else?)

○ *ME!*

"GOD GAVE US *TWO ENDS:* ONE TO THINK WITH; THE OTHER TO SIT ON. OUR FUTURE DEPENDS ON WHICH END WE USE. *HEADS* WE WIN — *TAILS* WE LOSE."

"Straight is the gate, and narrow is the way, which leadeth unto life, and few there be which find it . . . Wherefore by their fruits ye shall know them" (Matthew 7:14,20).

# JUDAS

## (WHO DIDN'T MAKE IT)

"Jesus was troubled in spirit and said . . . 'One of you will betray Me.' "

John 13:21

PHASE:     2 .. *Challenge To Live*
SECTION:   2 .. *"I" For Imaginary Or Real Salvation?*
MATERIAL:  .. *Analysis Of True Conversion*

It swings in the wind. It's a shell, an empty house. The one who once lived in this thing on a tree has gone out into eternity. Before it falls and breaks apart in the field we know what it is. It is a body — a dead human body. *Judas will never live again.*

*Judas* appeared to be real. He was a disciple. The Lord Jesus Himself chose him after a night of prayer. He did miracles with the other disciples. He was trusted by everyone, had the right language and appearance; but he turned out to be an apostate. *Judas* fooled everyone but Jesus. And now, how about YOU? Are you really a Christian? By the end of this section you will know for sure!

---

## GROUNDWORK — THE MAN IN THE MIRROR

---

Who *am* I? *Why* am I here? *Where* am I going? These are basic questions of life. The *Bible* answers begin *before Time itself,* and starts at the best place to find any answers — with *God.*

When everything began, God was *already there*, making it all happen. He said: "Light — BE"! and power beyond imagination exploded into reality; fiery energies spun into atomic chains. Undreamed of forces moulded matter out of nothing-ness. The Creator lit the fires of a million worlds at once, and the stars and planets all began. He set up *forces*, forces of *infinite precision* to guide His new Universe; we call them the "laws of Science" now, and study their awesome testimony to God's wisdom in the laboratories of the world (1 Chronicles 29:11-12; Job 37-38; Isaiah 45:5,7,12). Then He made a *special world*. There were already billions in His Universe, but this tiny, blue-green planet was to be *very* special in His eyes. God called His new and beautiful little world

*Earth* (Genesis 1:1-10; Isaiah 45:18; Exodus 19:6; Psalm 24:1).

*He gave Earth LIFE*, filling it with *plants, fishes and birds;* He made the *animal* kingdom, an astonishing display of His love and wisdom. To these creatures He gave *built-in control systems* geared to signals from the world around them. Each tiny creature, without ability of mind, was carefully *programmed* to carry out its tasks without mistake or error, from generation to generation; each performs complex actions in a mindless testimony to the Genius Who built them. We call these guiding forces "laws of instinct" (Genesis 1:20-25; Job 39:1-30; Psalm 104:10-30).

Then God was ready to *crown* His new creation with His most wonderful work. No one knew the love that existed in the fellowship of the Father, the Son and the Holy Spirit. There was no one like *Them* in the whole Universe; no one had ever experienced Their happiness. The whole creation was waiting for *another* creature who could share something with God. And so the Godhead decided to *extend* Their love. They said — "Let us make *man* in our image" (Genesis 1:26). Mankind was formed from the elements of the dust in supernatural creation, in *finite, miniature likeness* to God Himself. The first lovely pair of human people were created to begin a race destined for greatness as a part of God's very own life and family! Man was made a beautiful being, *perfect* in every respect. To understand just how far we have fallen from this perfection, we need to understand our own makeup. Our wonderful gifts make us the *only* creature made *in God's image*. Our three-fold nature is a reflection of the Godhead. It is represented in a very limited way by the following diagram. Just use it as a very rough picture of Man.

## MAN — A TRIPLE TRINITY

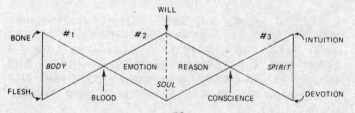

59

How would
the intricacies
of the human
body point
toward
evidence of
the Creator?

SECTION 1 — Your *BODY* — the "house" you live in.

*BONES* — A 206-part *structure* for *shape, support* of vital organs and some *protection* for delicate innards (Genesis 2:23; Job 10:11; Psalm 22:14,17; John 19:36).

*FLESH* — All *tissue* of the body — nerve, muscle, skin and hair. All "working parts" that give you *movement, feeling* and *appearance* (Genesis 2:7; Psalm 139:14-16; John 24:39).

*BLOOD* — The body's *life-factor* — carries *food, air* and a *police* and *garbage* disposal system! The "life of the flesh" is in the blood (Leviticus 17:14; Deuteronomy 12:23; Acts 17:26). The body begins from a tiny cell smaller than a pinhead. Following God's amazing built-in design code, new cells build in a pattern laid down before the world began.

SECTION 2 — Your *SOUL* — the real person. Every choice you make in life will help create this inner you — and help decide your destiny.

*EMOTION* — (*Sense, feeling, desire* responses of the body.) *Desire:* Job 23:13; 1 Samuel 23:20; 2:16; Deuteronomy 14:26; 12:20; Psalm 84:2; 42:1; 42:2; 63:1; 107:9; 119:20; 143:6; Isaiah 26:8-9; Ezekiel 24:21; Ecclesiastes 2:24. *Pleasure:* Psalm 35:9; 49:18; 34:2; 86:4; 94:19; 107:9; Proverbs 13:9; 29:17; 16:24; Ecclesiastes 2:24; Isaiah 55:2; (Amp.) Isaiah 61:10; Matthew 12:18; Luke 1:46; Hebrews 10:38; *Affection:* 1 Samuel 18:1; 20:17; Song of Solomon 1:7; 3:1-4; Deuteronomy 6:5. *Disaffection:* Romans 2:9; 2 Samuel 5:8; Numbers 21:5; Job 10:1; (Dby) Psalm 11; 107:18; (Dby) Jeremiah 4:31; 14:19; Job 33:20; (Dby) Zechariah 11:8. *Discouragement:* Numbers 21:4; Job 10; Psalm 42:5-6; 31:9; 6:3; 7:2; 44:25; 57:6; 88:3; 107:5; 116:7; Job 30:25; 27:2; 24:12; 21:25; 14:22. *Hurt or Grief:* 1 Samuel 30:6; 1:10; 2 Kings 4:27; (Amp.) Judges 10:16; 16:16; Job 3:20; 19:2; 7:1; Jeremiah 13:17; Isaiah 38:15; Matthew 26:38; Luke 2:35; John 12:27; 2 Peter 2:8.

*REASON* — (*Working out, thinking through* faculty; *thoughts* and *memory.*) *Knowledge:* Psalm 13; 139:14; (Dby) 143:8; Proverbs 19:2; (Dby) Proverbs 2:10; 2:3; 24:14; Isaiah 8:4; 58:3; Joshua 23:14; Acts 24:22; 24:8. *Thought:* Proverbs 23:7; Lamentations 3:20; 2 Peter 2:14; 2 Corinthians 3:14; 4:4; 11:3 (*mind* is the word *"thought"* in the last four passages). *Wisdom:* Exodus 35:35; 36:1; 1 Kings 4:29; Psalm 51:6; 90:1; Proverbs 2:10; 15:32; 24:14; 19:8; Ecclesiastes 2:26; Isaiah 33:6; Acts 14:22. *Mind:* Genesis 23:8; 2 Samuel 17:8; 2 Kings 9:15; 1 Chronicles 28:9; Jeremiah 15:1; Ezekiel 23:17; 24:25; 36:5; Deuteronomy 18:6; 28:65; 1 Chronicles 22:7; Jeremiah 51:50; Acts 14:2; Romans 14:15; Ephesians 4:17; Colossians 2:18; Philippians 1:27; Hebrews 12:3. *Memory:* Deuteronomy 11:1; Lamentations 3:20; Proverbs 10:14; Isaiah 43:26; Ecclesiastes 12:1; Matthew 5:23; Luke 16:25; 1:72; Philippians 1:3; 1 Thessalonians 3; 2 Timothy a:3,5; 2 Peter 1:13,15; 3:1. *Pride,* a disposition of the *mind* to think itself better or worse than it actually is is also ascribed to the soul (2 Chronicles 32:26; Psalm 24:4; Proverbs 28:25; Daniel 5:20).

How does man differ from the plant and animal creation?

*VOLITION* — (Power of *free choice;* ability to pick or choose between alternatives presented to the mind.) Often, the supreme choice of a man's life is called the *HEART,* being the center and source of all the moral life, and involving control of the *thoughts directly,* and to a lesser and *indirect* sense, the state of the *feelings.* The will is the command-post of the soul, the central headquarters of the personality. Man has the ability to originate his own actions.

*WILL* — Exodus 35:29; Deuteronomy 21:14; 1 Chronicles 28:9; Ezekiel 16:27; Psalm 27:12; 41:2; Isaiah 1:19; Mark 14:26; John 7:17; 1 Corinthians 7:37; 9:17; 2 Peter 1:21; 3:5; Colossians 2:23; 2 Corinthians 8:3; Revelation 22:17. A number of these words translated *"will"* are in the original *"soul".* *Choice* or *refusal:* Job 6:7; (Amp.) 7:15; (Dby) Psalm 77:2; Deuteronomy 30:19; Joshua 24:15; 24:22. 1 Samuel 17:40; 2 Samuel 24:12; Job 9:14; 34:33; Proverbs 1:29; 3:31; Isaiah 7:15; 66:3; Acts 15:40 *Lift up:* Ezekiel 24:25; Jeremiah 44:14; Habakkuk 2:4.

*SECTION 3* — Your *SPIRIT* — is not understood by many.

This makes man different from the animals. The Bible separates the *Holy* Spirit and the *human* spirit. God gave *of His own Being* to form a life-link from creation to Creator. This spirit formed *within* man (Zechariah 12:1) though a *distinct entity* from the Holy Spirit is a God-born faculty that connects us with the spiritual world, and returns to the Creator at death (Romans 8:16; Ecclesiastes 12:7; Luke

What is the
difference
between
conscience
and
intuition?

23:46). When a man is converted to Christ, the Holy Spirit  *indwells* his spirit; without Jesus, a human spirit can become the habitation of *demonic* forces. It is NOT merely the animating factor of soul and body. The Bible uses many passages like the following where the word *"pneuma"* cannot be translated just as *"wind"* or *"breath"*, although both soul *and* spirit are used to describe any INVISIBLE power at work (Mark 2:8; 8:12; Luke 1:47; 10:21; John 4:23; 11:33; 13:21; Acts 18:5; Romans 1:9; 8:6; 1 Corinthians 2:11; 5:3.5; 14:14, 15,32.)

Man's spirit has functions of *intuition, conscience* and *devotion.* It is the last part of man's being to develop as he grows from infancy to early childhood and morality.

CONSCIENCE — (A *comparison standard,* designed to *compare* revealed truth from God with the record of the mind). Like a sensitive watch, it is a useful standards' check *if* obeyed. A watch can tell time, but does not SET standards. It is *adjusted* to standard and needs to be constantly checked against this for accuracy. Conscience always gives the right "time" provided it is not seared or tampered with by *sin.* It serves as a built-in *alarm* system, *commending* or *condemning* man's moral choices and judgments (Deuteronomy 2:30; Psalm 34:18; 51:10; John 8:9; 13:21; Acts 17:16; 24:16; Romans 8:16; 9:1; 1 Corinthians 8:7; 5:3; 2 Corinthians 1:12; 2:13; 4:2; 2 Timothy 1:7; 1 Timothy 1:5; 4:2; Titus 1:15; 1 Peter 3:16,21).

INTUITION — (Ability to be *taught inside; direct sensing* of knowledge *without* the reason; "sixth-sense" or "E.S.P." is a function of intuition.) Here God reveals truth and the moral law directly to the mind of moral man after the "age of accountability," and this function is variously called *"light", "inspiration", "wisdom", "understanding",* sometimes of the *"mind"* (Psalm 43:3; 56:13; Proverbs 6:23; Job 32:8; Mark 2:8; Isaiah 11:2; Exodus 35:31; 1 Kings 4:29; Daniel 5:11-12, 14; Luke 24:45; John 3:19; Acts 18:25; 20:22; 1 Corinthians 14:14-15, 19; 16:18; 2 Corinthians 7:13; Colossians 1:9; 2:2; 2 Timothy 2:7; 1 Peter 2:9; 1 John 2:10).

*DEVOTION* — (The ability to *worship*, adore and praise God *in the spirit;* the faculties of the soul are inadequate to worship Him; He has given us a spirit so we may commune with Him directly without the limitations of human understanding or feeling). Leviticus 27:21; Isaiah 26:9; Zechariah 12:10; Luke 1:47; 2:13,20; 10:21; John 4:23; Acts 17:23; Romans 1:9; 7:6; 8:15; 8:16; 1 Corinthians 6:17,20; 14:15-16; Ephesians 2:18; Philippians 2:1; Colossians 1:8; 2:5; Revelation 21:10.

How does the function of the spirit and soul differ?

Although a number of Scriptures at first glance ascribe the same work to both soul *and* spirit (because under certain conditions either one can control the other) the Bible is most careful to distinguish *between* them. They are distinct in their function and very nature. Man has been made in the image of his Maker, he is a *tripartite* being who functions as a unity. Paul is careful to keep the distinction in 1 Thessalonians 5:23 when he prays, "May the God of peace Himself sanctify you wholly; and may your *SPIRIT* and *SOUL* and *BODY* be kept sound and blameless at the coming of our Lord Jesus Christ." The Word of God divides the SOUL and SPIRIT (Hebrews 4:12) again showing the distinction. Genesis 2:7 shows God breathing into man the breath of LIVES (*chay* — plural form). The *human spirit* and *earthly body* together form the elements of the central entity of the human being — his *soul.* 1 Corinthians 15:45 uses *'egeneto EIS psuchen zosan'* for "became a living soul" with the *"eis" local,* implying that the soul is the *meeting-place* of the body and the spirit. The soul, *once formed,* functions as an independent, indissoluble element from spirit and body.

*Before conversion,* the *spirit* of man is cut off from God, and often seems to function no differently than his *soul,* since it is completely controlled and directed *by* the soul (Genesis 41:8; Judges 8:3; (Dby) Proverbs 14:29; 17:22; Isaiah 29:24; 65:14; Daniel 5:20, etc.). God's way is for the spirit of man to direct the soul, while itself under the direction of the *Holy* Spirit of God.

Scripture shows man can make his *own* choices and is *responsible* for them: Genesis 3:11; Deuteronomy 11:26-28; 27:1,10,26; 28:1-2; 28:15,45-48,58; 30:15-20; Joshua 24:15; 24:20-24; 1 Samuel 7:3; 8:7; 1 Kings 18:21; Isaiah 1:19-20; 66:3-4; Jeremiah 18:7-10; 21:8; 36:3,7; Ezekiel 5:11; 20:7-8;

Matthew 23:37; Luke 10:42; 19:14; John 1:11; 3:36; 5:40;
7:17; Acts 7:51; Romans 6:16-18; Hebrews 11:25; 1 John
2:17. God has entrusted man with
the SAME ability of free choice
that *He Himself* has.

Man was given a *moral nature
like God.* Like the *Father,* he was
given ability to *create,* by *origina-
ting* his own *choices;* like the *Holy
Spirit,* he was given the capacity to
communicate in *direct spiritual fellowship* with God; like the
*Son,* he was given a *material body,* with the ability of *physical
senses.* Just as the whole Godhead act in *harmony,* man's
united being always acts as a *unity.* This total response was
given to us so that *all* of our beings could enjoy God's love.

The Father placed *witnesses to Himself* all around us that
speak to every part of our lives. As we grow, like Jesus, in
wisdom and stature, in favour with God and man, we
learn more and more of the wonderful privileges He gave us.

---

### GOD'S TESTIMONIES TO MAN

---

Look at the following four witnesses He gave for each of
our four basic endowments:

1. *OUR BODIES* — The Revelation of *NATURE* in
*CREATION.*

*Man's ENVIRONMENT* was made beautiful in the beginning. It is hard *not* to think of God when you look at the
sweep of the stars, feel the warm sun or smell a fragrant
flower. David said "The heavens declare the glory of God
and the firmament (the earth) shows His handiwork"
(Psalm 19:1). Day after day our environment was to speak to
us of God (Psalm 8:3-6; 24:1; 136:1-9; Jeremiah 51:15).

*Earth's ECOLOGY* — the close harmony of *our* life with
the *animal* and *plant life* of this world — was also designed to

turn our thoughts to God. Adam and Eve were placed in a garden to dress and keep it. They were given the animals to play with and love. All of God's other creations depend on Him for their life. Listen again to David: "Oh Lord, how manifold are Your works! In wisdom you have made them all; the earth is full of Your riches . . . these all wait upon You; that You may give them their meat in due season" (Psalm 104:24; 28; 65:5-13).

*All men* everywhere have seen *these* witnesses. They point unmistakably to God. No one has a good excuse for never thanking Him or worshipping Him. This is the point Paul makes in Romans 1:19-20, when he gives one reason why people who have never heard of Jesus can *still* be guilty of rejecting truth to make God angry with them (Psalm 19:1; Isaiah 40:26; Jeremiah 10:12).

*2. OUR SOULS* — The Revelation of *REASON* in *GOD'S WORD*.

*Our PERSONALITY* tells us a lot about the God Who made us. It is *this* that makes us sure we are not accidents of time and chance. Our thoughts, feelings and free will all provide equipment with which we can learn some things about life and our Maker. When we *think*, we can see in a very small way how *God* reasons. When we feel hurt or happy, we learn a little more about God's own feelings. When we are faced with a difficult choice, we can know on a tiny scale what our Great Friend has to do when *He* faces problems. Besides the testimonies of nature, the *written* Word of God (the Bible) appeals directly to our souls. It moves our feelings, enlightens our minds and challenges our wills. Although the Bible is not the only source of our knowledge of God, it is His *main* one. People who do not have the Bible will be judged according to the knowledge they DID have of God from other sources, but if we also know what God says in His Book we have far less excuses for hurting Him.

*TEMPERAMENT* is a testimony to the unique blend God makes of each person's inherited traits. Each of us are born with a *special balance* of feeling, thinking and directive abilities that set us apart from everyone else. These inherited balances influence the *way* we react to certain kinds of situations. Some of us tend to be more purposeful and fiery;

How do our own personalities reflect the image of God?

65

What problems would we encounter if we tried to change our temperaments?

others cooler and more careful. Some people are always acting cheerfully; others rather sensitive and melodramatic. Temperament is the *"soul's essential response to its surroundings."* It is good to recognize that not *all* people react to things in the same way. This is one more evidence of God's provision for keeping us unique and special. As we grow, we find we are absolutely distinct from all of His other children; our fingerprints, hair, voice prints and everything about us mark us out in His eyes from everyone else. How lovely of God to give us these distinctions!

Remember *this* about temperaments; God uses them *as* He has given them to us. Do not try to *change* yours. Temperament has nothing to do with your character, your love to God, or His love for you. You can do both good *and* bad things with your temperament. The same kind of *purposefulness* and natural strength of will that can make a man a fiery prophet for God can also be a real temptation for him to be *angry* or *mad* if things do not go his way. The one who has a *steady* temperament can tend to be *lazy;* the man who is always *laughing* can become *shallow;* the *sensitive* girl can get *gloomy* and *depressed* easily. Give your temperament *as it is* to God for Him to make the best use of.

As we yield our lives to the control and direction of the Holy Spirit, our personalities will be *shaped* by Him into the image of the Lord Jesus. We must often stay in God's Word to give it time to affect our whole beings. The truth of the Bible will flow through our lives, to be expressed by our temperaments in whatever work God gives us.

3. *OUR SPIRITS* — The revelation of *INTUITION* by the *HOLY SPIRIT*.

INTUITION is a function of our human spirits that can put us in touch with God and His truth *without* information from any of our five senses. God has made us moral like Himself. Since being moral involves *knowing* what *is* right, He has made sure that we would *instinctively sense* wrong choices. God did not only write His law in the Bible. Through intuition He writes it on *every heart*.

66

The *first function* of intuition is to make us *aware of God.* Just as a growing baby with *physical* hunger *expects* to be given physical *food;* and when developing intellectual hungers *expects* to find knowledge, so there comes a time in all of our lives when we sense a *spiritual* hunger and know that God is there waiting to meet us. We call this time of awakening in children "the age of accountability." It is probably *later* for children who grow up in non-Christian homes than it is for those who have earlier been exposed to the Gospel of Christ. But *all men* have it. Although non-Christians have not felt the indwelling presence of God, intuition gives all people a very clear witness to God's reality and claims.

What is the common moral characteristic of both the "civilized" and "non-civilized" world?

*Men also have the SENSE OF MORAL LAW.* God has written the clear understanding into our beings that we *should not be selfish.* Everyone starts off knowing right from wrong. It comes independent of our education and training, when we develop God-consciousness. God's moral law — the rule of right action — is given through our *intuition,* and through *conscience* directly appeals to our reason (John 1:9; 3:19-20; Romans 1:18-19).

It is a strange thing, but selfishness has *never* been admired. No creed or religion in history has thought well of the man who betrayed those who loved and helped him the most, or became a coward to save his own neck. Even dedicated Marxists have annual twinges of conscience. This rule God gave us — the rule of fairness — is known by *all races,* regardless of language, religion or training. Both "civilized" and "savage" know this inwritten law of happiness. As long as a person can function as a moral being, it will throw light on their conduct.

Now as this law directly appeals to our *minds* for acceptance, it can be fought off and its force dimmed by reasoning it away. It is not a *force* law like the instinct of animals. It directs by *influence,* not by *control.* If we do not want to obey it, we can always think up enough excuses why we shouldn't. Men can always "suppress the truth in unrighteousness" and be "taken captive through philosophy and empty deception according to the tradition of men" (Romans

67

What is the
universal
method that
God uses to
judge men?

1:18; Colossians 2:8, ASB). We can fight it or forget it for a while; argue with it or try to ignore it; but it is God's witness to right regardless, and we know it is there. Paul shows that in sinful men . . . "Their conscience also bears witness . . . their thoughts the mean while accusing or else excusing one another " (Romans 2:15; Acts 17:27-28; 2 Timothy 4:3-4).

While the Gospel greatly *adds* guilt to those who reject it, it is not God's original basis of condemning sin. The Bible shows us that God judges all men according to the DEGREE or amount of moral "light" they have. ("Light" is a Bible figure of speech meaning *that which shows us what we ought to do.)* The heathen may know far less about God than the church member. God will judge the heathen for what *he* really knew, and the church member by the same rule. He is perfectly fair and just with all men. GUILT is exactly *equal* to the *amount of light known and rejected.* ("There is no respect of persons with God; as many as have sinned without law [the Ten Commandments, or written, taught knowledge of right and wrong] shall also perish without the law . . . for when the heathen, which have not the law, do BY NATURE [moral law] the things contained in the law, these . . . are a law unto themselves.") (Romans 2:1-16; Luke 12:47-48; Matthew 11:20-24; John 12:35-36; 46-48; 15:22-24; 16:8-11; James 4:17).

4. *OUR SOCIETY* — The revelation of *WITNESS* by *CHRIST* and *CHRISTIANS.*

God has given us one more testimony of His love. When He first set up our human family, He made us so that we could learn from and enjoy *each other.* Human friendship is a *very beautiful* thing under God. Friends and sweethearts could both experience His goodness together (1 Samuel 18:1-3; Ephesians 5:24-25, 28-33; 1 Peter 3:7). He made us *"members of one another"* (Ephesians 4:25) and there is no closer link on earth than that between people who *really* know and love Him (Acts 2:41-47; 1 John 1:3-4; John 17:21-23). When others find out more about God, they can *share* their discoveries about Him. This gives us another way to learn about His greatness. All the different people that live in our world give God the chance to show *us* just how many ways He can meet our needs.

*Right EDUCATION* helps people know about God. The Creator gave us minds to learn, to be excited about the truths of His Universe. When we *start* with the right picture of our world, and find out just how God has fitted everything together, learning is a thrill. As we do one thing God shows us, we become ready to learn again. Each discovery should *add* to the excitement of the previous one; there was to be no end of this increase in happiness when man first followed His Maker. What we learn in our *souls* through our *intellect*, we should also feel right about in our *spirits* through *intuition*.

What should be the ultimate purpose of education within the family?

This is why God makes the *family* so important. We learn first of all what God is like by looking at our parents. They have a responsibility to give their children the right picture of Him. Our *souls* develop long before our *spirits*. The patterns we learn early in life should match the ones His Spirit will give us later. A child needs to see a little bit of what God's love is like when he sees that his father and mother love each other, and that they love him. When he begins to ask questions, his parents should tell him the truth in answers that will help him love and respect his Heavenly Father (Ephesians 6:1-4; Proverbs 23:22-25).

*Proper EXAMPLES* of a God-honoring life are also needed to help young people form pictures of what people who *do* love God look like. Two thousand years ago, God did the most wonderful thing possible to give us an idea of how to live. He Himself became a man, and walked on our planet for about thirty-three years. We have a record of His life in the Bible. He went through the same problems we do every day. He never broke His Father's law, and  He never hurt His Father's heart. He can give *us* the power to live in the same way. He was the best example of love our world has ever seen (Philippians 2:5-8; Hebrews 2:14-15; 4:15; 5:5-9; 1 Peter 2:22).

So also today, God needs people who will do what He tells them. This is the real purpose of the Christian's work on earth. People all around the world have not seen what God can do in a life. *We* must show them. They have witnesses of God from many places, as we have seen; but there is *nothing*

How do
common
knowledge
and
unselfishness
resolve
problems
between two
parties?

*more convincing* than a person who is actually DOING what they know deep-down inside they should do. God's plan for His runaway world is to *"re-incarnate" His Word* in human flesh as people surrender up their rebellion and accept His offer of life. The world needs *living* witnesses of God's love. *We* must be those witnesses (1 John 2:14-17; Acts 26:16-18; Matthew 5:14-16; Acts 1:8).

## THE CONDITIONS OF HAPPINESS

There are *two conditions* of human happiness. They are (1) *Common true KNOWLEDGE;* (2) *Common UNSELFISH-NESS.* There will never be unity or peace between people until they can at least meet these two conditions. If two *friends* do not agree, their *friendship* is in danger; if a *husband* and *wife* will not agree, their *marriage* is headed for the rocks; if a *nation* cannot agree, crime and anarchy will stalk the streets; and because our *countries* cannot agree, people are now afraid of nuclear annihilation. God says — "Can two walk together except they be *agreed?"* (Amos 3:3).

But take the *first* condition. How *can* a finite man agree with another as to what is true and valuable? He really is not *able* to, because he cannot always see what "valuable" *is.* That is why we all need *God.* He has promised to *show us* what we need to know, provided we will use this knowledge wisely. Although we are all finite, we have an *Infinite* Friend Who can answer any real problem. That is one reason why God has a *right* to all of our lives, whether we have given them to Him or not. If two people cannot agree using *their* limited knowledge, they can go to *God* or His *Word* and find a principle or direction for an answer. Not many people want to do this today. It is little wonder that our world is in so much trouble and has so many problems.

The *second condition* is just as important. Knowledge is not enough. Unless we are also willing to *do* that which we honestly see as the best thing, our knowledge will only get us into more trouble. Our world is generally rather clever today; it also is probably the most frightened and confused world of all time. It is not enough to *know* what is right; we must also be willing to *do* it. Begin with selfish *people;* and you will

70

always wind up with selfish *societies*, no matter *what* they call themselves, and no matter *how much* they know. That is *why* God has given us a law. It is not a suggestion, or advice; it is a *command*. God has made it a law because *all* happiness — not only His, but that of every creature in the Universe — depends on it. No one can afford to break it. God must be *sure* that everyone will obey it. If its direction was ever rejected by a moral creature, his selfishness left unchecked could end up turning the Universe into *Hell*. This law is called in the Bible — LOVE. There is no more important rule in all of God's Universe.

What's the difference between "law" and "advice" and why must we be aware of the distinction?

## THE LAW OF LOVE

We have already seen that God has an infinitely great Being and is an indescribably lovely Person. Now the next amazing thing we find out about God is that He is like this because He has *chosen* to be! God *Himself* has a law to keep.

God didn't just "make up" this law. It has *always* been in the Universe as long as God *Himself* has been here, because it is something just naturally true about His life. To understand it, we must see this *one simple idea; that God is valuable for His own sake.* We all know without really thinking about it that anything that *is* important must be worth choosing above something else *not* as important. Do you see that the VALUE of an object *IN ITSELF creates* the *reason* for us to choose it, if we can honestly see that it IS the most valuable object? Its VALUE obligates us.

Now *God's law is based* on this idea. It is not something He *invented;* but rather something that has *always* been true, in the very nature of things. The BASIS of this law is not God's IDEAS or WILL, but rather the *value* of *His eternal BEING*.

You know that God *thinks* (1 Samuel 2:35; Isaiah 1:18; 41:21; 55:8-9; Jeremiah 29:11; Exodus 32:7-14; 2 Kings

71

Does God's
law spring
from His will
or His being
and why is
this
important?

19:14-28; Micah 6:1-3) and *feels* like us (Genesis 6:5-6; 2 Chronicles 16:9; Psalm 78:38; 95:10-11; Isaiah 12:1; Ezekiel 6:9-10; Micah 7:18-19; Matthew 18:23,27,34-35; Luke 15:7,10). He can also *CHOOSE* between two things (Genesis 1:26; 3:22-24; 6:6,12-13; 9:11-12; Exodus 32:7-14; 20-33; 2 Kings 20:5-6; Isaiah 12:1; Acts 1:7; 1 John 4:14). He can *originate* choice. These qualities make up what we call His *MORAL* ATTRIBUTES. He *can* control what He does. He has power over His *own* power, to make amazing and infinitely wise decisions, directed by these powers of His incredibly wonderful personality.

But God's *BEING* functions quite apart from His *character*. He did not *create* this; He has *always* had this spiritual, self-existent Being, just like *we* have a body to live in. This infinite Being is distinct from His personality. Out of its powers He fashioned man and his world. With its energies He upholds the lives and happiness of all creation (Colossians 1:17). It is the *source of all life*; nothing would live if He withdrew His care from us. All of God's *powers* flow from His Being. Since everyone's happiness *depends* on these powers, God *Himself* has a responsibility to take care of them. And here is the *ultimate basis* of God's law. Since everyone's life hangs on *His* well-being, God MUST *will His own highest good* as the *wisest possible* act. If He decided otherwise, He would be *un*wise; His infinitely wonderful mind has never made a foolish choice. He is *obliged* to rule Himself and His creation for *everyone's* highest good. Just as *we* are responsible to love and take care of our lives, God is responsible to love and take care of *His*. You can see how this *is* the most valuable thing in the Universe.

God is not important just because He *said* so, but because He actually *IS* the most valuable person in the Universe. When we see that the Bible calls Him "good" it *means* something to us. God is good because He always *keeps* this law of valueableness. That is why *we* should all choose it, just as God does. God's love-law is *founded in His Being*, not His will. Since His being is *separate* from His will, the law *obligates* His will; He himself can *choose* to be good. That is why the words "God is love" mean something when applied to God. God has a law to keep Himself, and He keeps it. "Love" is not just something He invented. It is the way of a supremely intelligent life, and it is the way God *chose* to live. God has the greatest responsibilities in the Universe, and He

72

meets them ALL. There are few more awesome things in the Bible than knowing that.

Why was it necessary for Adam and Eve to be tested?

## WHAT WENT WRONG?

Adam and Eve awoke in a world of loveliness. Made as a tiny replica of their Heavenly Father, having in *finite miniature* the abilities and qualities of God, they were given His law of love to live by. The first man and his lovely wife walked and talked with God in the garden paradise that was Eden. There was no sickness, pain or death. There was no sin or rebellion in the world. Man was supremely happy, healthy and content. God saw everything that He had made was "very good" (Genesis 1:26-31).

Only one thing remained to be done. Before Adam was granted the gift of eternal life, he had to *prove* to God that  he could be trusted. A test of his loyalty was given him. A forbidden tree grew in the garden. Its fruit could extend his light *beyond that* which he had yet proved himself worthy to be given. Adam and Eve were *forbidden* to eat of it, lest they fall into the same selfish quest for power that had turned Lucifer, prince of the angels into Satan (Isaiah 14:12-15). God was very clear in His warning. He made sure that they understood how important their test was. It was the only way they could be tested for the glorious future God had in store for them. He guarded this most solemn law of the Universe by the *greatest possible penalty*. It was called — DEATH; it was an awful but absolute *necessity* if a moral being should ever do something *insane* as to break this protecting law. It would simply and finally *cut him off* from interfering with anyone else's happiness.

Incredibly enough, that tragedy *happened!* Eve, tempted by Satan in the form of a serpent, *took* the forbidden fruit. In a *perfect* environment, surrounded by everything he could wish for, Adam also ate the fruit, joining his wife in deliberate

73

Why was man removed from the Garden of Eden after his sin?

sin. It opened his eyes to evil. Right there man became both morally and physically *ruined!* Sin entered the world, and with it *death,* as Adam and Eve gave in to selfishness against the clear warning of God. The first pangs of guilt struck terror into our first parents' hearts as they heard, through the still air of evening, God's voice calling for them in the garden. In unspeakable sadness, God was forced to clamp down His Divinely-appointed penalties. Man was turned out of the Garden lest he take also of the fruit of the tree of life and become *immortal in sin* — a *second* Satan! The ground was cursed, so that man would have to labor in future to live; he would have less time for self-pleasing and resultant sin. Death began its deadly work, setting alight a time-fuse to detonate in every man's final exit from this life (Genesis 3:1-24).

---

## ME — OR ADAM?

---

It is vitally important to notice here *HOW* Adam fell, and the *consequences* of his fall. To understand present human depravity, we must first *define* the word "depravity". From the Latin *"de"* very, and *"pravus" crooked,* depravity means the *failure to meet an existing standard,* a fall from a place of original perfection. Adam became depraved in *TWO* ways; his SOUL first failed to obey God, then his BODY began to fail. The first depravity was thus MORAL, and was followed by the *second,* which was PHYSICAL, caused by Adam's selfish choice in spite of the clear warning of the penalty of God. These two depravities caused TWO kinds of DEATH; physical *and* spiritual. Although these are linked, they are *not* the same thing. Both deaths are states of SEPARATION; *spiritual* death being a state of separation from *God* (essentially, to *live sinfully* is to *be* spiritually dead 1 Timothy 5:6); and physical death being finally a separation from the *material world* of Earth.

*PHYSICAL DEPRAVITY* is the *inherited result* of Adam's sin. It has brought great tragedy to earth. Our bodies are all subject to these problems from it:

1. *DULLNESS* of mental faculties. None of our human "temples" function as well as they could. Our *minds* are not

as clear, our *feelings* not as capable of intense perception, our *strength* not as vibrant as our first parents. Our whole systems have "cooled" in their original vivid relationships and responses.

What do we inherit as a result of Adam's sin?

2. *DETERIORATION of HEALTH.* This is painfully evident across the world. There is no "perfect" health. All of us inherit bodies that are greatly subject to disease and sickness. Sickness is ultimately a result of Adam's sin, and we can reinforce our physical ill-health by our own selfish choices. The delicate way God balanced our physical and psychological systems make it easy for our *moral* lives to influence our *physical* beings.

3. *DEFORMATION* of innocent children. The moral disease of sin has invaded the delicate controls that influence the formation of new little bodies; sin has given us mis-shapen and tragic little forms that could have been beautiful babies.

4. *DISEASE* and *sickness* world wide are another limiting factor that tend to cut down the amount of moral damage selfishness can do. Consider the countries that turn from the Living God to serve idols. *Devaluation* of individual human life leads to *poor living conditions, uncleanliness* and *disease.* Sickness abounds, reducing the age of the population to a very low value. As the Gospel has come in to such places, *moral purity* has  been followed by *social changes,* leading to expanded life expectancy. This is another automatic law tending to curb selfishness.

*This physical depravity* is the power that makes our bodies *decay* and *die.* The first man had a perfect body. It was made to operate in flawless harmony and was constantly repaired and replaced cell by cell in wear. There is no *medical* reason for age death. We have a highly efficient set of repair organs that gradually re-make every organ and bone. Every *seven years* the ENTIRE BODY has been fully re-made. Science cannot yet explain why these "repairers" stop and the person gets old, feeble and dies. Physical depravity is a *failure of the way you are built,* of the *material* you are made of. It is an

Are the
inherited
results of
Adam's sin
basically
physical or
moral in
consequence?

"out of balance" set of once finely-tuned interdependent body functions. It is a physical breakdown of the laws of health, a fallen state in which healthy life is not kept going. This is *not* something of the SOUL; it concerns only the material of which the body is made that influences the soul. It is not sin, but the *fruit* of sin, our's and Adam's.

The Bible testifies to our *PHYSICAL depravity* by birth and circumstances, that make it easier for the will to choose self-gratification, but this is not the *cause* of our wrong action. It is obvious that man is in a weakened and unbalanced condition: Psalm 103:15-16; Matthew 26:41; Romans 6:19; Romans 8:3,23; 2 Corinthians 4:11; 5:2-4; 12:7; Galatians 4:13-14; Philippians 3:21; James 4:14. This simply gives him the *bias* towards selfish action, and is only an *influence* for sin.

Adam's terrible choice opened the lock to a tide of temptation, sin and death for his race (Romans 5:12; Hebrews 9:27). As man's sin increased, God slowly shortened his physical life span to help curb the resulting spread of destruction and unhappiness (Genesis 5:27,32; Genesis 6:3; Psalm 90:10). Mankind is a *fallen race*, not growing better, but progressively *worse*.

We are all victims of physical depravity and death, circumstances and environments that provide powerful temptations to sin, and *all men* follow the wrong choice of our first parents. Our own family lines, and ultimately Adam himself, are responsible for our PHYSICAL depravity. But this is, in itself, *not* sin. It is not the direct CAUSE of sin, so that we sin from some sort of physical *necessity*, but simply the weakened constitution and strong desires that give sin power and make men open to the tug of temptation.

"AT THE LAST FRONTIER THERE WILL BE NOTHING TO DECLARE — ONLY A PASSPORT EXAMINATION"

Why do you
think some
people think
of sin as
being "only
natural"?

# WHAT SIN IS NOT

1. *Sin is not NATURAL* — A common answer of man when faced with sin has been — "Yes, we *all* sin — *nobody* is perfect — we're only *human!*" Nothing could be further from the truth. Only by comparing ourselves with the perfect example of TRUE humanity — the *Lord Jesus* — can we see just how *un*-natural sin is. When God became man, He took on Himself a perfectly *human* body. Jesus was not God *disguised* as man, but God who *BECAME* man. Although He was conceived supernaturally, He was born of a perfectly normal human girl (Luke 1:31). He *grew, learned,* was *hungry* and *thirsty* (Luke 2:52; 2:40; Matthew 4:2; Luke 4:2). His body was as human as any man that ever walked the earth; it was in NO way more special than any other human body (Hebrews 10:5; John 2:21; Luke 24:3,23; 1 John 4:3). He *ate, drank,* felt *weary* and *rested* (Mark 2:16), and declared His body to be *flesh and bones* (John 20:20,27). He had a soul as human as any other man's soul (Isaiah 53:11, 12; Psalm 16:10; John 12:27; Acts 2:27; Matthew 26:38). *John, Peter, Paul* and *Isaiah* all called Him a *man* (John 1:30; Acts 2:22; 1 Timothy 2:5; Isaiah 53:3) and He called *Himself* a man (John 8:40). His *favorite name* for Himself when He walked this earth was — "The *Son of Man"* used *seventy-one* times in Scripture.

*Christ* was, of course, *always* God. He knew that He had come *from* the Father, and after that His earthly mission He would go *back* to the Father. His essential relationship with the Spirit and the Father was never removed. But *while He walked this planet,* to show us that it WAS possible to resist temptation and defeat the Devil with *only* the power of the Holy Spirit, the guidance of His Father, and the Word of God, the Lord Jesus used *NONE* of His Godhead powers. To be  fully "tempted in ALL points such as we are" and yet be "without sin" the Lord Jesus had to become *fully* human. To make Him *more* than this during His brief stay on Earth is to

What is the
great error
of the
sin-is-only-
natural
reasoning?

MISS completely the whole purpose of His life; not only to offer His body as a perfect substitute for our sin, but to show us the way a child of God was to live *in this world!* (Hebrews 2:14-15; 5:5-9). He *laid aside* His rights and powers as God to tread this world; (Philippians 2:5-8; Luke 2:52; Hebrews 5:7-9) although, His essential nature as God remained unchanged. *Understand* — the Lord Jesus had NOTHING available to Him on Earth that ANY child of God does *not* have available; His Father even arranged for Him to have some *disadvantages!* (Luke 2:7; John 1:46; 8:41). The Lord Jesus was our pattern of TRUE *human* nature, yet *He* was "without sin" (Hebrews 4:15); and He "did *no* sin" (1 Peter 2:22). GOD made human nature; God did NOT make sin!

*Sin is NEVER natural.* It is horribly *UN*-natural. Sin is NEVER "human." It is horribly IN-human. Sin creates *remorse, guilt* and *shame;* every time a man feels these three witnesses in his soul, they tell him sin is NOT natural. Even the simple *lie-detector* can tell us this. The whole body reacts *adversely* when a man sins. Sin is in fact, a kind of *insanity* (Ecclesiastes 9:3).

No one ever sins because they *love* sin. Even the *worst* sinner does not like to be *called* a sinner; he resents the fact of his selfishness, even when he *is* selfish! And even the worst of sinners cannot help but *admire right* in another, whenever that other person is sufficiently far away from him not to convict *him* of his selfishness (Isaiah 58:1-2; Ezekiel 33:32; Romans 7:22). Nobody sins merely *for the sake of* doing wrong. Sinning men and women *hate* themselves when they do wrong. A man sins only when he wants *something for himself more strongly than he wants to do right.* God never *planned* sin for man. It is the most *un-natural* thing in the moral Universe. To equate *humanity* with *sinfulness* is to make *God* the Author of His own *worst enemy;* to make God responsible for the thing that has brought Him unhappiness. Do not DARE say sin is "natural"! God *hates* sin with perfect hatred; He *loves* humanity.

---

## ARE WE REALLY UNABLE TO OBEY?

---

2. *Sin is not UNAVOIDABLE* — One of the favorite heresies of the past, that is rapidly now becoming the

favorite heresy of the *present*, is the lie of *Antinomianism* — What is antinomianism? that men cannot do what God expressly REQUIRES them to do; and therefore they may live how they like and still enter the Kingdom of God. In the midst of the greatest moral landslide the world has ever seen, in the midst of the most flagrant disrespect for law and order and government of any century, it is unblushingly proclaimed AS GOSPEL truth from pulpits across the nation that man *cannot* keep the law of God! In our wariness of the dangers of *legalism*, we have forgotten the perils of antinomianism; we have forgotten that the LAW is a *schoolmaster* to bring us to Christ (Galatians 3:24) and that "by the LAW is the knowledge of *sin*" (Romans 3:20). Gone is the preaching of moral responsibility that streamed from men like William Booth, George Fox, John Wesley and Charles Finney that made men *weep* with conviction; gone is the heartbreak of the Psalmist for the honour of God when he cried "Horror has taken hold of me, because of the wicked that forsake Thy law!" (Psalm 119:53; 119:37).

Many sincere men are saying, "God gave us *good* laws to keep," and in the next breath saying, "we are actually *unable* to keep them!" If this *is* true, then God's laws ARE *NOT* GOOD! *No* law is good that asks the *impossible* of its subjects. If God demands obedience to impossible laws then *God* is not just, for even *men* do not require obedience to impossible laws. If God demands such obedience under penalty of DEATH, then God is not only *unfair*, but *monstrous!* What kind of Being would pass laws upon his subjects they are unable to keep, then condemn them to *death* for their failure to obey? This is a blasphemy on God's character.

The Bible expressly declares that God has given *good* laws. *All* the laws of God are based on the one great *Law of Love*, that governs the actions of all moral beings in God's Universe — that every moral creature should unselfishly choose the *highest good* of God and His Universe according to their real, relative values; *God's* being *greatest, first* of all; then all others in the order of their true value under God. The *Ten Commandments* are just the letter expression of that law, given

If God's laws are impossible to keep, could He punish us for disobedience and yet remain righteous in doing so?

when men began to ignore the love law written on their hearts. They define man's obligations *Godward* in the first *three* commandments, then those of his obligations to his *fellow-men* in the last seven. The Lord Jesus summed these in His *two* commandments (Matthew 22:36-40; Mark 12:28-33; Luke 10:25-28) covering what Moses had already been given (Deuteronomy 6:5; Leviticus 19:18). *Paul* summed up the law into the one basic word *"love"* (Romans 13:8-10; Galatians 5:14; 1 Timothy 1:5; James 2:8-10). This law, expressed in different ways, is given as the unchangeable condition of happiness and holiness; it defines man's obligations and can *never* be changed or suspended in our present relationships (Galatians 3:19; Psalm 19:7; Matthew 5:17; Romans 7:12; 1 Timothy 1:8).

*Which* of God's laws are we actually UNABLE to keep — *if* we love the Lawgiver? Do we *have* to relegate God to some other position than King of our lives and put something else in His place? Do we *have* to take His Name in vain? *Must* we steal? What man has ever been born that could not help *BUT* murder? Do we have *no choice* but to commit adultery, to lie, to covet, to dishonour parents and refuse to honour God on a special day of rest? God says "His commandments are NOT grievous". Do WE say they are not only *grievous* but *impossible?* The Lord Jesus said — "My yoke is *easy* and My burden is light". Do WE say His yoke is not only HEAVY, but completely *unbearable* for any human being?

*No* saint in Scripture thought they were "unable" to keep God's laws. *Moses* didn't (Exodus 24:3; Deuteronomy 5:1; 6:24-25; 10:12-13; 11:22; 26:16-19; 28:47; 28:58-59; 30:8; 30:11-14). Neither did *Joshua* (22:5), *Ezra* (7:23-26), *David* (Psalm 19:7; 40:8), his psalmist friend (Psalm 119:165-168) or *Daniel* (9:9-11) or others! (2 Kings 17:13,7-18, etc.). The *Lord Jesus* Himself told men to obey His Father's laws, and that *this* was the test of being a true disciple (Matthew 5:17-20; 19:17; John 14:15,21; 14:23-24; 15:10). The *Apostle John* stresses this obedience (1 John 2:3-6; 3:18-22). Obeying God's love law simply means living for Him with *no selfish interest;* to live up to all the light you have with all the effort of will, mind and feeling necessary for the task in hand. For the Christian, obeying God and keeping His commandments are a *natural part* of his new life. Only the *sinner* finds it hard to walk in God's ways because he is trying to use the law as a means to his *own* end, the ultimate gratification of his own selfishness. He must fall.

Is a "sinful nature" necessary before a person can sin? Why or why not?

3. *Sin is not PHYSICAL* — Many think they have *explained* the fact of sin in the human race by using a phrase we shall call "Doggie Logic." It goes essentially like this: "A *dog* is not a dog *because* he barks; he barks *because* he is a dog. Thus, man is not a sinner because he *sins;* he sins *because* he *is* a sinner." The assumption is, of course, that all sin flows from a *pre-determined sinful nature,* and it is *this* nature that creates sinful acts of the sinner. Just as the bark of a dog comes undeniably from the fact that he *is* a dog, so man's sin will flow inescapably from the fact that he *is* a sinner, and was *born* so. It *sounds* nice; is it *true?*

There are, unfortunately, *two things wrong* with this logic. They are *serious* flaws because, once they are *assumed,* they actually *destroy* the basis of the very thing they seek to prove — that all men are *guilty* of, and *responsible* to God for, their sin. These logic flaws are — (a) *A Man is not a dog.* A dog's actions are *right* if he barks because God *created* dogs to express themselves naturally by barking. But God did *not* create men to *sin!* A dog's bark is *natural;* sin is *NOT.* The Bible everywhere represents sin as an alien invasion to a moral nature made in the image of God. Assuming that man sins *because* it is his *nature* to sin, also assumes that *sin* is natural. A dog barks because he is a dog. A man can *also* bark if he *chooses* to. Does this prove that he is a *dog?* No, it proves that he has *chosen* to do a thing he was never *created to do naturally.* If a man sins, it merely proves that he has so chosen to sin; and his sin will certainly be treated as *unnatural* in the eyes of God. (b) *Do we need a sinful nature to sin?* Is it *necessary* to have an "implanted sinfulness" to enable man to do wrong? If *one* sinner can be found in Scripture who sinned WITHOUT first having a sinful nature, the answer is *no;* and the case is closed. And of course, there are at least *three* moral beings who committed sin without sinful natures. *Satan* was the first. The first man *Adam* was the *second,* and his wife, *Eve.* The *angels* who were cast out of heaven were apparently before perfect. No moral being needs a sinful nature to sin; if he is given one that makes it impossible for him NOT to live right, he is not GUILTY but *helpless.*

81

## IS SIN A SOMETHING?

*Is sin a "thing"?* Are feelings or desires, for instance, good or bad IN THEMSELVES? The following diagram lists some common desires. *Mark* the column where you think each desire could be classed — as "right," "wrong" or "either."

| DESIRE FOR: | RIGHT (Moral) | WRONG (Immoral) | EITHER (Amoral) |
|---|---|---|---|
| MONEY | | | |
| SEXUAL LOVE | | | |
| POWER | | | |
| FRIENDS | | | |
| FOOD | | | |
| REST | | | |

*Did you think CAREFULLY?* You will find you can frame a situation for EACH where the desire in the question could be right OR wrong or an "EITHER"! This is because desires have *no will of their own*. They are built into all men in greater or lesser degree. There is no desire that cannot be used for God's glory, and no desire that *mis*used could not make you like the Devil himself. It is the PURPOSE behind the choice to indulge a desire that makes it right or wrong. That choice is carried out by the WILL, after consulting reason, conscience and intuition as to the rightness or wrongness of the action. DESIRES are NEVER wrong IN THEMSELVES. They are neither IMMORAL (bad, wrong) or MORAL (good, right) but AMORAL (having no morality or deliberate rule of right and wrong in themselves). Desires are God-given; used *rightly*, to ENJOY life; used *wrongly*, to DESTROY ourselves. The tug of desire is not sin *in itself*, but a natural feeling produced by stimulation and without direct control by the person.

## THOSE BRAINWAVES

*Are THOUGHTS right or wrong in themselves?* They, too, are AMORAL. The Lord Jesus Himself was given "wrong thoughts" during His dark wilderness temptation. But *He* NEVER SINNED (Hebrews 4:15).

Why isn't it wrong to be tempted?

A thought may be a *temptation* to do wrong, but it is NOT SIN until the *will* gives assent to the thought. It is not the feelings OR the thoughts that make men sin. Reason tells men right or wrong (using memory and conscience), but reason does not *carry out* decisions. Feelings tug, the mind advises, but neither DECIDE. Reason may *tell* choice the right, but has in itself no power to CHOOSE that way. Moral decision is under the exclusive control of the WILL, the key center of the whole personality. The *will's choice* makes a man sinner or saint in God's eyes.

---

## TEMPTATION

---

*Don't mistake TEMPTATION for sin.* Temptation is a suggestion to gratify a desire in an illegal way or amount. Temptation is NOT sin. *Jesus* was tempted (Hebrews 4:15). All men are tempted whether sinner or saint. "Every man is tempted when he is drawn away of his own lust and enticed" (James 1:14). The feelings ("Lust" — over-strong desire) tug at the will. The mind refers to memory and moral law for knowledge of right and wrong. The will is informed and is faced with a decision. If the reason tells the will that carrying out that desire would be RIGHT as well as *pleasant* and the will acts on this, happiness and harmony result. But if the mind gives a verdict of *wrong*, the choice can be caught in a struggle between the right, and the *pleasant*, but WRONG. There is always "pleasure" in sin of a very temporary kind (Hebrews 11:25; 1 Timothy 5:6). The mind knows right is best. If it should not know the choice made *is* bad, it is NOT SIN to the individual! It is for this reason that we are told not to "judge" another person. We cannot know how much light they have. Two people may be doing exactly the same thing; to one it is wrong, but to the other (as far as HE is concerned) it is not. This must not be confused with deliberate deceit. Not always are the actions of outward conduct the proof of a right heart (1 Samuel 16:7; John 7:24).

There is therefore *no such thing* as "unconscious" sin. God holds us responsible *for all the light we have and are able to get* — no more, no less. There is no sin that we know nothing at all about that God will judge us for. Men can sometimes do things that may be *legally* wrong, but in *ignorance*, without knowing they WERE wrong. A child's first defence against discovered wrong by its parents is invariably — "But I didn't KNOW it was wrong!" If *that* can be proved, he knows the case is closed. It is "to him that KNOWETH to do good, and DOETH IT NOT, to him it is SIN" (James 4:17). Should we sin in the eyes of the law through ignorance, it is only when we discover our mistake that we can ask pardon and forgiveness (Leviticus 4:2-3; Numbers 15:27-31).

For the Christian, *DOUBTFUL ACTIONS are sinful.* Doubt is nearly always a sign of some duty not done or some illegal choice about to be made. A man may have equal doubts on some things whether to do them or not. In such cases, he must act according to the best light he can get. But if he should go and deliberately do something of which he doubts the lawfulness, he is condemned. It shows a spirit of self-pleasing without careful regard to the Lord's glory. "Whatsoever is not of faith is SIN" (Romans 14:23). Any action that might cause another younger Christian to stumble falls into the same category. There are some things a Christian could do from a pure heart and right intent that outwardly could be misunderstood. Even of the Lord Jesus Himself it was said "He has a demon" (Matthew 11:18). Abstain from the very appearance of evil (1 Thessalonians 5:22; Romans 14; Acts 24:16; 1 Corinthians 10:32).

The condition of our *PHYSICAL depravity* gives great power to temptation. Consider two men, Dick and Jack. *Dick,* a non-Christian, always seems assured, well-balanced and at ease. *Jack,* who *is* a Christian, seems however to be run down, highly-strung and somewhat touchy. How can we account for this? Digging a little deeper, we find that Dick's parents are clean-living Christians who are reasonably well-off and physically in very good health. On the other hand, Jack's parents are unsaved, alcoholics, and his home is little more than a hovel. We can see it would not be too fair to condemn Jack for what he is *outwardly,* until we find out what he WANTS to be. We must also ask ourselves, not what Dick is like compared to JACK, but what Dick is like compared to *Christ;* or what better kind of man Dick could be if he WAS a

Christian. Give both Dick and Jack ten years or a set of tough circumstances and you will soon see there is all the difference in the world.

In *Romans 7:7-24*, the Apostle Paul *personifies* sin to show its power over the enlightened, but unconverted mind. The excited *love of conscious freedom*, wanting to have its own way, clashes with the judgment of conscience and the moral law; a conflict begins between the "law" (rule of action) of *sin*, and the law of *God*. Without the drawing power of Christ, the convicted sinner cannot free himself, until the *Gospel* comes  to deliver him (Romans 7:25; 8:1). But although Paul places the tug of this "law of sin" in his. *bodily members* (from where the excited desires sparked into unnatural strength by the habit of selfish gratification reside), he does not really make a case for any "physical" sin, as if this was his helpless *inheritance*. If sin WAS physical, in what *form* would it exist? Would it be *solid, liquid* or *gas*? If sin is *material*, it can be isolated in a test-tube. May we then see the phenomenon of a vial of sin concentrate? This is, of course, *absurd*. All efforts to trace actual sin to some organic connection with parents have failed of any evidence, medically or physiologically; at the most, ALL inherited traits from parents simply contribute *INFLUENCES* for later selfish choices.

*Neither does sin reside*, as some sincere men have stated, in the *blood. No* place in the Scriptures give the blood *morality*. It is a symbol of *life*, and as the electrochemical and circulatory system of the body, is the "life of the flesh" and the "circuitry" of the soul. As a symbol of a man's life, it is certainly a *precious* symbol of Christ's atoning *sacrifice* for our lives (Isaiah 53:10-12; Hebrews 9:22-23; Matthew 26:28; Acts 20:28; Romans 3:24-26; 5:9-11; Ephesians 2:13; Hebrews 10:10-14; 10:19-20; 1 Peter 1:18-19; 1 John 1:7). If it was true that moral characteristics *are* transmitted through the blood, then a blood transfusion from a *saint*, will make a man more holy, and one from a sinner will make a saint less sanctified. It will follow then, that a *prenatal* blood transfusion on a "blue" baby will give it a totally different nature!

85

Why can't
good works
change
a non-
Christian's
standing
before God?

## THE FINAL CONCLUSION

### WHAT SIN REALLY MUST BE

1. *Sin is UNIVERSAL* — Nothing is clearer in Scripture or in daily life. *World history* is a chronicle of wickedness. Every man prior to conversion is a *slave* to his own selfishness. Every unsaved man knows that he is selfish. The Bible shows the unsaved to possess *one common wicked heart* or *character:* Genesis 6:5; 1 Kings 11:9-11; 15:3; 2 Chronicles 12:14; Psalm 28:3; 66:18; 78:37; 95:10; Jeremiah 17:9-10; Ezekiel 14:2-3; 18:30-32; Ecclesiastes 9:3; Matthew 5:27-30; 9:4; 13:15; Mark 3:5; 7:18-23; 8:17; Luke 21:34; Acts 8:21 (18-24); Romans 2:4-6; 8:7; Hebrews 3:7-15. *All* men without God are *totally selfish* at heart; it is exceedingly humbling to admit that ALL a man's pre-conversion actions are not in the *least* virtuous when examined in Eternity's light. Man has nothing to commend him to God, when he comes asking for forgiveness.

The Bible further reveals that from the beginning of man's moral accountability,(seeing his spiritual responsibility to God and his fellow-men) man has made a choice to live supremely for himself, with *no exceptions* of true goodness, no pauses for really virtuous behaviour, no alternative weeks of true unselfishness before God. Many factors influence the *forms* of this selfishness; there are many "good" clean-living, outwardly moral sinners, as well as those who are humanly despicable and degraded. Man chooses the particular form of selfishness that brings him the greatest pleasure; and this includes deeds and actions usually considered "good" by society, *including* prayer, religious activity, Bible study and preaching! But all sinners from those who have done "many wonderful works" to those God has had to "give up to vile affections" have one uniform morality — "there is NONE that doeth good, no, *not one." This universal persistency* in sin is also shown in: Genesis 8:21; Psalm 10:4; 14:13 (53:1,3); 28:3; 94:11; Ecclesiastes 1:14; Isaiah 55:7-9; 64:6 Jeremiah 13:23; 17:9-10; Matthew 7:21-23; 12:34-35; Romans 1:21; 3:10-12; 3:23; 6:16-17; 6:20; Ephesians 2:1, 3; 5:8; Titus 1:15; 3:3; 1 Peter 2:25.

## YOU AND YOUR ORIGINAL SIN

2. *Sin is ORIGINAL* — There is nothing clearer in the Bible that man is VERY original in his sin! Sin is not a *transmitted* thing, it is *created* by each being with the elements of true morality — (emotions, reason, free will, moral light and spiritual perception of this).

Throughout the Bible, man's *moral nature* is shown to spring from his HEART. This "heart" is not your PHYSICAL heart that busily pumps life-giving blood to all the members of your body. It is an illustration of *the SUPREME PREFER-ENCE*, or ULTIMATE CHOICE of your will, just as the physical heart is the center and source of all physical life. The RULING CHOICE of your will is the center and source of all your actions, and is the one thing most entirely under your control. If God had made salvation dependent, say, on moving your body, or solving a problem, or even feeling a certain emotion, you may not have been able to do it. If you were paralyzed, your muscles might not be able to act. If you had little education, even on pain of death you could not solve a problem beyond your own reason. Even with a threat of everlasting torment, you would not be able to keep any emotion for long. But if God only asks for the *choice of your will*, all is brought within your reach. You can always give this "heart" to God. You can always CHOOSE so long as you have a rational mind and a moral nature. Every man born is faced with God's request to the awakening Adam — "My son, give Me your HEART" (Proverbs 23:6; 4:23; 3:5).

When men choose wrong, following Adam's example, they become guilty of the second kind of depravity — *MORAL depravity. All sin is moral depravity* — "missing the mark" in the ultimate choice of life. The Bible pointedly testifies of man's *free choice* in his life of sin, using a variety

of words that show explicitly man's guilt and total moral depravity. *No definition of man's moral depravity that tends to remove personal and individual blame or responsibility from each sinner is a definition inspired by the Holy Spirit of God.* ALL the Bible words used for sin show that man is a *REBEL*, not a subject of pity who has lost his ability of will to do right.

In your own words, define the term "sinful nature."

Who can study the penetrating pictures of sin in the Scriptures and make sin something small? From the very *least* expression (to "err, stray from the mark or path planned for man") to the *strongest* term ("utter evil, wickedness of the mind and heart") all sin is WRONG CHOICE (Numbers 15:27; Ezekiel 3:18; 2 Kings 8:20,22; 1 Kings 8:47-50; 1 Chronicles 5:25; 1 Samuel 12:13-15; Joshua 22:16; Isaiah 66:3; Jeremiah 7:24; Romans 6:14-15; Hebrews 6:6; Galatians 6:1; Matthew 15:2; Acts 1:25; 1 Timothy 1:9; Romans 6:19; 2 Thessalonians 2:10-12; 2 Timothy 2:19; 1 Peter 4:18; Titus 2:12; Matthew 7:17,18; Hebrews 3:12).

From this study of Bible words describing sin, we look *in vain* for evidence that sin is anything else than a *wrong choice.* There is always the idea of *movement, voluntary action, never* a static or inactive something *behind* the will, received by heredity, that CAUSES the will to act in sin. The Word of God protects itself from theological speculation like this; sin is a CHOICE.

*Without God.* man *does* have a sinful nature, but this nature is *NOT* physical. He inherits no causation from his parents or anyone else. Man is responsible for his *own* actions. His sinful nature consists in the *habit patterns* of a life lived for *self* instead of *God.* They flow from a wrong HEART, or *ultimate choice* in life. They need not be all pre-meditated to be sin. A man who has unyielded rights and resentment in his heart that has been allowed to build for some time does not have to coldly calculate to fly into a rage. If a man says an unkind thing, then tries to cover it by saying, "Oh, I didn't *mean* that," the Scriptures flatly contradict him by stating "Out of the abundance of the *heart* the mouth speaketh." He may not have meant it to be *revealed* in all its ugliness. But it WAS in his heart, and the unconscious action followed. Nature does *not* mean natural, as compared to *ordinary,* but that which is *common,* that which man does *AS A RULE.* If we say man has a sinful nature, we are not talking about some solid "thing" causing sin; but that AS A RULE OF LIFE, the sinner *always* behaves sinfully. His own heart is set on pleasing himself; out of *this* choice flows all his thoughts, actions and choices.

*Scripture reveals that NO sinner seeks God.* His selfishness has made him *run* from the call of God just like Adam did long ago: Genesis 6:5; 2 Chronicles 12:14; Psalm 10:4; 53:2

88

119:115; Ecclesiastes 8:11; Isaiah 9:13; 31:1; 59:4; 64:7; 65:1; Matthew 23:37; John 5:40; 6:26; Romans 2:4; 3:11. For this reason, he *cannot be saved* unless God invests great efforts in him to turn him back to righteousness.

What factors in a child's life can heavily influence later choices in his life?

---

### WHY DO CHILDREN SIN?

---

*How, then does a child* sin? One does not have to *teach* a child to do wrong. The explanation becomes clear if we carefully consider the development of a man. A baby enters the world as the object of its parent's fondness, unceasing care, and concession by those who guard it. In these circumstances, the natural, inherited appetites are *first* developed; and the child's natural love of conscious freedom begins to express itself. The feelings develop *long* before the *reason,* and both are deeply entrenched before the spirit begins to awaken to the claims of God. Much depends at this point on the *parents.* If they are faithful in their duty to God, they must train their child to yield up its own way when that self-willed way will interfere with the happiness of others. The child will learn at first obedience to its parents only in a love/discipline relationship; it is here that the habit of *response to authority* must be ingrained in the child's soul, so that later, when God opens up the spiritual understanding, the child will surrender to Him (1 Samuel 15:22; Proverbs 6:20-23; 10:17; 13:18; 15:5;31-32; Ephesians 6:1; Colossians 3:20).

Since the feelings develop *before* the reason and conscience, the will begins to form the *habit of obeying desire,* which deepens every day. The obvious consequence is that self-indulgence becomes the *master principle* in the soul of the child long before it can understand that this self-indulgence will interfere with the right or happiness of others. This repeated bias grows *stronger* each day before a knowledge of right or duty could possibly have entered the mind. Finally,  the moment of true *moral responsibility* arrives. The child is now old enough to understand wrong. (This will probably be

What truth
was God
attempting
to show
Israel in the
parable of
Ezekiel 18?

*earlier* in a *Christian* home than in a non-Christian one.) Does the child approach this test in a perfectly *neutral* state? If Adam, in the maturity of his reason, with full consciousness of the morality of his actions could give in to such temptation, is there any doubt that a *child* will not? The moment that child chooses selfishly, it *sins.* From this point on (and NOT before) God holds the child responsible for its own actions and destiny. It is significant that all words of the Lord to sinners begin FROM THEIR *YOUTH,* and NOT from birth, as some have supposed.

It may be objected — does not the *Bible* teach that man is *born* sinful? The answer is an unqualified *no.* A small number of verses have at times been urged to support this idea, but they will not stand up to careful scholarship, and have only been used because no better explanation of the universal sinfulness of man has been forwarded. God is *very plain;* He does NOT hold the child in any kind of responsibility for its parent's sins. "What do you mean, you who use this proverb: the *fathers* have eaten sour grapes, and the *children's* teeth are set on edge? As I live . . . you shall not have occasion to use this proverb in Israel. *All* souls are MINE; as the soul of the *father,* so also the soul of the son is *mine;* the soul that SINNETH, it shall die" (Ezekiel 18:1-3, 20—see also the whole chapter; Jeremiah 31:30; Deuteronomy 24:16; 2 Chronicles 25:4; Psalm 94:23).

In speaking of the *coming judgment,* we are told in the Bible that God shall judge every moral being for his *own* sins, no mention being made of the imputation of Adam's guilt: Psalm 9:7-8; 96:13; Ecclesiastes 11:9; 12:14; Isaiah 3:10-11; Jeremiah 31:30; 32:17-19; Matthew 12:36-37; 16:27; Luke 12:47-48; 20:46-47; John 5:27-29; 12:48; Acts 17:30-31; Romans 2:2-11, 12, 16; 14:10-12; Galatians 6:7-8; 1 Corinthians 4:5; 2 Corinthians 5:10; 1 Timothy 5:24-25; Hebrews 9:27; 1 Peter 1:17; Jude 14-15; Revelation 2:23. God has *specifically stated* He would *not* judge man for another's sin. Yet, *all* sin in Scripture is under the judgment of God. Man *cannot,* therefore, inherit sin from his parents *or* Adam.

Some Scriptures used to try to support this "inherited sin" idea have been pressed right out of context. In examining these, it will be important to adhere to some universally-accepted principles of Biblical interpretation. They are (1) interpret *each* verse or passage in the light of *ALL OTHER* revealed Scripture; (2) Examine each verse in the *CONTEXT* where it is placed, taking into account the *design, purpose, authority* and *author* of each passage; (3) Texts that can be used to prove *either* of two theories prove *NEITHER;* (4) Passages must be interpreted in a way (if they can be) by which they will not *contradict* each other. It is with these principles in mind that we shall examine the so-called Scriptural objections.

Why does Psalm 51:5 *not* allow for a transmission theory of sin?

(1) *Psalm 51:5,* "I was shapen in iniquity, and in sin did my mother conceive me." *David* speaks; he speaks from *personal experience,* and not for the whole *world;* and *who* is the *subject* of this sentence? NOT David, but his *MOTHER!* Pressed literally, this verse says that during his time of gestation and conception, his *mother* was a sinner; David is the *object.* There is a world of difference between being shapen *in* iniquity and iniquity shapen *in him,* just as there is a great difference between being born in *England* and England being born in *me!* What then, does this passage teach? *Three different interpretations* have been given, *none* of which teach the dogma of transmitted sin: (a) That David was *illegitimate,* as the *Jews* have always believed (David's *mother's* name is not mentioned; David was *not* with the sons of Jesse when Samuel came to anoint them; David's brothers seemed *embarrassed* by his presence); (b) That David came from a *lineage* in which there had been immorality, and remembered his "lineage" mother in comparison to his own sexual sin; (c) That David was simply deeply cut to the heart by his sin. and broke out in the extravagant language of *poetry* (cf. v. 3, 3, 7 and 8); in thinking back along his life, he broke out affirming that from the earliest moments of light he had been a sinner, and had come from parents who were sinners, without in *any* way implying that this sin had been TRANSMITTED down to him by his mother. In *no way* does this passage teach *"inherited"* sin, no matter which way it is interpreted literally *or* figuratively.

(2) *Psalm 58:3* has been pressed into service along the same lines; note that it is the *wicked* who "go ASTRAY", if the text is to be *literally* interpreted, it means that infants TALK as well as *lie* from birth! *Job 14:4* and *15:4* have been stretched to fit into this dogma, but both these two verses simply imply the *universality* of human sin and bodily frailty,

91

without any reference to the MEANS *by which* man sins; both may be used to *support* the idea that man is physically depraved, and by these influences will *certainly* (not *necessarily fixed*) sin. *John 3:3* can only at the *limit* state that that which is born of fleshly desire will tend to sin (when the will yields to its control), while that which results from the Holy Spirit's agency (in the sense that the will yields to Him), is holy. Nothing *here* about inherited sinfulness.

(3) *Ephesians 2:3* "By nature, the children of wrath" must be compared with Ephesians *2:1* which states man is dead THROUGH HIS *OWN* trespasses and sins; man's wicked nature has come *as the result* of his wicked walk in the way of this world, and as previously stated, the word "nature" does *not* mean the way we were born. God shows that a sinner goes *against* his nature in his sin (Romans 1:31; 2 Timothy 3:3; James 3:6) his "nature of wrath" is the *result* of his sinful *actions*, which have formed in his life a character that makes God angry with him.

*Romans 5:19 is an exact parallelism.* If the word *"were made"* means *"constituted"*, as some have said, then *all men will be saved*, BECAUSE of what Christ did, which is outright Universalism! However, this phrase occurs *21* times in the New Testament and in ALL other places where Paul uses it, it means *"to ordain, appoint, put in place of"*. It is used for the ordination of elders, bishops, priests or judges, and properly means "to put, place, lay down" or *"put in a position"*. With this qualification, the passage is clear; Adam's sin put all men *in the place of* sinners (dependent on *their* qualifying choices, as we shall see shortly) the Lord Jesus Christ's *death* put *all men* in the place of being righteous *IF* they will make the right choices! As Adam's sin was the *occasion* (NOT cause) of his race's sin, so Christ's obedience was the occasion, *not* cause of our redemption by grace through faith.

Every word in this passage (with the possible exception of v.17) where *"death"* is mentioned is manifestly *temporal*, or *physical*, and *not* spiritual death. This passage has nothing to do with proving that sin "descended from Adam." This interpretation was not found in the early church fathers; it was never given to the passage until the fourth century; was never adopted by the Greek church at all; and is wholly at variance with the design and scope of Paul's whole argument and presentation. Romans 5:12-14 shows that "death" was the penalty of disobeying God's law; but men *died* from Adam to Moses when there *was* no law; thus, the death that all men die is *not* spiritual, but *physical*. Because *Adam* sinned, all men *DIE;* they inherit not *sin,* but DEATH. In verse 17, Paul catches on *points of correspondence* between Adam and Christ, (cf. 1 Corinthians 15:45-49); the work of Christ *equals,* and even *surpasses* Adam's own failure, so that while Adam brought *temporal* death to his race, the Lord Jesus brought to man the gift of *ETERNAL* life. Nothing is said, as would be expected in verse 20, about Adam's fall extending to his race. Paul knew the word for "impute" *(logazomai)* meaning to count, reckon, and used it for *righteousness* (Romans 4:22); but a *different word* is used in Romans 5:13 *(ellogeo* — to bring into account). Verse 20 shows *instead* that the law came in as the *occasion* of universal sinfulness, implying that men sin *now* just as Adam did *then;* by intelligent transgression *of the known law of God.*

Man IS able to repent when faced with the love of God and the enormity of his sin, and *must* do so as a first condition of God's restoration to His family. This is directly asserted in both the Old and New Testaments (Isaiah 1:16-18; 55:6-7; Hosea 10:12; Matthew 3:2; Luke 13:3, 5; Acts 17:30-31). Because repentance involves a *facing* of, and *turning from,* sin, sin is ultimately a *MORAL* act.

"FALLING SHORT OF THE MARK DOESN'T PROVE IT OUT OF RANGE; THE AIM MAY NOT HAVE BEEN HIGH ENOUGH."

Thought: Falling short of the mark doesn't prove it was out of reach; the aim may not have been high enough.

---

## PROBLEMS SINCE THE FALL

Sin has deeply affected every area of life. The same *God-given endowments* that were to take us to the stars of joy and satisfaction have turned *against us* in sin. Our beings and our world form a unity that has been terribly degraded. Consider:

1. Our *BODIES* — Afflicted with *INTEMPERANCE* and *SICKNESS*

In what
sense are the
sins of the
parents
"visited"
upon later
generations?

*Physical depravity* gives great power to temptation. We cannot *help* our physical nature, and God does not *condemn* us for being born in such a condition without choice. Parents genetically transmit their blends of physical likeness; if they have lived clean lives for God's glory, the *child's body* will be similar barring hereditary mishaps or accidents before birth. To a large extent, a likeness of DESIRES and feelings will *also* be born in baby. Were his parents too fond of food? The child can be born with an over-strong eating appetite. The parents: greed may be *sin;* the child's *appetite* the unfortunate *result.* Thus the parent's sin is "visited" on the children, lasting *three* to *four* generations even if the child does not follow its parent's or grandparent's example (Exodus 20:5; Numbers 14:18; Deuteronomy 5:9). *Apart from God's transformation,* the world's sin will *multiply* in each generation. Our *ENVIRONMENT* has often been filled with smog, polluted rivers, grass buried under concrete, each removing a testimony of God's goodness; our *ECOLOGY* has rebelled, turning on man's selfishness in an ever-closing circle of destruction, as floods, famines, tornadoes and plagues sweep the world (Matthew 24:7; Romans 8:19-23).

## 2. *Our SOULS* — Filled with *PRIDE* and *UNBELIEF*

Moral depravity *deepens* every day in the lost. By sinning *much,* man has learned to sin *more.* The natural LOVE of CONSCIOUS FREEDOM God gave us has had no control or discipline; selfishness has flared through our world out of control. Two hundred years ago, the great statesman *Edmund Burke* warned: "Men qualify for freedom in *exact proportion* to their disposition to put *moral chains* on their own appetites. Society cannot exist unless a controlling power is put  somewhere on will and appetite, and the *less* of it there is *within,* the *more* there must be *without.* It is ordained in the eternal constitution of things that men of intemperant minds cannot be free. Their *passions forge their fetters.*" As moral control collapses, the natural drives governing *nourishment,* *reproduction* and *defence* take terrible power, resulting in the deadly sins of *gluttony,* (1 Timothy 3:3,8) *immorality* and immodesty. Once, before sin, nakedness did not induce lust; since the fall, God has commanded covering to reduce temptation and violence in this area (James 4:1-3). The chain of destruction involved in these misuses is described in Romans 1:21-32.

In your own words, define "worldliness."

3. Our *SPIRITS* — Open to spiritual *DARKNESS* and *DEMONIC WORK*

Our spirits have been affected by sin. Men have an *ignorance* of God, an insensitivity to His drawing love, a spiritual night that hinders Divine direction. He is now an *alien* to God (Ephesians 4:18; John 12:40; 2 Corinthians 4:4; 1 John 2:11; Matthew 6:23; John 3:19; Romans 1:21; 1:18; 1:25; 1 Timothy 6:5). His CONSCIENCE has become *defiled* and *seared* in sin (Isaiah 64:6; Titus 1:15; 2 Peter 2:20; Revelation 22:11) losing its sensitivity to His Spirit. He is open to demonic and Satanic *deception* and *delusion* (John 8:44; Ephesians 2:3; Titus 3:3).

4. Our *SOCIETY* — Degenerate through *WORLDLINESS* and *LUST*

The very relationships designed to make man *happy* have become tools of sin. Man has lost all true perspective of life under God with his fellow-men. He is shown to be a *self-satisfied* (Revelation 3:17) *slave of sin* (John 8:34; Romans 6:16-17, 20; Titus 3:3) who is *hypocritical* (Matthew 6:2, 5, 16; 23:13, 28) *hateful* and *envious* (Titus 3:3) and an *enemy of God* (James 4:4). The *WORLD* of sin is *not* the *earth* God made, but the *whole sinful system* selfish men have put together for their own pleasure that is opposed to God and righteousness (Galatians 1:4; John 7:7; James 1:27; John 14:30; Ephesians 2:2; John 16:8. Man is *pleasure-loving* or *worldly* in sin (2 Thessalonians 2:12; 1 Timothy 5:6; 2 Timothy 3:4) that leads to *fleshly lusts* being developed. The *FLESH* in Scripture, when referring to self-centered man, is a combination of this bodily *self and sin*, and refers to *man's concentration on emotional gratification* through the five senses. Man's worldliness is not a thing, a particular form of dress or behavior, but a *wrong heart-attitude*.

## A RACE OF REBELS

Should a man *continue* to please himself in deliberate rebellion against the moral or written law of God, his "heart" (supreme choice of purpose) begins to *harden* (Proverbs 4:23). By giving into desire he becomes a willing slave to it. The mind, building memories and thought habits for living, is torn between God's inbuilt moral law and the growing slavery to sin (Romans 7:21-24). Man is forced to *excuse* his actions, trying to justify his wrong choices and ignore the twisting knife of conscience. Torment, unrest and unhappiness all result. All unsaved men have in common evil hearts, "deceitful above all things and desperately wicked" (Jeremiah 17:9; Ephesians 2:3). Because all choices are made from hope or fear with respect only to self-pleasing, NOTHING man does can be "good" out of Christ. The broken law of God can only condemn him. Conscience rises up and points an accusing finger. Desire becomes a terrible dictator, turning body members into servants of sin (Romans 7:23; 6:12-19). The SAME God-given endowments which were designed for man's service now become his master. If we obey SIN, we become its slaves. All men, without exception, are in *one* of *two choices;* service to please God or slavery to pleasing self (1 John 5:12; Matthew 6:22-24). If we fix a pattern of self-pleasing too long, we can harden our hearts beyond hope (Mark 16:14; Proverbs 28:14; 29:1; 27:1; Psalm 95:8; Hebrews 3:15).

*WHAT then, IS sin?* Sin is not primarily the THINGS you *DO.* It is a state of will. It is a CHOICE of a strong ultimate end in life It is intent of purpose wrongly and selfishly directed. It is denying God's right to be God in your life. His Holy anger flames out against sin because it destroys all that is beautiful and good in life. Man living in slavery to sin is a hollow mockery of the holy being once made in God's like-ness and image. Yet we see Man from his first selfish choice forge an *unbroken* chain of deceit, pride, lust and rottenness. Without God in His rightful place as Center and Director of the heart, nothing a man can do will spare him from the righteous wrath of the King of Kings. All his actions, deeds and works are made for selfishness. Aware of his defiance of God's right, but choosing to be ruled by desire, a sinner lives

96

supremely to please only and ultimately himself. Every heart-beat of the life he borrows from God, he flaunts his rebellion in the face of ever-increasing guilt and coming judgment.

Thought: Sin, if it could, would destroy God.

*A deep sense of sin is sobering.* But the Bible never presents sin in such a way as seeing it in ourselves will lead us to hopeless despair. Jesus never condemned a sinner aware of his guilt, but wanting to change (John 8:11). In fact, it was only for those who had SEEN their sin that He offered hope! (Matthew 9:12-13; Romans 3:9-10; Luke 18:9-14; Matthew 21:31-32).

## GRACE

With all the race of Adam deliberate *rebels* against God's just and holy government, we could expect Him to have just vengeance in His heart. He sees His beautiful world broken and bleeding. Horrors of poverty, immorality and disease rage in men's lives. War, hatred and murder fill the earth with the stench of man against man. Monsters of suicide, insanity and fear stalk the corridors of men's minds. Who would blame  God for wiping out this corrupted world and starting all over again? All know right, but *choose* to sin instead. All know what is best, but insanely do wrong. Filled with lust to have, to do and to be, sinful Man strives to be as selfish as he can. Uncaring of the happiness of others or his Creator, he madly fights to please HIS god — himself.

God cannot forgive man by *waiving the demands of universal justice.* In His position as Director of the Universe, God must mete out exact justice to all, regardless of their relationship to Him. To do less would disqualify Him to be Judge of the Universe. God's laws are GOOD. There is nothing wrong with THEM. God had to set a penalty for breaking them to bar men from rebellion against the law. Without a *penalty,* law is only ADVICE. The Ten Commandments are a written expression of a law God Himself keeps; willing the highest good of His Universe and its creatures according to their

97

relative values. They are rules of life to show man the right way of holiness and happiness. If broken, their rights *must* be upheld by punishing the law-breaker. A penalty shows the seriousness of disobedience and tends to prevent the law from being broken again. The penalty of sin is DEATH, separation from the privileges of fellowship with God, the Source and Substance of all life. God must be true to His own holiness. To set aside the penalty of a broken law would be to throw out the law itself. *Justice,* the letter of a broken law, can only CONDEMN the law-breaker. We cannot turn to the law for pardon. It excludes pardon and forgiveness and has no power to reform the guilty (James 2:10; Romans 6:23; 7:7-12; Matthew 5:17-20; 1 Timothy 1:8).

Since the Fall, MERCY, not only JUSTICE is God's rule of action for man. The Bible pictures God as pleading with man, waiting to suspend judgment at the slightest sign of repentance. God longs to forgive and relax all claims against our race of rebels.

*Yet — a problem!* For God to freely forgive would weaken the strength of justice and encourage future rebellion and disobedience. Others could say, "If those law-breakers could get away with it, so can we." God has no way to forgive a sinner without *transforming* him. How could God resolve these two great opposites of mercy and justice?

*God has given us a Book.* With amazement, we discover in its pages what is without doubt the most amazing truth in the Universe!  The BIBLE, God's wonderful revelation to man shows us that despite the ruin of His world and the great grief man's rebellion has caused the Godhead — *God is LOVE!* God's problem in forgiving man is NOT *personal,* but *governmental.* He has conquered all vindictive feelings of bitterness and vengeance towards His wayward creation. His heart longs for man to be reconciled; restored to the warm fellowship He once had in Eden. God is not only willing to FORGIVE, but having found a way to be just and pardon too, is willing to FORGET! (Psalm 86:5; Nehemiah 9:17; Lamentations 3:22; Nahum 1:3; Titus 3:4; 1 John 4:8)!

God needed a substitute for the penalty of the law that would uphold the law and yet have *as much effect* on the law and the law-breaker as the penalty itself would have had. Faced with terrible difficulty, the Godhead's infinite wisdom found the only possible way to satisfy both the demands of justice and their loving choice to show mercy and pardon.

How does the death and resurrection of Christ restore the broken God/man relationship?

"THE VERY NAILS REJECTION DRIVES, KEEPS GOD'S HANDS OUTSTRETCHED."

| THE CROSS |
| --- |

## MERCY AND JUSTICE FUSED

The *Lord Jesus,* Himself part of the law-giving Godhead, humbled Himself and became man (Philippians 2:5-7; John 1:14; Luke 1:26-35). He lived a spotless life in perfect obedience to His Father's will (John 8:29; Hebrews 5:8). He went about "doing good and healing all that were oppressed by the devil" (Acts 10:38). He healed the broken-hearted, preached deliverance to the captives, brought sight to the blind and set at liberty them that were bruised (Luke 4:18). For just over three years, the Prince of Peace walked the sin-scarred streets of this world as a living demonstration of God's tender concern for man. He gave man a glimpse into the Father-heart of God (Matthew 6:26-30; John 6:39; 14:9; 16:26-27). He gave the ultimate demonstration of God's love for His sinning world, when before a sobbing Universe He bore in His own body on the cross of Calvary, God's just punishment for sin. The earth shook, the sky screamed as the Son of God bled and gasped out His life. The Father hid His face as His Son showed *how much sin really cost God.* He, the Holy One Who knew no sin, became sin for us (1 Peter 2:24; Hebrews 9:28; 1 Corinthians 15:3; 2 Corinthians 5:21).

On the lonely Hill of the Skull, a windswept cross draws

99

an unforgetable picture. Once seen with the eyes of faith, it magnetically draws man to God in tearful love and broken repentance.

The Cross reconnects the smashed relationship of man and God. He can now forgive because His only-begotten Son provided the great Substitute. The agony of the worst torture in history wrote God's grief and hatred for sin in letters of blood. To see the cross both upholds the law and forgives the repentant sinner (John 3:14-17, 12:32). "He was wounded for our transgressions, He was bruised for our iniquities; the chastisement of our peace was upon Him; and with His stripes we are healed. All we like sheep have gone astray; we have turned every one to his own way; and the Lord has laid on Him the iniquity of us all. Who shall declare His generation? For He was cut off out of the land of the living: for the transgression of my people was He stricken" (Isaiah 53:3-12).

When a man discovers the truth of the cross, he sees how *bad* his sin really is. His own guilt is penned in the torn flesh and broken heart of the Son of God. The cross defines the reality man is running from. The soul-shaking shock of understanding the seriousness of sin strips away deceit and pride. Words from the parched lips of the dying Son of man take on a terribly *personal* meaning . . . "Father, forgive them; for they know not what they do." We see it is not THIS Man Who deserves to die — but US! The cross does all that God's holy justice and tender love could not do apart from it. It makes a blood atonement for sin (Hebrews 9:22; Ephesians 1:7; 1 John 1:7). It provides a substitute for the penalty of the law (Galatians 3:13; Romans 8:3-4). It throws up a roadblock of love in the life to possible future sin. You can go *free* if you will — the Man on the middle cross took your place!

## CONDITIONS, OF COURSE

*God has done all He can to save you from sin.* There is nothing more left in heaven or earth God can use to set you free with, to live and to love Him forever. He has met all HIS conditions for mercy and justice. Have you — WILL you — meet YOURS?

Could a condemned criminal successfully *bargain* with the judge who passes sentence?

If you have seen the Truth and you are NOT really God's child, conviction has gripped your heart. The Holy Spirit makes REAL your deceit and lays bare to you the awfulness of selfishness! Your heart is NAKED before your Maker, Whose all-seeing gaze penetrates every lie and every excuse. You will not just want to "accept Jesus" — you will cry out from the bottom of your being for the Lord Jesus to accept YOU!

Your guilty, rebel heart has been an enemy of God *too long*. Nothing you could ever do could make up for the pain and sorrow your sin has caused God and His world; you and I are utterly unworthy even to ask forgiveness of the gracious King of the Universe. Yet, He loves you, despite your sin! And He offers you a FREE PARDON — if you will take it now!

## "What must I do to be saved?"

*Give up your rebellion against reality. Admit* your sin. Forsake the gaudy little god you have made of your selfishness. It is not enough to "feel sorry" or to merely admit these facts to be true (James 2:19). You must utterly and totally renounce all future claims on your life — time, talents, money, possessions, friends, career and future (Luke 13:3). Choose with your will to serve and love Jesus Christ and to take sides with Him against your past sin (Luke 13:3). Determine in your heart from this day onwards to love Him, obey Him and follow Him forever. Your heart will never be broken, your doubts will not clear up, you will never die to the world until you trust, surrender, BELIEVE Him from the HEART. Pledge to your Heavenly Beloved to "cleave only to Him, for richer or poorer, for better or worse, in sickness or in health" and you will never part at death (John 8:51).

# NOW, READY?

THERE IS NO TIME LIKE NOW ...
GOD HAS DONE ALL HE CAN FOR YOU ...
THE NEXT MOVE MUST BE YOURS!

In your own words, describe what it means to "become a Christian" or to "accept Christ."

"God, I've been selfish; I've been proud; I've been nothing but a Hell-deserving REBEL, and I'm sorry! I see *NOW* what sin has done to me. I'm *sick* of my old life, God; I really WANT the change You promised me."

"Please God — *FORGIVE* all my sin. I *need* you Lord! I surrender my will; I give You my *heart.* Send me Your Holy Spirit; make Jesus *real* to me now. From this day on I want to live to please You. Make me Your own child; be my *Lord* and *Master.* Amen."

To do this from your heart is to *"believe to righteousness."* The moment you grasp the things of Christ, by receiving Him into your heart's throne as King, you will see in the light of eternity the emptiness of the world, of reputation, riches, honour and pleasure. Take hold by faith His forgiveness and His righteousness; surrender to Him all rights to your life. Make a step of committal to Him with the faith that works by love, purifies the heart and overcomes the world. All that you need you will find in the Lord Jesus (1 Corinthians 1:30).

From this moment on, *tell the world Who you belong to.* "For with the *heart* man believes to righteousness; and with the *mouth,* confession is made to salvation" (Romans 10:10-13).  When Christ is enthroned in your heart, He will recreate in you His own life. It will no longer be a life lived for selfish "I"; but Christ Who "dwells in me" (Ephesians 3:17). As far as is in your power, make right that which is wrong (Luke 19:8). Show the world your new ownership by a changed, transfigured life; that you are a man or woman *for* whom Christ *died,* IN whom He *dwells* and THROUGH whom He works (2 Corinthians 5:19; Colossians 1:17; Philippians 2:13). Then, and only then will you know the joy and peace of forgiveness — the fellowship of the Godhead in eternal life (1 John 5:1-5; 5:10-13).

"GOD PAID THE WORLD'S HIGHEST PRICE FOR THE SCRAP OF BROKEN MEN."

What is the
one sin God
can't
pardon?

## A WORD FOR THE FOOL

Either our God is the LORD *or* our god is OURSELVES. We can pretend a hypocritical sort of self-righteousness; but there will always be the nagging certainty that it is "appointed unto man once to die, but AFTER DEATH, the judgment" (Hebrews 9:27). Should you choose to stay selfish and reject the light God has given you, you multiply your guilt and deserve your final destiny (Romans 2:4). *Your* god is the person or thing you think most about, that to which your thoughts return when there is nothing else at hand, the *center of your life*. If it is the Lord Jesus Christ, you will one day share the unspeakable privileges of ruling and reigning with Him in the Kingdom of Heaven. If it is *yourself* and you will *not* obey the pleadings of the Holy Spirit to repent and believe, you have spurned your last chance for life. *You can only come when He calls you.* Without the drawing of the Holy Spirit, you will never WANT to obey God (John 6:44). Reject His tender call and you are in great danger of committing the one sin God CANNOT pardon — the final and ultimate rejection of His love.

We have only short years to decide before the curtain of death will draw life to a very permanent close. Life is so short — eternity is so long! If, like the rich young ruler, you must here turn away "sorrowful," the Lord Jesus too will be grieved — but He will LET YOU GO (Mark 10:17-22; Ephesians 4:30). If you will not give up your rebellion against the King, we must here sadly say goodbye to you — but *do you know where you are going?* (2 Corinthians 4:3-4; 6:2; Psalm 14:1; John 14:2; Mark 16:15; 2 Thessalonians 1:7-9; 2:10-12).

Thought:
God is not
nearly as
concerned
with our
perfection as
He is with our
direction.

## STICK TO IT, SAINT!

There is no hint in the Bible that God promises forgiveness of FUTURE sins. He hasn't planned any cycle of sin and repentance for His disciples! You  are not infallible, but neither are you *expected* to go back into sin. God will keep you safe and protected, but KEEP GOING ON with Him! (Luke 9:62).

Should a man fail God, his heart will condemn him. The law will again bind him to its terrible penalty as long as he persists in his wilful rebellion. If the penalty no longer applied to a disobedient "disciple", it is no longer law, but *advice*. Such a man would have no rule of right or wrong any more, not being good OR bad. No such Christian exists in Scripture or life. The express teaching of the Bible is to live a *life of victory* over sin out of love to God (Matthew 5:13-48; 7:12-27; Mark 12:28-34; John 15:8-14; Romans 13:9-11; 1 John 3:3-11). No other life is truly Christian. All of us will be faced with temptation, weakness and failure. But by God's grace we can HABITUALLY overcome.

Should *you* ever disobey, go in deep, total repentance to ask forgiveness of your Father. God covenants with His children to draw them back to Himself should they stray (Psalm 89:30-34; Hebrews 12:4-11) but never DARE "use" His mercy and grace! Should a so-called "disciple" despise God's love, return to the vomit of past selfishness and die in rebellion trading on His mercy, such a hypocrite will find Hell waiting for him (1 John 2:1-6).

We have a great High Priest Who is able to "save to the uttermost" (Hebrews 7:25). If any man sin, we have Him as our Advocate (1 John 2:1). But *nowhere in the Bible is* forgiveness AUTOMATIC as long as sin is persisted in. Thousands of so-called "Christians" are fooled by thinking they can "do what they like" now they have "believed," when *their* "like" is nothing like God's *love*. A lot of lukewarm, half-hearted church members are going to get shocks

104

on the Day of Judgment. STAY TRUE — STICK TO IT, SAINT — GOD WILL HELP YOU! (Exodus 32:30-33; 1 Chronicles 28:9; Ezekiel 18:19-32; 33:12-19; Matthew 5:22; 18:32-33; John 5:14; 15:1-6; Acts 8:18-24; Romans 6:12-16; 8:13; Hebrews 10:26-31; 12:14-17; James 1:12-15; 5:9; 2 Peter 2:20-22).

A VOW:
BY THE GRACE AND LOVE OF THE LORD JESUS CHRIST, I WILL STAY TRUE TO HIM WHO FIRST LOVED ME AND GAVE HIMSELF FOR ME.

(Signed) .....................................................

"Blessed are the PURE IN
HEART: for they shall see
God" (Matthew 5:8).

# BARTHOLOMEW

## (WHO WAS WITHOUT GUILE)

"Because I said . . . I saw
thee under the fig tree, believ-
est thou? Thou shalt see greater
things than these."

John 1:50

What is the
difference
between
biblical
purity as it
relates to
sexual
expression,
and
*puritanism*?

PHASE:       3 .   *Disciples in Clay*
SECTION: 3 ..   *"S" For Seeing God Through Heart Purity*
MATERIAL:    *Consecration For Clean Morality Christianity*

He was under a fig tree when Jesus saw him. He expected a
Messiah of miracles, and Jesus did not disappoint him.
"Because I said to you,'I saw you under the fig tree', do you
believe? You shall see greater things than these." *Nathanael,*
called *Bartholomew,* was one of the first disciples chosen to
follow the Lord into a life of miracles.

How did *Bartholomew recognize* Jesus? God links those
who see Him with the eye of faith with those who are PURE
IN HEART. Of *Bartholomew,* Jesus could say — "Behold an
Israelite indeed, in whom there is no guile." We cannot know
God if we are morally unclean. We all need clean, clear hearts
for the adventure into discipleship.

---

## DRIVE TO LIVE

---

God planned in us *three basic drives,* to work in harmony
and grow together in balance. They built the youth of the
Lord Jesus. "Jesus increased in *wisdom* (the *PERSONALITY*
drive) and *stature* (the *PHYSICAL* drive) and in *favour with
God* (the *SPIRITUAL* drive) and *man* (the *SOCIAL* drive —
a natural result of controlling the other three) (Luke 2:52).

The most powerful emotion-influencing part of the physical drive is that of SEX. Without this inbuilt direction to be
"fruitful and multiply" we would last only one more generation (Genesis 1:28). This is the Father's most sacred gift to
man — the power to re-create life.

*GOD CREATED and ORDAINED* sex. It is *NOT* "evil" or
unholy. The Bible does not hesitate to extol the joys of a
God-given, God-directed sexual love in marriage. Sex is *God's*
idea; *He* made it up. It is a *symbol* from the innermost being
of the Father's heart of some of the most sacred relationships
of Scripture. *Christian marriage* represents on earth the holy
love the Heavenly Bridegroom, Jesus Christ the Lord, has for
His Body, the Church (1 Corinthians 6:18-20). A *Christian
family* is the earthly pattern of God's longing for *spiritual*

sons and daughters to rule and reign with Him. In its God-designed place, sexual love is the most beautiful relationship on earth. It is His special gift to signify His ultimate purpose  for man; to be in the Father's house and family, living in love and fellowship through eternity (1 John 3;1-2).

What were the two basic reasons God gave us sexuality?

Because God made sex in human beings such a special relationship, He set definite *differences* between *animal* and *human* sex drives. Animal reproduction is sparked by automatic *instinct laws* that operate at certain times of the year. There is no *love* in these sexual couplings, just blind instinctual desire. *Human desire* for sexual love and children is quite different. It has been placed by the Creator *at the direction of* the *human will* and *thought*. It is NOT automatic. God designed it to both awaken and function under the control of the personality. In early years the force sleeps, hidden from our attention, but as we begin to mature it makes its presence felt in our lives.

Sex was given for *two major physical* reasons: *re-creation* of the race by reproduction (Genesis 1:27-28; Psalm 127:3-5) and as a source of deep *spiritual and physical pleasure* between husband and wife (Matthew 19:4-6; Genesis 2:24-25; 24:67; Ecclesiastes 9:9; 1 Corinthians 7:2-5). The same Bible that gives stern *warnings* about the *misuse* of sex (Proverbs 5:1-8, 20) clearly describes how sexual needs *should* be met, to bring us great happiness (Proverbs 5:15, 18-19). The Bible teaches PURITY, not Puritanism! A husband is to be "intoxicated" with his wife's love; this is not only described by the Holy Spirit as a part of *wisdom* (Proverbs 5:1); but God is seen to know and approve of this sexual union (Proverbs 5:21). God made sex to be tenderly beautiful.

"THE FLESH OF THE GODLIEST SAINT IS NO MORE DEPENDABLE THAN THAT OF THE VILEST SINNER."

## MARRIAGE — TOTAL TOGETHERNESS

*True marriage* is a FUSING of *all three basic drives*. Each

109

Of the two charts on this page, which describes your dating practices?

drive has its own corresponding love relationship. Man and wife thus become "one" in body, soul and spirit. God plans courtship and marriage in three stages —

| RELATIONSHIP | TYPE OF LOVE | GOAL OF RELATIONSHIP |
| --- | --- | --- |
| Courtship "Dating" If practical, then | "Agape" — spiritual love — Giving, not getting from each. | Each purposes to bring the other closer to the Lord; Boy LEADS; GIRL inspires. |
| Betrothal Engagement If practical, then | ADDS) "Philia" — Soulish — Friendship; Sharing, not selfish. | Share, compare plans for future; calling, ministry; find out if both emotionally, mentally suited. |
| Marriage Instituted and Ordained by God | ADDS) "Eros" — Physical — sexual love. Blessing, not bitterness. | To come together in one flesh for mutual comfort and to have a Christian family to bring up for the glory of God. |

Satan, bitterly jealous of man's ability to create, designs to degrade and destroy the beauty of this relationship. He plays up the PHYSICAL attraction and evilly reverses the above God-designated order, sending thousands of friendships onto the rocks:

| RELATIONSHIP | TYPE OF LOVE | GOAL OF RELATIONSHIP |
| --- | --- | --- |
| Conquest "Dating" | Over-stimulated, sexual, physical love; Getting, not giving. | Dates to "have fun" — gratify the sensual at the expense of God's moral law and consequences. |
| Engagement Often forced | Ill-defined friendship, understanding; selfish, not sharing. | Attempt to find "real person" of other fails because of barrier of guilt through involvement. |
| Marriage Necessity not thrill | No real spiritual bond apart from the grace of God. Bitterness, not blessing | If it "works out" makes it a "church wedding." Such marriages usually full of disharmony, frustration. Often ends in divorce or some separation. |

110

## NEW TESTAMENT DATING

*We have more books on sex* than ever before; more information on "making love," more data on being a sexy "swinger," but we have *left out God* and are paying the price for it! Sex is a special part of life, and precious; it was not designed to be treated as part of every meal-time conversation. Precious things are not to be used too often, but treasured for special *times;* you must learn to direct the power of sex and preserve it in purity, or you will join the ranks of the lonely and bitter.

*Sex is like a fire.* A fire is amoral; the *same flame* that *warms* a home can *burn* it down. There is no difference between the fire that comforts and the fire that kills; each burns the same way. But in one case it burns *in its proper place* and time, and in the second, it burns *out of limits* and *out of control.* The same built-in joys God gave sex (in the right way) can become raging fires of destruction.

Listen to these burning words of *David Wilkerson* from his message to youth on dating that he calls — *Parked At The Gates of Hell:*

"I want to talk to you about a *fire;* a fire that is burning in the hearts and minds of literally thousands of young people, Bible college students included, across this nation. It is spread from Hell itself having been vomited on this nation to enslave innocent young people with uncontrolled emotions. This fire now scorches tne lives of young people from all walks of life; the socialites, the slum-dwellers, the middle-income class and even ministers' sons and daughters. This raging fire is now bringing shame and sorrow to young people from the best of Christian homes; children of parents who are respected in the church and community.

This flame burns out of control across the nations of the world. It is fed from Hell itself by the fuel of unclean stories, smutty books and pornographic photographs shamelessly disguised as art. It smoulders from restricted age movie films and suggestive dancing, it flares in the lives of young people parked in the seat of a car away from the eyes of the law and the public in lonely, secluded back roads."

111

How can a
person avoid
emotional
disaster
through the
misuse of sex
in a dating
relationship?

*Sex goes wrong* for the *same reasons* that a fire destroys.
It can be *lit too soon* (getting emotionally involved before
God's time) and *in the wrong place* (some form of pre-marital

sex). To avoid the first, follow
these dating rules of thumb:

1. *Avoid the "steady" relationship until God's time.* The biggest
problem with this form of dating
is that after you spend a *lot of time*
with the other person you can get
*too familiar* with each other, and

like each other too much to think about the facts. This
invariably leads to you letting down your guard, lowering
your moral codes, ignoring the warning of your conscience
and inviting trouble.

2. *Keep busy and active.* David fell through *laziness.* If he
had been out on the field with his men doing the job God
had called him to do, he wouldn't have been sleeping around
his palace and having too much time on his hands. Fill up
your life with activities that you can enjoy under God and
you will save a lot of pressure.

3. *Stay away from "bad scenes."* A "bad scene" can be
defined as any place that brings two kids who like each
other *close to nature* and *away from the eyes of civilization.*
Watch out for unchaperoned beach, hunt, ski or fishing
parties; any place that can still the voice of reason and God is
a *trouble spot* — stay away! A *particularly* bad scene is a *car;*
it can very well act as *transportation* away from safeguarding
publicity, *mood music* and a *bed on wheels* all combined.
Stay away from parked cars on dates like they were filled
with tarantulas and scorpions!

4. *Don't get serious with ANYONE* until you are *ready* for
marriage *physically, emotionally* and *mentally,* and above all
*spiritually. Girls:* If you value your love, don't give it unre-
servedly to *any* guy until you are *both* quite sure you are
God's choice for each other. *Guys:* Don't you *dare* lead a
girl on to think you love her when you are only "putting her
on" for your own pleasure. Girls get hurt very easily, and
very deeply. *No guy* has a right to say to any girl "I love you"
until he is prepared to say in his next breath — "Will you
*marry* me?" If you can't make the second statement, don't

112

*bother* making the first. It isn't true.

What is the difference between love and lust?

5. *Don't get involved* with anyone until your wedding date is set. If you cannot be satisfied with spiritual communion and conversation, with just that desire to be with each other and to keep your life holy and pure, you are *NOT IN LOVE! Lust* can only wait five minutes; *love* can wait for five years. Now you may *think* you are in love; you may even call it *spiritual:* but *IS* IT? Take this little test to search out your own level of commitment in GOD's kind of love.

TEST:

CAN I LIST FIVE WAYS IN WHICH I
AM NOW SEEKING TO DRAW MY
FRIEND CLOSER TO THE LORD?

◯ YES (I am in love)

◯ NO (I am not)

---

### KEEP YOUR TEMPLE CLEAN

---

*When confused with true love,* trouble with physical stimulation can strike so quickly that irreparable damage is done before the person (or the bewildered parents) realize it. Sexual desire is a tremendously POWERFUL physical and emotional force once fired. Young people are *not old enough to date* until they understand fully both the *purpose of courtship* and the *dangers of physical involvement.* Unless they are both committed to the total Lordship of Jesus Christ so that in both courtship and/or friendship relations they "glorify God in their bodies and their spirits, which are God's," (1 Corinthians 6:19) they should not be allowed out together. Thousands of scarred lives and shattered dreams are terrible testimonials to the reality of dating dangers.

*Getting physically involved* is like igniting a *built-in bomb.* The trouble with necking and petting *outside* of marriage is that it was designed by God to lead into sexual intercourse *in* marriage. In a frenzy of kissing and hugging and petting, the natural flame that God has put into the heart of every young man and woman begins to burn out of control before God's time and without God's approval, and the Devil keeps whispering and urging on, saying, 'It's all right, you're in love, you belong to each other, you have a right, and even if you do get into trouble he'll stick with you, she'll stick up for

113

What are the risks of premarital sexual activity? Why do these risks usually go unperceived until *after* sin has been committed?

you — everything's ALL RIGHT!" One minute everything can *seem* right and good, and the next minute you know you've gone too far, and all that seemed so sweet and pure  shows up as the *filth and dirt of sin.* The pleasures last only a short time, and then the roof caves in; suddenly, as emotions are brought under control everything becomes soiled and wrong; one moment you thought it was *real love* and *now* you see it for what it really was. Don't *ever* start experimenting no matter how close your friendship, or you will set the fuse burning down to the end God designed it for, long before you are ready for it or can afford it.

*Petting just isn't worth it.* Necking has a bad habit of getting *heavier;* each time you light the fuse, *it will burn* — and next time you light it, you will begin *where you left off.* To stay *clean,* stay *away.* It's as simple as that. Petting can — (1) Make you feel *guilty and ashamed* of yourself for breaking God's laws and heart. (2) *Ruin your reputation.* It only takes a *little* "talk," it doesn't all have to be *fair* and it doesn't even have to be all *true;* but once done, you may be *marked for life.* (3) *Cause you to lose your sweetheart.* Girls, get *this* especially; after your boy friend goes too far he may decide you are *cheap,* or getting him too deeply involved and simply *leave you* finally and forever. And if you *give* in, you *will be* cheaper. (4) *Break your parents' hearts,* or get you married too *early,* too *soon* or to the *wrong* person. Sexual involvement is a binding relationship; it's hard to cut it off once begun. (5) *Ruin your date-life.* Even *if* you break off your relationship before you go "all the way" you will create *bitterness, frustration* and *loss of respect* between you. The "magic" in your dating relationships will simply vanish, leaving them ugly. You will forget everything you ever saw in the person the first time you met them. (6) Worst of all, you will wreck your *spiritual* life. Any form of "love-making" like this will throw up immediate barriers to spiritual growth. You will *feel* guilty and wrong, because you ARE guilty and wrong! *You* know it, and be sure GOD does too.

COURTSHIP is to be a *SPIRITUAL experience!* In courting, the couple must take up responsibilities they will later share with privileges should they marry. The MAN is to be the *leader*. He should point the way to new heights in God, so that AS A COUPLE they are drawn closer to Christ. He should find and plan ways to lead the girl he is dating into a finer, purer walk with the Lord. The GIRL, on the other hand is to *inspire* her man to launch out for his Lord. She is to uplift, strengthen and refresh his leadership. She becomes his "help-meet." Unless a dating couple can be satisfied *in Christ alone,* they are NOT in love.

What should be the spiritual goal of any Christian friendship?

God made man and woman to respond differently in physical involvement. In marriage, the girl is aroused much later than the boy, and this delay is intended to underline the supremacy of human love over mere animal desire. Primarily, a *boy* is excited by a LOOK; a *girl* by a TOUCH. The fellow should thus guard his eyes as well as his thoughts and the girl should take care in the way she dresses, to be modest and pleasing to the Lord Jesus. She should avoid any physical contact that could lead to lighting a fuse of desire and he should keep his hands and lips from committing sin.

Morality has degenerated to such a point where suggestions such as these could be met with incredulous stares and protests about the "change of times". But to follow these rules is neither old-fashioned or outdated. Moral purity is a rare gem, that must not be bartered for the approval of a God-rejecting society. *One night of stolen pleasure is not worth a lifetime of regret!* (Judges 16:4-31). Results of dis-

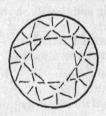

obedience to the moral law are painfully obvious — moral filth and perversion are at an all-time high! It is time Christian youth set an example of purity and holiness worthy of the Name by which they are called (Job .31:1; Matthew 5:28; 1 Corinthians 10:31; 6:18-20; 1 Timothy 2:9-10).

## SENSUALITY OR HOLINESS?

*Moral freedom* has been defined as "Not the *right* to do what you WANT, but the *power to do* that which is RIGHT." As temptation presents itself, the Christian is faced with a

Why could
Jesus say,
"Whosoever
looketh
on a
woman to
lust after
her hath
committed
adultery with
her already
in his heart"?

CHOICE between selfishness and love. The choice for God gives the Christian true sex freedom — the choice for *selfish desire* enslaves the heart in lust and moral bondage.

## WHERE "NO" ISN'T HOLY

Beyond the point of *committing the will to indulge desire* against moral law, *any* form of self-denial can no longer be moral or holy. Once the WILL gives in to desire, the choice is AS BAD as the act itself in God's eyes. The only reason the actual ACT is not carried out in such a case is some motive based on *hope* or *fear,* not on God's law of love. Among such forms of denial preventing much OUTWARD immorality are the fear of consequences, fear of discovery or social disapproval or strict environmental standards. Unfavourable circumstances prevent much *outward* sin, but thousands of human hearts are still inwardly nothing but sewers of lust (Matthew 5:27-28; Mark 7:20-23). A sure sign of the heart's committal to lust is a steady mental diet of cheap, sensuality-exalting literature. You can tell a man by the books he usually reads. Show me a person who feeds their mind on filth and I will show you someone under the bondage of lust.

| SEX-ORIENTATED ACTION PRESENTED | MORAL STATE OF PERSON IF | |
|---|---|---|
| | YIELDED TO | DENIED |
| LOOK (Boy) TOUCH (Girl) If yielded to, can lead to: | Natural curiosity; like Eve listening to serpent in Eden, God only forbids learning in area of wrong (Romans 16:19). | Innocence: no temptation present to sin. (Adam and Eve before being shown tree of knowledge.) |
| DESIRE awakened: (Temptation to gratify awakened sensuality.) If yielded to, leads to: | Conscience alarm shrills - Warns "Knowledge of this is out of bounds" (Romans 2:15). | Peace — Conscience will approve choice to deny the gratification — "Flee" is to turn from mind (2 Corinthians 1:12). |
| INTENT (Will commits itself to desire). Lasciviousness begins. | Sensual desire grows strong to satisfy awakened lust. RESULT: SIN (James 1:15). | Spiritual desire deepens to glorify God in body. HOLINESS (1 Corinthians 6:18-20). |

116

*TRUE REPENTANCE* must precede deliverance, and this is not just "feeling sorry" over the RESULTS of breaking God's moral law. All kinds of moral impurity stem from *lasciviousness*, this initial will surrender to indulging sexual desire out of God's ordained limits. *Any form of tendency to excite sexuality* by *an act of the will outside of marriage* is *SIN*. Unless it is confessed as such, the desire will build further and further, leading a person deeper into immorality, even to the point of "no return" from God. EVERY sexually immoral action *scars the personality* in a total involvement that God considers quite more serious in effect than any other sin (1 Corinthians 6:18).

Describe the downward spiral of uncontrolled lust and why this is so tragic.

## THE GROWING GIANT OF LUST

Lasciviousness develops into *worse forms of sexual deviation*. The terrible, terrible, power of misusing God's creative gift brings a harvest of havoc in the moral life. Lasciviousness always develops into deeper and deeper forms of impurity. It quickly develops into a giant that enslaves the heart. Lust will continue to forge a steel chain of habit over the will, until only the power of the Living Christ can free the man from bondage. Once *lust* begins to take control:

| IF YIELDED TO | ACTION | IF DENIED (Unholy "No") |
|---|---|---|
| Rationalizes away feeling of wrong; self-justifies motives, excuses are made to the reason. Convinces self of "right" to be satisfied. Desire for stimulation increases; previous wrong looks less guilty. | SUB-CHOICES to get physical thrill or gratification. Stem from lasciviousness . . . leads to: | (For instance, by Truth given by a Christian to show guilt.) Anger looks for reasons why sensuality can be "justified." Argues over Scripture, moral responsibility to God, others. |
| Concupiscence — overstrong sex appetite which "must" be satisfied; Unable to concentrate; extreme embarrassment; accuses others of wrong motives to shift guilt. | SENSUAL ACTION: "petting" in everincreasing depth leads to: | Envies those who can "get away with it." Denial causes a retreat into a world of evil imagination, fantasy and self-delusion; hazy thinking. |

117

| Why is masturbation a misuse of the God-given sexual drive? | IF YIELDED TO | ACTION | IF DENIED (Unholy "No") |
|---|---|---|---|
| | Fornication or some form of masturbation. Building up of nervous tension from stimulation demands release in the system. Habit grows stronger, deeper. | RELEASE; Temporary form of satisfaction. | Defraud morally — both self and other person cheated; Intense frustration develops unsatisfied emotions, bitterness and loneliness begins. |

MASTURBATION is one such result of a heart-committal to sexual desire. This problem affects thousands of young people, and even more especially *religious* young people because the church-goer cannot afford to be discovered in some form of *fornication* like his unsaved or unchurched neighbor. Because his mind is so informed about God and right living, the church youth's guilt is a *double* misery. The Christian's body is the *temple of God.* Its sexual nature gives it grace and force, firmness to the will and radiance to the personality. A God-controlled sex-life brings a *drive* and *enthusiasm* to activities in life; to our sexual impulses we owe our love for bright colors, graceful forms, rhythmic motions and sounds. It gifts the emotions with the affections and instincts of a lover and sweetheart. But self-abuse *ruins* all this. Self-abuse by masturbation is a form of *self-love,* out of God's perspective, in which the tremendous powers of the emotions are thrown away. To find deliverance and have that emotional love power channelled back into life and to the Lord is an experience anyone delivered can only *feel* to understand. Masturbation wastes and spends the power of this life-drive.

*All* Christians can experience the temptation to such desires at times in life, but this is normal. In this defiling *habit*, passions have taken over and the flow of constant strong sex urges *cannot be controlled.* The body is bound in *concupiscence.* This abnormal mental condition destroys normal sexual feelings and substitutes hyper-inflamed desires that drain the whole system of the substances in the sex organs that aid in developing the mind and body, when re-absorbed without use. *It is easy to recognize;* nothing so destroys the will-power and vital energy. Habits become sloppy, the attitude insipid and melancholic; the whole personality sheepish, reclusive and embarrassed. Young men

118

lose their *personal magnetism;* young women their *attractive-ness.* The eyes appear languishing, without expression, and the whole face takes on a vacant look. Often the person grows irritable and touchy, and may try to get involved in some kind of *religious activity* as a guilt compensation.

What are the outward evidences of a life that is out of order sexually?

The majority of young men afflicted with this habit soon begin to realize the effect it has on their system and put up a  battle against it. The only way to break this is a determined *re-setting of the will* to follow *Christ,* and the willingness to *spend time* in breaking the power of the body habit. It may take from *six to eight* months for nature to check the nervous and physical waste caused by self-abuse. Restoration can only come through DETERMINED *ABSTINENCE.* Follow the deliverance program given at the end of this section if you have this problem and want freedom.

---

## THE PRICE OF PRE-MARITAL SEX

---

*Every society* LOWERS THE STANDARD of the previous one. What one generation will ALLOW, the next will ENJOY! God made the sexual act to bring fulfillment in a *total harmony* of body, soul and spirit. Those playing fast and loose with sexual desire will find less and less emotional release and pleasure as their responses become brutalized and guilt scars develop in the personality. The sexual love God gave man was made to be an *OUTWARD* expression of an *INNER* submission. All kinds of barriers are thrown up by premature sexual involvement, such as:

1. *GUILT* — God has placed the alarm of *conscience* in our souls to warn us of impending danger to our personalities. Some primitive peoples exist in our world without much inhibition of conscience; it is significant that they have stayed in a primitive state. The conscience alarm can protect us from emotional upheavals and insecurity because it *safeguards* us from losing trust in ourselves or others. Do *you want* to carry with you to a marriage altar guilty hands and a soiled mind?

119

Why does
premarital
sex make it
so hard to
establish
mutual trust
later on in
the
relationship?

**2. FEAR** — You can't *love* someone you are *afraid* of. Love without fear means being able to fully TRUST the one you want to love. If a couple experiments with sex before publically committing themselves to each other in marriage, how can they be sure that either will remain faithful AFTER marriage? After all, they each broke their *own* moral controls in a place of trust *once;* how will they know that it will not happen *again?* If either "jumps the fence" *before* marriage, who is to say that neither will jump it again *after* with *someone else? Self-trust* and *trust* of each other is *vital* to a successful marriage. Sexual sin destroys trust.

**3.DILUTION** — Sexual love is such a deeply profound act that it is impossible to do without *investing* a part of oneself in the other person. It *always* involves a mutual sharing, even with a prostitute. This is why it is so serious to take the body and use it for sexual sin. No Christian dare join the temple of God with a harlot (1 Corinthians 6:15-20). And here is *another barrier* to sexual fulfillment — If you give *away* yourself each time you do this, *how much* of yourself is *left* when you have thrown away deep parts of your personality on casual relationships? This is why the philosophy of "try before you buy" is *worse* than useless with sex. The *less* you have given of your inner self to others, the *more* you will have to share with someone who will reward your investment with love and trust. The "free sex" idea isn't *free,* and isn't Biblically *sexual.* The only way to measure the success of a stupid set of excuses for lust like this is to compare its premises with the current *divorce rates* and the skyrocketing *suicides* from the "fulfilled."

The *boy* who *thinks sex sin "does no harm,* as long as you don't hurt anyone" is a *fool.* The chief pleasure of a "sexual conquest" for a male is not physical, but primarily psychological . . . the thrill of "putting it over." Such a conquest not only degrades God's purpose but enslaves him to lust, sows the seed of distrust in his partner of any future marriage and can never *really* satisfy. It can never achieve the heights of a real love relationship like that which God planned for man and wife — one of mutual trust and confidence.

Likewise the *girl* who gives her body to a boy "in love" with her, expects to be rewarded with understanding and affection but will always be disappointed. Without God-ordained sanctions, there can be no mutual giving of devotion and tender affection, no leisure to develop a warm relationship and a guilt-free happiness together. The majority of marriages that fail begin with this kind of *physical involvement BEFORE marriage* that scars the ability of each to love their partner as God intended — deeply, wholly and purely.

Is homosexuality inherited or acquired?

## HOMOSEXUALITY — THE FINAL HORROR

*Deliberate rejection* of God's moral law with *continued indulgence* in sin is very dangerous. In many cases, dissatisfaction with an ungodly sexual experience leads to experiments with *others* of the *same* sex. One sin for which God destroys a nation is that of *Sodomy* — *homosexuality* or *lesbianism*. No homosexual is born — he LEARNS his sin! By sinning *much*, he learns to sin *more*. Rejecting Godhead authority in  order to carry on in lust, many sexual perverts build cases for their sin. They do not want to retain God in their knowledge (Romans 1:21, 18). Their scarred senses demand more excitement from illigitimate sexual relationships with those of the opposite sex, which does not come. Still burning with unsatisfied lust, many walk through the door of experimentation with those of their *own* sex. If men and women reach this level, and God can do no more to win them back He gives them up to their heart's committal to lust (Romans 1:24-25).

*Homosexuality* is very prevalent today. Many so-called "church leaders" have argued for, and actually tried to *leagalize* it, pressing for the "rightness" of such unnatural filthiness! Men are calling it *"sickness,"* but God calls it SIN. Our own generation is on a road to doom. Homosexuality is advancing its cancer at a frightening rate in thousands of lives. It cannot always be recognized by visible symptoms, but some of these are:

| PERVERSION | CHARACTERISTICS | INNER LIFE CONFLICT |
|---|---|---|
| Homosexuality or lesbianism (sex relations with those of the same sex). | Short interest span; overly-emotional; gushy; flowery talk; attracted to sense stimulating clothes, loud, bright ornaments. | Intense frustration; deep loneliness, jealousy. Great bondage of will to the habit of lust. Mind ruled by sensuality. |

| What is the first step of deliverance from sexual perversion? | PERVERSION | CHARACTERISTICS | INNER LIFE CONFLICT |
|---|---|---|---|
| | HABIT PATTERN FORMS DEEPER (Titus 1:15-16). | Highly destructive guilt feelings; tries to "make up" often by doing good deeds, "religious" work — (2 Timothy 3:5-9). | Gets progressively worse; restlessness, turmoil and fear; Personality breakdown begins (Job 18:5-14). |
| | END RESULT OF CHARACTER — (Ephesians 4:17-19). | Argues over truth, Bible and moral responsibility (Titus 3). REPROBATION — (God gives up). Unable to feel naturally or think anything else but lust (Romans 1:28). | Complete slavery; scarred, dead emotional life; "flat" look of face; speech strange; suicide thoughts strong (2 Timothy 3:1-13; 1 Timothy 1:6). |

The *real* horror of homosexuality is the utter *bondage* it makes on the will. It is harder to break free from deep homosexuality than from almost any other selfish lust. A Sodomite becomes a *worshipper* of human flesh. He defiles and profanes the God-given sexual relationship between man and woman. EVERY CIVILIZATION freely misusing sex has degenerated by the result of continuously re-lowered standards until almost the entire society has become reprobate. At EVERY POINT of such history God has quickly allowed the total DESTRUCTION of this civilization before its perversion spread to others. It was so in the days of the *Flood, Sodom, Greece* and *Rome.* It will be so *again* in *our* generation unless the tide is checked by a revival of purity.

*A homosexual CAN be saved* (1 Corinthians 6:9-11) but he must DEEPLY repent and honestly ADMIT his guilt, *hating* his sin. Any conniving at sin, excuses of "weakness" must be faced for what they are. He must *totally renounce* his past life (and partners) asking Christ with *all his heart* to cleanse and deliver him. A deep and searching revelation of his wrong and the power of the Lord Jesus to save must come to his life from the Holy Spirit. Often the counsellor must seek the mind of God to discover the *starting-point* of the homosexual's steps to his present degraded life, so confession and repentance can strike at the *core* of his sin. FASTING for an

122

*extended time* is a most effective tool for physical victory over the unnatural "love of the flesh" and should be put into action immediately after repentance. IF a homosexual will respond to the call of God by wanting to change, *God is able* to deliver him. The road may be rough, but Christ is able to "save to the uttermost" (Jude 23-24; Hebrews 7:25). Tragically, most do not WANT to respond, preferring to live without apparent remorse for their sin against God and human nature.

*Every child of God* must learn to "keep his body under" lest when he has preached to others, he himself becomes a castaway (1 Corinthians 9:27). Obeying God's love-law will prevent untold deep damage to the moral life. There are easily-recognized symptoms marking a person with control (or lack of it) over their sex-lives. These forces *yielded to Christ* become a tremendous tool to give drive and fire to the personality in God's work. *Check your own life out* against this chart.

Immorality can usually be uncovered by the discerning Christian. It is one of the most prevalent sins of our time and unfortunately affects thousands of Christian young people not properly instructed in dating relationships.

*Who but God could know* what goes on in parked cars and secluded woods and parks across this nation? Who but God could really know what goes on in the minds of church-going teenagers and twenties; who but God could see what sweethearts are allowing in their lives; what privileges are being demanded; what risks are being taken; who but GOD could see the whole picture? "Can a man take fire in his bosom and *not* be *burned?*"

Why is a man who whispers, "I love you," to his sweetheart before taking sexual advantage of her, a hypocrite?

123

Which areas on
the chart best
describe *you*?

| | |
|---|---|
| **YIELDED OR UNCONTROLLED DYNAMIC** | |

| AREA | RESULTING PERSON WHEN SEX-LIFE IS |
|---|---|
| **EMOTION** | YIELDED: Devotion — Intense love for Christ; freedom in showing love and affection to others.<br><br>NOT SURRENDERED: Roller coaster life — moved by feeling, opinion and not by God's direction; emotionally unstable. |
| **REASON** | YIELDED: Intelligent — Relatively quick to grasp spiritual truth; deep insights consistently into Scripture.<br><br>NOT SURRENDERED: Philosophical bent; prone to argue over Scripture and doctrine; questions any authority. |
| **VOLITION** | YIELDED: Forceful — Consistently on the move for God, taking the lead whenever needed.<br><br>NOT SURRENDERED: Hasty — Impetuous, inconsistent; full of contradictions; little or no discipline of will or body. |
| **PHYSICAL** | YIELDED: Dynamically creative — Quick to use new situations and opportunities to create roads for Truth.<br><br>NOT SURRENDERED: Listless, powerless, seemingly continuous apathy and dullness. No concentration, shifty eyes. |

Sexual immorality is the *fastest-striking* sin of youth. Perhaps more than any other uncontrolled desire, it backlashes in all areas of life, causing a total circle of destruction. If *YOU* are, right now, morally unclean, you may have to use the following weapons against this sexual leprosy. It is a complete program for *every area* of your life. Use EACH area where you know your life or the lives of others have been affected.

How can
depression be a
possible
warning of
"dangers to
come"?

---
**BREAK FREE OF THE FIRE**
---

*SPIRITUAL*

1. *Start by being BRUTALLY HONEST with yourself.*
Ask God for forgiveness from your SIN. Stop calling it
"weakness," excusing it by saying "God knows our hearts,"
or "I'm only doing what is natural." Stop baptizing it with
any soft names. Call it SIN, and be willing to repent of the
sin ITSELF, and not simply be sorry for the *trouble* it has
caused. It is impossible for you to live a Christian life in the
grip of lust. God can free you, but you must be willing to
take sides with Him against it. Go NOW, and don't wait until
conviction subsides and you feel cold and hard again (1 John
1:9).

2. *Make a present of your love to the Lord.* Ask Him to
wash away the guilt and the stain of your guilty past and to
give you the courage and strength to clean up your wrong.
Throw your problems completely into His hands, and ask
Him for a new heart to love Him and serve Him as you ought.
(Ezekiel 11:19-20).

I HAVE HONESTLY CONFESSED MY SIN AND ASKED GOD'S ◯
FORGIVENESS

3. Seek God's face for a *filling with His Spirit.* The HOLY
Spirit will make *your* life holy. Unless you are supercharged
by Him, you will, like Samson, be "weak as any man". If you
will claim from God His promised enduement of power from
on high, you will be able to "walk in the Spirit" and not
fulfil the lusts of the flesh (Galatians 5:16).

I SHALL TRUST CHRIST FOR A DAILY FULLNESS OF THE ◯
HOLY SPIRIT

4. *Beware of the danger signal depression.* It is part of
God's alarm system given to warn you of approaching temptation. Life runs in cycles (Galatians 6:7). Temptation from
physical desire can return at certain times of every day, week,
month or even year. When you sense depression, prepare for
possible trouble. Take it as a sign from the Lord to spend

125

What are the possible dangers of face-to-face confession of past sexual sin?

time in prayer and meditation on His Word. Sometimes depression is a warning of sin against the Lord (a "cloud" across the conscience) or a returning desire to sin that has been sparked off by a reminder of past wrong actions. Ignoring the warning will nearly always lead to over-confidence and most probably a complete failure again.

I WILL BEWARE OF THE WARNING OF DEPRESSION ◯

I'LL BE O.K., I CAN HANDLE MY OWN PROBLEM MY OWN WAY ◯

## SOCIAL

1. *MOST* IMPORTANT — *CONFESS to the other person(s) involved*. WRITE A LETTER, *without describing* the nature of your moral offense to the other person. They already know it was wrong. Use the format of the confession letter outlined in MT-15 for the three basic sentences, and simply ask forgiveness. It is not necessary to elaborate on your wrong. Use "not being an example of a Christian" or "failing to set a decent standard" as your wording for the *specific sin*. Avoid confession *in person* if possible, as this may lead to emotional involvement that could start your problem all over again. Whenever necessary (and remembering the law of the highest good) be willing to *break off* the past relationship. [See MT-19] If you are engaged, you will have to seek God's face as to whether it is best to honestly confess to each other and then pledge to stay clean and pure for each other and God until you can marry, or to completely *finish off* the engagement. Ask God's direction, *but be willing to act* on the answer. This may be very difficult — possibly the hardest part, but it *has* to be done (Matthew 5:28-30).

LETTER HAS BEEN WRITTEN ◯

2. *Set up a prayer-covenant* with another Christian friend. If they do not know about your problem, just tell them you have a great need for victory in your life and you would appreciate their prayer support. If you are still involved with the other person who is a Christian (for instance, an engaged

couple who have over-stepped the boundary of purity but who have now decided to stay true to the Lord together) pray with each other (James 5:16).

## A COVENANT HAS BEEN ESTABLISHED ◯

3. *Keep away from sources of temptation.* Avoid places where you will be alone together, or stay away from the person who was party to your problem. Avoid too much spare time on any future dates, *plan* your outings and wherever possible, at least until you are fully free, stay with Christian friends as a GROUP when you go out together (1 Thessalonians 5:22).

## PERSONAL

1. *WILL* — Be ready for a *battle!* Whenever temptation comes, try to *divert your attention* to *Christ.* Get right out if it is too strong (Genesis 39:7-12). The SECOND look is the one that destroys. The fight will be tough, especially if you have been deeply involved in immorality, but in times of the *severest* temptation, a firm NO and a SINGLE LOOK to Christ will bring victory (Psalm 16:8; 37:24; 1 Corinthians 10:13; 2 Corinthians 8:12). In faith make a complete committal of your will to Jesus. This done, look for no new feelings, but step out in life with confidence that He has begun a work.

2. *MIND* — *Every attack* begins here. When a sensual thought enters, do not play with it. Toy with it for a *second,* and all your good intentions are doomed to fail. Second thoughts on moral issues are almost always defections to the Enemy. Do not fool around with a dirty thought. Kick it right in the face with a Scripture. *One second* of an honest "Lord, help me" and it will flee in fright. *Resist* the Devil by shying a good rough Bible verse at him in the Name of Jesus (1 Corinthians 10:13; John 8:36). Start *spring-cleaning* your *memory* with the tool of *meditation* on Scripture. Build bulwarks in your subconscious mind by filling your soul with *praise* to God, singing or shouting a "Hallelujah!" of victory every time you feel under pressure. *Memorize verses* in the area of moral purity, especially *just before sleeping,* repeating them over and over until they begin to wash your conscience. BURN any books God points out as wrong; don't save them "just in case" you fall again — go NOW and get rid of them!

127

How does
1 Corinthians
6:20 apply to
the area of
sexual
purity?

Begin some *Christian biographies* instead that will fill your thoughts with the way God works with men (Psalm 119:9, 11; Philippians 4:8; 2:5).

3. *FEELINGS* — Prayer is your best outlet for the strong reaction of feelings. Call on the Lord to help still any storm of raging emotions. IF you have taken care of the *mind*, your *feelings* will soon subside. David's *Psalms* mirror every major feeling of mankind and how God feels about us. Use them as your own Scripture voice in expressing the battles of your heart (Psalm 120:1; 121:1-4; James 4:7).

T O DO:

> WRITE OUT PSALM 119, VERSES 9 AND 11
> MEDITATE AND MEMORIZE THEM BOTH

## PHYSICAL

1. *Make a present of your BODY to the Lord.* Give it to God to use for His glory, presenting *part,* by *part,* each section of your physical being. Offer Him every part that you have misused before, and promise Him you will keep it clean in future. Your body is *GOD'S* HOUSE. You are NOT your own if you have given your life to the Lord Jesus. Begin NOW with your *hands.* "Lord, *take my hands.* They have been defiled, and your Word says 'Cleanse your hands, you sinners' (James 4:8). I give them to You for cleansing. Help me to keep them from doing wrong.' Then take your EYES. They have got you into trouble too many times. 'Lord, here are my EYES. I am shaken by Your Word which says — 'If your eye *offend* you, *pluck it out;* it is better that you enter life with one eye than having two eyes to be cast into hell fire.' (Matthew 18:8). "I make a covenant with my eyes and You right now. I will not use them lustfully' (Job 31:1). 'Take my *LIPS.* I remember that *Judas* betrayed You with a kiss. I do not want to do the same thing. I promise You that I will keep my lips to speak your praises, and save my kisses for the one you have for me." Do this *carefully.* Consciously give *everything* (Romans 12:1-2).

2. *Get into some solid WORK or exercize,* especially if you are a man. Throw yourself into all your activities with as

128

much energy as you can muster. This will help *channel* your physical drives into useful outlets, and help release any possible tensions; besides, it will make your activity more fun. Set yourself a tough deadline on everything you do, and challenge yourself to *meet it* for God. Lethargy is a well of carnal desire that can be emptied by hard work at solidly challenging tasks. Develop more activities under God (Ecclesiastes 5:12; 1 Corinthians 9:27).

What are the potential "trouble spots" that dating couples should be aware of?

3. *FASTING* can be used in especially difficult cases. Use the instructions found under *Simon The Zealot*, and spend a week-end in prayer and fasting with the Lord, reading the Bible and memorizing verses. Take this manual away with you, and carefully go through this clean-up program part by part. Do not scan quickly through it and omit to do most of it, or you may not find full deliverance. Sexual sin needs a *deep* and *thorough* cleansing on *many* levels of your life, and sometimes takes more than one Bible principle for use in deliverance.

Take *two simple rules* with you when you date. *Use* them and 90 percent of your problems of temptation will be avoided. *Ignore* them and you are almost *certain* to fall.

*GUYS:*   (1) You will *have* problems being excited by a *LOOK,* so watch your *EYES.* Keep a "Job's covenant" (Job 31:1) and you will keep your mind.

(2) You will *give* a girl a problem by *TOUCH,* so keep your HANDS *to yourself.* Take conscientious care of your eyes and hands and enjoy your date.

*GIRLS:*   (1) You are going to give a guy problems by the way you *DRESS,* so watch it! *Don't* dress to stir lust; dress like you were going to be ushered into Heaven *right on your date,* and Jesus will not be ashamed (1 Timothy 2:9-10).

(2) Keep a *"hands off"* attitude. It may be hard to say "No" but you *must.* No heavy necking or petting can develop this way. If your boyfriend does not understand, *repeat* it a couple more times then use this "emergency prayer":

129

How does
Christ's
relationship
to the Church
portray a
husband's
relationship
to his wife?

*Extend your free hand* from your shoulder, pull it *back behind* you. Then pray silently, "Lord, give me *strength* for this task." Then slap him! (If he asks for Scriptural justification for your action, show him Ecclesiastes 9:10.)

---

## LEAVING AND CLEAVING

---

### FOR HUSBANDS AND WIVES

*Study the relation* of Christ to His Church and you will discover the perfect marriage relationship. The wife gives up her *own* name and takes on her *husband's;* she merges her *life* with his; she recognizes him as her head, and looks to him as her *support, protector* and *guide.* She devotes her *whole life* to his happiness, and to carry out his will in her love for him; she naturally looks to her husband to *protect her* from injury,  insult and want. She *hangs her happiness* on him, and expects that he will protect her; and he is bound to do it. Their reputation and interests become *one;* what affects *her* character or reputation affects *his.* This faithful *husband* loves, cherishes and honors his wife; he gives of his time, his labor and his talents to promote the interest of his bride. And the faithful husband is jealous for his wife's good name, and feels deeply when her feelings or reputation are injured. *Christ* is the perfect picture of the faithful *husband;* His true church is the perfect pattern of the loving *wife.*

Because true marriage is essentially *spiritual,* as well as personal and physical, staying in love is primarily a *spiritual battle.* It is for this reason that surrender to God is so important for a happy love-life. Statistics indicate that a church-attending couple have *fifteen times* as much a chance to stay together than those who have no faith. *Mutual agreement* is the essence of harmony. To live happily together, we must *agree* together. To agree together implies *common knowledge* and *common unselfishness.* When either or both of these conditions are *not* met, destructive disagreement may result.

If two *friends* cannot agree, their friendship may die. If two *lovers* cannot agree, their love may grow cold. If a husband and wife cannot agree, their marriage may be headed for disaster. To take two people from different walks of life, with different backgrounds, different patterns of living and different ways of looking at life and marry them is one of the most difficult ways of achieving agreement in the world! Yet it is done every day, without so much as a course in college to show people *how* to do it.

Two people often need a third party before a quarrel can be settled. What is it about God's nature that makes Him the best third party we can possibly have?

*Common knowledge; common unselfish* choices for each other's highest happiness; these are the two essentials of home harmony, or unity in *any* group. Here is where the power of God can help a home so much. It is first of all, completely *impossible* for *any* group to have *total* common knowledge. No two people in the world think alike; no two people in the world have exactly the same amount of information. In a situation where two people cannot agree, they must appeal to someone who knows more about it than *they* do who can direct them as to the wisest choice. Here *God* is the only Person in the universe Who is totally qualified, with His infinite wisdom, all-knowledge and a heart of love. He can guide each family member to the best course which will bring a harmony to the home. Secondly, the power of Jesus Christ can save a person from the destructive force of *selfishness;* that is the essence of sin and the chief cause of home conflict. He cannot only forgive the guilty past that causes so much home quarrels, but come and live His life through the man or woman who surrenders completely to Him. The love He gives can deliver completely from the power of selfishness. With *Him* to ask direction and to give power to do that which is best, peace and love can fill a home.

*The key reason* why so many couples have lost the power to stay in love lies here. Unless husband and wife both belong to Christ, and have learned from Him what love is *really* like, both their marriage and their lives will suffer. *Every marriage has a soul* — an inner life which is lived out by both partners when they are alone together. This is shared by special *"voices"* used in private, that reveal what the other person is REALLY like when no one else is listening who

131

What are the possible results of unfulfilled responsibilities?

needs to be impressed; by certain *"looks"* and little *actions* that form a whole language only the husband and wife know. Is the "soul" of *your* marriage *Christian?* Is your home a practical demonstration of two people who are following Christ Jesus, and trying to do as He asks for each other's happiness? *Husband,* are you a follower of Jesus, who knows how to take *care* of your wife, to *love* her and *protect* her, or are you a self-centerd, demanding dictator? Do you take the *leadership* and your proper share of responsibility and give a good example for your family to respect and follow? Or have you become a coward in your own home, hiding from your responsibility in business, in social company or selfish pleasure? It is easy to convince yourself that your *wife* is to blame for your conduct. But you are a man responsible to *God* for the vows you took at a marriage altar. Have you *kept* them?

And *wife* — what of *your* life? Have you truly *given up your rights* to run an independent life, and gladly invested your time, talents and energies in your *husband* and his work? Do you *obey* him, or do you fight to be in a leadership place that does not belong to you? Do you accept him *as he is,* or is your love for him *conditional* on what *you* want to *make* him into for your own happiness? Are you God's example of a wife who is gentle, tender and submissive — an inspiration to your man? Or are you bossy, hard and domineering, filled with self-pity and self-justification and criticism? These are hard questions to answer, but if you will face them honestly, God can show you how to stay in love. And there is nothing more like heaven than a home that is in love with each other and God.

---

### BIBLE LAWS FOR STAYING IN LOVE

Your love-life *can* be a happy one! To successfully combat the pressures that have been able to destroy so many homes and divide so many marriages, you must follow God's laws for family responsibilities. Even if you have so far *failed* to

132

make a success of staying in love, by God's help you can begin again. If you are not a Christian, your own unhappiness and the misery you have brought into the lives of others should be reason enough for you to be willing to allow Jesus Christ His rightful place as Leader and King of your life. If you are sorry for your failure to do what is right in His eyes, and you really *mean* to stop living for yourself, He will *forgive* you and *help* you. *There is no happiness in a home that is not built upon His love and His leadership.* Will you get on your knees right now and tell Him that you want to start again like a little child? Ask Him to *forgive* you and *cleanse* your heart from sin. Ask Him to come into your life and give you the power to be the kind of person you should be in your home. He *will* help you! Do it right now.

If you are already a Christian, His laws will not be hard for you to keep because you love Him (1 John 5:1-4). If your *mate* is not a Christian, you must pay even more special attention to God's behavior laws, for if you faithfully do what He asks, there is the very strongest probability that *they* will also give their lives to God. It may be difficult to apply these laws if you have not done so before, and have acted wrongly for a long time. But if you are willing, God will give you all the strength that is needed (2 Corinthians 8:12; Philippians 4:13,19). If you are *not* willing to do what the God Who loves you asks for the highest happiness of your family and His families across the world, you are not yet a Christian and need to ask God to forgive you before anything on this sheet will be of any help to you. Ready? *Men first.*

## RESPONSIBILITY OF THE HUSBAND

God has set up the *husband* to be the *leader* of the home under Him. He is to make the final decisions that involve the well-being of his family and wife. He himself is to be a subject of his King, Christ Jesus. His *effectiveness* as a family leader will be *directly proportional to his willingness to follow God's directions.* If he cannot learn to *follow*, he will never make a good leader. If he refuses to follow a loving, concerned God, he will fully deserve the trouble that his foolish rebellion will bring to his home and his life. God has given the husband the privilege and responsibility of leader-

Why is selfishness intensified in a family situation?

133

What is the first temptation that will come to a husband after an argument with his wife? How can such a temptation be overcome?

ship because he was made to be physically *stronger* to protect, provide and serve his family. His basic *role* in the home is to *LEAD*. God's basic *command* for him is to *LOVE*. It is his *nature* to lead, and if he is stopped from this, he will become angry or bitter. It is easy for him, however, to become mad or hurt over something his wife does, and to *withdraw* his love from her. If he gives up his responsibility or breaks God's basic command for him, he will bring trouble in his home and his life (Ephesians 5:23; Genesis 3:16).

1. *DON'T hold back your love!* "Husbands, *LOVE* your wives" (Ephesians 5:25). You must love your wife as your own body because you are both in the sight of God "one flesh" (Ephesians 5:28a, 5:31). You must learn not to behave harshly or to become selfishly angry with your wife if she should fail, but be tender, gentle and kind in every trying situation (Colossians 3:19). If you want to be boss of your household, first learn to be boss of your own *temper!* Give your wife honor and consideration as the "weaker vessel" (1 Peter 3:7). You may need to ask her forgiveness for your hateful temper. *Swallow* your stinking pride! If you call yourself a child of God, your life should be marked by *love.* If you cannot learn to love your *wife* you do not really love *God* at all (1 John 4:7-8). Give her your love at *all costs.*

This love will not always be a *feeling* of *affection.* There will be times when you feel anything BUT affection for her, if she does something foolishly or unthinkingly. But love is not primarily a feeling, but a *choice* for the *other's highest good.* Get control of your feelings. DO that which is *right.* Learn to *forgive* "seventy times seven" (Matthew 18:21-22). If your wife begins to wrongly assert leadership, your reaction may very well be to *withdraw* your love from her to "teach her a lesson." You are UNDER *command* to love her in this case. If you need to *reprove* her, do it, but do it in *love.* Your first duty is to be *Christ-like* to your wife. This means you must not only be a man of prayer, a man of the Word of God, a man of the church and a man of honesty and integrity, but you must be a man who shows *Christ's* love. Without it, your marriage will be doomed to failure.

134

# LOVING YOUR WIFE

"Love your wives — as *Christ* loved the church" (Ephesians 5:25). What is the church? The *church* is a body of people who once did not care about God, who showed Him no love and gave Him no obedience. But He loved *them* into caring, and He loved *them* into obeying. He still pleads with His Bride when she, the church is imperfect; He rebukes and chastens at times, but always in love. He loves and goes the limit, taking the guilt on Himself, for He can bear it when His Bride cannot. Do *you* have this love? If you do, you will not justify your actions by saying *"She* did it first" or accuse your wife *"You* started it, and I'm not going to say sorry until you do!" Christ always works to bring His Bride to see her faults and repent, and He is always there to help and *begin* the reconciliation. If you are going to be leader, begin by taking the leadership in asking *forgiveness.* Do not bury your head in the sand and sulk until *she* admits her faults! Take the lead; help her by carrying the load of her faults. Forgive, be considerate, and thoughtful, lovingly try to lead her to a better way of life. This love is described in *1 Corinthians 13.* Measure your love against this.

Perhaps your love is *dead* already. God is the God of the Resurrection! He can make your dead love live again! *Hosea* was God's man, but his wife was an adulteress. Hosea loved her so much that he brought her back from slavery that her sins had sold her into. He would take her back, live with her, love her and plead with her to be faithful. He did this simply because he loved her and was concerned for her. He did everything he could to win her back. He did *not* rush her to the divorce court. Read Hosea's story for an example. If you will be willing to *act·*as if you loved her, God will give you the love you need. This is not pretence; it is *obedience* to Christ's commands. *Begin your honeymoon* all over again. Bring her presents, flowers. Take her out on a date again. Court her all over again. God can make your dead love flower into new life and restore it into full blossom!

2. *DON'T BE BOSSY or domineering.* "For the husband is the head of the wife, even as *Christ* is the head of the church; and he is the saviour of the body" (Ephesians 5:23).

135

A husband's greatest temptation in asserting his leadership is to *abuse* his leadership and use it in imposing on his wife. Jesus is head of the church, but *He* is not bossy or domineering. He exercises authority without dictatorship. He voluntarily became a *servant* for us (Philippians 2:5-7). The Christian husband should seek likewise to *serve* his wife, not as a "hen-pecked" man but as unto the Lord (Luke 6:38). He should be willing to *work* to earn her appreciation and respect. He should be as willing to offer his help to *her* as he *wants her* to help him.

Husband, you do *not* lead in a haughty, superior manner. This is not the Spirit of Christ; this is not meekness (Ephesians 5:22-26; 6:1-3). To lead your wife in love is to guard her own happiness and to plan her best interests under God. This is *not* slave-driving. Christ's leadership is one of tenderness, care and love; He sets an example and loves us into following it for Him. If you were YOUR wife, would YOU want to  obey yourself? If you want her to obey you, you must be the *kind* of man who is easy to obey. Your wife is *part* of you, and if you love yourself and her, take *care* of her (Ephesians 5:28).

". . . Many couples begin their married life with the attitude that their *mate* must make them happy and that it is the mate's *duty* to do so. They enter holy wedlock *looking* for something rather than with the intention of *giving* themselves to one another. '*Submitting* yourselves *one to another* in the fear of the Lord' (Ephesians 5:21). *This* is the Lord's way. People who enter marriage with the attitude of *getting* instead of *giving* are quick to find fault with one another. Little things irritate and disturb them, such as personal habits, ways of speaking and mannerisms. These lead to quarrels and tension mounts while the divine pattern of 'love' is ignored."

## CONSIDER YOUR CO-PARTNER

*Husbands MUST treat their wives with consideration.* Ephesians 5:22 does NOT mean that you can treat your wife

136

as you please *without* respect and care for her. *Henry Brandt* says — "The relationship between wife and husband can be likened to the relationship between the president and vice-president of a bank. Only one can be president; both carry heavy responsibilities. The vice-president knows the policies as well as the president. He helps make them, is in accord with them, and is limited in his decisions by them. He can step in and take over at any time and the bank will function as in the past . . . *Freedom* comes through submission and subjection to bank policies. It is a friendly, interdependent relationship. Occasionally, new circumstances arise. The president calls his first vice-president together to ponder the question. It is a serious moment when a meeting of the minds is not possible. Such an occurance is rare, but when it comes, the *president* must make the final decision not according to personal whim, but in the best interest of the bank. Once the decision is made, everyone, including the president is bound by it. If later, the decision proves not to be in the best interest of the bank, it can be changed" (*Balancing Your Marriage*, page 24).

What is the difference between submission and slavery?

"Too often the moral downfall of men is blamed on some failure of their *wives*. That is a cowardly evasion of moral responsibility. The man of disciplined character does not have to have a warm, responsive wife who caters to his every impulse, to keep him in the path of virtue. He keeps *himself* there, by the grace of God. If his relationship with his wife is *happy*, he is *grateful*; if it is *not*, he simply appropriates more grace and demonstrates the man he is. A *weak* man is a poor risk however warm is his wife; a *strong* man will keep himself pure even if it means total abstinence the rest of his life . . . Some marriages are less than ideal in their physical aspects. Some bodily or psychological impediment prevent the fulfilment of that romantic ideal . . . *So what?* Must there therefore be irritability and constant tension, and perpetual teetering on the brink of moral infidelity? . . . Such conditions are often the rock on which the marriage is shattered. But they may also be the rock on which the marriage is *built* into a stronger and finer edifice. In these very problems the couple may find a deeper meaning of love and a truer, richer stability . . . The marriage is not just "saved," it is often *stronger* than marriages wherein there have been no deep struggles and decisive conquests" (*The Disciplined Life*, Richard Shelley Taylor).

*Don't abuse your wife physically.* The Bible commands the husband to live considerately with his wife, giving her *honour* as the "weaker vessel" (1 Peter 3:7). Men must not be harsh or bitter with their wives, but gentle, tender and kind in every circumstance (Colossians 3:19). This means *self-restraint*, especially in the area of sex. Christ is the "Saviour of the *body*" (Ephesians 5:23) and your wife's submission to you is *no excuse* for undisciplined, selfish and unrestrained sexual promiscuity. Sexual love is to be a warmly-shared and tender privilege between you and your wife, not an occasion for you to abuse her body as if she was nothing more than an object of gratification for your over-indulgence. God makes no grounds for moral flabbiness, especially in marriage. *Self-control* is one of the fruits of the Spirit (Galatians 5:23-24). If you cannot learn to bring your desires within sensible and considerate limits, you are in grave danger of *giving in to* temptation outside of marriage when domestic stress, long illness or marital "fridgidity" in your mate, or separation for some time puts pressure on your morally feeble controls.

3. *DON'T abdicate your responsibility.* True leadership is a labor of love (1 Corinthians 13:4-7). Man was made to lead, provide and defend. He was made physically stronger to protect and care for his wife. To do this he must *stick to his task.* It is not easy to be a leader. It is by far easier to *give up* when things get tough and leave things to his wife when she was not designed to bear such a burden.

"In a home, the *husband* is responsible for the family. He should have the total picture in mind — financing, training,

housing, planning for the future. He must depend heavily on his wife for carrying out the *details.* To do this, he may need to delegate much of his responsibility to her. At times he must act decisively when a difficult decision is up to him. The husband has the responsibility of setting godly standards for the home, and leading the way up to them himself, just as *Jesus* set the standard for His followers (John 14:15). A husband should rule his household according to the best interests of his wife and family."

138

*You*, husband, are to be the kind of man that is dedicated under God to your wife and family even to *death* (Ephesians 5:25b). Your duties are [A] *DIRECTIONAL* — as the head directs the body, so you are responsible to God to lead the affairs of your family. Make it a *family rule*, that after careful, prayerful discussion together, if husband and wife cannot agree, it will be the *husband's* decision that will carry. God will hold you responsible for your family management, not your wife. [B] *PROVISIONAL* — you must make adequate provision for your family. The first share of your earnings must go to your *household*, for God holds you responsible for their well-being and care. You have no right to force your wife into taking care of financial provision for the house, while you spend your earnings on self-gratification. "If any provide not for his own, and especially for those of his own house, he has *denied the faith* and is *worse* than an infidel" (1 Timothy 5:8). If you fit into this category, you had better take steps to set this situation right, for you are in a bad place with God. [C] *CHIVALRIC* — (1 Peter 3:7). This society needs a *rebirth of chivalry;* men need to study and practice it, and women should expect it and ask for it. Opening doors for the wife, allowing her to enter first, showing simple courtesy and honor is all too often simply *neglected* by the husband. Wives are usually generous in understanding, but they do not want to have to "understand" *too* many things — especially neglect. [D] *SPIRITUAL* — The husband has a home responsibility to lead the house in prayer, family devotions and worship. This leadership does not come out of half-hearted directions to do this out of a sense of duty.

One of the best teaching aids is example. Why would this be so valuable in a family situation?

*Keith Miller* says — "If you want your children to read the Bible and pray someday, get up and do these things *yourself* — because *you WANT TO*. They'll know if you are *really* interested or just doing it out of a sense of duty" (*A Second Touch*, page 39). "A husband's job is to be head of the house in religious matters. If you don't have a family worship at home, it is the *husband's* fault. If you don't have prayer in your home, table grace and family worship you ought to be ashamed of yourself for your sin against God. It will make all the difference in the world. Every problem you face in the family will be solved if you pray together" (Billy Graham). The husband should be in the forefront of spiritual interest, devotion and cultivation. If anyone in the home has to urge another to go to church, it should be the *husband*. He is the head, as Christ is the *head* of the church, and should busy

139

Thought: If we expect nothing from our partners, can we ever be disappointed if we don't receive it?

himself with his *duties* rather than talk about his rights.

The husband's *greatest* temptation to give in to the spiritual pressures bent on destroying his home is to *withdraw his love* from his wife under provocation. He may be persuaded  that his wife does not love *him*, that she will be "just like" some other unfortunate female example in his family. But he does not DARE give in, and withdraw into a selfish shell. "Love is *never* jealous, envious, haughty or proud . . . it is not irritable or touchy. It does not hold grudges and will hardly notice when others do it wrong" (1 Corinthians 13:4-7). In his tract *"Marriage Can Be Happy"* Gordon L. Van Oostenburg writes —

"When you feel neglected, feel that you have been overlooked or ignored, it only reveals your lack of love. When you are so easily upset or disturbed about your partner's mannerisms, it only reveals your lack of love. When you become suspicious and think evil of your mate, it only reveals your lack of love. When you feel you have "gone far enough" and you are ready to quit, it only shows your lack of love. "Love *NEVER* faileth." This is the secret. Love so that you expect *nothing* from your wife, but go all out to please your partner, always making it your aim to please her and make her . . . happy. It is the only pattern for a Christian marriage."

*Dr. Oswald J. Smith* says "there are *two kinds of wives.* There are those who love to demonstrate their affection. They meet you at the door, throw their arms around you and give you a welcoming kiss. They go to you of their own accord and crawl into your arms. If there is anything between you they make it up at once. They are like a clinging vine, and they are priceless. They know just how to make you love them and to make you happy. Then there are the *other* kind. They are reserved. *You* have to take the initiative. They may love you deeply, *more* deeply than the first, but though they express their affection for you in their letters, they do not show it when they are with you. If there are any misunderstandings, they just suffer and wait until YOU make up. Their love is true, but undemonstrative. You will have to go more than half-way if you want to be happy. They have much to give, but they do not know *how* to give it, and you

140

must teach them. You must win them. You must go the second mile. They may even resist you. Their response may be disappointing. But it will pay you to persevere." *(How To Win Your Family To Christ).*

How does a woman's emotional makeup lend itself toward harmony in the marriage relationship?

## RESPONSIBILITY OF THE WIFE

The *wife's* responsibility is to *submit* herself to her own husband in the Lord. Her relationship is at the same time  *equal* and *unequal*. She may be his equal as far as *intellect, conscience, service, freedom* and *happiness* is concerned; but she is *not* to take the reins of *leadership* in the home. It is not a question of superiority, but *authority* She cannot effectively do a man's job under God, just as her husband cannot effectively do hers. One of the reasons for this law is her difference in make-up. A woman usually reacts more by her *senses*, rather than *logic*. God made her this way, with the capacity to experience, feel and enjoy so she could pass on her inspiration to her husband. She is usually better able to "sense out" an experience than a man; he is more *matter-of-fact* in his approach to life. *Spiritually,* she is often more able to see the whole picture than the man, but is *not* able to dissect and analyze its *worth* as well as her husband. This gift is both an advantage and a *disadvantage*. When protected from deception under the leadership of her husband, she is free to inspire and challenge him in ways he could never see without her. If she is left *unguarded* by his "spiritual umbrella" (see 1 Corinthians 11:3-12) and assumes the *false* responsibility of implementing and approving her *own* discoveries, she is left tragically open to satanic or other form of deception, leading both herself and her husband into danger (Genesis 3:1-6; 1 Timothy 2:11-14).

For this reason, a woman fulfils her role in the home only when she makes it her ministry to *INSPIRE. God's basic command* for the wife, to protect her against the temptation to try to implement her unchecked ideas is to *SUBMIT* to her husband's authority; to OBEY him. This safeguard, intro-

What are the
primary
scriptural
responsi-
bilities
of the wife?

duced after the fall, is underlined *right through* the Bible. She is to submit in *everything* (Ephesians 5:24) except specific orders to sin (Ephesians 5:33; 1 Peter 3:1,2).

1. *STAY HOME where you belong* (Titus 2:4-5). Being a wife and a mother is a *full*time job. Whenever possible, the wife must spend the *majority* of her time with her home and her children. Some women spend all their time away from home simply to escape their God-given responsibilities. Others will get involved in business careers *God* never gave them, so they can boss their own lives and not be dependent on their husbands. There is no greater possible danger of them *losing* their family love. Wife, did GOD call you to the work you are doing outside of your home? It will be easy to justify your actions by complaining that your husband does not make enough money to "keep up with the Joneses". You can buy a whole houseful of new carpet and *still* lose your children and your husband in the process. You may build a wide circle of social friends, but if you fail in your home responsibilities, you have failed the most *basic test* of your womanhood.

*Be willing to learn from older Christian women* (Titus 2:4). This is a further test of your submission. They can teach you to "love your husband, love your children, to be discreet, chaste, keepers at home, good, obedient to their own husbands, that the Word of God be not blasphemed." To properly honor and appreciate contributions from older women of God who have learnt from the school of time, is a way for young wives to save themselves from many foolish steps and possible heartaches. Perhaps the greatest lesson they can teach you is the importance of your role in the home.

You, as a woman, have a basically *different make-up* than your husband. Your *body* is different; you cannot do the rough hard labor that is the lot of many men. God never intended you to. Your *mental attitude* is basically different. Men are usually naturally aggressive — leaders. You have been made to *follow* in love. All being considered, you are usually higher in personal qualities than your husband because God made you for your man to be proud of you. You are made to be more patient, understanding. You are able to stand greater hardship, difficulty and pain. You can comfort and sympathize better, and are more even-tempered. Do not try to do a man's job, in a man's way. You will only succeed in *cheapening* the qualities that set you apart, *coarsen* the things that make you most beautiful and grieve God. You cannot attempt to act like a man without losing the *very things* that make you uniquely different, and better suited for your own work than him.

When would the wife not be required to submit to her husband's authority?

2. *STAY IN SUBMISSION as a Christian* (Ephesians 5:22). Giving in to God as a sinner is often hard, and a direct parallel exists in *your* need for surrender to your husband's leadership. If God begins to plead with you in love for the rights of your life, you may try to put Him off and convince yourself that surrender to Him would leave life dull, tasteless and frustrating. But if you finally surrender to His loving con-

trol, what a surprise awaits! All things become new; your whole attitude changes completely. The old, rebellious life of self-dependency seems like slavery in contrast to the new joy, peace, contentment and serenity His care and watchful protection brings you. You become *free* for the first time to be what you were meant to be. Just so is the way of submission to your *husband's* leadership. Without this surrender, the few selfish "kicks" you get out of "wearing the pants" in the family will lose their lustre and leave you bitter and disappointed. How much more lovely is the wonderful way of God (Hebrews 13:17; James 3:17-18).

*If your husband is not a Christian,* do not despair. You are still to submit in his leadership, in EVERYTHING (Ephesians 5:24) except *direct, specific* commands to commit *sin.* In this case, you are under *higher law* (Acts 5:29; Mark 12:28-31) and must not follow him into sin. This is not applicable in cases where you "feel God would have me do this" without *specific* direction from the *Word of God.* God will show you ways *around* your husband's directions that involve compromise without actual *transgression,* so you will be able to turn these into a chance to witness or some other work for Christ. If you feel God wants you to do something, but have been ordered not to by your husband, use Proverbs 21:1 and pray — "Lord, I think You want me to do this, but my husband will not allow it. If You do, then You must change my husband's mind, because You have asked me to submit to his authority." Under *no circumstances* are you to

143

What is the
great
temptation
facing a
Christian
wife with an
unsaved
husband?

overrule his authority simply because you are a "Christian" and he is not. You will not be part of God's *answer* in your home, but part of His *problem*. God never breaks one of His basic laws so that He can fulfil another. Go the way of loving submission (Romans 13).

---

## WINNING YOUR UNSAVED HUSBAND

---

*Dr. J.C. Brumfield* gives some sage advice to help you win your husband to Christ using 1 Peter 3:1-6. "The wife *can* win her husband to the Lord if she meets *God's conditions.* He gives directions affecting *three things: attitude, appearance* and *adornment* . . . the body, the soul and the spirit. 1 Peter 3:1 is a direct reference to 1 Peter 2:18 where servants are asked to be subject to their master. *Wives* are to practice this same obedience with their husbands. If the wife finds herself married to an ungodly or even a cruel husband, she is to bear her suffering just as Christ did, trusting God to take care of injustice suffered (cf. 1 Peter 2:18b).

"I have the *utmost sympathy* for the woman who has to live with an ungodly man. Her love has been betrayed, her romance has faded, her dreams have vanished, her hopes are shattered and her heart is broken. My purpose is to help you  claim God's promise and *win your husband* to the Saviour. To do this, I must speak frankly; some things I am going to say may hurt. God requires you to be in subjection to your *own husband*, not some stranger! (1 Corinthians 11:8-10; 1 Timothy 2:11-14; Ephesians 5:23,30). Every time the Word of God uses 'obey,' a special Greek word meaning 'one's own *dear* husband is used.

"Be in subjection to 'your own dear husband.' That is not *unreasonable* is it? Of all men, you have chosen *him* to be your life companion, to share sorrow and happiness, to be the father of your children, to be the protector of your home and the provider of your needs. You left father and mother . . . to live with him in preference to all other men. God gives a wonderful promise to the faithful, loving submissive wife. 'They *may* (oldest manuscripts — *'shall'*) be won.' God is saying that if you carry out his directions, your husband 'shall' be won. The word *conversation* does not mean much talking' . . . but the *behavior, manner* of *living,* the *conduct* of the Christian wife. A nagging, irritable, complaining, careless, unpleasant woman will never win her unsaved husband to Christ . . . You preach to him that Jesus can free him from his sins, help him overcome drinking, swearing and the use of tobacco; but unless you *show* him that Jesus can cure that temper of yours, your tongue and disposition, your words will have little effect on him.

How could a wife's appearance help win her husband to Jesus?

"The *second condition* has to do with *appearance.* Nowhere does the Bible condemn a wife for being clean, neat and attractive. I suggest very kindly that if some women spent about ten minutes looking in the mirror, they might discover why their husbands do not make love to them any longer. There seems to be some connection between cleanliness and godliness which some Christian women have not discovered . . . Christian women should not cheapen their appearance by gaudy ornaments and worldly attire in order to attract attention. But nowhere does He condemn a woman for making the best of her personal appearance in order to hold the love and admiration of her husband. Mere outward adorning however is not the only way — 'the *ornament* of a *meek* and quiet spirit' will reach his heart. A meek spirit does not create a disturbance, is not officious or 'bossy.' A *quiet* spirit is one which bears with patience the disturbance caused by others and is gentle in word and action."

"Be careful that your desire to win your husband is prompted by the proper *motive* — the glory of God. Many sincere Christian wives want their husbands saved so that their lives will be happier and their homes more peaceful. Because they have a selfish motive, God has not answered their prayers. Ask God to give you a *concern* for the soul of your husband, that whatever it might cost you in sacrifice or suffering, his soul might be saved for the Lord's glory."

"*When your husband comes home* this evening, meet him with a smile. Have your hair done, and a clean, becoming dress on. Try to look just like you used to when he came to take you out on a date. Be sure the house is spick-and-span and homey-looking. Have an appetizing meal on the table;

145

What are the
dangers of a
wife
withholding
sexual love
from her
husband?

serve his favorite dish. Be sweet, kind, cheerful, soft-spoken and submissive to him. He may faint; but when he recovers, he will like it. If you continue to act in this way, according to God's promises, your husband will be won to the Lord."

**3.** *Give him LOVE at all costs* (Titus 2:4). In too many marriages, no "hugs" can break down the invisible wall of reserve and reproach. Get on your knees and ask God's forgiveness for your self-pity and critical attitude. Only *Christ's love* can break down the walls and bind your hearts together again. Men are won to Christ by *Marys*, not *Marthas*. *Oswald Smith* comments — "Take time to *express* your love. Give him a chance to enjoy your affection. Go to him often. Make love to him even if he is old. Be so indispensable that he will never even think of anyone else." This includes *physical love* (1 Corinthians 7:1-5). The sexual relation is holy even if the wife has an unbelieving husband. The wife's body belongs to her husband; one purpose of sexual union is to avoid fornication (1 Corinthians 7:2). If the wife tries to defraud her husband out of a spirit of spite, or to show disapproval of something he has done, she runs the risk of *losing a husband* to some other girl who gives him cause to be tempted. This is *specifically forbidden* in Scripture. "Do not cheat each other of sexual intercourse, unless, of course, you both decide to abstain temporarily, to make special opportunity for fasting and prayer" (1 Corinthians 7:5 — Phillips).

It should be mentioned in passing that this command of Scripture is a powerful force to weld a marriage strongly together. There are many hidden blessings when the husband obeys God to regularly meet his wife's sexual needs, and the wife does likewise with her husband's needs. The beautiful Song of Solomon poetically and reverently describes some of the joys of this physical/ spiritual blend of married love (Song of Solomon 6:1-10; 7:1-9; 2:3; 8:3). Many Christian people have not made a careful study of the Bible on this subject and get the unfortunate impression that sex is a necessary, but unholy duty. Nothing could be more damaging to the love-relationship God planned for husband and wife. Marriage is to be held in honor, as the highest gift of love God has given a young couple (Hebrews 13:4).

146

*Resist the temptation* to *goad, manipulate* or *"nag"* him. Don't undercut his leadership by taking sides with the children against him. Stop *comparing him* with someone else's man. Above all stubbornly deal with the sin of *self-pity.* Love is your only necessary weapon and defence and you must draw on Christ to be able to use it consistently and sincerely. "If you *love someone,* you will be loyal to him, no matter *what* the cost. You will always believe in him, always expect the best of him, and always stand your ground in defending him. All special gifts and powers from God will one day come to an end, but love goes on forever" (1 Corinthians 13:7-8a — *Living Letters).* God *help* you to — "stay in love!"

"Blessed are the POOR IN SPIRIT; for theirs is the Kingdom of Heaven" (Matthew 5:3)

# MATTHEW

## (WHO SACRIFICED TO FOLLOW)

"If any man will come after Me, let him deny himself, take up his cross and follow Me."

Matthew 16:24

What is the
function of
memory and
why can this
be either a
blessing or a
threat to us?

PHASE:     3 .. *Disciples In Clay*
SECTION:   4 .. *"C" For Confession And Restitution*
MATERIAL  .. *The "How" Of Humility*

That despised tax-gatherer! If any man was an unlikely prospect for discipleship, *Matthew* was. No one liked tax collectors. Like Zaccheus, *Matthew* probably had no real friends. But Jesus passed by his money-table one day and called him to follow. *Matthew* swallowed his pride, left his past life and joined the wondering disciples. No matter what men thought of him — *JESUS* had called him! That made all the stares and the sneers worthwhile. *Matthew* called a feast at his house. Was he trying to show the whole world that he was different? Did he try to say "I'm sorry" for the past? *Matthew* proved he meant business when he left all and followed. Like Zaccheus, he could say, "If I have taken anything from any man by false accusation, I restore him four-fold." Have *you?*

The hardest death to die is *death to self*. The most difficult thing to do is to admit wrong and get the past cleaned up. Is there something in *your* life you wish had never happened? Do you still *remember* something you would much rather forget? Did anything happen once to you that you wish you could now *change?* Then there is probably some work for you to do in this section. You could have an *unforgiven past* that needs the cleansing of confession and restitution. We have ignored this Scriptural teaching too long.

## CLEAN CONSCIENCE CHRISTIANITY

*WHY confess past sin against others?*

God has designed our memory to *record the past*. Our conscience ties in past actions with our present thinking and God's moral law. When our conscience is clear, the mind is undisturbed by guilt and free from uneasiness. But past *sin* is also recorded in the mind. This shows what deep damage sin does to the personality because our memories usually forget mistakes and problems to build on the good. These "guilt deposits" must be dealt with, or every time a similar temptation to the recorded sin takes place, our minds will refer to *that* past surrender of will to selfishness for guidance. At once failure and defeat will crowd our thoughts, preparing us to sin again the same way. This is the reason so many people cannot seem to resist temptations.

What is the purpose of confession and restitution?

Although this "law of sin" has terrible strength (Romans 7:14-24) God has given us two deeply powerful principles to overcome it. They are the moral forces of *confession*, to bring self-honesty and forgiveness, and *restitution*, to right wherever possible the harm that has been done by selfishness.

The *PURPOSE of confession* is to *restore* a *ruptured relationship.* Too many Christians have over looked the fact that when we hurt both God AND man, it will be necessary to make things right with BOTH. We have ignored what we have done to harm *others* by our selfishness, and wondered why we did not feel justified after only asking *God* for forgiveness. No wonder so many of us lead such miserable lives! Without confession and restitution we can never —

## 1. OVERCOME TEMPTATION —

Satan uses the memory of unforgiven sin to remind you of past failure and prepare you for bigger defeat. He "trades" on the past, using your unerased sin to drive you deeper and deeper into bondage (Psalm 32:1-5; 1 Corinthians 8:7; Acts 23:1; Hebrews 10:12; 9:14; 1 John 3:21-22).

## 2. OBEY GOD —

Unforgiven sin BLOCKS FAITH. When sin is constantly brought to the mind, we lose sight of God's purposes and fall into despair. The promises of God no longer hold a richness. Multitudes of young people fall by the wayside in Universities and colleges because of *dirty pasts* that corrode faith. Clean consciences help you face anything, confident that there are no secret weeds of unrighteousness that have not been rooted out and burned. Past failure conquered means present power to beat temptation (1 Timothy 1:5-6; 1:18-19; 3:9; 1 Peter 3:15-16).

151

## 3. OVERFLOW WITH JOY —

A sure sign of an unclean conscience is a *loss of joy* in the life. Unforgiven sin strips away freedom from the spirit and life becomes most obviously miserable. The conscience, uneasy and restless, will not let the mind be at peace. The forgiven past is a chief source of rejoicing for the liberated Christian (Acts 24:16; Hebrews 10:22).

## 4. OVERCOME THE WORLD —

"He that covers his sins shall not prosper; but he that confesses and forsakes them shall have mercy" (Proverbs 28:13). Leave anyone in the world you live in with some sin you have done against them not righted, and TO THAT PERSON AT LEAST you are NOT truly a Christian. Every time you try to speak for God your past *testifies against you.* When previous selfishness is confessed to others who were wronged, you can speak boldly and surely of the power of Christ Jesus to completely deliver from sin.

---

### CLEANING OUT CLOSET TIME!

---

Skeletons . . . in YOUR closet?

*How do you get them out?* Memory is highly efficient in remembering wrong. Although it forgets unpleasant and worthless things (like the last time you tripped over or missed what you were aiming for) it NEVER forgets unrighted *sin.* Much mental illness today can be traced to guilt never wiped from the mind by confession, restitution and forgiveness. Shock, drugs and other medical and psychiatric treatment tries to take  such guilt memories from the mind, but *God's* method is the only really effective one — FACE each wrong with its full load of guilt — but *don't* HOLD it! Bring it out into the open before the Lord Jesus, confess it to Him and to those "others" involved — then receive healing *forgiveness.* Now

152

this will NOT be easy (and that goes especially with the "others"). But — reread the *results* of a clear conscience just outlined. Do you NEED these to live as God wants you to? Do you want to live a normal, happy, guilt-free life? Then you NEED to do this and gain a clear conscience. To confess your wrong will kill your PRIDE stone dead. It is going to HURT, make no mistake! But try to go on in peace without getting that past of yours right and you'll *never make it.* Take a deep breath . . . ask the Lord for some "intestinal fortitude" . . . READY?

When asking the Lord to "search our hearts," why is it important to be alone?

---

## GETTING STARTED

---

Go and get a *paper* and *pencil.* Next, go and find a place where you can be truly alone — where no one will interrupt. If possible, go out into the country somewhere, or lock yourself in some quiet room where you can meet God. This is a *special moment* — make a special time and place for it.

Spend a little time at first, just quietly WAITING in His Presence. Don't *say* anything.

Wait there in the stillness until you begin to feel His Presence. As you sense His Holiness you may start to feel your own worthlessness, but this is good preparation.

*Now — ask Him to start digging!* Ask the Lord to search your memories and to bring to your mind unconfessed past sin. As they come to your mind, do not give in to the temptation to ignore them and look for something else. *Admit them* one by one as God shows them to you, and most important — WRITE THEM DOWN! ("Ug! Surely not — someone might find the paper and . . .") WRITE THEM DOWN — *ALL* DOWN!

And they *will* come, one by sordid one, drifting reluctantly through the fog of your consciousness, the things you have run away from for a long, long time. Strangely enough, you will find yourself remembering a lot more of the unforgiven past than you ever had thought possible. Write them all down, using if you like the following spiritual diagnosis

153

sheets. After rereading your list, add any others that come to your mind.

Go over it a *THIRD* time, and you will find still others connected with these. You will remember this way, NOW, things you didn't think you would remember in *eternity*. Go over the list slowly, thoroughly and carefully — *just as if* you were about to die and stand before the Judgment Bar of God Himself.

---

**SPIRITUAL DIAGNOSIS SHEETS**

---

*CHECK LIST NO. 1 — Personal Sins of the Past*

1. *STEALING.* Can you remember taking belongings, property or money that was not rightfully yours? Did you

STEAL from neighbors, school, shops or from your own home, family or relatives? LIST everything you can remember taking, large or small, and determine you will try to pay each back (Exodus 20:15; Leviticus 19:11; Zechariah 5:3; Romans 2:21; Ephesians 4:28).

Yes [ ]　No [ ]　Unsure [ ]

2. *CHEATING.* Did you get anything from anyone unfairly? Did you cheat at school to pass an important test or examination so that someone knows or suspects you, or you have a qualification that you do not deserve? Did you rob someone of their fair share of money or praise for a job? Did you embezzle money from anyone? (Deuteronomy 24:14-15; Job 31:13; Jeremiah 22:13; Malachi 3:5; James 5:1-4).

Yes [ ]　No [ ]　Unsure [ ]

3. *LYING.* Any *designed form of deception* for selfish reasons. "If you design to make an impression contrary to the naked truth, you LIE." Dishonesty in action, word or appearance is an abomination to God. Lies cause distrust and suspicion. Confess your deceit — make a resolution to right any damaging falsity of the past (Revelation 21:7-8,27; Leviticus 19:11; Colossians 3:9; Ephesians 4:25; John 8:44).

Yes [ ]　No [ ]　Unsure [ ]

4. *SLANDER.* Back-biting, speaking evil of another. Have you talked "behind someone's back" in such a way to hurt

their character, or in a way you would not be willing to do before their face? You do not have to LIE to slander. Any form of malicious gossip — telling the truth with design or intent to hurt or injure is slander. "A WHISPERER separateth chief friends" (Proverbs 16:28; 6:16-19).

Yes [ ]  No [ ]  Unsure [ ]

5. *IMMORALITY.* Are you guilty of past immorality? As a child, teenager or recently; in outings, dates or at other times, did you light sexual fires which could not righteously fuel? You have deeply wronged both God and the other person. Your lust could have caused a complete chain of sin that can affect many lives. Moral impurity causes great guilt. You will have to be ready to both admit your guilt and ask forgiveness (Matthew 5:28; Job 31:1; 2 Peter 2:14; 1 Corinthians 6:18, 9-10).

Yes [ ]  No [ ]  Unsure [ ]

6. *CENSORIOUSNESS.* Are you guilty of bitterness? Did you speak of others without love? Did you judge motives, think the worst of a situation involving someone else and spoke cuttingly to them about it? (John 7:24; 1 Corinthians 4:1-7; 6:1-8; Galatians 6:1; Matthew 7:1-5; 5:21-24; Colossians 3:8).

Yes [ ]  No [ ]  Unsure [ ]

*CHECK LIST NO. 2 — Sins Discovered in Attitudes*
("How do *others* behave towards me?")

1. *LEVITY.* Needless frivolity, silly talk, speaking or acting like a fool. Jests that tend to undermine sacred standards of life like birth, death and sex; empty unprofitable conversation or "Bible" jokes that make light of God's Holy Word achieve nothing but a dangerous devaluation of the Christian's word and his authority. Have you been insensitive to others' needs because of foolishness? Real humor is a gift of God and will always prepare a heart for the work of the Holy Spirit; the stupidity of levity is sin (Proverbs 15:14; 24:9; Ephesians 5:3-4).

Yes [ ]  No [ ]  Unsure [ ]

2. *ENVY.* Envy is "the rottenness of the bones" (Proverbs 14:30). Behind talk about others' faults and failures is rotten envy. Did you gossip and boast to exalt yourself at the expense of others? Does it *hurt* to hear certain others praised? BE HONEST! If you have harbored this spirit of Hell, repent DEEPLY before God or He will never forgive you (Job 5:2; Proverbs 14:30; 27:4; Galatians 5:25).

Yes [ ]  No [ ]  Unsure [ ]

3. *PRIDE.* It is nothing but *selfishness personified.* It is thinking and pretending you are more or less than you  actually ARE. It is not being willing to have both yourself and others take you at *heart* as well as face value. Have you paid more attention to your LOOKS than you have to the state of your SOUL? *Contention with others* is almost always a direct result of pride. Do you constantly "cross" with others? Is there a divisive, trouble-stirring spirit in your heart? Then YOU are PROUD. Admit it! Humble yourself before God and ask those you have hurt to forgive you (Proverbs 16:5,12,18; 21:24; 29:23; Titus 3:9; 1 Corinthians 1:26-31; 1 Peter 5:1).                    Yes [ ]   No [ ]   Unsure [ ]

4. *INGRATITUDE.* How many times have others gone out of their way for you, made personal sacrifices to help,—and you have treated them like dirt under your feet? Did you take favors as a matter of course? Get this sin right! Untold bad attitudes are bred in ungratefulness. Friends? PARENTS? (Romans 1:21; Malachi 3:8-11; 2 Timothy 3:2; Exodus 20:12; Ephesians 6:2; Colossians 3:15).
Yes [ ]   No [ ]   Unsure [ ]

5. *ANGER.* Have you been *bad-tempered?* Did you lose self-control and not show gentleness and patience? It's no good blaming your "Irish background" or "bad circumstances." Provocation only reveals the true state of your heart, not makes it like it is. If you kick a barrel of *acid,* all that comes out is *acid;* kick over a barrel of honey and all that spills over is sweetness! Nothing comes *out* of your heart but that whichis already IN there! Besides — it will do no good to say "I didn't *mean* to say it" if you have *sworn* or taken the Lord's Name in vain. Scripture says "Out of the abundance of the heart the mouth speaketh." Have YOU denied someone Christianity by your attitude? (Proverbs 15:18; 22:24; Ecclesiastes 7:9; Matthew 5:22; Colossians 3:8).
Yes [ ]   No [ ]   Unsure [ ]

6. *CURSING.* Have you hurt others by using *gutter language?* Swearing has no place in the life of a child of God. Never use exclamations that begin with *"G"*, *"C"* or *"J"*; they are usually substitutes for curses with God's Name. Have *you* failed to guard your speech? (Deuteronomy 5:11; Matthew 5:33-37).                    Yes [ ]   No [ ]   Unsure [ ]

## CHECK LIST NO. 3 — Sins of Damaged Witness
("What am I like in the eyes of others?")

1. *HYPOCRISY.* Have you lived before others so as to make all you have said of Christ and His Gospel a lie? Is there "Pharisee" in your attitude? You believe, you have said that "the Bible is true." Then have you LIVED by it? To have said one thing and done another makes you a hypocrite. If you want to move on for the Lord, you will first have to admit your failure to live according to Bible standards to any you have turned from Christ by your lukewarm life. Think hard — have you? (Matthew 6:5-6; 7:3-5; 23:28; Luke 12:1; 1 Timothy 4:2; 1 Peter 2:1).    Yes [ ]   No [ ]   Unsure [ ]

2. *HINDRANCE.* Hell is full because so-called Christians block and hinder others from doing God's will. If you have destroyed their Christian confidence in you by your self-centeredness, or needlessly wasted their time with non-essentials, you have been a hindrance. Have you? (Ephesians 5:16; John 9:4).    Yes [ ]   No [ ]   Unsure [ ]

3. *HARDNESS.* Have you fought back, grumbled or returned evil for evil? Was your behavior un-Christlike when someone in the past wronged you? To them you may as well have been like any other unsaved, rotten-natured man. Vou will have to go back to them, confess your attitude as s·: and get it right. Were you hard and stubborn? (Exodus 16:8; Philippians 2:14; 1 Corinthians 10:10; 1 Thessalonians 5:15; 1 Peter 3:9).    Yes [ ]   No [ ]   Unsure [ ]

4. *HALF-HEARTEDNESS.* Can you remember occasions where at work or on a job you shirked your full share of responsibility? Have you been lazy or half-hearted about something which was entrusted to you? Have you shirked times of secret, family or public prayer meetings because it would have cost you a little time? Perhaps you have prayed in such a way before God as to have offended Him even more than missing  it out! Did you stay away from revival or soul-winning influences out of some pretence of business? You have stood by and let souls go to Hell while you please *yourself?!* (Ezekiel 33:8; Proverbs 24:12).    Yes [ ]   No [ ]   Unsure [ ]

5. *HOLDING BACK.* "There are many professors of religion who are willing to do almost anything that does not call for self-denial; but when they are called to *deny themselves*, Oh! that is too much. They think they are doing a great deal for God, and about as much as He ought to ask in reason; but are not willing to deny themselves any comfort or convenience whatever for the sake of serving the Lord. They will not deny themselves the LUXURIES of life to save a world from Hell" (Finney — *Revival Lectures*, page 41). Have you given only of your abundance, and never of your NEED that others may hear the Gospel? Have you looked on your possessions and property as if it were really YOURS, and you had a right to spend it or hoard it without a thought of GOD'S rights and a world's needs?

Yes [ ]   No[ ]   Unsure [ ]


6. *BROKEN VOWS.* Here lies the reason why so many Christians have spiritual relapses after spiritual conventions; their *consecration is incomplete.* They made a vow to God and failed to *keep* it; they do not realize how serious an offense that is. They think that it is only their *failure* and concern if they forget; but they are wrong. God considers it a serious breach of fellowship. Is there a vow you made to God that you have not kept? Did you promise Him something you have since forgotten or gone back on? (If it was unwise,you had better ask His forgiveness and release.) (Ecclesiastes 5:1-2; 5:4-6; Acts 5:4).

Yes [ ]   No [ ]   Unsure [ ]

NOTE: ALL "UNSURES" COUNT AS A "YES"
(READ ROMANS 14:23 TO SEE WHY)

Take each one slowly and carefully. *Check* each area that is a "sore spot" and on your *own* paper write out what you will have to do to get it right. *Confess them* to the Lord one by one as He shows you them. When you have *finished*, REREAD your list again and *add any others* that come to mind. Don't give in to temptation to pass quickly over any area that hurts. Take your courage in your bare hands; FACE your sin. *This first part will be painful.* Let God furrow your heart and break up all the hardness that has formed from unconfessed sin. If *tears* begin to come, *let* them. "Godly sorrow works repentance," and tears may soften your heart for God to work with it (2 Corinthians 7:10; Psalm 38:18; 34:6,18; 51:17; 147:3; Ecclesiastes 7:3; Ezekiel 34:16; Luke 4:18).

"Go thoroughly to work in all this. Go *NOW*. Don't put it off; that will only make matters worse . . . Don't think of getting off by going round the stumbling blocks. Take them up out of the way. Things may be left that you may think *little* things, and you may wonder why you do not feel as you wish to, when the reason is that your proud and carnal mind has *covered up something* which God required you to confess and remove. Break up all the ground and turn it over. Do not balk; do not turn aside for little difficulties; drive the plow right through them, beam deep, and turn the ground all up, so that it may all be mellow and soft, and fit to receive the seed and bear fruit a hundred fold "(*C.G. Finney* on *Hosea 10:12*).

*Deal with your sin in TRUE repentance;* this means to *SEE* it; *HATE* it; *FORSAKE* it. Your sins were *committed* one by one; *think over them* one by one. This is the way to feel and see your guilt before God; this is the way the Holy Spirit can open your eyes to the deadly work sin has done. Do you *SEE?* Now then, choose. *Tears* are not enough, *feeling sorry* is not enough, you must decide NOW to make a total TURN from these hateful things that hurt God. It means you purpose NOW to give up every filthy habit, selfish ambition, bitter feeling and ungodly friend, and to get right everything on your list! Until you do you will never have peace with God. Do not dare use any of the following excuses:

---

## EXCUSES OF PRIDE

---

1. *"Getting it right will mean putting back something I don't have."*
Better to have an honest DEBT than an accusing past. God always makes a way to provide IF you sincerely want to get it right. Arrange to pay back debts in some kind of installments if need be—but ARRANGE TO PAY THEM BACK!

2. *"They probably won't understand."*
You'll probably be surprised! Your job is to GET IT RIGHT — the "understand" is between THEM and God. If they don't seem to, they may realize that they also need to ask your

159

Thought:
Excuses
don't bring
peace; they
only prolong
the problem.

forgiveness . . . BUT don't you DARE ask for it when you go!

3. *"I'll do it — but not just now . . . some other time . . . "* NOW is the accepted time! (2 Corinthians 6:2). The LONGER you put it off, the HARDER it will be to confess. Get it fixed up between you and God, then go as soon as you can.

4.*"It was so LONG AGO — surely it doesn't matter NOW!"* Then WHY do you still REMEMBER it? If it still gnaws your conscience, then it is not forgotten — OR forgiven. Go back and get it right as best you can.

5. *"It was only such a little thing . . . "* It IS big enough to bother your conscience. After getting the "big" things righted, a "silly, little thing" may be the VERY reason why there is still no peace or sense of complete forgiveness. One little "bit" in a runner's eye may cause him to lose the whole race. *Don't* try to cover it. Dig it out — confess it.

6.*"The old problem is different; situations have changed; everything is O.K. now."* This can be God's method of preparing your way to get the past forgiven. He may have changed others' attitudes so your confession will be accepted. Don't use it as an excuse for not going.

7. *"They — well, uh — they aren't there anymore."* Come on, now! Surely they have left friends or relatives if they have moved. Get their address from one of them. You can phone them or write a letter if they are too far away. If you honestly CAN'T trace them, why not ask God to help you find them? If it is important, He could work a miracle to make your confession possible.

8. *"Why bother confessing? I know I'll only do it again."* If you say this, you admit *two things:* (a) *You have not REALLY repented.* Repentance is not just feeling *sorry* for your sin, but DETERMINING before God that by His grace

160

you will SIN NO MORE that way! Don't you DARE ask forgiveness while secretly deciding to do it again! Such a wretched excuse for repentance is a MOCKERY to God. (b) You have never asked forgiveness in the right way. Did you honestly NAME your BASIC sin? Did you repent and ask forgiveness for THAT or just the RESULTS of it? The agony of self-humiliation when the sin itself is confessed blocks the way back to it far more effectively than trying to control yourself in NOT doing it.

Are *you* presently using any of the excuses listed on this page?

9. *"It's no use going now. They're dead."*
If necessary, you can go to the *nearest relative* or closest friend, but ONLY if the sin concerns them in a direct or indirect way. *Personal* offences can be left buried.

10. *"These people aren't Christians. What will they think of me?"*
Don't be worried about your testimony now. It is the PAST you are getting right BECAUSE you want to be different in the future. They will probably think you ARE a real Christian. Honesty is rare and usually respected. God will help. Go and do it.

11. *"The OTHER person was MOSTLY in the wrong. I'm only partly to blame."*
How MUCH wrong did they do? Was it, say 80 percent or 90 percent THEIR fault — or quite a lot LESS? Write down how much YOU were to blame — say 10 percent, 25 percent or 50 percent. Then you go and ask forgiveness from them for YOUR SHARE of the wrong. Don't mention their part. They have to live with their past. You have to live with YOURS. The step of humbling self must be taken by someone. You do it — they may follow.

12 *"If I just don't do it again — can't I just FORGET it?"*
No, you CAN'T — and that's part of the problem! Besides future determination will not wipe out the past. Your new behavior towards the one you wronged without the first step of confession and restitution will be misunderstood by the one you have wronged. He will think it is all some kind of "goody.goody" act to buy your way back into his favor. You cannot heal INSIDE hurts by doing good things OUT- WARDLY for the one you have wounded. Bitterness poisons every eye of judgment, so the one wronged can see only the *worst* in the one offended until he is forgiven. You go, and

Why must care be taken in the proper wording of a confession to another person?

humble yourself. Do what you know to be right.
NOTE:
IF YOU HAVE ANY MORE "EXCUSES", WRITE THEM IN HERE ▢

---

### WHAT AM I GOING TO SAY?

---

1. *You MUST NAME your BASIC sin!*
Most problems in confessing past wrong to others start right here. Until you get totally honest with yourself (and that means being willing to NAME WHY you did what you did) when you actually do go to ask forgiveness, you won't get it. Envy, for instance, might make you gossip or talk behind someone's back. Later, they find out that you have been "saying things" about them. These are the RESULT of your sin, not the sin  ITSELF. Can you see it will be little use to say "I'm sorry for 'saying things' about you"? You can't change the results of sin and neither can they be forgiven. A spiteful word, an unloving action, a hasty judgment all go irresistably out into time making their black marks on history. You cannot undo these any more than you can recall Time. Don't ask forgiveness then for "gossip," but for ENVY. Confess the sin that CAUSED your words or actions. If you don't confess this *basic* sin (God will show you exactly what it is if you ask Him) you may only deepen the split between you and the other person. Now, be brutally frank with yourself. WHAT WAS the REAL wrong that you did? Write it down, so you can see it. Are you sure *that* is what it is?

2. *When you do go to confess, make sure the WAY you ask is right!*
Wrong attitudes cause half-hearted and worse than useless confessions that may quite probably only aggravate the wrong. Such "confessions" as these show that the root of PRIDE has not been exposed and destroyed:

(a) *"I WAS wrong — but you were too!"* Pride AND bitterness lie under this weak attempt at apology. Of course, it is worse than useless. Get before God and ask Him to conquer your pride and hurt.

162

(b) *"Forgive me — IF I have wronged you."* You missed on HUMILITY. Say this kind of thing, and you show that you haven't seen your wrong in all of God's light. Be honest!

Why should a confession not contain too many words?

(c) *"I'm sorry, but it wasn't all MY fault, you know."* You are not blaming THEM (at least, directly) but you don't want to shoulder the blame either! Take ALL your guilt squarely and honestly. Be brave — face it.

(d) "I'm sorry . . ." or "I apologize . . ." They could get angry at seeing you and spit back — "I'm sorry to!" Most tries at confession only get as far as this. That last step of self-humbling is always the hardest, and coward pride will pull this as a last-ditch to escape crucifixion. Problem? The sin is not NAMED. Until it is, forgiveness can never be real or total. NAME it!

### 3. *The RIGHT WAY.*

Here are three BASIC SENTENCES for correct confession that contain all the elements of a proper, pride-humbling step for forgiveness: (a) God has convicted me of something I did against you . . . (b) I've been wrong in (Insert your BASIC SIN) . . . (being envious, stealing, etc.) . . . (c) I know I've wronged you in this (here, add any steps you want to make in paying back where necessary) . . . and I want to ask you — will you forgive me?" These three basic sentences, spoken in the right attitude are sure to get results. Don't TALK TOO MUCH — the more you say, the greater the danger that you will start to shift the blame off yourself, or say something wrong. Beware of any "but" that creeps into your mind (Proverbs 6:2-3).

"EXPLORING OUTER SPACE ISN'T AS IMPORTANT AS DIS-
COVERING INNER PEACE."

---

## THE RIGHT MOMENT

---

1. *TIME*

  (a) Do you know the *basic sin* you have to confess?
  (b) Have you *thought through* what you must say?
  (c) Is it *convenient* for the person to see you? (Don't go if they are busy or still angry.)
  (d) Can you be *alone* for a few moments when you ask?

Why does
the present
attitude of
the other
person play
an important
role when we
are asking
their
forgiveness?

In most cases, privacy is best in confession to avoid any embarrassment they may feel. If others are there when you go, ask if you can see the person alone for just a minute.

## 2. *ATTITUDE*

(a) Is *your* attitude right? If they sense insincerity, bitterness or pride, your words will mean almost nothing. Think of all the real hurt and loss your sin has caused. As you think about this deeply, asking God to reveal its results, the proper feelings will come. Your attitude in confessing will be a sincere tone of voice, asking quietly for forgiveness with a bowed head.

(b) Is *THEIR* attitude all right? Are they in a reasonably good mood to forgive? You cannot always guarantee their tempers, but don't try to confess if they are still in a state of bad feeling that will not listen to reason. If they get angry when you try to talk to them, wait quietly and humbly in a repentant attitude. When their temper is more under control, ask their forgiveness (Proverbs 22:24).

---

### DANGERS — DANGERS — DANGERS

---

1. *DON'T* SET THEM OFF AGAIN! Any words you use to take blame or attention *off yourself* will surely relight the other person's anger or bad feelings.

2. *DON'T* involve others. If you are asked to, simply point out that YOU are the one to blame; and it would mean a lot to you if they would forgive YOU.

3. *DON'T* wait too long. Make a *special time* for it. Don't try to "fit it in."

4. *DON'T* try to witness as well. NEVER witness during confession or restitution, unless you are actually and specifically questioned about salvation. Your act of restitution is witness enough for the time being. Later, you may be able to tell them more about the WHY of your confession. First things first.

164

5. *DON'T* play down your own *guilt.* If you don't fully realize your own wrong, the one you ask to forgive you may think you are insincere. This happens because:

(a) Our *conscience* becomes SEARED and weakened in sin (1 Timothy 4:2). Wrong does not, after a while, appear to *us* to be as bad as it actually is.

(b) The *OTHER* person we have hurt tends to think MORE of our wrong than it may actually be. They feel strongly offended; YOU were to blame. Remember it.

"ALWAYS LOOK TRUTH IN THE FACE, HOWEVER ATTRACTIVE HER PROFILE."

---

## SOME SPECIAL QUESTIONS

---

What are the legitimate boundaries concerning confession and restitution?

1. *HOW FAR does confession and restitution go?* As a general rule, you should confess *ONLY AS FAR as the EXTENT of your sin.* If you have sinned only before and against God, confess only to HIM. Sin against another and you must confess it alone *to that person.* If you have sinned against a GROUP, the GROUP should hear your confession. There is no point in confessing sin that is unknown to  others who are not concerned in it. Such confessions are morbid, self-centered and will *hinder* your testimony, not help it. If you do this foolishly, you will do more harm to yourself than good.

*Restitution* should only go as far as the person can humanly repay. You will NEVER be able to undo all your wrong. God only expects the repentant one to do all in his power to restore that which he has taken from others, no more and certainly no less. We must be TOTALLY COMMITTED to restore that which took place before our sin. God asks of us the WILLINGNESS to go, if need be, to a hundred people to restore a relationship. True, total repentance is to do that which is right up to the *full limit* of our ability. It concerns only that which is KNOWN and RECOGNIZED to be sin by the repentant one. Often, others

165

Thought:
True
repentance
doesn't wait
for feelings—
it just obeys.

who see your sincerity may make *exceptions* to any claims they have for restitution, but you will have to trust your case to the hands of God Who does all things well.

2. *"I don't really feel sorry for my sin. How can I repent?"* You haven't really seen it as God has. Have you asked Him to show you your sin — as He views it? Be ready for the shock of your life — if you can stand it!

You cannot make feelings, however, by WANTING them. The Holy Spirit can convict by recalling from your memory IN DETAIL all the results of your wrong. Go over your sin always IN DETAIL, never in general. General repentance is usually no repentance at all. As you think deeply about the effect of your sin, FEELINGS will come equal to your guilt.

3. *"What say I fail and do the same thing all over again?"* It will rarely happen if your repentance has been real and deep enough the first time, but if you do, then you must humble yourself and confess it AGAIN. Jesus taught and the disciples practiced this principle, building it into their lives (Matthew 6:15). Confession is God's all-covering method of dealing with sin and throwing up a blockage to future wrong.

4. *"What happens if those I confess to don't forgive me?"* Again, this would be a rare exception if the initial confession is deep and sincere. Should it occur, you must prove by your changed life and attitude that you really MEANT what you asked. Your good works will convict them of truth. You will need to ask the Lord for much patience and lots of love (Romans 12:20-21).

5. *"Those who are in authority over me won't let me ask forgiveness."* If, for instance, a parent or boss stops you from making something right, you must obey them and ask GOD to change their attitude. "The king's heart (the boss) is in the hand of the Lord — He turns it whatever way He wants to." God can change their minds, but you must NOT defy God-given authority and take matters involving them into your own hands. The only permissive defiance of authority is against a command to deny the Lord Himself, or to commit a definite act of sin. In all other cases, you must rest your case in the hands of God and wait patiently for an opportunity to make things right when the time comes (Numbers 30:2-16; Matthew 10:32-37; 1 Corinthians 10:23, 27-33).

166

**6. Why is it so important to add restitution to confession?**
Society is *disintegrated* and *destroyed* through sin; restitution

is the integrating and restoring reverse process; and nothing makes a more powerful impact on a selfish world! It is the best way of testifying to the world of the change that Christ can make; it gives the new Christian a good start in the lessons of humility and unselfish "peace-making." It is actually the Bible way of taking "revenge" on sin. If this was taught as part of every new believer's responsibility to his world, *Christian* social revolution would catch like fire (2 Corinthians 7:10-11).

What is the first step in restoring the reputation of one whom we've cut down?

*STOLEN THINGS* — Many new Christians will be reminded by the Spirit of God about things they have *stolen* that they could return or repay. Spiritual revolution for *you* may mean humbling yourself and being willing to *return* the stolen goods or money, or being willing to *confess* it, even if it means honest *debt* or even some kind of *punishment*.

*FRIENDSHIPS* — Perhaps there are *friends* of yours that need letters of confession and restitution; this is especially true in the area of sex and dating. If you have done things on dates that you have never apologized for, *write a letter* asking forgiveness and use "not being an example of a Christian" or "not setting you a decent standard" for your wording as to specific wrong. If you have a non-Christian boy or girl friend you need to *break off* with, first give them a chance to stand for Christ, then if they see what God has asked and will *not* obey, say "By rejecting Christ as the center of your life, then you have rejected me, because He is the One I love most."

*OTHERS* — If you have cut down someone's *reputation*, you must apologize for your envy or whatever sin caused the criticism; then go about *building up* their reputation again. If you have hurt your family, you must apologize, then determine to repay good for evil, by *helping in the home*. If you have been *bitter*, write *letters of gratitude* to those who have helped you, then go and apologize to the one who hurt you for your attitude.

"BEFORE DECIDING YOUR CONSCIENCE IS CLEAR — GIVE IT A GOOD SHAKING AND HAVE ANOTHER LOOK."

## OUT OF THE PRISON OF GUILT

*Forgiveness is always costly,* but it tears down the wall of a stubborn, proud will. Once you have asked forgiveness from God and others, confession has been made to all concerned, the promises of God for complete and total deliverance from the accusing finger of past sin are yours.

Wrong actions cannot be wiped from our minds. But we CAN *change* them for the memory of forgiveness! Every time Satan attempts to recall the dark part to discourage you, you will be able to recall a bright memory of confession and forgiveness to turn the shadow of accusation into happiness. The words of pardon from others who have accepted our confession (and forgiven) can put wings on our hearts and move us mightily to praise God for His forgiveness. Joy and peace will flow like a river through the soul that has been cleansed by the blood of Christ.

### 1. *The INWARD look:*

Pray for a heart-search by the Holy Spirit whenever you feel doubt or discouragement. The revealing of selfishness is  His task. He searches our inner lives, dredging up all that is not of the Lord. We must not *always* morbidly look inwards for faults; this will FEED selfishness, not kill it! But self-searching is a valuable tool *IF* you sense the warning of spiritual DEPRESSION, DOUBT of God's Presence, love or assurance or lack of *power.* Sometimes some of these things may be present in your life even when there is no known sin. At such times, ask God for further light, cling hold of the promises of God by faith and learn to smile out the grey days that are sent to teach us obedience in difficulty. However, should it be SIN that has clouded your relationship with God, a deep heart-search by the Spirit will reveal the cause, that we might bring it to the light of God's judgment.

## 2. *The BACKWARD look:*

If the Holy Spirit shows us sin, we must go back to the place where the Lord first met us. It is the *cross* again. We see the Lord Jesus once crucified — for THAT sin — bearing our penalty. A line of blood trickles down from its splintered base. The sight shocks us, grieves us, and we see the awfulness of God's judgment. This is not the *law,* representing God armed with holy wrath and determined to punish the sinner without hope or help, but LOVE demonstrated in the infinite cost and sacrifice God is willing to go to in order to save us from sin. It is the most terribly beautiful picture of the Gospel, showing God's hatred and heartbreak over man's selfishness. When we sin, we again nail Christ to the Cross. We tear open again the wounds of the Saviour and make His redemption a mockery. Well might "Heaven put on the robes of mourning and Hell hold a jubilee." All God's care and love — and DARE we *still* sin?

*Why is it necessary to not only receive God's forgiveness after hurting another, but forgive* ourselves *as well?*

## 3. *The FORWARD look:*

*Remember — God has called you for a purpose.* Don't let failure make you lose hope. Never let yourself be discouraged  from your high calling. Failure to *overcome* is but a step towards maturity. Like a runner that stumbles in a race, you cannot afford to stop and cry over a fall that costs you lost time or opportunity. CONFESSED and REPENTED of sin is FORGIVEN sin! God help you to forgive *yourself* when HE has forgiven you! Are YOU not satisfied when *God* is? Man, of all the Creator's creatures, was made to stand perfectly upright. You must press towards the mark of the prize. Learn from failure, but then get it right and FORGET it. Begin the sprint for the victory tape.

*Will you do this now?* Will you go to your gracious and loving Father as a little child and humbly ask His forgiveness?

Many millions are jailed in their own guilt this very day in your world, not knowing what to do or who to turn to. To some of these, the last road of *suicide* seems the only possible

169

escape. Minds are snapping under the terrible load of guilt from a filthy past. It is up to *you* now, to put into practice that which you know must be done. Your testimony of complete and total deliverance from the penalty and power of sin through the grace and mercy of Christ Jesus can be the means of opening up the prisons of guilt for at least some of these who are on the pathway to a lost, bitter eternity. Don't just READ this — in the Name of Christ, go and *DO* it! This is the *only way* you can be free to love with God's love that others may see and believe that Jesus is the Christ, the Son of God, and that He can truly save His people from their sins (Matthew 1:21).

FORGIVENESS IS COMPLETE ◯

MY CONSCIENCE IS CLEAR! ◯

DEBTS PAID:

(Signed) _____

"WHEN YOU ASK FOR A WASHING, DON'T OBJECT TO THE WRINGER."

"God hath chosen the foolish things of the world to confound the wise; and God hath chosen the weak things of the world to confound ... the mighty; ... that no flesh should glory in His Presence" (1 Corinthians 1:27, 29).

# JAMES THE LESS

## (WHO WAS ALWAYS THERE)

"Those members of the body which seem to be more feeble, are necessary; and those members ... which we think ... less honorable, upon these we bestow more abundant honor."

1 Corinthians 12:23

What are the two basic forms of pride? Why does God hate them?

PHASE:     4 .. *Faith In Action*
SECTION:   5 .. *"I" For Individuals In The Body Of Christ*
MATERIAL   .. *Living With Yourself And Others*

He was the son of *Alphaeus.* His name was *James,* but it was easy to get him mixed up with the more well known brother of *John* in the team of disciples. We shall call him *James the Less.* Not once in the New Testament is his work for the Lord recorded. But he WAS always there! He was there when the Master chose Twelve. He gathered with the hundred-and-twenty on the day of Pentecost. He knew when he was wanted, and he was there because he was NEEDED. *James* had a talent for "fitting in." He didn't seem to go "on stage," but he did God's will. God used him AS HE WAS. And you? Are YOU a *"James the Less?"* Did you know that you count for God?

## PRIDE ISN'T ALWAYS PUFFED UP

*What is pride?* It is thinking we can act apart from God. It is saying we don't need Him in all we do. It is acting as if no one in the Universe is more important than us. But basically, it is simply the *refusal to acknowledge that we are what we actually are in the eyes of God.*

*Pride appears in subtle ways.* There are two basic kinds; the pride of the *"big wheel"* and the pride of the *"worm."* The first is the most obvious; it is the "humility-and-how-I-achieved-it" type. It shows in the way people look, dress or speak. God *hates* a proud look (Proverbs 6:16-17). It can stick up its ugly head in business, athletic or social life. The worst kind is the most widespread, because it goes around in Christian  clothes. We can preach on the pride of *race, face,* and *place;* but the most deceitful is pride of *"grace."* You do not have to look far to spot it in most churches.

One such form trades on the *goodness* of God. It involves "reminding" Him of how much you have done for Him in the past. You suggest to your conscience that since you have accomplished some great things for God, you are entitled to a small moral holiday. This is *not funny*. God is *not* going to overlook any kind of sin, no matter how much you have done (Ezekiel 18:24; Philippians 3:5-8). Too often his children fall RIGHT AFTER they have done some *really significant* work for Him. Grace cannot be "stored" so you can "sin a little" on your reputation. The *higher* you get to God in the eyes of men, the more *carefully* you must guard your life because He will judge you *more severely* as a leader for failure than someone else with less light (James 3:1). He will not "balance out" present sin against past faithfulness. Neither His faithfulness *or* love are altered by our actions if we do wrong, He will chasten us, no matter how good our spiritual reputation. Paul counted his tremendous accomplishments as LOSS (Philippians 3:7-9). He lived for *TODAY* and *"THAT DAY"* (2 Peter 3:10-14) when Christ would return. The past is to be *forgotten* as *formed*. God is easy to please, but hard to satisfy. "No man" said Jesus, "having put his hand to the plow and LOOKING back is fit for the Kingdom of God" (Luke 9:62).

Why is it necessary to exercise care in our spiritual walk after some significant spiritual victory?

*Self-dependence* is the pride sin that felled *Lucifer*, the beautiful angel of light in charge of God's wisdom secrets, and turned him into *Satan*, the Devil (Isaiah 14:14; Ezekiel 28:12-17). As long as there is someone bigger and better than he, the man with the "big wheel" pride can never be content. Now God is always going to be infinitely greater than any man can ever be. A man who wants to be King of his own universe NEVER wants to meet God. That is why a lot of people waste a lot of time and words arguing that He does not exist. They really wish it were true because one day they know they are going to have to answer for their false estimates of their own importance.

On the other hand, overdone *self-condemnation* can be pride too. This is pride in the robe of humility. It seems very self-abasing. Very few of us are multi-talented people. Most of God's people only have a small gift here and there that God uses. But such words as "Oh, I would never consider myself to be a saint!" or "I am too, too UNWORTHY to work for God" can be symptoms of spiritual *disease*.

173

The pride of the "worm" devalues what *God* says we are worth in *His* eyes. He does *not* annihilate our personalities; He cares for us regardless of our lack of greatness because He made us and knows what *we can be* in His hands. Now when we compare ourselves to *His* greatness, we do seem very small and rather insignificant. Like Jacob we can know what it is like to *feel* like a worm in contrast to the infinite power and glory of God (Isaiah 41:14; Job 25:4-6). But remember, God *HIMSELF* became man. He made us IN HIS OWN IMAGE. Jesus Himself, Lord of glory, King of Kings, *now* has a body like ours will be (Luke 24:39; 1 Corinthians 15:35-55). And the Lord Jesus has called us not just servants, but *friends* (Luke 12:4; John 15:13-15). We are in His Royal Family (John 1:12; 2 Corinthians 6:18; Galatians 4:6; Hebrews 2:10-11) and inherit all the riches of His sonship privileges (Ephesians 2:4-7).

Too many people are unaware there *is* a "pride of the worm." But it is this *hesitance,* this lack of holy boldness, this failure to grasp the hand of God and plead His promises, that hinders His purposes. We are not the Lord, but if He saves us and equips us for a task, we *can* do it! We cannot stand around on the sidelines murmuring sanctimonious things about being unworthy, when Christ has given His army *standing orders* to fight for righteousness. God values each one of us. What *we* can do is just as important to Him in terms of our faithfulness as what any other man or woman can do. And we should stop thinking of our *limits* and start thinking about *His resources.* God has had enough of self-pity in the mask of humility. The Lord Jesus was as dependent on His Father's power in the days of His flesh as you and I are now (John 5:17-47). He simply did His work, giving glory to His Father (John 12:26, 28). *True humility FORGETS self, not debases it.* When a man is caught up with Christ, he stops being self-conscious and starts being God-conscious. And *this* is true humility: being willing to be *known* and *accepted* for what you REALLY ARE in the sight of the Lord.

*Satan uses both extremes* in his attacks on Christians. If he cannot *puff you up,* he will try to *push you down.* He will alternate thrusts of great *elation* or great *depression* following spiritual *victories* or *failures.* Watch out for these two kinds of pride, *recognize* them for what they are, and *resist* them. The safest way a Christian can think of himself is as a

FORGIVEN child of GOD. This will keep you from both of these extremes. And remember too, the *secret* of dealing with self is not *wrestling* with it, but getting so caught up with the Lord Jesus and His work that you *forget* it.

Why is the wearing of a mask equivalent to lying?

## MEN IN MASKS

Almost everyone wears a *mask* to cover the real man — our true inner souls. Behind many a smile lies defeat, discouragement, and despair. *We live in a pretend world.* Daily, people practice their smiles in the mirror and go out to live with other masked people. It often seems like no one understands us and our problems, for most everyone we meet seems to live a relaxed life. Finding no one with problems like ours, we  cover the lines of guilt and worry, fix our smile up carefully again, and go on back to pretending. From *childhood* we are taught to be unreal; to look as if we are happy when we aren't; to laugh when we feel like crying; to act as if nothing has happened when we are hurt; to carefully cover the tears and go on with the business of living again.

But it is this kind of automatic deceit that makes it hard for God to get through to us. He wants to *show us* what we are. It may take Him a long time, but once He has begun He will complete His work. And He cannot begin to help us until we learn the *truth* about our old lives; that in US there is "no good thing" (Romans 7:18). Sometimes it takes a man a lifetime to realize that he IS what God *says* he is without Him — a SINNER. We always find reasons why we are better than the Bible says we are; if we get too good at these, we can simply never be saved.

"FAITH SUFFERS LITTLE ON THE LAUNCH-PAD
TESTING-TIME COMES WHEN IT IS FIRED INTO THE UNKNOWN."

Why is it
that we as
Christians
must be
willing to
accept the
truth about
ourselves?

## YOU ARE WHAT YOU REALLY ARE

When the Lord Jesus came, *He wore no mask.* He was wholly what He seemed to be. In Him was found no guile. People came to Him pretending, but found they couldn't fool Him! He looked into their souls, showed them without saying that He understood why they wore their "mask." Gently, He helped them take it off, and the man behind it saw light as he faced the world honestly for the first time. When Paul saw himself as GOD saw him, he said "I am *chief* of sinners" (1 Timothy 1:15). In God's army we are *all* chiefs no indians!

*God wants to show you what you are.* It may take Him a long time, but He will stop at nothing short of perfection once you have let Him have your life. He can't start until you know the *truth* about yourself — "In me there lives no good thing!" Sometimes it takes us a lifetime to realize we ARE what God says us to be — "sinners!" Once realized, we can start being really dependent on God to make us all He wants us to be. We are like the ugly duckling. Until we despair of ever changing ourselves, God cannot make us into beautiful "swans."

*"Taking off the mask"* is rather frightening and a little bit painful. But when we learn to do this TOGETHER before God, we take a giant step to family unity as children of God. Immense personal problems grow out of this root — failing to believe that I AM WHAT I AM. Check out your *own* life for this:

1. *CROWD FEAR* — *"Nobody wants me; nobody likes me; nobody accepts me."*

Afraid of meeting others? Self-consciousness is *pride.* The less you think about what others think of YOU, the more power and freedom you will have in your Chrisitan life as you walk before the eyes of the Lord. If you are like this, you have not accepted yourself for the way God made you (Psalm 56:4).

**This is me: Yes [ ] No [ ]**

2. *CONCERN FOR LOOKS* — *"I hate the way I look; my hairstyle, clothes, face, etc."*

176

If His people spent even as *much* time on their *hearts* as they do their LOOKS, God could meet much of the world's need. If YOU could CHANGE the way you look, *would* you? Without surgery even — you *CAN!* Your *looks* reflect the

What are some of the outward evidences of an inner "mask"?

state of your *heart.* When it is honest and free from guilt, your face will be lit with the radiance of God. A person who is truly beautiful INSIDE, will be attractive OUT-SIDE. *Clothes,* like lives, must be simple and clean. Very gaudy or "showy" dress is a sure sign of a lonely, self-centered heart. A Christian must not be a slave to the fashions and customs of the world. Live like the world and you scream to the streets, "Give me dress, give me fashion, give me flattery and I am happy." Take care of the INSIDE and the *outward* appearance takes care of itself (2 Corinthians 3:18; 1 Timothy 2:9-10; Romans 12:1-2, Phillips translation).

**This is me: Yes [ ]  No [ ]**

### 3. CRAZE FOR SPIRITUALITY — *"Nobody really understands me and God."*

Some people seem to try *too hard* to be Christians. They appear intent on being "super-holy," wanting to do everything "spiritual" or acting as God's judge of the sins of the world.

Yet *those who know them* "smell a rat." Their zeal doesn't ring *true.* The fruit of the Spirit is strangely absent. Wrapped up in themselves, their over-spirituality is a shell covering a desperate need of being accepted.

It can often begin from *personal deficiency* by birth or accident. It need not hinder their spiritual life, but THEY think it must. Such needy ones blame their parents or God for what has happened. But NEITHER should be accused (John 9:1-3). God can allow such things for a demonstration of His power and glory in weakness. If it is a God-allowed "infirmity" it must be accepted (2 Corinthians 12:7-9).

**This is me: Yes [ ]  No [ ]**

### 4. CRITICAL SPIRIT — *"Nothing I seem to do turns out right!"*

What are the
outward
manifes-
tations
of a critical
attitude?

*Criticism* shows you have not taken your proper place in God's order, and learned to live with yourself. It can show against *others* — envy, jealousy, back-biting or in the civil war of your own life. (Frustration — never seeming to make it.) You want to be like someone else you like a lot, but can't; or you wish someone else would think you are something which you know you are *not*.

Doing this is really *blaming God* for the way He made you. You feel a failure because you hate yourself for what God intended you to be (Ephesians 5:29).

This is me: Yes [ ]    No [ ]

---

### GET OUT OF THE RUT!

---

Are *you* on the list?

Then *stop running from reality*. FACE YOURSELF. Take off your mask. You *are* what you *are*. There is no use pretending differently. You have blamed others and God long enough. Once you really accept yourself for what you are, frustration will vanish and you'll be ready to be moulded into all that God intends you to be (Psalm 73:26).

When you *don't* accept yourself, your problem is often made more complex because of sin CAUSING or CAUSED BY this lack of self-acceptance. Check out the following list in order, and sincerely right with God that which in the past you have pretended was acceptable.

### 1. CONFESS AND TOTALLY REPENT OF

(a) *Bitterness.* You have blamed God, your parents or someone else for the way you are. The seed of hell is sown in your heart, and you will reap its fruit unless you uproot bitterness. Admit it first to God and ask His forgiveness. Then put it right with any others by asking their forgiveness.

Guilty? Yes [ ]    No [ ]    Forgiven now [ ]

(b) *Secret Sin.* You have practiced *secret* sin that only you or perhaps one other knows about. Your spirituality is a *cover-up* to make people think you are working for God when you

178

know all the time you are a hypocrite. Confess that sin NOW to God! Don't run from facing it. Deal with it *honestly,* bring it to the light and claim His forgiveness.

Guilty? Yes [ ] No [ ] Forgiven now [ ]

(c) *Judging.* You bitterly passed sentence on others because you saw in them either something you wanted but didn't have, or some fault you yourself had (or still have). You thought that people would notice the latter in you, so you criticized the other person to shift all the blame onto *them.* You are guilty of the same thing you accused them of (Romans 2:1). Ask God's pardon and confess your envy to the one you backbit or slandered.

Guilty? Yes [ ] No [ ] Forgiven now [ ]

## 2. COMPLETELY AND WHOLEHEARTEDLY

(a) *Yield any denied right to God.* Whatever right(s) you have held back from the Lord must be given to Him. Write them out and "burn" them before Him. It may be your right to be thought pretty or handsome, the right to be popular, the right to be known by the world. God can never use you or own you fully until you completely consecrate all you have and are.

(b) *Exchange your reputation for — Christ's.* You must be willing to be seen by the world as they saw Jesus. Are you ready to be misunderstood, maligned, and even murdered for your unswerving obedience to the Father? If you have *no* reputation you can't *lose* it! Jesus made Himself of "no reputation and took on Himself the form of a servant" (Philippians 2:7). You should come to a place in your heart where you are willing to go WHEREVER GOD WANTS YOU — "onstage" in the spotlight of the world, or lost to all men in some stretch of uncharted green jungle. Your *Lord* was a servant. To follow Him, you must identify yourself with Him (John 15:18-20; 1 Peter 4:12-16).

Am I ready to go anywhere — anytime? Yes [ ] No [ ]

(c) *Thank God for the way He made you.* Get on your knees and tell Him you are sorry for the way you have thought of the life He gave you to demonstrate His glory. Confess, if need be, that you wanted to be the star of the show, that you wanted to be like someone else when all the time He wanted

If we seek to please only the Lord, can the opinions that others hold about us really bother us? Why or why not?

179

Can separation ever be a *good* thing? Why or why not?

you to be *YOURSELF.* And thank Him — THANK HIM FOR THE WAY YOU ARE, for that scar, that deformity, that infirmity! Until you can truly thank Him for what you actually are, He can never fully use you. Do it now (Proverbs 19:15; 2 Corinthians 12:5-10).

Once you have taken your place in God's order, you can start getting *excited* about life. It will be just as you need — a Christian life of truth, controlled by the Holy Spirit and in conscious dependence on the power of God. You will actually discover *true humility* — being nothing more or less than you *are.* You no longer need a mask to hide the real you. Your life will be seen by all the world — clean, honest and glowing with the power of God.

## WHY DIFFERENT CHURCHES?

*Why are there so many denominations?* Why can't Christians agree on a common set of ideas and all unite? This question puzzles and must be answered in our working together to reach a world. DIVISION often does come from SIN (1 Corinthians 3:3) and is marked by the fruit of strife, envy and bitterness (James 3:14-18). But earthly division without sin is, strangely enough, essential to UNITY because:

1. *We are limited in knowing each other.*

Only *God* has *all* knowledge. This is why He is qualified to be Moral Judge of the Universe. He knows that which is right in every case, and we can refer to His authority. *Agreement* comes from *common understanding.* This means that we should have at least the same *amount* of knowledge each on every point in question.

But *this* is impossible! We have not all grown up together, learning the same kind of life situations. We don't all respond the same way to different things. And this is not *necessarily*

180

wrong. We shall not agree if we do not understand alike. Time is too short to grasp the whole reality of God. Each of us must obey that small part which God reveals to us, shaping our lives to change the world. We need *eternity* to learn and share all God wants to show us as a Christian family (Isaiah 55:8-9; Ephesians 4:13; Romans 11:33; 1 Corinthians 13:9).

What basic element must two people be able to agree upon before they can work together as a team for God?

### 2. *We have different personalities.*

Some of us are naturally quiet, others active. To some God has given gifts of speaking in public — to others ministering in loneliness. Much of this depends on the way we were brought up and natural hereditary factors. God does not change these personalities when He saves us, but only *redirects* them for His glory. We cannot all *act* alike because we were not all *born* alike (1 Corinthians 3:3-11).

### 3. *God chooses men to work together* on the basis of their being able to *AGREE* together.

If they differ basically in their understanding of how to PLAN the work God sets them to do, they cannot work as a team (Matthew 18:19; Luke 10:1). Remember, the *Goal* is always the same — It is *God Himself!* We *all* agree on the goal (Luke 9:59). *Subchoices* to reach the goal are *man's* decision made by available knowledge of situations. We may NOT agree on these.

If we feel before the Lord we can serve Him best one way, we should team with those who agree with this choice. There is neither need nor sense to quarrel over the *means* to accomplish the goal (Mark 9:40). If Christians cannot agree in PLAN, it is not *sin* to part but SENSE. Separation here lets us carry out God's work for each of us in the best way possible (Acts 13:1-3; 15:36-40).

### 4. *The world has different needs.*

Christ has set different offices in the church to take care of the various spiritual needs of the world (Romans 12:3-9; 1 Corinthians 12:4-28). Often a particular form of witness is needed to reach certain kinds of people. You cannot practically reach "everyone" effectively as possible because others by background and training are *better qualified* to

181

present truth in some ways than you. *No man* is sufficient by himself. All of us need each other just as we need the Lord. A native preacher is usually better able to communicate than a stranger who does not know the language or the customs. God raises up a work and fits people into it. As long as it doesn't become formal and stagnate it can do a task no one else can do.

---

## MULTIPLICATION BY DIVISION

---

One of the most important principles of power in God's Word is *DIVIDE TO MULTIPLY.* Too often Christians unwittingly fight God by trying to "herd together" a large group. God wants Christians to SPREAD OUT THIN so that the message of the Gospel might touch many lives. Seed must be *spread,* or plants will choke each other in growing. Some reasons why we *should* divide:

### 1. *Small group unity*

The SMALLER a group, the more chance of *unity* in understanding. Jesus always concentrated on a *FEW.* They were easier to teach, correct or discipline. Evangelism must be built on trained and dedicated *leaders.* A few so fired with truth will shake the world for God. Communism proves what Jesus demonstrated — multitudes can be won if you give them *disciplined leaders* to follow. We *learn* best in small numbers. We *pray* best in "twos and threes" because we can believe for one thing together better than in a crowd.

Words used of *unity* in Psalm 133 — *"dew", "ointment"* — are all materials in a FINELY DIVIDED STATE. God divides to multiply.

### 2. *Fixed group comfortability.*

"Armchair" Christianity is not *God's* Christianity. Selfish, lazy natures demand indulging and pampering. When a work has been done for God, we tend to "rest on our laurels." Comfortable religion is NOT discipleship. If we dig in our heels. God will dig us *out* again. The disciples began to "hole up" in Jerusalem. God allowed persecution, scattering them

What are the possible dangers of large group meetings? How can these dangers be avoided?

to the four corners of the world (Acts 11:19-21). When useful believers get *too settled* in one place, God may stir up trouble or persecution to break them up and move them out where the need is (James 1:1; 1 Peter 1:1).

### 3. *Large group formality.*

The *larger* the group becomes, the greater its tendency to drift into a rut of *formalism.* Organization in the New Testament was always SIMPLE, and only used when absolutely *necessary.* The NEED determined the structure. With God the *simpler* the *better* (2 Corinthians 1:12; 11:3).

If a work gets too large, there is a greater chance to ignore the *spiritual* and push the *material.* Group METHOD becomes more important than God's MESSAGE. If it gets *too* complex, He must break it up so it again becomes workable. God has used this method all through history. Object to our *own* structure being shattered and God may leave it alone — and us too. All that will remain is a *monument to failure.*

---

## THE SCATTER PRINCIPLE

---

The Lord Jesus *commanded* — "Go ye *into all the world* and preach the Gospel" (Mark 16:15). The person is YOU. The command is *GO!* Christians today should have guidance to STAY HOME rather than wait to be *told* to move out. Jim Elliot said "Most Christians don't need a call — they need a kick in the pants!" You don't become a missionary by crossing the sea, but by *seeing the cross.* Every Christian is a

*missionary;* every sinner a *mission field.* When God gets ready to change history He uses the SCATTER PRINCIPLE. The

Can you think of any hindrance that would keep *you* from a foreign field commitment?

sower scatters seed; and the seed is men (Matthew 13:24-30; 36:43).

The Gospel has always made greatest impact by an *alien* to a nation. A Jew brought it to Rome; a Roman took it to France; a Frenchman to Scandinavia; a Scandinavian to Scotland. A Scotsman took it to Ireland; and an Irishman made mission conquest of Scotland. The Englishmen, John Wesley and Whitfield, took revival fire to America.

The Lord Jesus Christ ordained Twelve, that they might "be with Him" and that He might *send them forth* to preach (Mark 3:14). *Evangelism* is telling a world the good news of the Cross. Christ calls men today and He has *not* changed His technique. Going OUT for God makes your presentation of the Gospel more effective for reasons like these:

1. *A Spirit of Adventure.*

The challenge of new fields demand that the disciple give his utmost to the task. There are new conditions, new people

and new perils to face. Routine tends to produce rusty or dusty Christians. Fresh situations draw out the best in discipleship (Mark 3:14; Luke 9:1-6; 10:13; Acts 1:8).

2. *A Sense of Abandonment.*

Called to leave all that is naturally close and dear, the disciple has a chance to *prove* the reality of his consecration. All of us have only so much time, talents and devotion. By moving out from our settled home conditions we can give God and unreached others, that which we would have used on those who perhaps have already heard. Going out for God very practically *burns all bridges behind you.* When there is no God-given *home* responsibility, there is NO REASON for you to *stay.* To tell the Lord we have "given Him all" yet cling selfishly to the safe, comfortable life, is hypocrisy (Matthew 10:37; Mark 10:45; Luke 9:23-25; John 20:21).

3. *A Stranger is Accepted*

Men tend to ignore the authority of a *local.* Almost every

184

prophet of God has been rejected by his own nation. In Jesus' day, men refused to accept His message because they knew His lowly background (Matthew 13:53-58). "A prophet is not without honor, save in his *own country,* and among his *own kin,* and in his *own house*" (Mark 6:4). We are to be strangers in the earth (Hebrews 11:13). The unknown element attracts. When a newcomer brings a message he claims is important, he draws the curious. God can use this to attract sinners to the Truth by sending His disciples to "regions beyond" (Acts 17:18-20). 17:18-20).

Why would a young Christian probably feel more "at home" at a small group meeting?

---

## GOD'S GARDENS

---

*If the "seed" God scatters is men, how can "new plants" take root?* There must be *growth* before there is *reproduction.* Crowd work is effective in mass evangelism, but not in training and teaching to any great extent. How can new disciples be taught truth, built up in the faith, and trained for world conquest? There are grave problems in starting a nucleus of Christian life. Unless faced honestly and realistically, young Christians will die.

## 1. GROUPS MUST BE SMALL —

(a) Everyone *learns* better in a small group. When there are questions, answers are found for them rather than being missed or ignored.

(b) Larger groups have a greater danger of *formality,* set pattern and boredom. Small groups are flexible and adaptable.

(c) *Everyone* should take part. Each member of the "body of Christ" has something to contribute. Everyone, even the shyest and youngest, needs a chance to add to the team's effectiveness.

## 2. PEOPLE MUST BE AVAILABLE —

(a) *For INSTRUCTION:* Young Christians tend to have problems at unpredictable hours. There is an urgency in some

How does
Christ's
parable
remind us of
a structural
problem
within the
Church today?

that cannot be put off for another time. The team must be able to meet daily to help each other in difficulties and trials.

(b) *For FELLOWSHIP:* A fire burns best when all the wood shares the flame equally. God wants *no* man totally independent. We all need the Lord Jesus and we all need each other. A place must be found where we can meet to worship God and share our love for Him.

(c) *For REFUGE:* Never forget — true Christianity always brings *persecution.* The meeting place must also be a *place of*

*safety* from the enemies of the Gospel, who, having been faced with the living truth and rejected it, must either run from or destroy it to live unaccused. The disciples lived always in constant peril of their lives.

### 3. MONEY IS SCARCE —

Building takes up *too much* of the Lord's money. We put fortunes into bricks and wood that have no *spiritual* result directly in evangelism. The greatest single hinderance to expansion and evangelism in needy areas today is a *lack of funds* to build and buy land for Christian meeting places. The cause of Christ goes *begging* instead of *beginning.* Yet how can man meet without a building?

---

### BACK TO A BIBLE SECRET

---

How did the *early church* solve these? Has God left us in the complex mess we have today without a word of instruction? We have lost a vital secret somewhere. The question is not only *"Is* there an answer?" but "Are we willing to *use* it?" New wine must be put into new wineskins. When ideas are *set* by tradition and habit they are "old wineskins." It is better for such who are set in their patterns to KEEP what they have, rather than try to change. "New wine" would break up so much of the old traditions that it would DES-TROY instead of help (Matthew 9:15-17). For those, how-

186

ever, who have yet to face such problems and are willing to be a "new wineskin" — God has an answer to *ALL* these difficulties!

What were the two basic scriptural divisions in the early church and how does it compare with what we see today?

*The early church thrived* under this Scriptural method of meeting. Personal evangelism was practiced daily, and follow-up of new converts took place with naturalness and ease. Like all of God's answers, it is *simple in principle,* but *far-reaching in practice.* It costs nothing, yet meets *every* need. It can never become too big. The perfect place of Christian fellowship is — the HOME!

*The CHURCH IN THE HOME!* Throughout the Bible the home is central. God uses the illustration of the church as a family many times. He is the Father, we are "children." The home is the basic unit of society, the real strength of a nation. God planned Christian life to begin in the home.

Think of the beautiful *simplicity* of the home fellowship. It is a perfect place to invite even unbelievers. Informal, natural, without stigma, people could meet there simply without stuffiness. The door of a home was always open to needs in Bible times. No one had to put on special clothes to go and hear a special man in a special place. Home fellowship is *effective* because it isn't *artificial.*

*CHRISTIAN COUNSELING* is always easier in the home. No mass meeting can ever take the place of the honesty and hunger for truth that reveals itself in the home. Early disciples NEVER used the temple or public place of worship for fellowship. It was used as a public witness and as a place of prayer. Fellowship was in the *houses of Christians.* God recognizes only *two scriptural divisions for a church:*

(a) *A CITY LOCALITY* — "The church at Corinth" . . . "at Thessalonica." In God's eyes, an *earthly church unit* is defined by *city limits,* or divisions. When a man was saved in the city of Thessalonica, he was added to the "church" in Thessalonica. If a missionary from Ephesus won a man to Christ in Galatia, the young convert was added to the church in GALATIA, not to the "CHURCH of *Ephesus* IN Galatia!"

*Church names* are traditional, defining doctrinal stands, but not scriptural. Much of the complexity of mission work

187

could have been avoided if we had understood earlier this idea of "adding to the church."

The Bible definition of a "church" is a "company of believers" or "called-out ones" — a witness to God's power and glory. It is not a building or a "name", but a group of Christian *people* however they meet. The *way* they are organized or *methods* they use are unimportant. The *Name*, the *Person* around which they meet is their supreme common ground (1 Corinthians 1:2; 2 Corinthians 1:1; 1 Thessalonians 1:1; Acts 7:44-50; Ephesians 2:19-22).

(b) *A LOCAL CHRISTIAN'S HOUSE — "church in the house"* is *four times specifically mentioned.* The home is already built and needs no extra funds to keep it going. Money that was available could be used for missionary expenses and for the poor. Men could meet at any time in a moment. The church, under heavy persecution, could not use a public meeting-house as it would have been burned down or invaded, and believers taken and killed. *The home was perfect for meetings — unobtrusive and to some extent* private; disciples gathered to worship the Lord beside the streets filled with vicious enemies of the Gospel (Romans 16:5; 1 Corinthians 16:9; Colossians 4:15; Philemon 2; Matthew 10:11-13; Mark 6:10; Luke 5:29; 10:5-7; Acts 9:11; 10:6; 2:2).

*In the small group*, a home could hold checked temptation for a man to be self-important in ministering. Pride is a very real danger with those God puts into places of leadership. The home meeting does not foster pride. A man has to be real, instead of having to put on any "show" to impress a crowd. *Teaching* was clearly easier. People could get personal attention to their needs (Acts 16:15).

When the group got *too large*, it very naturally split. This was part of God's plan. Another home was opened — another group began. Dividing to multiply, the early church evangelized by leaps and bounds. In just TWO YEARS *all Asia* was reached with a Gospel witness (Acts 5:42; 20:20;

188

What are the financial advantages to meeting in a home?

19:20). If a group of believers got carnal and dead, the meeting just naturally broke up. There was no building expenses to keep going, no dead mechanical system to grind on without God; no visible sign of failure to the world. *Christendom is cluttered* with useless buildings and systems because sin has come in, God has left the movement and only pride or organizational structure keeps people from closing them down.

What kind of world conditions could force the church out of her buildings and into homes?

---

## MAKING IT WORK

---

A *"church in the home"* is *radical for many*. Tradition is easier to follow, but tougher in the long run, as mounting  problems financially and organizationally tax time and talents to the limit. This coming generation has a chance to use the "church in the home." It is the needed answer if young men and women will put it into practice. *God is behind this idea.* Many around the world, hungry for real fellowship, are *meeting in homes* for prayer and Bible study. God is getting ready His world-wide family for the greatest evangelism thrust of all time. Those not understanding God's way will seek a UNISON of carnal church-goers banded together at the cost of the great truths of faith (Revelation 18:1-5). But those with "eyes to see" shall witness an immense *UNITY* of believers, rising up to contend for the faith "once delivered to the saints."

*The Book of Acts is about to live again.* Persecution from religious authority backed up by the power of a world government is readying to lash out at an awakening church. We must be ready for this. It shall be done by *God* and not by man, but we must be willing to MOVE WITH HIM. If we continue to cling too long to the ways of the past, we may be left without oil in our lamps when the Bridegroom comes.

"SHALL WE OFFER GOD OUR LABORS IF WE HAVE LET HIS ROSE-TREES DIE?"

How would
you define
stagnancy?
What are
some of its
evidences?

## THE COMMITTAL PRINCIPAL

Why do many moves of God "peter out"? What causes stagnancy?

God asks us to be *channels* of His power. A channel TRANSFERS material from one point to another. When a channel merely absorbs that which it was designed to transmit, it loses its usefulness.

Too many church-goers are not *channels*, but *sponges*. Their entire philosophy is self-centered: Their world revolves around good to themselves, instead of good to *others*. They ask God for blessings, but fail to realize that a "blessing" cannot truly bless until it has been PASSED ON (Matthew 10:8).

*Consider a puddle and a stream.* The puddle keeps water to itself. Big puddles grow slimy and stagnate. The water gets dirtier and dirtier and breeds bugs. The thirsty air sucks away at it and it dries up, inch by inch, until only a spot of wet mud marks the place where it once was.

A stream *passes on* all it gets. It keeps nothing for itself, but gives everything away. It is this very life giving that makes it a refreshing source of life. It is connected to the source and gives life to all it contacts. WHEN THERE IS A LACK IN YOUR LIFE — LOOK FOR SOMETHING TO *GIVE AWAY.* Blocked channels are caused by selfish conservation of blessing. Unless you are a *stream* for God, you are doomed to dryness (2 Corinthians 9:6-7).

This principle holds true in all areas of a disciple's life . . . it is underlined right through the Bible. If you lack *money*, stop holding on to the material wealth entrusted to your stewardship, and *invest* in God's house and God's work. If you want God to give to *you*, give to God! (Malachi 3:10). If you lack *time*, spend *more time* with God; the moments you spend will show you what is imperative and what can be disregarded. If you lack love, look for someone who is un-

190

lovely; give *love away* to them; and it will grow greater. Especially is this true of the *ministry*. If you want God to *work with* you, work with *God;* if you want Him to *speak* to you more, speak to *Him* more; if you want to *hear* from Him, let Him *hear from you!* Whatever you sow, you will reap; and if you sow sparingly, you will reap the same way (Galatians 6:7; 2 Corinthians 9:6; Proverbs 11:24-25).

What is the difference between "giving" and "committing"? What are the implications of this for a Christian?

God has placed in *our hands* the limits of our ministries. There is no limit to the task we can do for God except that of our *faith*. We are to "attempt great things for God; expect great things from God." We can bring our ideas to Him, and He will grant whatever is for His glory. The Lord Jesus said — "According to your *faith*, be it to you" (Matthew 9:29) and "Ask what *YOU* will, and I will give it to you" (John 15:7). Where are the men who will dare great things for Christ? The *only conditions* on these promises are that we *abide in Jesus* and that *His words abide in us.* That means we are to live in His love and His Word (Matthew 7:7; 18:19; Luke 11:10; John 14:13; 15:16; 16:23-24; James 4:2; 1 John 3:22; 5:14-15). If we make *God* happy and delight ourselves in Him, He will give us the desires of OUR hearts! (Psalm 37:4; 1:2; 119:24, 77, 143,174; 40:8; 112:1; Jeremiah 9:23-24; Proverbs 11:1,20; 15:8). God will fill whatever size vessel we bring to Him, but He will not give us more until we use and give to the limit what we already have. "Give and it shall be given you."

*Paul gave Timothy* this commital principle — "The things that you heard of me among many witnesses, the same commit to faithful men who will be able to teach others also" (2 Timothy 2:2).

God never *gives* a blessing — He *commits* it. Giving stops short at the person to whom it is given. Commital *goes on* from person to person, so many more share the Word of Life. God has not merely "given" you eternal life. There is a mighty *"GO"* in the word "Gospel"! He commits to your trust the "true riches," that you might share with others who have never heard. That which *you* learn — COMMIT. God bless you as you do!


TO DO:
BEGIN A HOME BIBLE STUDY OR PRAYER GROUP EXPERIMENT.

If discipleship
is basically a
learning
process,
what
attitudes
could block
that process?

## DISCIPLES ARE LEARNERS

*There are no experts in the Body of Christ.* The only
authority is *Christ.* All of us follow Him. All of us learn from
Him. A disciple is first and fore-
most a *LEARNER.* The single thing
that the Twelve had in common
was their *willingness to learn.*
Listen to these burning words from
*George Verwer* -

"The Lord Jesus said — 'Follow
me and I will make you fishers of
men.' This is but one place where He exhorted His disciples to follow Him. *He would say the same to us, His
twentieth century disciples.* The burning desire of each of us
should be to follow Him. We should not follow men or men's
ideas but Christ and His ideas."

"To follow Jesus means that we must also be disposed to
follow the person or persons whom God has *put in charge* of
various parts of His work. God knows His people need
leaders, therefore He raises up men equipped with gifts
necessary for leading His children into victory. No local
church is stronger than its leaders and history has proved this
to be true. We need young men who have been chosen of
God to take on definite responsibilities of leadership in both
spiritual and practical realms."

"The *greatest need* is for *followers.* The first requirement
for a good leader is that he be a good follower. Some individuals might feel they should be carrying some position of
leadership. To such individuals I would say — "Then learn
how to follow." Learn to bury your own plans and ideas,
allowing someone else to make decisions which you will
wholeheartedly carry out. And soon you may find yourself
being asked to make decisions. There is no room . . . for the
person who has all the answers. We must take the position of
followers."

"We must take the position of *learners*, for a *disciple is a learner*. Wherever he goes, he has his "L" plates with him. A disciple is always willing to listen to another's point of view and to esteem it better than his own. He does not covet a position of leadership, but only desires to be a follower of Jesus."

What is the greatest problem a leader can face?

Very often, those who have desired to be *leaders* never developed into real leaders, while those whose one desire was to follow the Master have been chosen by Him for some task of responsibility and leadership. I know of no better way to help a person be a good leader than to give him a group of good followers. On the other hand I know of no better way to destroy the effectiveness of a leader than to give him a group of *unco-operative followers* who refuse to submit to his authority in accordance with the Word of God. If you are a good follower, your presence on the team will be a constructive factor, strengthening the unity and the effectiveness of the entire team."

"If you are not a good follower, then you will more likely be a destructive element, *creating* problems rather than *solving* them. You must not expect that you will always agree with your leader or see in him perfection, for remember, he is as you are, just a follower of Jesus."

I PLEDGE — TO BE A LEARNER — A FOLLOWER OF JESUS.

"Blessed are they that hear the WORD OF GOD, and KEEP it" (Luke 11:28).

# THOMAS

## (WHO WANTED TO SEE)

"Except I shall see . . . I will not believe."

John 20:25

195

What is
intuition and
how is this
evidence of
God's
existence?

PHASE:    4 .. *Faith In Action*
SECTION:   6 .. *"P" For Positive Faith in God*
MATERIAL:   .. *Truth And The Word Of God*

Like *Thomas*, the heart of every disciple is questioning. All men are hungry for reality. To discover Truth is the center of man's thousand different searches — the voiceless quest for God Himself. *Thomas* said "Unless I see I will not believe." So he was met by a Living Lord and placed his fingers into His risen, riven side. There were tears, and a choked confession of penitent loyalty.

The voice of *Thomas* is speaking still. We have not yet seen the Lord in all His glory. It may not be long until the Voice of the Bridegroom will whisper — "Rise up My love, and come away." But until we see Him face to face — "Blessed are they which have NOT seen — yet have believed."

## WHAT IS — TRUTH?

Pilate asked it; so have a million others. What IS Truth? Is there any ultimate reality in life? This section will give you some answers!

God has written into our beings some things we can "intuit" about Truth. Our generation is in deep trouble, because it has ignored these witnesses. Now these built-in testimonies are an essential part of our thinking process. Anyone who trys to use logic to deny them will have to use them as he thinks. They cannot be disproved because they are always assumed in every argument. They underlie all searches for reality; we assume these two things:

1. *Truth EXISTS.* We have to *assume* this; it cannot be proved. All our logic chains of thought are based on a few things we *are* sure of. We may be wrong about the things we *do* decide are true; we also do not usually realize that we are

assuming anything. But consider; if anybody really tried to live as if no truth of any kind existed, he could not think, argue, talk about it or prove it. He could not be sure of anything, including the things he was using to prove his point; his premises, logic or words. And that would be horrible.

The denial of truth is a self-contradicting philosophy. Why?

Think of a man climbing a cliff. Before he can take his feet or hands from the place he stands on or holds, he must first be sure of his grip in the new place. If he lets go *all* holds at once, he falls. The same thing happens to a man who plays games with words by trying to philosophize away this concept God built into our beings. If he gives up all the things he is sure of at once, he has nothing left to stand on or work from. He loses all grip on reality and falls off the cliff of life to destruction. Reality exists; it is a simple concept, but absolutely basic to life. Before we can find anything, our search must start by our assuming that perhaps it *is* there to find. The alternative to this is a form of madness; that everything is an illusion, a dream-and-shadow world.

2. *Truth CAN BE KNOWN.* This follows from the first assumption; we believe that if and when we find the reality we looked for, we can recognize it. Consider a scientist searching for an answer to a problem. He assumes there is an answer. He thinks of ways to look for it. Then he assumes he will be able to identify the solution from the evidence of his senses which can be extended through his instruments. He thinks about what he wants, looks for it and is able to say "This is it!" when he finds it!

What about the person who says "There is no such thing as reality; reality cannot be known"? Think about what he has done. He said "There is no such thing as reality" but ASSUMED that what *he* said was real; he said "It cannot be known" BUT ASSUMED that *you knew* what he was talking about. That is why both must simply be accepted as first truths, or facts. Challenging them very quickly turns any argument or debate into complete nonsense.

And where do you think GOD begins when He gives the essential conditions for knowing Him? He asks that we assume only that *He* can be known. Hebrews 11:6 says:"But without faith it is impossible to please Him; for he that

197

What is the definition of "invention"? How does that definition prohibit us from saying "truth can be invented"?

comes to God must believe that HE IS and that HE WILL REWARD them that diligently seek Him."

Certain things follow these two assumptions. We think also that Truth would be both UNIVERSAL and ULTIMATE. Firstly, we expect something that is true to be as valid under the same conditions "here" as it is anywhere. What is truly "true" now should be just as true in future. People have looked for a long time for such an ultimate reality that would serve as a basis to correlate all art, humanities and sciences. We can expect applications of truth to change as conditions do; for instance, the law of gravity we consider universally "true" although its outworking gives a man a different weight on Mars and the moon. The law itself does not change; we do not expect it to. It describes a relationship between mass and space; as either variables change, relative gravity changes, while the law remains true.

Secondly, we expect truth to be ultimate. We do not want to keep on finding hidden things behind what we *said* was true that change our picture again. We want something absolutely basic, something final. That means true truth could be *discovered*, but never *invented*. Invention is simply the use of facts already known in new ways. We assume that such facts, like science laws, do not change; and that they can be endlessly repeated with the same results. If we discovered that they *did* change, everything would lose its framework; and all our logic and study would become totally meaningless. *Life* is like that. Study can help us DEFINE truth, but at best only clears up our understanding of it. We can deny truth, but will never be able to alter it. Our generation has tried to do *just* this with God's absolutes; we already see the awful price it has paid for tampering with our built-in concepts of reality.

---

## SPOTLIGHT ON REALITY

---

*The Bible*, written revelation of the Infinite God of all Knowledge, *reveals* what is "true truth." Jesus said: "If you continue in My Word you shall know the Truth, and the Truth shall set you free" (John 8:31-32). In the pages of

God's Holy Word, we find the ultimate answer to man's search for Truth. The Bible is the only Book in the world that can sanely claim absolute authority to ultimate reality because it comes from the One True God. Other faiths on earth have described at best, a SEARCH for truth; but the Lord Jesus said "I AM the Way, the TRUTH and the Life; no man comes to the Father but by Me" (John 14:6). God's spotlight on reality is His Word. It shows us the nature and character of Truth; we see from it that Truth is —

What is the "mystery" of atomic physics and in what manner does the Bible address itself to it?

## 1. SPIRITUAL

We could expect this from a study of atomic physics. The atoms that build the energy chains we call matter are simply energy bundles held together by a yet "unknown" force. This central power defies analysis, yet without it our entire Universe would collapse. The Bible reveals what this Force is; it is the power of God (Hebrews 11:3; Colossians 1:16-17). The heart of the Universe is spiritual; it is not subject to change or decay.

*Science tells us something eerie.* If it were possible to alter the basic atomic frequencies of our material Universe, our world could CO-EXIST in the same space and time with *another* world, each equally real and "solid" with its own flowers, buildings and people, each world freely passing THROUGH the other, but NEITHER world being aware of the other's existence! Parallel this with the *Bible revelation;* man is more than matter, he is also a spiritual being with the capacity to contact a spiritual world in Heaven or in Hell, and be a citizen or denizen of either when he passes out of his earthly existence. We ARE in contact with these parallel dimensional worlds; we ARE bound for one of them, and beings from both have invaded our earth, that the Bible calls angels and demons (Genesis 19:1-16; 28:12; 2 Chronicles 32:21; Luke 2:13; Matthew 13:39; 12:24-26; 2 Thessalonians 1:7; Hebrews 13:2; Ephesians 6:12; Mark 5:1-9).

## 2. COMPREHENSIBLE.

Truth is grasped by the *mind* (Luke 24:27; Colossians

199

Why does
the vastness
of the
universe
militate
against
secular man's
attempt to
find a "unified
field of
knowledge"?

2:2-3; Hebrews 8:10; 1 Timothy 2:4; 2 Timothy 2:7; 3:14-15). No finite mind could grasp ALL of Truth, since it must cover every field of knowledge; only God knows all reality in this sense. But we have been gifted with reason and intuition to help us tap this field. We *can* grasp anything put into our minds that is in a small enough portion for us to properly compare and relate it to everything else we learn. Where our sense-thinking fails, God can use our *intuition*.

Whatever God reveals will be *truly* "true," although, it will not, of course, be *exhaustive*. We can only learn a little at a time, but what we do learn from Him will always prove ultimately valid in ANY area of life. This is what a secular man searching for a "unified field of knowledge" must first recognize; only the Infinite God of the Bible can help us put things together correctly. We have no way to "prove" any starting-point is valid when we are too limited to see that small point in the context of the whole Universe. The Christian simply *trusts* the revealed love and character of God, and accepts that what God reveals will always ultimately prove to be wholly right. Jesus said God's truth in His word had power to "free" us. *Excitement* follows discovery of truth. Given only that we could be saved from death and decay, our capacity for knowledge and corresponding excitement is limitless as eternity. Think of the marvels God has ready to show us if we obey Him! (Proverbs 22:21; Ephesians 4:11-24; 1 Corinthians 2:5-16; Colossians 1:25-28).

### 3. REVEALED BY GOD.

The Bible shows us that Ultimate Truth is GOD HIMSELF. As First Cause of all Reality, Truth must be centered in God's uncreated, eternal Being (Deuteronomy 32:4; Psalm 100:5; Jeremiah 4:2; Zechariah 8:8; 1 John 5:6). It follows that He is the *only One* Who *can* reveal it to man; unless He does, we could *never* know truth in any real sense. The Unseen God cannot be discovered by unaided human reason (Job 11:7-8). God is a God Who hides Himself (Isaiah 45:15). He reveals His Presence only to those who are honest enough to admit their sin and surrender to His love (Isaiah 59:1-4; 56:6-7; Hebrews 11:6). He can be discovered only when He *wants* to be. It would be *sin* for God to give more truth to a person who could not be trusted to use it rightly. No member of the Godhead will reveal Himself unless we meet His conditions (Luke 10:21-22; Deuteronomy 29:9; Proverbs 1:23; Isaiah 45:3; Matthew 18:3; John 12:36-40).

What is the difference between the discovery of material truth and the discovery of spiritual truth?

If a scientist considers *one basic discovery* worth a *lifetime* of hard work, think of the worth of knowing *God*, Who is the *source* of all Truth! *Moral* truth requires the *same conditions* of discovery as *material* truth, with one difference; moral truth also requires a *cost to the self*. With God, KNOWLEDGE = RESPONSIBILITY (James 4:17; Luke 12:47-48;23:34; John 9:41; 15:22,24; Matthew 11:20-24). When God gives us moral light, He expects reaction for or against it. Truth is revealed so that we may react and respond to God. *Acceptance* will mean a further and more profound insight into the ways of God; *rejection* will not only result in a darkened understanding, but also a gradual loss of *present* reality as God continues to blind the sinner on even-deeper levels (Matthew 13:12-15; Psalm 82:5; Isaiah 59:1-9; John 9:39-41; 1 John 2:9-11).

The way to abundant life is *OBEDIENCE TO TRUTH.* Do what God shows you, and you begin to build your life on eternal foundations. As one block of truth is laid and cemented in place by continued obedience, God gives you another. *Reject* any "block," and He will give you no more. You will from that point on have to make your OWN of "wood, hay and stubble" (1 Corinthians 3:9-15). These will perish when we one day stand before Him Whose eyes are as a flame of fire (Revelation 1:14). God longs to give us the precious and the everlasting. If refused, especially the Foundation Stone Himself (1 Peter 2:5-7), we shall have no house for eternity.

---

### FAITH COMES BY . . .

---

*Loyalty, trust* or *obedience* to revealed truth is Bible *faith that saves.* This is NOT HOPE. *Hope* is an expectancy, or a

201

trust without a promise. Many people think they have "faith" when it is either intellectual assent or hope. Faith is founded on *authority*. Bible BE-LIEF is based on DEFINITE PROMISES. *Saving faith* is *LOYALTY TO THE WORD OF GOD.* God's Word is both LIVING (The Lord Jesus) and WRITTEN (The Bible — John 1:1-3; 2 Timothy 2:17). Faith is *not* just the mind accepting a fact. Satan himself "believes" in this way! Faith that delivers is *obeying* Truth. God makes man a promise by His Word. The promise works IF a man *responds* to that Word. Trust is always tied in with action in Scripture. Faith DEMANDS action! Faith without works is dead — a faith without life. Trust without expression is a mere mental "yes" to Truth without a real "Yes" of WILL. Belief is based on PROMISES and linked with ACTION (Hebrews 11; James 2:14-26; Matthew 7:21-27).

*UNDERSTANDING REALITY* is called in the Bible "Light" or "Knowledge of truth" (Ephesians 5:13). The illustration of light in darkness is clear. Our "darkness" is MORAL. We hide ourselves from Christ because our deeds are evil (John 3:19). We pretend, living in self-deceit and hypocrisy. God switches on His "searchlight" (Proverbs 20:27) of moral intuition. The Holy Spirit uses Truth to flood-light our sin. Caught dirty and naked, we can either throw ourselves in sorrow onto His mercy, or flee in fright further into the darkness. Truth shows us who we are. Whether we face it or run is up to us. Truth HURTS! It does not gloss over sin. Reality is not easy to face; but unless we admit it, we disqualify ourselves for eternity. A *Christian* is the world's only true REALIST. His world is real. His life is real. His destiny is sure. Anyone else is either running from reality or still searching for it.

---

## REJECTING LIGHT

---

*All men ARE* ABLE TO UNDERSTAND Truth and God's moral law (John 1:9; Psalm 71:17). If they obey it, more light will be given. Should a "heathen" man try to live up to the light he has, God would find a way to reveal Himself to him (Romans 1:19-20; Acts 10:1-35; 16:6-10; 8:26-39). Obeying truth will bring more light on our life. If, however, we DISOBEY, the *same Truth* revealed to save us will JUDGE us (John 12:46-50). It is interesting to see what the Bible says about *HOW* God judges a man or woman. We reveal our own relative knowledge of true right and wrong when we judge *someone else*. God *records* these value judgments we make; they will be the basis of His examination of our lives when we one day stand before Him to give an account (Matthew 7:1-2; Romans 2:2-3).

Why would it be important in the proclaiming of the gospel to clearly distinguish between intellectual assent and biblical faith?

If a man rejects God's Truth, he begins to search for something to take its place. He knows life is not complete; but is not willing to accept Reality, knowing it demands a change in his own selfish action. Trying to "plug" this gap in his life, he will work out his own more convenient way of thinking (one that does not cost him his sin) making his OWN religion — *even his own GOD!* He begins to build a life on false foundations. When he exposes these to hard Life, they must crumble. He will have to search again. There will always be an emptiness, an inner void (2 Timothy 3:7).

He may become a "free-thinker," a "rationalist," a member of a great number of men who have likewise rejected Truth. He becomes a "man of philosophy and vain deceit, after the rudiments of the world and not after Christ" (Colossians 2:8). He will probably not admit that he is also a rebel against God, a moral coward and a fool as well (Romans 1:22).

"FAITH ISN'T SOMETHING YOU HOLD, BUT SOMETHING THAT HOLDS YOU"

On which
side of the
chart do you
belong?

## FACING IT — OR FRIGHTENED OF IT?

Should a man have *rejected* light for some reason, his life will show it. There are obvious signs to discern between the truly obedient and the self-deceiving rebel:

| OPEN TO GOD —<br>FACING LIGHT | HIDING FROM GOD —<br>FEARING LIGHT |
|---|---|
| Eager to learn truth. | Skeptically questions truth. |
| Active in seeking for truth | Avoids all effort to discover truth. |
| Develops a working life philosophy with firm foundations. | Constantly looks for other ideas rather than truth he KNOWS to build life on. |
| Open to new ideas — always ready to revise previous opinions in the light of more knowledge. | Mind sees only what it wants to see; resists truth even when powerfully proved beyond reasonable doubt. |
| Flexible theology, growing humility. Willing to adjust or modify. | Increasing pride; "concrete" theology — very mixed up and set hard! |
| Transparent life, clean conscience. | Secret sin; defiled, weakened conscience. |
| Growing zeal for God. | Zeal dies under falsity, unreality. |
| Life becomes more Christ-like. | Life becomes more selfish. |

## ANSWERING THAT ATHEIST

An *atheist* is someone who has *rejected known reality*. The Bible says, "The FOOL has said in his heart — there is no God" (Psalm 14:1). He has actually said, "No God for ME!" An atheist has DELIBERATELY rejected reality. He hides from Truth. He sees it, but will not act on it. He orders his life *as if* there WAS no God. No man arrives at "atheism" by calm, logical and unprejudiced reason. Honest reason leads to

204

discovering God (Hebrews 11:6). The moral law is written in every "atheist" heart. With every other man on earth, he acknowledges right, approves moral goodness and dislikes his own selfishness. An atheist "front" is always a brazen EXCUSE for a life of selfishness and rebellion.

*Four major problems* make a man or woman call themselves "an atheist." There is really *no such thing* as a logical, honest atheist; no one can prove God is NOT there without omniscience. Use the following ideas to help with "atheist" sins of —

1. *PRIDE:* When a man rejects truth to build his own philosophy, he may often say "I don't *need* a crutch like God." His pride makes him blind to his weaknesses; use a piece of paper and pencil like this to lovingly show him how *silly* unbelief sounds:

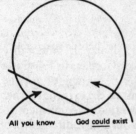

All you know    God could exist

*"ATHEIST":* "Believe in God? Ha! There *is* no God!"
*YOU:* "There IS no God?" (Repeat it to him slowly.)

*Draw a circle.* Say: "This circle represents *everything there is to know.* Do *you* know everything?" (Say with a smile.)
*"ATHEIST":* "No, of course not." (Unless he IS insane!)

*Draw a line* cutting off a small segment of the circle.
Say: "This part of the circle represents all that YOU know."

*Draw an arrow* into the rest of the circle.
Say: "Will you *admit* that God COULD EXIST in that part of the circle YOU KNOW NOTHING ABOUT?"

This will prick the balloon of his self-importance and humble his pride. He can no longer say "There is no God." He cannot call himself an "atheist" any longer. He must admit that he is an *agnostic* — not knowing whether there is a God or not. Share now your own personal experience of Christ. This will NOT prove God's existence positively. It is only useful to sweep away a silly excuse for a deceitful heart.

2. *BITTERNESS:* Some people reject God because of a deep hurt in life — a "root of bitterness." Although not

205

How could a
false view of
the nature of
God cause a
root of
bitterness to
spring up?

always realized by the would-be counsellor, their rejection of
God is based on an improper picture of His true nature and
love. They say in their hearts — "If there WAS a God — why
did He let this happen to me? There cannot be a God." Their
bitter denunciation shows a deep hurt. For this type of person —

YOU: "Tell me about the God you don't believe in." Be
sure to show real sincerity and interest in their reply. They
may reveal the real cause of their bitterness towards God.
Prompt further by showing your concern for their hurt heart.
Let him see that you really CARE. Then say:

"I don't blame you for not believing in that God. I don't
either." Help by probing for and pointing out the cause and
result of their bitterness. Then direct the person to ask God's
forgiveness for blaming the work of self or Satan on the One
Who loves him and is grieved deeply over the tragedy of sin in
the world.

3. MORAL IMPURITY: A person living in immorality
often claims atheism. Their rejection of God or His Word is a
REBELLION AGAINST AUTHORITY. Anything or anyone
who interfers with their personal pleasure chase is thus either
ignored or rejected. This type of person finds it convenient to
"deny" God rather than face Him. Your Spirit-directed presentation of truth will cut away his excuse.

YOU: "Suppose for a whole week you DID believe in God
(or the Bible). You decided to follow Him (or it). (Look him
directly in the eye). Would you have to CHANGE some of
the things you are doing?"

HIM: "Yes" or "I suppose so." (If he says "No" let him
know he is being dishonest. Look him straight in the eye
again and say — "Be honest now! Would you?")

YOU: "Then it's not really a question of whether you
BELIEVE the Bible, or God or not. It is a question of
whether you want to FOLLOW Him. That's right, isn't it?"

As with problem 2, the cause of their so-called "atheism"
will be evident from other symptoms you can usually recognize, as described in chapters treating such problems in

full. If you are alone with the person, it is often effective to point out the real cause for their so-called "rejection" of God. To see their sin written down and the reason for it often coaxes them to be honest with God and repent.

What is the difference between the honest inquirer and the skeptic?

4. *TEACHING:* Young people brought up in a God-denying environment sometimes claim atheism to conform to society or to the stand of their parents. This "atheism" is least serious, as it is an empty profession caused by taught arguments and not the result of self-studied thought growing out of some controversy with God. Our hearts are hungry for reality. When the life of a witness demonstrates the Lord Jesus and brings Truth to light on the mind, such so-called "atheism" will crumble. It takes *more faith* for such an *atheist to NOT believe!*

## DON'T SKIP THE SKEPTIC

The "skeptic" has to a *lesser* degree all the opposition of the "atheist." His unwillingness to listen is the natural war of a blinded mind against the Holy Spirit. His opposition is spiritually-centered in a rebel will. Truth presented IN PRAYER by the convicting power of the Holy Spirit is your only effective weapon to bring conviction. You must be first convinced of Truth and TOTALLY GRIPPED by it yourself. A doubt-  ful faith will make no impression. Your OWN GRASP OF REALITY is crucial to *HIS* GRASP of the Gospel. The effort a man puts forward to attain a desired end is always *directly proportional* to the clarity and desirability of that end. Does he SEE JESUS in your life?

Don't worry about the hundred-and-one arguments he may bring up. Don't even bother to *answer* them. Make the skeptic see that ALL his oppositions and excuses, ALL his contradictions and insincere questions are *false.* If he is in-sincere, throwing up "smoke-screens" to avoid the real issue between him and God, don't argue, but *show him* (and *tell*

What is the
best answer
for the skeptic?

*him)* that he IS insincere in doing so. Pour in the FACTS of his rebellion against God, his need of a Saviour and his responsibility to accept or reject the Great Substitute. Face him with inescapable Truth. Your loving concern and deadly earnest must lay before him what God expects OF him, right *then.* You need not know all the answers to his cavil to be able to witness effectively, "A man with an experience is never at the mercy of a man with an argument." Your understanding of salvation, your personal prayer-life keeping you in a vivid touch with God and your earnest manner of presenting the Gospel are of key importance.

*"Proof" of the Bible's Divine Authorship* is almost useless to the atheist and the skeptic. His rejection of God and the Scriptures are not because he has no REASON to believe, but because he does not WANT to believe. Others, however, may have been misled by some ignorant rebel into thinking the Bible is "full of mistakes" or "all nonsense." Not bothering to look for themselves, this false impression becomes an excuse for a sinful heart.

For such, there is *abundant evidence* that the Bible is all that it claims to be . . . "For the prophecy came not in old time by the will of man — but holy men of God spoke as they were *moved* by the Holy Spirit" (2 Peter 1:21; 1 Thessalonians 2:13; 2 Timothy 3:16; 1 Corinthians 14:37; 2:7-13; 11-13; Ephesians 3:1-10; 2 Peter 3:16; 1 Peter 1:10-12).

---

## IS THE BIBLE THE WORD OF GOD?

---

*Make no "mistake" about it — the Bible is here to stay!*

The Bible is a Book *from* God *about* God — the story of His love for man. Its central Figure is *Jesus Christ,* God robed in humanity; the record of His origin, birth, life, death and resurrection. Its *message* is stranger than fiction; that the God Who spun the worlds in space once visited earth to provide a way to heaven; and that man may share a new Kingdom in His very own family. *The Bible is no ordinary Book* — it is strangely *different* because it was written by men who

208

listened to the Voice of God. The words they penned were *more than human.* They live like fire to each new generation, fresh as wind and pure as rain.

What is the basic content of biblical revelation and why is it so offensive to the world?

It is not a book of *history;* although, its records have been accurately substantiated by modern archaeology. It is not a book of *poetry;* although, it has been the inspiration of countless songs and poems through the centuries. It is not an *adventure story;* although, few novels have matched the sheer drama of its pages. It is not a book of *ethics* or *morality;* although, civilization's finest and fairest laws have been forged from its principles. It is not a *text book,* but it still astonishes scientists and scholars from fields as widely-differing as genetics, geology and nuclear physics. The Bible is a unique record of man's problem and God's own *answer;* the Good News of *salvation from sin through Jesus.*

"What man has *produced,* man can *exhaust* . . . we have outgrown every other book that belongs to the past; but instead of out-growing the Bible we have not yet grown *up to*

 it. The Bible is not only up-to-date, but it is always *ahead* of date" (C.A. Benham). Centuries of study by the most able scholarship have not begun to exhaust its riches. The profoundest study has only revealed unfathomable depths of wisdom. *Mark Twain* said "It's not the things I *don't* understand in the Bible that bother me; it's the things I *do* understand!" This accurate insight exposes the *real* reason most people are afraid to study the Scriptures; they are afraid they may meet the *Author,* and they know that they are not *ready* to do so. For many people, objective evidence as to the authenticity of Scripture is almost *useless;* their "atheism" or "skepticism" is merely a convenient excuse for moral cowardice and wilful blindness. Such a rejection of the Word of God does not stem from *lack* of *evidence,* but from lack of *honesty,* integrity and moral purity.

*THOSE "CONTRADICTIONS . . ."*

. . . are largely *myth.* Few people who criticize Scripture actually know what it *says.* Even *fewer* have the necessary qualifications to pass any accurate, objective verdict on its message.

Thought:
The next
time a
skeptic tells
you that the
Bible is
"full of
contradic-
tions,"
ask him to
give you ten
examples.

*Most* have never really read it at *all,* and their assertations of
to pass any accurate, objective verdict on its message. *Most*
have never really read it at *all,* and their assertations of
"mistakes" or "contradictions" are largely *heresay.* Any man
or woman who would like to give an intelligent opinion or
conclusion on the Bible should *first* spend enough time in
personal, intensive research to see what it actually *says.*
Simple but honest investigation will *harmonize* the majority
of *apparent* discrepancies from *shallow* reading.

The Bible does not attempt to *defend* its claim to Divine
inspiration; it simply *states* it. The writers of Scripture continuously claim their message was not *human opinion,* but
*Divine revelation.* Genesis opens with the words *"And God
said . . ." nine* times in the first chapter; the statement *". . .
saith the Lord . . ."* appears *23* times in the last Old Testament book, *Malachi. "The Lord spoke . . ."* appears *560*
times in the first *five* Bible books; *Isaiah* claims at least *40*
times that his message was from God, and *Ezekiel* and
*Jeremiah* do also, *60* and *100* times respectively. At least
*3,800* times in Scripture, writers declared their message
*Divine* in origin.

The *Lord Jesus* quoted from at least *24* Old Testament
books. He referred to *Daniel* 22 times, *Isaiah* 40 times, the

Pentateuch 60 times as well as the
*Psalms,* never implying that the
events or people recorded there
were mere fables or folk-lore. In
Luke 24:24-27, Christ claimed
Himself to be the subject of prophecy all through the Old Testament. Many times He stated that all
things in Scripture *must* be fulfilled
(Matthew 13:14; Luke 21:22; John 13:18; 15:25; 17:12). He
claimed His *own* words were inspired (Mark 13:31; John
6:63; 8:42-47; 12:46-50) and that "the Scripture cannot be
broken" (John 10:35). His *own* claims to Divine origin and
the claims of the *Bible* stand or fall together. If *He* cannot be
proved a *liar* or a *lunatic,* the Bible *is* God's Word.

New Testament writers who knew Christ likewise claimed
Divine inspiration. *Paul* declared his message came *from* God
in God's *power* (1 Corinthians 2; Galatians 1:11-17), and
*Peter* says Paul wrote by "wisdom given to him" (2 Peter

3:15-16). At least *600* Old Testament quotations and references in the New Testament interface and interlock both parts in a united whole. God says *He* called scribes to write (Matthew 23:34) and *commanded* His followers to teach what He said (Matthew 28:19-20) sending the Holy Spirit to help them beyond human observation and memory. Their understanding (Luke 1:3; John 16:13-15) of past and future records came by His Spirit's guidance and control (John 14:26). The Bible is full of such data infinitely beyond its human authors' knowledge. Scripture inspiration is like a *composer's* relationship to a *conductor;* the composer writes a score from which the conductor produces music according to his *own* personality. It is like a painter who selects raw materials available to him to blend and prepare colors for his masterpiece. *God* is the Composer and Master Painter; His author friends the "conductors" and the "colors" (2 Timothy 3:16).

Honest scholarship by skeptic and saint alike will result in overwhelming evidence of its authenticity. Consider some of the following evidences of inspiration —

## 1. *Its SURVIVAL* —

*WHY* has the Bible survived century after century of *determined persecution?* No ancient book has such a vast number of surviving copies than the Bible; there are *thousands* of Old and New Testament manuscripts. Variations between these are minor and insignificant and great care must have been taken in copying them. It is said that Jewish scribes would use a new pen each time they came to the word "LORD" and at that point carefully compare *everything* they had so far written with the original copy. Men have been killed for owning copies in every century. Each era brings a renewed attempt to stamp it out, but history shows it has been impossible to destroy the Scriptures. *Voltaire* said "In one hundred years, this book will be forgotten." *Voltaire* is forgotten. *One hundred years* exactly after his boast, his house was being used as the headquarters for the *Geneva Bible Society.* Jesus said "Heaven and earth may pass away, but *My Word* will *never* pass away" (Matthew 24:35). God's Word is "quick" or LIVING (Hebrews 4:12). It has stood the test of scholarship, centuries and the trials of all enemies.

How does the personal integrity of the Lord Jesus lend credibility to the Old Testament Scriptures?

211

Why is the
structure of
the
Scriptures
one of the
best
evidences for
its validity?

## 2. *Its STRUCTURE* —

Take about *40* different writers over a period of about *1,500* years of time. Use men from many walks of life — doctors, shepherds, kings and some fishermen. Pick them from miles and generations apart. Give them little or no chance to communicate. Cut most of them off from the church organizations of their day. Ask them to write on religion — poetry — health — ethics — science — morality — philosophy. Ask them to make predictions of future events; the meaning of life; the mystery of existence; man's final purpose. *YOU* be the editor! Collect, condense and couch it in common language. Divide it into books, chapters and verses. Now — *what have you got?*

LITERATURE *HASH!* No man on *earth* could make unified *sense* out of such a mass of outdated ideas, wild speculations and hopeless contradictions. But the BIBLE was written just like that; and any honest reader who has carefully examined its message has found it to be *one amazing WHOLE* from Genesis to Revelation, united in theme, consistent in concept, logical in development and agreed in doctrine. In real-life illustration, parable and prophecy, recording historical people who lived and died, the Bible is the love-story of history — God seeking rebellious man.

## 3. *Its SCIENTIFIC ACCURACY* —

The God of the *Bible* is the God Who created the *Universe. True* science and Scripture will *always* agree — they both have the same Author! Science has had some centuries to examine the statements of fact in Scripture. Although the *opinions* of men about *Nature* and the *opinions* of men about the *Bible* have sometimes clashed, NO fault has been recorded in Scripture. The Bible does *not* tell fairy-tales. Its statements are *true,* able to stand the closest tests. It is a matter of *historical record* that *science has never developed significantly anywhere* except where there was a *Christian influence.* The scientific method and motivation for enquiry is really a *child* of the Scriptural concepts; that the Universe is the *orderly product* of a Divine Mind, and that man *can* discover the secrets of His creation, since he is made in rational, finite miniature of his Maker. Science has *mainly extended* in areas where the Bible was most freely read.

Galileo, Newton, Pascal, Copernicus and many others knew the Bible and its Author.

Before *Columbus* sailed around the world, Scripture records the *spherical nature* of earth. (Isaiah 40:21-22). When "Science" as a baby thought the world to be held up by "three elephants on the back of a tortoise," the Bible factually established its *free float in space* (Job 26:7). The *moon* is shown to be a *reflector,* unlike the radiating sun (Job 25:5). Modern precision telescopes have charted a "runaway" star in space, *Arcturus.* Drifting with all its planets in tow it travels silently through the Universe at twenty-seven and one-half miles a second. The Bible recorded its wanderings *centuries before the telescope.* The Bible record of *creation* is a master example of the harmony of geology, biology and Scripture. *Three hundred years ago,* it was discovered that

 physical *life* was resident in the *blood;* the Bible recorded it *3,500* years ago (Leviticus 17:11). *Meteorology, geology, aeronautic* principles are hinted in Scripture (Psalm 135:5,7; Job 38:4; 28:5). *Atomic energy* and *radiation effects* are "old stuff" with the God of the atom (2 Peter 3:10-12; Isaiah 13:13; Joel 2:30 — the word *"pillars"* is in Hebrew, *"palm-trees").*

Science can *tabulate* for us the *"What,"* analyze the *"How"* and probe for the *"Why;"* but it cannot tell us the "Where *from?"* nor the *reason* for which the Universe exists. It cannot say *who* you are or *why* you are here; it can tell us what we are *able* to do, but not what we *ought* to do. Here God's revelation in *Science* is superseded by His revelation in *Scripture* (Psalm 8:3-6; 19:7-14; 91:1). One shows His *power;* the other, His purpose.

## 4. *Its SPAN OF TIME IN PROPHECY* —

If there is *one* thing the Bible dares do that *no other book in the world does,* it is to *accurately predict the future.* God arranges the situations of history to bring about His glory in the lives of those who respond to His call. Working with the moral choices of men, He directs circumstances together into

How does
prophetic
revelation
in the
Scriptures
help to
validate its
claims?

a *pre-planned series of patterns* laid down before the foundation of the world. The *outline* of many of these patterns is
revealed in the Bible. There are about *3,856* verses directly or
indirectly concerned with prophecy in Scripture — about *one
verse in SIX* tells of future events! God's challenge to the
world is "Prove Me now — I am the LORD . . . I will *speak;*
and the Word that I shall speak *SHALL* come to pass"
(Jeremiah 28:9; Ezekiel 12:25; 24:14; Luke 21:22). Bud-
dhists, Confucianists and the followers of Mohammed have
their sacred writings, but in them the element of prophecy is
conspicuous by its absence. The *destruction of Tyre,* the
*invasion of Jerusalem,* the *fall of Babylon and Rome* — each
was *accurately predicted* and fulfilled in the smallest details.

*In the life of the Lord Jesus Himself* there are over *300*
fulfilled prophecies. The chances that these would all coin-
cide by *accident* in one person are laughable. By the laws of
chance it is ONE in a number followed by *181 zeroes!* To
give you some idea of the size of this immense figure, think
of a ball that is "packed solidly" with *electrons* (two and a
half million BILLION make a "line" about one inch long).
Now in your mind imagine this ball expanded to the size of
the Universe we know — some *four billion* light-years in
diameter (a light-year being the distance light travels in a year
at the speed of over *186,000* miles a SECOND). Multiply this
by 500 QUADRILLION, then remove just ONE electron,
"coloring" it red. "Stir it" in for a hundred years with the
others. Then blindfold a man and send him in to "pick it
out" *FIRST* TIME. *Impossible?* This is the SAME chance
order that Christ lived and died *according to Scripture* by
*accident.* The Bible specifically predicts events and happenings that are as modern as tomorrow's news release.

### 5. *Its SOCIAL INFLUENCE —*

A book's *true* nature is revealed by the *effect it has on
society.* The Bible gives laws for human relationships that
have never been *excelled* or *equalled.* Whenever the Scriptures have been taught and lived, they have transformed
nations. The Bible has brought consideration for others,
tenderness and compassion for the old, sick and the needy. It
has dignified womanhood and guided childhood. Whenever
the Scriptures have been freely circulated in the language of a
people, it has released astonishing power for good, elevating

society, overthrowing superstition and opening the door to progress in the sciences, arts and humanities.

Are there any problems in my life that a renewed biblical study might help?

The *Bible message* has delivered thousands from the chains of fear, sickness and sin. It is the *most powerful book* in the world for the renewal of man. *Practically* applied, it teaches and inspires industry, fairness and justice; it stands for the welfare of the individual, the family, the community and the state. It has created more *benevolent enterprises* than any other book in history. *Study for yourself* the record of history. Watch what has happened to the nation that has honored the Bible and its Author; see what has happened to *progress* in countries that have tried to suppress, reject or misinterpret its message. Wherever the *Bible is loved and applied, the nation is exalted.* Whenever men become forgetful of its Author and ignorant of its truths, fear, war, disease and hatred will stalk their streets. The Bible injunction is clear — *"Happy* is the nation whose God is the Lord."

### 6. Its SUPREME APPEAL —

The Bible is a Book with a *universal message* for all men. It is the only volume that a *child* and *scholar* may find equal

delight in. Its simple, life-related principles can work in any country, transcending barriers of culture and race to bring peace, love, joy and forgiveness. *Only the Bible* can make bad men good *inside,* transforming the rebel and the rotter into the saint and servant of humanity. It appeals to all men.

### 7. Its SUPERNATURAL SALVATION —

The *greatest* proof of the Bible is the *difference* its message makes in lives. It is indeed the written revelation of the God Who made us; its claims, origin, historical records and prophetic fulfillments point unmistakably to the secret of eternal life.

God has *promised* to answer the earnest seeker. Bible Truth must be revealed by the Holy Spirit (John 16:13; 1 Corinthians 2:11-14). Let the "doubter" but pray honestly

215

What is the
first step in a
disciplined
reading of
the Scriptures?

from his heart, "God,, I don't know if You are real or not, or if this is Your Book or not, but if it is and You can help me, show Yourself to me through its pages as I read" — and God will meet him in conviction (John 20:30-31).

"Then shall you find Me — when you shall seek and search for Me, with all your heart." All God requires is *HONESTY* towards Him. If a man is willing to face the demands of Truth, God is more than willing to lead Him into the reality he needs! (Jeremiah 3:4-5,12-13).

---

## MEANING FROM YOUR LIFE-MANUAL

---

Your Life-Manual — the Bible — is the most *important* Book in the world. It holds the key to life and to your every problem; it is the letter from your Great Friend and your Manual for Miracles; your passport to power and a text-book for Triumph! Yet "devotional drop-outs" are all too common in countless Christian lives. How do you get OUT of the Bible what God has put IN to it for you?

*Get a Bible.* Look at its *SHAPE.* It has *four EDGES* or sides, and *two FACES,* or covers. We will use this to symbolize our study of God's Book.

The *four "edges"* will be (1) *READ;* (2) *RESEARCH;* (3) *MEDITATE;* (4) *MEMORIZE.* The *two "faces,"* applying it to help your (1) *SOUL (personal);* (2) *SOCIETY (ministry).*

Let's look at these in detail:

---

## [1] READ ...

---

To be able to read and understand the Bible you should:
- (a) *DESIRE* to know God *through* His Word (Matthew 5:6).
- (b) *DETERMINE* to seek God by His Word (Psalm 27:8).

(c) *DISCIPLINE* your life to find God *in* His Word (John 8:31).

Thought: Beware of half-truths; you might get the wrong half.

An impressive *poem* to help you understand Scripture —
  "Read on, read on, read on, read on,
  Read on, read on, read on,
  Read on, read on, read on, read on,
  Read on, read on — read on!"

*READ IT!* "Soak" yourself in Scripture. Carry a Bible or New Testament wherever you go. Take "bites" in spare moments, standing in a line, waiting for a friend, travelling. You cannot understand much if you do not READ much. Make a habit of reading for a certain time or cover a determined amount each day. The Bible is your spiritual food.

How you treat your BIBLE is the *attitude* you have towards CHRIST! Your attitude to its message underlines your present relationship to the Lord. Do you love God's Word? Spend time with it? It is the only visible link between God and man given to every child of His. If you are not faithful to your Bible you are not faithful to the Lord Jesus Christ.

*HOW MUCH should you read?*

By reading it about *FIVE MINUTES* a day, you can finish the *entire Bible* in LESS than a YEAR. It takes only 70 hours and 40 minutes to read it ALOUD completely through. The Old Testament takes 52 hours 20 minutes; the New, 18 hours and 20 minutes. If you spend, say, on holiday, 8 hours a day with it, you can finish it in just NINE days!

Or perhaps you would rather read *chapter-wise.* The Bible can be completed in about *18 weeks* at just *TEN* chapters a day. The Old Testament in 14 weeks, the New in only 26 days. The Gospels (Matthew, Mark, Luke and John) together with Acts take just 12 days; the Epistles and Revelation only 15. Of course, you may not have *that* much time, but HOW MUCH TIME *DO* you have? Are five minutes or a few chapters a DAY too much to give back to God in Bible study and prayer?

"BEWARE OF HALF-TRUTHS; YOU MIGHT GET THE WRONG HALF."

What are the
dangers of
interpreting
the *clear*
passages of
Scripture by
more obscure
and isolated
texts?

## RULES FOR UNDERSTANDING THE BIBLE

Use these simple *seven rules* as master-keys to unlock the secrets of Scripture. You will have no difficulty in understanding the Bible with the Holy Spirit as your Guide and Teacher, as long as you keep in mind these basic principles in interpreting God's written Word:

1. Interpret *EACH* passage or verse in the light of *ALL OTHER* passages or verses you can find on the same subject. Failure *here* has led to trouble for hundreds of otherwise sincere, searching Christians. Get plenty of PERSPECTIVE on verses or words by comparing them (with the help of a concordance) to others on the same subject. Use *major* sections to interpret *minor* ones; *literal* sections to throw light on *symbolic*  ones; *specific* passages to explain *general* ones; and use verses that teach with *fact* and *logic* to interpret verses expressing *feelings* and *experience*.

2. God's Word means *EXACTLY* WHAT IT SAYS. Whenever possible, take the meaning of a verse exactly as it is written (literally) unless the surrounding verses (context) show clearly the language is only symbolic or a word-picture for illustration.

3. Think of *each* verse in the light of SURROUNDING verses; the PURPOSE of the passage you are reading; the MESSAGE (if any) of the entire chapter; and if necessary, the DESIGN of the whole book. In other words, *read every verse IN CONTEXT.* Never pull non-existent meaning out of a verse by pulling the verse out of its *obvious* meaning IN ITS SETTING. "A text out of context is a pretext."

**"HELL IS TRUTH SEEN TOO LATE."**

4. Texts that prove *either* of two theories on Scriptural truth you are looking at prove NEITHER. Different passages must also be understood if they can be, in a way by which they will not *contradict* each other. Truth is NEVER contradictory; such verses are most usually like two sides of the same coin. Failure to understand such texts correctly may lead to APPARENT contradictions until the Holy Spirit clears up the difficulty. Never FORCE meanings into verses if they do not fit; study something else instead until God sees fit to show you its real meaning. Things "hook and eye" together after a while; like a last piece in a jig-saw puzzle, the difficult text can fill in a gap and you suddenly "see" a new picture of Truth in all its beauty.

Why would historical context be an important factor in the interpretation of the Scriptures?

5. Use your *HEAD*. God gave us common sense. He used ordinary people to write the Bible in common language. Read it like you would any other book. Keep in mind WHO says WHAT; is it man, demon, angel, sinner, saint or God? HOW does he feel when he says it? WHAT resources, interest and abilities does he have to carry out any promise or judgment he makes? WHERE is this being said? WHY is it being said? WHEN can I expect it to happen? Some promises are for our future life in glory with Christ; most have become due since the birth of the early Church. When you find one that you think may apply, ask God to make it real and use it.

6. The *FIRST time* anything is mentioned in Scripture is usually the key to understanding its BASIC or primary meaning when it is used *anywhere ELSE* in the Bible. This is quite true for words, phrases, things, happenings, numbers, objects, ideas or people. Also keep in mind that anything repeated UNDERLINES its importance; there are no non-essentials in God's Word or needless padding. Pay special attention to those passages, words or ideas that are mentioned many times in Scripture; God considers them important to us.

7. *Promises or judgments* are conditional on man's response to God's *conditions*. Whenever God makes a promise, He reveals a PRINCIPLE of UNIVERSAL APPLICATION to all persons in like circumstances. He is no respector of persons. All His promises are "Yea and Amen in Christ Jesus" (2 Corinthians 1:20) and are founded on and expressive of, the great unchanging principles of God's government. Thus,

219

What are the
benefits of a
good
concordance?

promises are not restricted in their general application to the
person or persons to whom they were given, but may be
claimed by ALL persons in similar circumstances. What God
is at one time, He ALWAYS is. What He has promised at one
time to one person, He promises at all times to all persons
under similar circumstances.

---

## [2] RESEARCH . . .

---

It's not enough to see what the Bible SAYS — you should
have some ways to *STUDY* it. The Holy Spirit will guide you
into all Truth if you ask Him (John 16:13; James 1:5), but
you must be prepared to pay a price of DIGGING IN! Unless
you put in some time and effort to search out the great
Truths of Scripture, you will never grow up for God. You
study for school or work. You study to improve playing
skills. And to be a powerful Christian, you had better be
ready to study to *show yourself approved unto God* (2
Timothy 2:15).

Most people never get started because they don't know
HOW.

### WHERE DO I BEGIN?

Here are *five basic tools* most scholars and students of
God's Word have used. For any real research into the Bible,
you should invest some money in
any of these.

1. *A good CONCORDANCE.*
This is a sort of "Bible index." Perhaps best will be *Young's Analytical Concordance.* This lists where
words are found in the Bible and
gives you their meaning in the
original language. More complex is *Strong's Exhaustive Concordance;* this lists EVERY WORD of the Bible but is harder
to use for the beginner. *Crudens Complete Concordance* is
good, but does not give as much meaning in words. Con-

cordances are expensive, but well worth while. Sometimes Bibles have a small concordance in the back that you can use. It will help you locate verses of which you can remember only a few of the words of the verse, but not the reference. Simply look up a key word as you would in a dictionary and go through the list until you find the wanted verse. It saves much weary searching for needed verses you cannot place.

Why must commentaries be read with care?

2. *A reliable DICTIONARY.* Use a well-known, approved type, for instance, *Oxford* or *Websters* revision. With this you can look up words you don't understand and get some fresh ideas about others.

3. *Other TRANSLATIONS.* The well-loved *King James Version* sometimes uses words that have since changed their meaning. Other versions may help you understand a certain difficult passage, but WATCH those that are "interpretive," giving notes to tell you the "real meaning" of the verses! Some of these are comments by fine, godly men, but such "notes" are NOT the Word of God. You want the Holy Spirit to be your main Teacher.

4. *Other HELPS.* A Bible *ATLAS*, Bible *Encyclopedia*, Bible *DICTIONARY* and other study helps can be added to your library as need and funds allow. However, these are not needed for most things God can teach you from His Word. BEWARE of the *"commentary"!* They CAN be helpful, but often become a "crutch" supplying a ready-made answer after the tradition of men rather than the Truth of God. Some are almost useless in many areas of study. The BIBLE throws a lot of light on many commentaries! STAY SIMPLE in your study.

5. *NOTEBOOK.* You will need some way of RE-CORDING your studies. Use a well-bound, loose-leaf folder if possible, or if funds permit, a loose-leaf or wide-margin Bible. This will keep a record of your "Venture into Truth". Books of the Bible can, as they are most times in this Manual, be abbreviated. Use just enough letters to *clearly identify* the book; i.e."First Peter" can become, in short form "1 Pt." or "1 Pet." Put the *chapter* first, then any verses following it, i.e. "The First EPISTLE of John, chapter one, verses nine through to ten," becomes — "1 Jn. 1:9-10."

221

.What would
be the best
method of
Bible study
for a
beginner?

---
### VENTURE INTO TRUTH
---

Try one of these methods used by the world's greatest Bible scholars for study:

#### 1. *The WIDE look: (Analytical)*

Take a whole Bible BOOK (a short one for a start!) and *read* it *through three or four times.* You may start with a modern version that reads easily, then use the *King James, Revised* or *New American Standard* versions. Examine the PARAGRAPHS (natural divisions of thought) of the book. Write on a sheet of paper in your *own words* what you think each paragraph talks about. Don't be concerned about detail — try to  find the GENERAL IDEA of each part. Look for *repeated words, names,* or a *related series* of thoughts. Now, in a note-book, draw up a chart with divisions marked at each paragraph. Write in each section what you think the verses say. Underneath these, try to *group* the paragraphs into larger divisions or parts. This will give you an even wider view of the book's message. Both PARAGRAPHS and MAIN DIVISIONS should contain ONLY ENOUGH WORDS in their titles to *JUST* DESCRIBE THEM — no more or less. Finally, write out one sentence of a few words that SUMS UP the book's purpose and put it at the top of your study as the main THEME. Author, date and setting can be found with other helps.

**When tried, check here [ ]    Helpful? A lot/a little**

#### 2. *The DEEP look: (Inductive)*

Take a paragraph or chapter and this time pay more attention to DETAIL. Write down the BASIC THOUGHT in each sub-section of this passage. THINK! Put them down, with their chapter/verse reference on the far left-hand side of a sheet of note-book paper ruled into 3 columns vertically as shown: (page TS-29).

222

Now put *questions* beside each of these. Ask "Why? What? Who? Where? When? How?" using those which have bearing on the part under study. Now try to find *answers* to these questions and again write these down this time in the third column. Note down also *important words* in the passage. Look up their *meanings* in your concordance and dictionary. Put these under the words studied, leaving space in case you want to add something later. WORK NEATLY. Each study will then be very useful.

How can a color code be helpful in biblical studies?

| REFERENCE | QUESTIONS | ANSWERS |
|-----------|-----------|---------|
|           |           |         |
|           |           |         |

When tried, check here [  ]   Helpful? A lot/a little

### 3. *The BROAD look: (Topical)*

Using a Bible you can mark, trace *words* through a book or even the entire Old or New Testaments. Use one *color* for each word you study, changing the METHOD of marking when you run out of colors (e.g. underline, circle, bracket, star . . .). Try to trace *"believe"* through John; *"overcometh"* through Revelation; *"love"* in 1 John; *"Father"* through the Gospels. Find important words for study by looking for those nouns or adverbs used a large number of times in a *concordance* (listed under a particular book or chapter). Take a verse at a time. Ask yourself: "What does *this* word mean *here*? In what situation is it being used? How many *times* is it used here? How important is it to *God?*" Check the MEANING of the original word by looking it up in an analytical concordance. SUM UP your findings on separate pages of your notebook.

When tried, check here [  ]   Helpful? A lot/a little

You may want to MARK OFF verses having the same THEME or IDEA right through your Bible to help you in counselling or study. A basic *color code* will be helpful to show you at a glance what kind of verses a passage contains after you have studied and marked it. Here is one such coding system you might find useful if you have not worked out one of your own:

In your own words, define the "personal approach" to Bible study. Why must great care be taken in it?

| COLOR: | IDEA: | USE: |
|---|---|---|
| Red | Danger | Warnings; danger of sin or rebellion. |
| Orange | Warmth | Colorful verses; basic truths, oddities.; |
| Yellow | Bright | Prophecy, future promises of glory. |
| Green | Safety | Salvation, deliverance promises. |
| Blue | Calmness | Christian instruction for service and devotion. |
| Purple | Royalty | Precious promises of grace from the King. |

### 4. *The PERSONAL look: (Inter-weave Analysis)*

Some parallel passages of Scripture raise puzzling questions. The accounts of some sections *differ* in details from other accounts describing the *same* incident. How can we answer these problems in study? One important key to such places is the *"inter-weave"* method of analysis. We should remember that the people recording Scripture sometimes *left out* details that other inspired writers *put in*. The Holy Spirit did not "dictate" the words God wanted, but GUIDED expressions according to their own personalities. Accordingly, each author recorded a slightly different picture of the same scene from his point of view as he responded to the direction of God's Spirit.

The *Gospels* reflect their human authors' cultures and backgrounds. *Matthew,* a *Jew,* saw Christ as the promised *Messiah,* King of Israel, and his gospel is full of Old Testament prophecies fulfilled; *Mark,* a young *Roman,* saw Him as the *Servant of God,* and his story picks out Christ's actions and deeds. *Luke,* a *Greek* doctor, saw Jesus as the *Son of Man;* he picks out much of the warm, human side of the Lord. *John* saw Him as the *Divine Son of God,* Who was the Lamb taking away the sins of the world, in all His majesty and power.

Accordingly, the Gospel accounts are like an intricate *jigsaw puzzle.* To get a whole picture of what Jesus did or said, we must take each separate picture and "inter-weave" it into the fabric of the whole account. To harmonize difficult passages, simply *rearrange·* all events recorded in the *proper sequence of time* and *insert new details* from different accounts at the proper place that will give a smooth, consistent description of what actually happened. Leave out *all but one* of the repeated sections of description, or you will have superfluous material in your final study account. Remember, the writers of the New Testament did not hesitate to *paraphrase* Old Testament scriptures when they used them in their messages, nor draw back from using *general* prophecies as ground for *specific* fulfillment in the New. It is important only that the essential *content* and *sense* of the passages remain the same, not the wording of it.

What are the dangers of prayerless Bible study?

### 6. *The HIGH look: (Knowledge Without WISDOM)*

*WATCH OUT* for *this* one! (Psalm 18:27). All study must be balanced by a corresponding amount of PRIVATE PRAYER. Truth *without prayer* will only harden a person in conviction when you witness, and truth STUDIED without prayer will not break up the fountains of your heart to taste of the Waters of the Word of God. There is always a danger of making Bible study ITSELF the *end* of your work, instead of the *glory of God.* Learn the *Living* Word with the *Written,* and you will become a man of God *and* a man of the Book.

Adam's sin was not in learning, but failing to learn in the light of God's counsel. Never implicitly accept everything, even if it comes from the pulpit. You have a responsibility to test every doctrine and teaching against the Word of God (1 Thessalonians 5:21; Acts 17:11; Isaiah 8:20).

Here are *three tests* for all new knowledge you are given:

1. Is it *taught, expressed* or at least *implied* RIGHT THROUGH Scripture?
2. Is it *practical, exciting* and *logically consistent* within God's premises?

225

What are the
evidences of
"truth in
action"?

**3. Does it help me *love* the Lord Jesus more, and more deeply *hate* sin?**

Truth can easily be recognized by the clean Christian. It is simple; it lifts the heart closer to God; it is consistent with all other facts of Bible and natural revelation. When obeyed, it results in growth and personal holiness, an increasing sense of your own ignorance, and a deeper dependence on Christ. Truth makes a man more excited about his life, his world and his Lord; it never contradicts other plain statements of Scripture, nor denies reason, sound thinking, or God's unchangeable justice and love.

*Theology* is simply the study of God and His Word. If a man's theology makes him cold, proud or bitterly inflexible, it is non-Christian (James 3:13-18). True theology helps from the spirit of the Lord Jesus, Who humbled Himself and "Became obedient . . . . even to the death of the cross (Philippians 2:8). If your doctrine has not made you more like the Lord Jesus, you need to do one of two things immediately; *obey* it or *change* it. The Sadducees of Jesus' day didn't get their theology straight; the Pharisees had all the right rules, but didn't obey or even know the Ruler. We still have Sadducees and Pharisees today. Christians are neither; they live out the rules because they know and love the Ruler. Keep close to the middle path of Bible balance.

---

### [3] MEDITATE . . .

---

*George Mueller*, the great saint of faith, was a man who knew God and His Word. What was the secret of *his* Bible understanding? In his own words . . .

"It has pleased the Lord to teach me a truth I have not lost the benefit of for more than fourteen years. I saw clearly . . . the first great business of the day was to have my soul *happy in the Lord*. I saw the most IMPORTANT thing I had to do was to pray after dressing in the morning and give myself to the reading of the Word of God and to MEDITATE on it. Thus my heart might be comforted, encouraged, warmed, reproved and instructed."

226

Search every verse for a blessing. Get *food* for your soul. Say to each text or passage — "I will *not* let thee go except thou bless me!" (Genesis 32:26). You may then be led BY THE WORD to confess sin, pray for others or ask for some need, then go on and read another. Keep the idea of "reading as feeding" in mind as you read the Bible. This way you will stop wandering thoughts, straying attention and "other things" that might turn you from seeking the Lord's Presence. Christ is IN every page of Scripture — in picture, parable and personality. Look for your Beloved's face in the Book He has written for you.

Describe the process of scriptural meditation.

Meditation is a *"chewing the cud"* with Scripture so that God's Word becomes a vital part of us. It involves *rethinking*  all our daily experiences in the expressions of Scripture, using God's own language to talk to Him. Meditation is *spiritually digesting* the Bread of Life, feeding and building the "inner man" of the spirit.

Meditation is a cleaning stream for the mind. Many will not read the Bible because they say they "don't remember any of it." Take a dirty glass. Fill it up with water and pour it out again. There may be little left in it, but the glass is *different.* It is *cleaner!* In the same way, thinking God's thoughts after Him purifies the thought life. The living sacred Scriptures are guidelines for clean, clear thinking.

One of the meanings of "meditate" is to *"mutter".* To help grasp the meaning and fullness of a verse, READ IT ALOUD. Repeat it to yourself a number of times. This constant repetition is like dialing a familiar telephone number — remembered through habit. Many blessings are given through the discipline of meditation (Joshua 1:7; Psalm 1:2-3; 1 Timothy 4:15).

"SAY IT SIMPLY — SAY IT OFTEN, MAKE IT BURN!"

What are
some of the
practical
benefits of
memorizing
God's Word?

## [4] MEMORIZE .

Memorizing Scripture should be a part of every Christian life. It is the process of "hiding God's Word in the heart" that we might not sin against Him. Memorising Scripture is like loading a weapon of the commando for Christ. It enables you to:

### 1. *Route doubt and defeat the devil.*

When the Prince of Life met the Prince of Darkness in the Wilderness temptation, He didn't bother to argue or reason. The Lord Jesus met every subtle accusation with a flaming arrow of Scripture. "It is written . . . it IS WRITTEN . . . IT IS WRITTEN!" It's no good learning how to use your "gun" when the Enemy is on you! Memorizing Scripture is the Sword of the Spirit (Ephesians 6:17; Psalm 119:11; James 4:7).

### 2. *Put cutting conviction into your witness.*

"Let the high praises of God be in their mouths and a two-edged sword in their hands!" Great men of God have been men who were saturated with Scripture. God blesses HIS *WORD* — the *more* we learn and use, the *deeper* and more effective our Christianity (1 Peter 3:15; 1:23; John 6:63; Psalm 19:7; Hebrews 4:12).

### 3. *Equip for Christian service.*

No man can do the work of God without a knowledge of the Word of God. It is the foundation, the superstructure and the building-block of witness and service for Jesus Christ. You do not need to be clever, sophisticated, witty, talented or popular — but you do need to memorize the Word of God (2 Timothy 2:15; 3:15,16; Psalm 119:42).

*HOW do you memorize?* Your memory banks have three related functions:

228

1. *LEARN* — "Feed-in" of information. One of the best ways to do this is with a card system. Prepare a set of *Scripture flash-cards* like this —

What are the three related functions of memory?

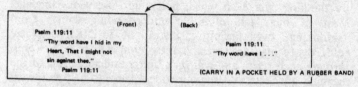

*Use as many senses as possible* by *writing out* the material and *reading it aloud* at the same time. This way your eyes, hand and lips all play a part. Carry your cards with you, and "ruffle through" them at spare moments like travel from work or school in a bus, plane or train; when you sit down to eat or relax. Go through them just before sleep at night and first thing in the morning (Deuteronomy 6:7). You can also put them up one at a time on your mirror or car dashboard, where your eyes will fall on it every time you come to use it.

2. *RETAIN* — by the "over-learn" process. Simply carry on memorizing AFTER you feel you have properly learned it. This "extra" makes results "print" far better in your mind. If you are doubtful of a Scripture, don't hesitate to flip the card over and reread the correct wording. Don't guess. Review "learned" Scriptures at least a couple of times again before you begin on new ones.

3. *RECALL* — Getting back what you put in. It will be a great help if you can make some sort of vivid picture on the card or in your mind that ties in with the thing you are trying to learn. Use your *imagination.* The more vivid, the better, you will easily remember the picture, then by association, the material. The card system lends itself to easy recall; repeat the Bible references twice as shown.

TO DO: WRITE OUT PSALM 119, VERSES 9 AND 11
       MEDIATE AND MEMORIZE THEM BOTH.

---

**TO YOUR SOUL**

---

*The PERSONAL look at Scripture — (Inspirational, devotional)*

Take a verse that interests you — one that you think you understand. Read it through at least SIX times to get the feel of it. Now, WRITE OUT the verse IN YOUR OWN WORDS. Try not to use many of the original terms of your verse, but by thinking over each word, put it into everyday language. Most of our lack of Bible understanding comes from "skimming" over Scripture, instead of THINKING as we read. By trying to rewrite a verse, you will have to *think through* each term, and will get a better understanding of the meaning of the verse. Use your concordance to help you with the basic meanings of the word, and use other translations if you are "stuck" for a synonym. *Ask yourself* — "Does what I have written, SAY what the verse MEANS?" Have I used words unsaved people can understand? How could I use this verse to help someone?"

*When you study the Bible, DON'T:*

1. Tempt God by asking an impossible or unreasonable kind or degree of evidence.
2. Defend *error* for the sake of argument.
3. Call in question *first truths* or attempt to prove them.
4. Get impatient at the ignorance or stupidity of others.
5. Be *ambitious* to excel them in study or argument.
6. Adopt an argumentive or cavilling state of mind.
7. Fail to *PRACTICE* as fast as you learn.
8. Let your *head* get ahead of your *heart.*
9. Grieve the Holy Spirit.
                    (C.G. Finney: *Hints For Fruitful Bible Study*).

---

## TO YOUR SOCIETY

---

(Tips for those who must speak in mass meetings or public platforms the Word of God).

When you are preparing a message:

1. *READ YOURSELF FULL:* Stay constantly in the great truths of the Word of God and you will not need to hunt for texts; texts will hunt YOU! "Make your Bible the Book of books; study it much upon your knees, waiting for divine

light." Whenever you select or prepare passages or texts for preaching, expect the direct leading and teaching of the Holy Spirit, and never fail to present the subject He lays on your heart for the people. Keep a collection of illustrations that have PERSONALLY meant much to you; stories and phrases that illustrate the truth of God. Talk often with all types of sinners; learn FROM THEM their opinions, needs and errors, that you may meet such needs with truth.

How does writing down sermon material relate to our witnessing to the lost?

2. *WRITE YOURSELF CLEAR:* After God has given you an idea or text and your mind is beginning to fill with illustrations, take a sheet of paper and *write out* what is on your heart. Make a very loose outline on paper, leaving *plenty of space in between;* fill in the gaps with other Scriptures and illustrations as they come to mind. Use the clear, strong truths of Scripture; stay away from opinion and theory. State what you  have to say and say no more than you can show beyond doubt to be the Word of the Lord. Leave *no* point until it is clear; understandable and gripping. Use a SANCTIFIED IMAGINATION to put truth into vivid pictures. "The task of the preacher, gentlemen, is to *see clearly* and to tell what you say in a *plain way*" (Peter Marshall). Anticipate objections and answer them. When you have written all you have, go digging again for Scripture and illustration, adding to your outline. Finally, ARRANGE it in logical, progressive and proper order. This should be in the form of an OUTLINE message, and NOT memorized like an actor's lines. You should be free to adapt your message at any time to the need, even while speaking. All preaching should be conversational, in common language and indwelt by the Holy Spirit.

Good preaching is marked by *REPETITION* — not just of words, but of *ideas.* Draw a "fence" of words around each idea by *repeating the basic thought* while using new facets of it. If you have something important to say, spend more *time* drawing your "fence" because most people will not get an idea the first or even second or third time they hear it. Study carefully the messages of the men God used and you will see the same basic repetition. When you use the "inter-weave" method of study in the Gospels, you will see that *Jesus* did this too. Make your *sentences very short*, and be sure to use words that everyone can understand, even the children. Their *interest* will be your best criterion of effective communication. And talk TO your hearers, not ABOUT them! The more direct and personal you are, the more powerful your words.

"ATHEIST — MAN WITHOUT INVISIBLE MEANS OF SUPPORT."

"That they all may be ONE; as Thou, Father, art in Me and I in Thee, that they also may be ONE IN US; that the world may believe that Thou hast sent Me" (John 17:21).

# JOHN

## (WHOM JESUS LOVED)

"There was leaning on Jesus' breast one of His disciples, whom Jesus loved."

John 13:23

What is the
supreme task
of God?
What is the
means
whereby He
accomplishes
this?

PHASE        4 .. *Faith In Action*
SECTION:     7 .. *"L" For Love, Producing Unity And*
                  *Motivation*
MATERIAL:        *Forgiveness, Fusion And Obeying The*
                 *Law Of Love*

If Jesus *did* have any favorites, this boy was. The Book calls him "The disciple whom Jesus loved." He had been close to the heart of the Lord even before he leant on His breast at the Passover supper. Love begets love. *John's* simple secret is the mark of true discipleship — deep, devoted love to the Lord Jesus Christ.

## WHAT IS LOVE LIKE?

*The love of God is the greatest force in the Universe.* God's love loosed on the world shook it to its foundations. The early disciples were not tied together in organization, sworn together in doctrine or frozen together in tradition. They were *melted* together in love.

God's supreme purpose is to *unite His children with Himself.* God's love can move a world. There is nothing more powerful in Heaven's armory — God *is* Love. A Christian without love is an impossible contradiction. "He that loves not, does not know God — for God IS love" (1 John 4:8). Love draws the lost. Love is our *greatest single weapon* for world conquest.

In the soul-searching "Lord's prayer" of John 17, Jesus relates *love* to *UNITY*. Purposely He allowed His disciples to hear Him pray this. It was His "last request" before the cross. God wants us to be *one.* The *means* of doing this is not by plans or programs. It will show VISIBLY ON EARTH what is ALREADY TRUE IN HEAVEN — that the "Church" is a single BODY with Christ as the Head. If the Church acted like a love-linked family, the world would see reality.

LOVE is neither a state of mind or a kind of feeling. The love God asks of men is based on His moral law. It is a direction for the will. It is the rule of unselfishly willing the highest good of God and His Universe. Love is the law of right choice, of unselfish action, a standard all men understand and assume everywhere.

The Ten Commandments can be divided into two basic groups. How did Jesus summarize them?

The *TEN COMMANDMENTS* is this moral law *worded*. The *first four* act *vertically:* man— God; the *last six horizontally:* man — man. They show what general course to take. Every other Bible command does the same. God has not given us a detailed "rule-book," but an *outlined sketch* of the right path. The Ten Commandments given to Moses are the *letter expression* of the *spirit* of the moral law. These ten general rules of action can never be broken or disobeyed without penalty. They are a BARE MINIMUM of right to build out or upon (fulfilled) — never to be "done away with" (Matthew 5:16-20).

*The Lord Jesus* expressed the SAME moral law in two simpler, more searching rules:

1. Love the Lord your God with all your:
   *HEART* — ("Moral" heart — supreme choice of the WILL)
   *SOUL* — (Used here for the senses — FEELINGS)
   *HEAD* — (Thoughts — the REASON)
   *STRENGTH* — (Physical actions — the BODY)

God simply asks us to *put Him first* in all we choose, feel think or do. We are to will His highest good in every situation involving choice between two things. We must do that which is right *as far as we see our duty:* God asks us to do that only which we *know* we should, and use our lives wisely for His glory.

2. *"Love your neighbor as yourself."*

This does not necessarily mean we will always feel *good* about them or we will have to ignore or excuse their sin. To love your "self" is simply wanting to be cared for and happy. *Self-love* is not sin. Selfishness is wanting "just to take care of me" no matter how others feel or are concerned. A selfish man disregards the rights and happiness of others, unless these can somehow help HIM. Self-love is *needed;* but selfishness is *sin*.

Loving your neighbor as yourself, then, means to will doing good for others just as you would take care of your own happiness and well-being. This "neighbor" may be very nasty to you; he may do things against or to you that not only make you hurt or angry, but are positively wrong. To love such a neighbour *doesn't* mean that you must pretend that he wasn't really as bad as he seemed, or that the things done didn't really happen. It means to WILL HIM GOOD *despite* your own natural feelings — to conquer bitterness and revenge and be as concerned that he be cared for as you are for your self. To do this is to love as God loves (Romans 13:7-10; Matthew 5:44-48).

The *two commandments* are *further condensed* in the church letters to a *single word — "love."* LOVE is the *fulfilling of the law* (Romans 13:10). It is the basis of right and goodness — the inbuilt law of decency and honor — to will the highest good for God and His moral creatures as the ultimate goal of life.

*This love is a free, intelligent choice of the will.* It chooses right in *itself*, whether to do this brings personal gain or not.

It enjoys everyone's good things; if practical, shows as much care and concern for a stranger as a friend; it chooses the highest good for all in general in any situation. It produces clean lives and good actions and flames deliberately in opposition to sin. Love is just and firm, not weak or sentimental. It holds up under pressure but longs to pardon or show mercy whenever justly possible. Love is *honest* and does not pretend; willing to help even the dirtiest dregs of humanity with a "hem in its garment that touches the very dust." Love *self*-sacrifices, even the dearest rights to do good, to others in need of God (Romans 5:5-9; 8:28; John 8:42; 13:1; 14:3; 15:17; 1 John 4:7).

*To follow God's law of love is to be perfect in His eyes.* It is to do all that we know we *can* and *must* do; to live up to all the truth God gives us; love is not a *feeling* or a *thought* but a *choice* made with intelligence and consideration. It is to "do to others as we would have them do to us." It asks us to use only *what we have when* it is needed, demanding no more than what we are able to give. God's commands are not grievous — "And now Israel, what doth the Lord thy God require of thee, but to fear the Lord your God, to walk in all His ways, and to love Him, and to serve the Lord thy God with all thy heart and with all thy soul. To keep the commandments of the Lord and His statutes which I commanded thee this day *for thy good?*" (Deuteronomy 10:12-13).

TO DO: READ 1 CORINTHIANS 13 EVERY NIGHT FOR A WEEK.

What is the biblical definition of forgiveness?

---

### WHY DISUNITY?

---

*Disunity* caused by sin is the *headache of heaven.*

*Fellowship* is the *presence of the Holy Spirit between believers.* Sin cuts off Spirit-communion. God cannot accomplish His purposes in double-minded men. The uniting love of God is today's desperately needed dynamite for world impact. How do we go about having it?

*LACK OF FORGIVENESS* is the *greatest cause* of disunity. The Lord Jesus linked love with forgiveness. *His* pardon from the cross calls from us our first responding love. Forgiveness is God's method of dealing with the guilt of sin — to give all just claims against the one who injured without any further thought of compensation or "paying back." *Without* forgiveness there can be no joy. God wants us to pardon others as He does us. If we will not, we cannot expect *His* pardon.

*UNFORGIVING SPIRITS* destroy unity. Christians get disappointed in each other and nurse a poisonous grudge in their hearts. When this happens barriers go up, usually *felt* rather than spoken. We cannot pray and work together as a family like we used to. It doesn't seem the same any more. The whole business seems less like an adventure than a silly game. Bitterness is DEADLY.

Jesus said, "If you bring a gift to me and remember that you have something against your brother — *first* go and fix it up with him. When you've got that right — then come and offer your gift." We have a lot of gifts at altars, unacceptable.

237

What is the
destiny of a
bitter person?

*Forgiveness* is essential for *fusion*. If we don't — bitterness will kill us.

*WHY SO HARD?* Why does God condemn bitterness so much?

*All of us change by the way we think.* God plans to make us like Jesus. By thinking of Him we become like Him, and the more we do this the greater the change from "glory to glory."

When we are disappointed by someone, our thoughts go off the Lord. We begin to think over and over again of their offending actions and attitudes.  Our minds feed on bitterness. The poison seeps into the soul — and our very thoughts begin to destroy us. "As a man thinketh in his heart so is he." Think about an enemy and you will change — you will become *just like him.* You *become like* the one you despise. You *recreate* his faults until there are not *one,* but *two* hateful men — your enemy and *yourself!* (James 5:9).

---

## WHAT HAPPENS TO THE BITTER MAN

If you lose sight of *God's* standard and think about those of your *enemy*, your own standards begin to change. You *compare* yourself with them, leading to *pride.* You keep changing (oh, so slowly) until you wake up to realize you are acting the *same way!* But you *still* hate. Your mind excuses itself, and you say "at least I don't do the same *things* as he does." Yet you have the *same attitude.* Bitterness is one of the characteristics of Satan. It infects multitudes who profess to belong to the Lord.

TO DO: READ 1 CORINTHIANS 13 EVERY NIGHT FOR A WEEK.

# THE CURSE AND THE CAUSE OF BITTERNESS

Bitterness is a *"wounded spirit,"* a keen disappointment in someone. It is a natural response to wrong done by another. It can be real or imaginary, one big thing or a whole lot of little things. Very often it starts in the *family*, leading from there into all kinds of rebellion and hardness. You can recognize bitterness by the following signs. A number of these will tell you that a "root of bitterness" is the cause of the problem:

TO DO: TAKE A GOOD, LONG LOOK AT YOUR FACE IN A MIRROR.

## SIGNS OF BITTERNESS

1. *Hard features* — Jaw line is tight, and the eyes are deep set.
2. *Unable to show concern* — inconsiderate and selfish attitude.
3. *Ungrateful air* — expects favors but shows no appreciation.
4. *Flattery* — over-praises some, viciously judges others.
5. *Withdraws from transparency* — cautious in meeting others.
6. *Possessive in friendship* — pays too much time and attention to a narrow circle of friends. Has an unnatural fear of losing a close friend.
7. *Surface happiness only* -- highly sensitive, "touchy" nature.

## CAUSE OF BITTERNESS

God promises *special grace* if we lose confidence in others. We get bitter if we refuse to respond to it, and forgive them as Christ commanded. Many people we meet in life can either knowingly *or* unknowingly offend us. If we forgive them as Jesus has asked us, we begin a great force for good in their lives as well as ours. If we do not, we trigger off a process of self-destruction. When someone hurts us, God will give us power to forgive. This turns our hurt into a chance to HELP them. Self says "get revenge" instead. At the moment of being hurt, we can choose either way.

239

Using the chart on this page, check your own attitude.

## PLANTED HELL IN PRACTICE

This chart shows what happens when someone is bitter and will not forgive.

| YOU CAN SEE | GOD CAN SEE | THE BIBLE SAYS |
| --- | --- | --- |
| Unshared thoughts by word or attitude. An unseen barrier goes up. | A "root of bitterness." Deeply wronged, hurt; real or imagined. | "A wounded spirit who can bear?" (Proverbs 18:14). |
| Ungratefulness; no sign of appreciation. | Broken regard; love is alienated, cut off. | "Men will be . . . ungrateful . . ." Sign of last days (2 Timothy 3:2). |
| Stubborn, sulky attitude, appearance. | Rejects authority of persons "over" him. | "Rebellion is as the sin of witchcraft" (1 Samuel 15:23). |
| Openly rebels; now refuses to obey authority. | Takes own authority; becomes own "boss." | "I will exalt my throne . . ." Satan's sin (Isaiah 14:12-14). |
| Gets into bad company. Wrong friends associate. | Needs other "rebels" for encouragement. | "Taking pride in what should cause shame" (Philippians 3:19). |
| Defends wrong. Asks: "What's wrong with . . .?" | Carries out secret desires for wrong. | Bring results of a selfish life. Fruit of sin. (Galatians 5:19-21). |
| Starts to condemn others to try to shift guilt. | Deep guilt, conviction from broken moral law. | ". . . Wherein you judge another; you condemn yourself" (Romans 2:1). |
| Alternate mood extremes — ecstasy, depression. | Sees no way out. Begins to think about suicide. | "My soul is weary of life . . ." Wants to end it all (Job 10:1). |

(Bill Gothard — Youth Conflicts)

# ROOTING OUT THE SEED OF DESTRUCTION

Can you think of any experience in your life within the last two years that could have been an occasion for bitterness?

If YOU recognize bitterness in your own life, you must confess it to the Lord. When it has been thoroughly repented of and dealt with by the blood, you MUST then forgive the one that hurt you. "Forbearing one another, if any man have a quarrel against any — even as Christ forgave you, so also do you" (Colossians 3:12).

*Steps back to forgiveness:*

*STEP ONE:* Make a LIST of all those who have wronged you. Write down their names and relationship to you.

*STEP TWO:* Under each name, list the FAULTS of the one causing your grudge . . . Take your parents, for instance, if you have a family bitterness against them:

*THEY* —
(a) Promised me something, but didn't keep their promise.
(b) Punished me for things I didn't do.
(c) Are too strict in punishing me for things I DID do.
(d) Gave more attention or love to other members of the family.
(e) Set me a poor example.
(f) Told ME not to do things I saw THEM doing.
(g) Expected too much of me.
(h) Tried to make me into something I just wasn't.
(i) Weren't there when I needed them.
(j) Took out their frustration and bad tempers on me.

*STEP THREE:* List all YOUR faults! People usually suffer from a bad memory here. In case you do check your life against this list:

List (ha!) completed [ ]

1. *Poor attitude.* If your parents were asked to rate your attitude around home, would THEY say it was above or below average?
2. *Laziness.* How NEAT have you been? How often have you wasted time watching T.V., listening to the radio or

241

records, or just lazing around when you should have been doing something else?

3. *Ungratefulness.* When did you last THANK your parents for ordinary things they do for you — giving you meals, working to keep the home, etc.?

4. *Untruthfulness.* Have you done anything behind their backs that would make them distrust you or lose confidence in you? Have you at times told them only part of the truth so they would go along with what you wanted to do? Have you decided something for yourself when they should have been asked or done it for you?

5. *Stubbornness.* How do you react when they ask you to do something? Do you (a) Do it immediately; (b) Tell them you'll do it later; (c)Ask them "Why can't somebody else do it?" (d)Ask them "Why does it need to be done?" (e) Tell them you can't do it; (f) Tell them you won't do it?

6. *Bitterness.* Have you nursed this seed of Hell in your heart for things you think they have done to hurt you?

Be VERY HONEST with yourself here. Forget your *feelings* for the moment and concentrate on the FACTS. Have you done something to hurt THEM? Write it all down on your list. This is the biggest part of your problem.

List (gulp!) completed [   ]

*STEP FOUR:* Ask God's forgiveness for the things on YOUR own list. Don't try to excuse anything. DEEPLY REPENT of them. These things are poisoning your life. Make no light job of this. Get your list as forgiven and clean as you would want it to present to God on the Day of Judgment. This is going to be hard, but it must be done (Matthew 6:12,14-15).

Have asked forgiveness from God [   ]

*STEP FIVE:* PURPOSE in your heart to ask *THEIR* forgiveness. This is the most difficult step of all, but without it you will never fully clear your life of bitterness. This must be done humbly, sincerely and honestly. Unselfishness forgives — and forgets. Holiness has a very short memory when others do it wrong. Be TOUGH on self. Don't *think about* your act of forgiveness of them after carrying it out, or you will feed self ("How noble, how generous of me to do this great and condescending thing!"). As long as you deliberately bring their offense back to mind, you are FOOLING YOURSELF in thinking you have really forgiven. If the thought of their wrong afterwards comes back to mind in a strong temptation to nurse the old grievance again, compare your OWN wrong past with God's standard, and think about how much GOD was willing to forget and forgive (Matthew 18:21-35). The rule is to *WILL* the highest good, not try to FEEL.

Why does Satan seek to destroy family unity?

**Have asked their forgiveness [  ]**

---

## UNITY IN THE HOME

Foundational to all Christian unity is the HOME. The church assembly is no stronger than the home-life of its pastors and elders. A Christian who has not learned the lessons of home harmony will have a difficult time doing anything worthwhile for God outside of it. The family is God's testing-ground for us to teach us love and discipline relationships. Begin here if you want to learn love!

*Nobody really knows what goes on in your home as well as God.* His eye is in every place, seeing the evil and the good. Every wall is transparent to Him. Whatever is hidden carefully from the prying eye of the world is not hidden from *His* sight. He knows all about your family. Most of all, He CARES how you feel. He really understands what makes you hurt and sad, afraid and alone (Deuteronomy 5:29; Psalm 11:4; Jeremiah 17:19-21; Proverbs 15:3; 1 Peter 5:5-7).

If Satan wrecks your *home* he can ruin your *life.* From a thousand secret ambushes, he springs traps on your family.

He worries at the love-ties that bind a happy home together. He works on your *parents* when they are tired, ill or bound by habits, hoping to slash apart their love and split your family in two. He tries to turn brother and sister against each other over stupid little differences that grow into explosions of hate and bitterness. And too often he has done it!

*How do you think GOD feels when He sees YOUR family?* *He* first planned the home-life for happiness. *He* began the first marriage, blessed the first home. From the beginnning

243

Describe
God's
"chain of
command"
in the family
and how
each family
member fits
into it.

He chose to *direct us* through the structure of a home that loved and obeyed Him. *His basic home laws:*

1. *PARENTS should love Him with their LIVES as well as their lips.* They should be REAL people all through, who can teach their children to work and play and love and laugh. God wants them to be a source of strength and guidance. Home should be a place of peace, love and security. God longs for your parents to be like this even more than you do. Are you HELPING Him to change their lives by doing your part? "Honor your father and your mother" He commanded. Are you doing that? (Deuteronomy 5:16; Matthew 15:4-6; 19:16-19; Ephesians 6:2).

2. *The LORD JESUS is to be First "Boss" in your family.* DAD and MOTHER are to be next, *IN THAT ORDER;* the rest of the family subject to their authority. DAD is to LEAD the home under God and *provide for all its needs,* both physical, mental and spiritual; MOTHER is to be the INSPIRER. She should stand behind Dad in love and *encourage* him on in his work and leadership; be there when she is needed for comfort or advice (Ephesians 5:22-23; Colossians 3:18-19; 1 Peter 3:1-2; Titus 2:4-5). If this is not true of your family, do you want it to be? If so, are you willing to OBEY God?

3. *YOU are to love, honor and OBEY your parents as you would obey the Lord.* He wants to work THROUGH your parents to use them to teach you how to live rightly. God has set up this "chain of command" so He, by using them, can direct your life. "My son, *hear* the instruction of your father and *forsake not* the law of your mother" His Word commands (Proverbs 1:8-9). The question is NOT "Are one or both of my parents *unsaved?*" "Are they doing things that make *me* ashamed of them or hurt?" The question is — "Have *I* done what they asked me to do?" (1 Samuel 15:22; Proverbs 6:20-23; 10:17; 13:1; 15:5,31-32; Ephesians 6:1). *Loving them* means swallowing your hurt or pride and doing RIGHT even when it is hardest to. *Honoring them* means respecting their God-given authority on your life, even when you think you know better. *Obeying them* means DOING WHAT THEY TELL YOU even when you would most like to do something else! God has a way of dealing with problems. But as long as you keep fighting and struggling and rebelling

against your parents, you are fighting HIM too! He hates trouble a lot more than *you* do. He WILL do something about it in your home. *But get on His side.* Nobody ever fought God and won in the end. That fight is for ultimate losers only.

What is the only exception to parental obedience?

4. *Trouble in the family is to be taken IMMEDIATELY to God.* If someone is in the wrong, HE will deal with that one. If your parents ask you to do anything that you do not like, you must take it to *God* and ask *Him* to change their hearts (Proverbs 21:1). You have NO RIGHT to disobey ANY of your parents' instructions EXCEPT when they command you SPECIFICALLY to break the law of God. All else MUST be done, and you must trust the Lord to straighten out problems. If they *are* wrong, God will help you (Psalm 27:10). But if you refuse to obey them, God has no choice but to take sides against *you* as well.

---

## WHEN A BROTHER SINS

---

Perhaps the most *disobeyed* command in the entire Bible is in Leviticus 19:17 — "You shall not hate your brother in your heart; you shall in any wise *rebuke* your neighbour, and not allow sin on him." Christians have forgotten how to reprove and rebuke sin. They have sat quietly by and let the world rush on to Hell without a word. There is such a fear of man in the church today that the average Christian seems to have to *apologize* for being holy! Yet REBUKE is a DUTY of every Christian; to fail to reprove sin is to *disobey God.*

*Most people have a funny idea of love.* They imagine that it is a warm *feeling,* and fellowship and compassion is a pleasant state of sensation between two people. In this dream world, the shaft of rebuke is the very *opposite* of Christian fellowship. Nothing could be farther from the truth. To truly experience love and fellowship we must *give* ourselves and share ourselves, and this means telling the *truth* about ourselves. We have a general idea that love and unity would be very wonderful, but we are not willing to pay the *cost* of it. The cost is chiefly the pain of being willing to give *and* receive the corrective of reproof. Without this, there will be no spiritually true unity; without unity in truth and love we will never experience a spiritual awakening on any national scale. Reproof is the *most neglected* cost of revival.

*The Life of the Lord Jesus was the life of love in action.* Yet His actions were *starred* with rebukes aimed in all directions. Jesus was not a comfortable person to have around if you cherished secret sin. He rebuked sin no matter how high or low a man was in society. He was a man with *no* reputation with a single eye to His *Father's* glory. He not only rebuked runaway *Nature* (Matthew 8:26), *demonic* forces (Matthew 17:18), and *sickness* (Luke 4:39), but *sin* in every guise. He rebuked religious materialism (John 2:13-25) in church and even a proudly patronizing religious leader when sitting as a guest in the man's dining room! (John 7:36-50). He cut into religious hypocrisy in terms so scathing that the men who were exposed took counsel together to kill Him (Matthew 23:13-33). He rebuked the *disciples* (Mark 8:33; 10:14; Luke 22:24-30). If Jesus was the living embodiment of love, why don't Christians rebuke sin today?

Reproof is *ESSENTIAL.* God teaches us to *respond to His authority* through reproof. The discipline of the *family,* essential to divine order in the church and the nation is based on this (Proverbs 6:20-23; 10:17; 15:5,31-32; 29:15; 12:1; 13:8; 1:23). The most critical test of a Christian is his growth in the ability to *give* and *receive* reproof. If we *give* but do not *take* reproof, we are bossy, critical and obnoxious. If we *take* it, but do not *give* it, we are doormats. The man who does not want to do *either* is a *phony;* he fears *man* more than he loves *God.* Christians become one in only *one* way: when they deal truthfully with each other, speaking the truth in love, receiving it from others if it hurts or not, and giving it even if it *costs* us to do it.

*Love to God* plainly requires that we reprove. *Sin* is God's greatest enemy. Holiness is hating the things God hates and loving the things God loves. Sin cost God His Son, and Christ His life. If we really love God, we will hate sin enough to rebuke it. Rebuke is a *measure* of love. The more deeply we love God, the more effectively and directly we will rebuke sin. If we love our *community,* we will reprove sin. "Righteousness exalts a nation, but sin is a reproach to any people." Bad examples tend to corrupt others; they must be

246

firmly rebuked. If we love our *neighbor* (anybody in our influence) we will reprove him if he sins. It is cruel NOT to rebuke him! The man who sins is injuring his reputation, his respect, his integrity, his business, family or body. If you see a man's house on fire and he is sitting there insanely laughing in the flames, is it "love" to pass him by without a warning? If a man has done something mad and continues in it, endangering

himself and others, will you "care" so much that you just *smile* with him and go on as if nothing is happening? Sin is *moral* madness. If a man is in his burning house he will lose his life; if he is living and dies in sin, he will lose his life and *soul* also! Is it "kind" to let a friend go on in sin until the full justice of God must be unleashed on him? Are your feelings so tender you cannot *warn* him of his terrible peril and spiritual danger?

God *EXPRESSLY* REQUIRES it. There is not a *stronger* command in the whole Bible. It is not only stressed in the Old Testament, but underlined and underscored right through the entire Scriptures (1 Timothy 5:20; 2 Timothy 3:17; Titus 1:13; 2:15; Luke 17:3). To *refuse* to rebuke is rebellion against the Word of God and to refuse to receive reproof is rebellion against the control and direction of God. You *MUST* rebuke! The man that sees the law of God flagrantly broken on all sides and does nothing to oppose or prevent it is a traitor to the Christ who died to purchase men from sin. Can you see these Scriptures and pay no attention? You may as well pretend to have a clear conscience and get drunk every day.

It will always be *hard* to reprove, especially with a close friend. But we must, like Nathan, have the courage to put principles above personalities (2 Samuel 12:1-14). The secret of reproof is to do it *ON GOD'S* BEHALF, not as some personal complaint or injury against *yourself*. If you will but rebuke FOR HIS SAKE, you will find it far simpler and more effective. The idea is — "That hurts *God*," not, "This hurts ME." Your own *personal* displeasure is not the issue, and if you bring it in, you will appear meddlesome and bossy.

247

What are the possible "emotional risks" to the one who rebukes? How can this fear be overcome?

*When faced with a choice* to *rebuke* for Christ's sake or be *silent,* you must see that the question is not, "What shall this man think of me if I rebuke him?"  but — "What will *God* think of me if I don't?" The issue is: "Shall I be *faithful* to God and risk being embarrassed by this man and others, or *deny the Lord,* allow this man his sin and keep my reputation at the cost of spiritual cowardice? Will I spit in Christ's face so this rebel can slap me on the back? Do I care more about my great *Father's* reputation than my *own?*" It will not matter, once you have settled this question, that you may be *reproached* by the one you rebuke; you have done what you could for the one you serve; and *He Himself* will share your reproach, because it is really against *Him. You* are not at fault for making the sinner feel uncomfortable; HE is at fault for breaking God's laws and God's heart; and he must be *reminded* of it. The reproach you suffer is for Christ; HE will share and suffer it with you (1 Thessalonians 5:24; 2 Corinthians 12:10; Hebrews 11:26; 13:13; Luke 6:22). We are to be *happy* if men reproach us for Jesus' sake (1 Peter 4:14; Matthew 5:10-12).

## HOW DO YOU DO IT?

*If you are in the right place with God,* you will always know when God is asking you to reprove for His sake. The Holy Spirit will give a clear urge; and if you do not obey, you will feel a sense of *loss.* For *fellow-Christians,* the proper Bible method is to first go to the sinning party IN LOVE, wanting to help him back to a good place with the Lord. If he listens, you have gained a brother (James 5:19-20). If he does not, after concerned prayer, take *one or two witnesses* with you, who are also grieved over the hurt this brings God. If he *still* refuses to repent, the matter must be brought up with him before the *whole church* (Matthew 19:15-17). In ALL of this, there must be NO censoriousness or destructive criticality. If he will not repent even before the church, he should henceforth be treated as a "heathen." What kind of attitude does *God* have over a "lost" man? Not ruffled-tempered resignation; not an "I-give-up" attitude, but GRIEVED, deep CONCERN over the sin causing separation, with an obvious willingness to forgive and forget at the least sign of contrition or repentance by the rebel. Always reprove *in the Holy Spirit* so the offender will feel as if the reproof came from *God Himself*. God's feelings are HEARTBREAK over the sinner, and eagerness to forgive. Are there *tears* behind YOUR reproofs? Can you *weep* over the one in the wrong? (Jeremiah 9:1; Luke 6:21; Philippians 3:18; Acts 20:31)..

Describe the scriptural method of reproof.

You should use more or less *SEVERITY* in your reproof, according to:

(a) Your *RELATION* to the one sinning. Reproof will not always be in the same strength or form; you must take into consideration the relative *age* of the person you rebuke; older men or women must be treated with respect (1 Timothy 5:1-2, 19); the *authority* and *familiarity* that exists in your relationship must also be taken into account.

(b) The *KNOWLEDGE* an offender has, if they are relatively *ignorant* of spiritual light on the area of their wrong, reproof should be more in the form of *instruction* or *advice*; if sinning against much light, much *greater* severity must be used to be effective (Matthew 23:13-33).

(c) The *FREQUENCY* of the offense. Use more *sharpness* in rebuke for those who are doing wrong out of habit, *accustomed* to sin, and knowing much spiritual light *without* obeying it.

---

## DON'T REPROVE THESE

---

Scripture records only *four cases* when a word of reproof would only *aggravate* a situation. In such cases, a *grieved silence* is often more eloquent than words. We are *not* to reprove the *scoffer* (Proverbs 9:8; 15:12) as it will only make him more hateful and bitter; the *self-deceived heretic* (Titus

249

Why do
Christians
shy away
from the
ministry of
biblical
reproof?

3:10; Ephesians 5:11) — when a man rejects truth and begins to TEACH the same, he is to be warned *twice*, then left alone; the *rebel* who is known to be a hater of God or authority (Ezekiel 3:26-27; Matthew 7:6) as rebuke may only provoke violence; and finally, the *extremely self-righteous* (Matthew 15:14; 27:12) who are so full of pride, conceit and so satisfied with their own wisdom and goodness that all reproof will only bring argument. *In all other cases,* we are to firmly follow the direction of the Spirit of God to rebuke sin.

*Avoiding rebuke* is really evidence of a *people-pleasing heart.* Only *God* can deal with the "fear of man" that brings a snare! (Proverbs 29:25). This fear of man is basically a *love of reputation;* being more concerned about your *own* rights than *God's.* It means that you are too afraid of what people might say or think about you to stand up for *right* when it is not popular. It will *NEVER* be easy to rebuke; every disciple will be faced with the temptation to "cop out," but *if we love Jesus,* we will love Him enough to *speak out* for Him. There may come a time when far more than our *reputations* are at stake, but our very *lives;* what will we do on *that* day? We must be willing to DIE to our own pride, our own self-seeking, our own reputation, and *live crucified* for Christ. He has commanded us to *forsake* our love of reputation for the love of *righteousness;* if we become slaves of what people think of us, we will never change our world (Isaiah 51:7; 51:12; Jeremiah 1:6-8, 17; Romans 8:15; Hebrews 13:6; 1 John 4:18).

## DARKNESS OR LIGHT?

One basic problem that occurs in rebuke is that of knowing the difference between true Christian rebuke and reproof and the critical, fault-finding spirit that is *sin.* When you are not sure which attitude YOU have in a critical situation, take the following test. It lists for you the differences between *JUDGMENT* and *DISCERNMENT. Two different words* are used in the *Greek* language; we are commanded to avoid the first and do the second, although the different words are translated by the *same* English word *"judge"* —

Studying the chart, what do you see as the basic underlying attitude on each side respectively?

| WRONG | RIGHT |
|---|---|
| Giving verdict; conclude, condemn or to damn. | Search, examine, discern; make a difference between, investigate. |
| Believe what anybody says about wrong-doer; guess at what seems to be the "reason" for the problem (John 7:24; Proverbs 18:13). | Keep questioning until you know all the important facts about the situation (1 Corinthians 2:15). |
| Be shocked, show alarm at what you hear; make snap judgment (1 Corinthians 4:5). | Look for the real CAUSE of the trouble — do some digging for FACTS (Proverbs 25:2). |
| Get proud about your own "spirituality"; boast about your own "victories" to the sinner, so he feels hopeless (Romans 2:1). | Look for a similar problem YOU beat in your life; use their problem to reflect your past wrong (1 Corinthians 4:7). |
| Don't bother to go and talk to the one you hear has sinned; talk ABOUT him to all your other "faultless" friends (John 12:47-50). | Pray and look for a good time to be able to talk with the sinner over his problem so you can help him back to Christ. |
| Rush right up and tell him — "Now look, you are wrong here!" (James 4:11). | First get their confidence and then share a way you beat the problem (1 Corinthians 6:4). |
| Tell God about everybody else's sin and failure compared with your "little bit." | Ask God to bless the one in the wrong, to help him back (Matthew 5:44). |
| Never beat the same problem you judge in your OWN life (Matthew 7:3-5). | Go over your own steps to victory in past and help him up again (1 Corinthians 11:31). |

TEST: HOW LONG DOES IT TAKE YOU TO "CHANGE GEARS INSIDE" WHEN YOU SUDDENLY HAVE TO PRAY?

251

## RECEIVING REPROOF

A *characteristic of a saint* is his ability to receive reproof. God teaches to stay on the "trail" through reproofs designed for our instruction. Such reproof can come from many different sources. Learn to recognize God's hand in these corrections which could come from:

1. *Scripture* — The Word of God will often give you a dose of solid rebuke when you are backsliding in heart (2 Timothy 3:16).

2. *Spirit checks* — The Holy Spirit puts "brakes" on inside if you go off the trail (Proverbs 1:23).

3. *Conscience* — The inner voice of the moral law is an ever-present reproof against sin (Hebrews 13:18).

4. *Circumstance* — The very *results* of sin are a powerful reproof to the sinner (Jeremiah 2:19).

5. *Chastisement* — When God uses the rod! He allows others to punish us for correction for our own good (2 Samuel 7:14; Hebrews 12:4-11).

6. *Friends* — Never think less of a friend if he points out a fault you should correct. Such a man is a rare companion (Proverbs 27:5-6; 6:3).

7. *Foes* — Sometimes more honest in rebuke than friends. *Always* listen.

8. *People in Authority* — Those God has set over us in civil affairs; police, judges, teachers, kings, and presidents (1 Timothy 2:2; Titus 3:1).

9. *Pastors and church leaders* — Those who have been entrusted the care of the flock of God (Hebrews 13:17; Ephesians 4:1-16).

10. *Parents* — We learn to obey God by learning to obey our parents. We must learn to take reproof from them (Proverbs 13:24; 23:12; 6:20-23).

Concerning these seven basic needs, which do you feel is the strongest and the weakest in you home?

---

## FAMILY RULES FOR PARENTS

---

Because God can teach us so much through the *family, parents* have a great responsibility to train their children correctly. Today the family is under great stress from many different quarters. The strength and moral fiber of the home is the true foundation of the strength of the nation. Many parents have not followed God's laws for home unity, and great trouble has resulted. They will answer at the judgment seat of Christ for what they have done with the life of the child God lent to them. Young people have *seven basic needs* which can be met in the home: (1) *Security* — from seeing a mother and dad in love with each other and them; (2) *A sense of belonging* — having the kind of family life that is fun to be in; (3) *Desire to accomplish* — being praised for what they do well, and encouraged in their interests; (4) *Freedom from fear;* (5) *Freedom from guilt* — by learning to live clean lives before God and get things right that go wrong; (6) *LOVE* — to be accepted for what they are and encouraged to the best; (7) *Knowledge of truth,* to know what is real in a world filled with hypocritical living and speaking. They must thus —

1. *Be taught truth by word AND example.* The child needs to be able to trust his parents implicitly. Nothing false or unreal should be told children that later discovery will fix doubt of the parent's trustworthiness in their minds. Such fables as "santa," "fairies," "the stork brought you here," etc. may be pleasant little fantasies but can harm (Psalm 51:6; 78:4-8; Proverbs 12:19-22; Isaiah 26:2; Ephesians 4:15; 3 John 3:4; 1 Timothy 4:7).

2. *NOT be pampered.* Children should feel loved and wanted, but *never* be worshipped or indulged. Let them understand their rightful place in the family with its privileges AND responsibilities. If parents foolishly worship their child and treat baby as if it is the most important person in

the world (no matter how much it may SEEM to be at the time!) they will deserve later displays of selfishness and rebellion.

When a child misbehaves or sins, it should be corrected in love. For *first-time* wrongs, reproof should take the form of stern advice. *Second-time* wrongs then should always be punished after explanation and NEVER in anger. The parent's punishment should not be to take out their feelings on the child, but to correct him for wrong. All teaching is best done by EXAMPLE. Whenever possible TAKE TIME to undo any  selfish habits, showing him right ways of repentance — confession, restitution, asking forgiveness, etc. Begin EARLY. Where such training and reproofs are resisted, stern physical punishment should be given; hard enough to hurt but not damage. It is never "love" to deny a child a whipping for doing wrong in the face of a family law made under God (Proverbs 13:14; 22:6; 31:27-29; 1 Thessalonians 2:7).

3. *Respond to AUTHORITY.* The child will learn to obey God first of all by learning to obey his parents. God's plan for the growing child is to teach him to respond to those who are best in a position to direct and guide his life. God's whole Kingdom is built on a *chain of authority* headed by Himself. The Centurion recognized this fact when he came to Jesus for the healing of his servant (Matthew 8:5-10). God is Ruler over kings and all those in civil authority (Daniel 4:17,25; Psalm 75:7; Romans 13:1-7; 1 Peter 2:13-14). *Parents* are all responsible through these ultimately to God, and must not disobey civil or national law. In each home, *Christ* is to be head of the family. The *husband* is to be head of the *wife;* the children are to *obey their parents* (Ephesians 5:22-24,33; 1 Peter 3:1-2; Titus 2:4-5).

 NO child has any right to disobey the law of his parents as long as he is under their care whether they are SAVED OR NOT! The ONLY exception is an order from a parent that *specifically* contradicts the law of God, or one to clearly commit sin. Untold volumes could

have been written on the bad attitudes and heartbreak caused by the failure to obey family rules in the delusion that salvation for the child has totally excluded them from any need to obey their unsaved parents' instructions. Disobedience to those God has allowed to be your "bosses" is rebellion ultimately against God HIMSELF! No matter how badly your parents may carry out their home and family duties, you are *before the Lord* bound to obey. Leave all other restrictions in the hands of the Lord (Proverbs 21:1; 6:20-23; 10:17; 13:8; 15:5,31-32; 1 Samuel 15:22; Ephesians 6:1; Colossians 3:20).

*When is a child old enough to understand and respond to the claims of Christ?*

4. *Taught to live God-centered lives.* The moment a child is old enough to understand sin, he is old enough to be converted to Christ. Children can be taught to be unselfish, to trust in the spiritual rather than material riches of life and encouraged early to surrender their lives to the Lord Jesus. A respect for God and His commandments, honor to parents and elders and a way of life that is decent, cheerful, honest and hardworking can all. be fixed at an early age into the child's heart, if parents will only TAKE TIME to LOVE and teach their children the right path. "Train up a child in the way that he should go, and when he is old, he will not depart from it" (Deuteronomy 32:46-47; 11:18-19; Proverbs 22:6; Matthew 21:16; Ephesians 5:1).

---

## SPECIAL RULES FOR P.K. HOMES

---

Much bitterness begins in homes where parents are involved in the ministry. All too often "preachers' kids" are treated wrongly because of the special stresses the work of the Gospel can place on parents. Parents should observe the following special rules:

1. Live a life of *true discipleship* in front of your kids. *Practice* what you *preach.* Walk before God as truly honest people. *Never* lie, by life or mouth (2 Thessalonians 1:10-12; James 3:13).

2. *Pray WITH FAITH for your kids.* Do not complain to God about them. Do your best before Him, leave them in God's hands, and ask that He shall be glorified in their lives.

Why are
there special
areas of
responsi-
bility
for children
in a pastor's
family?

3. Where *you* are wrong, APOLOGIZE. Proud, arrogant and unbroken teenagers copy their proud, unbroken parents. Have *your* kids seen *you* break before them, and humble yourselves before them when you have been in the wrong? YOU do it FIRST (James 4:10).

4. NEVER tell them to behave *BECAUSE* they are "P.K.'s." If you are concerned about your reputation, it is high time you became like Jesus and *lost* it (Philippians 2:5-7). No kid can stand living under the cloud of having to be "special." Base your family laws on what is RIGHT, not on reputation. Never use *that* comparison in your home (Colossians 3:21-25).

5. Spend *TIME* with your kids! Your home is your greatest *mission-field*, your most important *congregation.* If you have not learned God's lessons of love and discipline in your own home with your own children, you are disqualified for ministry (1 Timothy 3:4-5,12).

6. Balance your time *on the field* with your time *at home.* Do not forsake the needs of your family for the needs of your world. God has placed you closer to your home; your first responsibility of ministry is *there.* Who will reach them if you do not? (1 Timothy 5:8).

7. If Dad is *traveling* for long periods, Mother should be careful to use the time alone with the children wisely, in uplifting his ministry before the children and in prayer to God with them. Bitterness to a traveling preacher is usually picked up from the *one at home.* If GOD has called a person away for a time, GOD will give enough time with their family. The one that stays home must be loyal to the one travelling, and guard their attitudes.

8. *Don't force* your children into personal sacrifices you think you could make. *Provide* for them, so they will not be in want BECAUSE of the ministry. This is *non-Christian.* It has turned thousands of young people away from God's work (2 Corinthians 12:14; Luke 15:12).

"IF THE GOSPEL WERE HARD AND NARROW, GOD WOULD NOT
RECOMMEND IT FOR FOOTWEAR."

## WHEN CRITICIZED

Thought: When you step on a snake it will strike back — a worm never does.

What happens when you are criticized? What attitude should we have? A.W. Tozer shares some helpful hints on receiving admonition:

1. *Don't fight back against criticism* and defend your church or organization. FALSE criticism can't hurt you; honest criticism will HELP. Listen to it and do something about it. Friends don't need your "defence," foes won't listen to it! (Proverbs 26:4).

2. When reproved, *don't pay attention* to WHO the criticism came from. Don't let decisions be influenced by the possible motives of the person who gave you reproof; friend OR enemy. "An enemy is often of greater value to you than a friend because he is not influenced by sympathy" (1 Peter 2:23).

3. *Don't make the same mistake* the children of Israel made; that of being *unable to take admonition*. This diagram sums the danger:

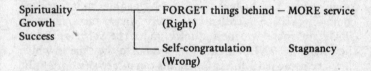

Spirituality / Growth / Success ——— FORGET things behind — MORE service (Right) / Self-congratulation (Wrong) — Stagnancy

"Leaders come to accept themselves as the very chosen of God. They are special objects of Divine favor; their success is *proof* that this is so. They MUST, therefore, be RIGHT, and anyone who tries to call them into account is instantly written off as an unauthorized meddler who should be *ashamed* to reprove his betters."

*Our attitude must be* — "We are *unprofitable servants*; we have done that which was our duty to do" (Luke 17:7-10).

257

What are the
avenues to
true biblical
unity? Why
is revival
impossible
until such a
unity is
restored?

## CONDITIONS OF REVIVAL UNITY

*TWO CONDITIONS* mark *every* revival of history. No people will experience a true spiritual awakening unless BOTH are present. They are *PRAYER* and *UNITY* (Acts 1:14; 2:1; John 17:20-23; Matthew 18:19-20). We have seen that unity can come by *love* expressed in *forgiveness, discipline*, and the willingness to receive *correction* and *criticism*. It is also important to understand the two forces that shape a deep spiritual awakening.

1. *VISION* — Proverbs 29:18. People need to SEE, to *experience*, to feel that God is at work in an active vital way. Whenever God wants to bring a vision, he looks for a *man*. This man is the man who *wholly wills to do the will of God.* Vision is born out of *true prayer* and *genuine unselfish love.* It comes when people get thoroughly cleaned up from all sin and begin to pray that God will supercharge them by His Holy Spirit (Joel 2:28; Habakkuk 2:2).

2. *KNOWLEDGE* — Hosea 4:6. The *experiences* of vision must be married to *facts* of revelation. The second condition of unity is *agreement in knowledge.* We must be sure we know *what* we believe, and *why;* people unite around common facts. To create true unity, these facts must be TRUE, or there will be no unity under the *Spirit of Truth;* they must be VALUABLE — important to the time in which they are preached. Unless Christians can *discern and obey* the truth, no revival is possible (Romans 10:2; Proverbs 22:17-21).

*DIVISION* comes when these two essentials are *split apart* from each other. People can get *experience*-centered or *knowledge*-centered. These divisions mark every strata of the Christian church. If there *is* no awakening, complete revision must be made in *both* areas. REVIVAL is simply Christians *returning to obeying God;* this is where VISION comes from; returning to what God has SAID in His *Word* is REFORMATION of knowledge. We must learn what it means to LOVE the Lord with all our *heart* and *soul* and *mind.*

# THE EYE AND THE EAR

Disunity among Christians is also caused by us *not understanding* our relationship in Christ. "Our bodies have different parts, but all together make up the only one body. With Christ it is just like that" (1 Corinthians 12:12 — paraphrase).

Scripture teaches that when we enter God's Kingdom, our connection with the Lord Jesus is like the link between the

HEAD and the BODY. The two *belong to each other*; neither can work separately. Jesus Christ is the Head of the Church; Christians all over the world make up the rest of His "Body." God counts all who love and serve Him as PART of Christ (Ephesians 1:22-23). *We* need HIM — He needs US! Think about the following things with this in mind:

## 1. *The HEAD is the MOST important.*

All body functions are directed and controlled by the head. The mind ties together all the actions of various parts of the body to enable a man to carry out his work. The HEAD is center and source of all operations, linking into unity all the various abilities of the body parts. So with the Lord Jesus. *HE* must be *Center and Source* of all our fellowship, labor and devotion. As a mindless body is helpless and powerless, so "without Him we can do nothing" (John 15:4-5; 1 Corinthians 1:30-31).

## 2. *No one is "MORE" important.*

Eyes see; ears hear; feet walk. Each does the job it was designed for. No ONE member of the body can do *everything* that needs doing. We cannot really compare an "eye" with an "ear" to find out which is "better." *ALL* are BEST — as long as they do the job they were created to carry out. The eye

259

**Why are there no insignificant members in the body of Christ?**

cannot hear and the ear cannot see. We in the Body of Christ must never forget this. Comparing ourselves with *others* is a root of division (1 Corinthians 1:26-29).

### 3. *All ARE important.*

God makes EVERYONE "princes," but only the *Head* can wear the crown! The church has limited God because people have mistaken NUMBER of talents for *importance*. There is only one pituitary gland in the human body. It is small — no bigger than a thumbnail. Yet without it working, a man has only a few minutes to live! Some Christians "sulk" because they cannot be like some other part of the Body. Because they can't do *ONE* thing, they refuse to do ANYTHING! It isn't *lack* of FIVE-talent men, but *laxity* of ONE-talent men that ties God's hands. In surgery, a hand that is hindering and poisoning a body by its uselessness is cut off. Be like *Mary* — she "did what she could" and though she never preached a sermon, was worthy in God's eyes of a thousand messages on His grace (Mark 14:8-9). EVERYONE in the Body has a vital part to play. *You* do *yours* (1 Corinthians 12:19-21).

### 4. *The condition of ONE member affects ALL the Body.*

A *living unity* connects all believers in Christ. We tap this invisible unity link when we pray for each other. By being all  connected to the Head, we must also be connected through Him to *each other*. A thousand pianos all tuned in to the same tuning fork are also in tune with each other. Are you tuned for harmony? What YOU do affects the "music" of all the Church. If you want to build up the *Church*, get YOURSELF in top working order . Your devotion to God will spark off a revival unity with all others you touch in spirit (Romans 12:4; Ephesians 4:11-16; 1 Corinthians 12:26).

"A ROSE WILL DO MORE THAN A PACKET OF SEEDS TO MAKE A MAN WANT TO GROW FLOWERS."

## COUNT IT ALL JOY!

What is the difference between confession *to* Christ and confession *of* Christ?

Every now and then you meet a trial that doesn't seem to do what it should. You ask God to take it away, but it still *stays* there. You think that perhaps it is the Enemy. You resist him in the Name of Jesus; but if it IS him, he doesn't seem to flee! What is the answer to trials like this? "Count it all JOY!"

### COUNT IT ALL JOY!

"Rejoice in the Lord always and *again* I say to you — rejoice! Have a reputation for gentleness, and never forget the nearness of your Lord. Don't worry over anything whatever; tell God every detail of your needs in earnest and thankful prayer, and the peace of God, which transcends human understanding, will keep constant guard over your hearts and minds as they rest in Christ Jesus" (Philippians 4:5-7 — *Phillips*).

You can go through *anything in the world* with two firm assurances; consciousness that you are in the *will of God* and that *He loves you.* Everything that happens to you has been filtered through His hands. The only thing the Devil can do to you is to TEMPT you — and he has to get permission from God to do that!

PRAISE is a *habit* formed by *practice.* You BECOME what you think about. We ignore another kind of confession we need to practice just as much as that used over sin. It is not confession TO Christ — but *OF* Him! Daily confession of His glory and grace will bring daily deliverance from the more subtle sins of depression and doubt. PRAISE is the *positive confession of the faithfulness of God.* It is the outward expression of "counting it all joy" (Psalm 22:23; Proverbs 23:7; Philippians 4:8; Psalm 42:5,11).

The early disciples were a little band filled with hope and enthusiasm, utterly possessed by a desire to save their world. Jesus and His team were no grim company. Their preaching

What are the
benefits of
praising the
Lord in all
things?

and teaching was an exciting series of surprises. Christianity without enthusiasm is like a body without life. Discipleship is NOT dreary resignation. The early disciples were beaten, but rejoiced that they were "counted worthy to suffer shame for His Name's sake." Paul and Silas in prison prayed, sang praises and started a *church* right where they were! Even the Lord Jesus went to the CROSS *for the JOY* that was set before Him. In discipleship, the pearl and not the *price* is important (Hebrews 12:2; Matthew 13:44-45; Acts 16:25-32).

Praising God is letting your life thrill to Him. When you rejoice, you demonstrate true discipleship to a darkened, hopeless world, convincing sinners more than any words the priceless gain of life with Jesus your Lord. Joy draws like a magnet. When you praise, you:

### 1. *PROVE YOUR FAITH* —

Nothing shakes a sinner more than to see the joy of a Christian even under heavy trial. When you are supposed to "moan" and *don't*, he knows you have something awfully *real*. Praise is a living expression of *faith*. NEVER speak *negatively*. Words SPOKEN have great power to produce attitudes. We are ruled by our words more than we realize. Don't build strongholds for the Enemy by confessing a feeling of defeat! Talk about Satan's power to hinder, and you give HIM glory! Say you can't do it and you are beaten before you begin. Speak your fear of trouble and you call Hell into action. Don't be snared by the words of your mouth (Proverbs 6:2). Talk of doubt, fear or worry and a thousand shades of bondage will grip your heart. God is NOT in the grave! You follow the Christ of the empty tomb, Who walks in an Easter morning gladness (Psalm 100:4; Ephesians 1:12).

### 2. *EXPRESS GRATITUDE* —

*Praise keeps requests in perspective.* We tend to think more of our *troubles* and less of our *Father*, Who is closer than hands or feet. The Devil cannot get you if he cannot *discourage* you! Praise is a song of deliverance, a hymn of victory sung before the battle is joined. Nothing is more disturbing to Hell than a little band of disciples singing over conquest *before* the encounter, with perfect confidence in their Captain. Never wait to feel capable to do the job God calls you to do. That is cowardly. He enables with every call, but strength is supplied IN service, not before. Praise keeps Christ *King* in your life. Murmuring, complaint, worry and doubt nail Him again to the cross and bury Him in a tomb.

Young People can best learn praise by filling their hearts and minds with *music.* Do not complain about the older generation's music; get your heart right before God, and full of praise and love for Him, and write your own. If you like some tune, put new words to it. If you are musically talented, write music to Psalms or new sounds to old hymns (Ephesians 5:19).

You may face giants you cannot conquer, needs you cannot meet. But GOD is on your side. Your battles are HIS

 battles! Fear and depression disintegrate under the power of praise. It brings *Christ-consciousness* into every problem. WHY should you say "Thank You Father" for trials? You NEED them, to learn to throw yourself onto Him. As soon as you stop having a thankful, joyful heart, something gets into your spirit and defiles it (1 Peter 1:7).

You MUST praise . . . even when you feel *least* like doing so. All of us have our "gray days" when God's light goes behind a cloud. Are you trusting in FEELING or in your Father's love? Rejoice in the Lord, and you affirm your faith in His unchanging *promises* regardless of changing feelings and seemingly-impossible circumstances. HOW do you praise? When trouble comes, *look back on your blessings.* If need be, WRITE a LIST of what God has done for you. Praise is a sister to prayer. It lifts hurt hearts into the very Presence of Christ.

A PRAYER:
"LORD — THANKS FOR THIS TRIAL. THIS IS MY CHANCE TO PROVE TO YOU I MEANT IT WHEN I SAID 'I LOVE YOU' FROM MY HEART."

"But as many as are LED
BY THE SPIRIT OF GOD,
they are the sons of God"
(Romans 8:14).

# PHILIP

## (WHO LISTENED TO THE VOICE)

"And the Angel of the Lord
spoke unto Philip and said
'Arise, and go . . .' and he
arose and went."

Acts 8:26-27

Thought:
Before you
can *know* the
will of God,
you must be
willing to
*accept* it.

PHASE:         3 .. *Faith In Action*
SECTION:       8 .. *"E" For Establishing Purpose*
MATERIAL:        .. *Meekness Isn't Weakness*

Out of *revival* into the loneliness of a desert. *One man* more important than a multitude. *Philip* listened to a Voice and the Voice sent him into the wilderness.

Are we where we should be — the right place at the right time? *Philip* had ears for the silent Voice of God — he knew the secret of day-by-day guidance.

---

## THE WILL OF GOD

---

If you haven't asked it by now you are probably not a Christian.

"How can I know the will of God for my life?"

Walk through the halls of Time and study the men and women of God who changed history. They were not often special people, or wise after the wisdom of this world. But they all had one thing in common, they knew and did the will of God in their generation; and they changed all of history.

Scripture is the record of common people who found God's will. He spoke to them then, and He has not changed. God is still looking for a man; at every crisis of history He has found him. He is the man who wholly wills to do the will of God. And you can be God's man, God's woman! He has no favorites. If you will faithfully apply the Bible principles of guidance, you can know the Voice of God and do His will as surely as any man or woman of God who ever lived. And you may be God's chosen man or woman for this hour.

"FEAR KNOCKED ON THE DOOR — FAITH ANSWERED — AND
THERE WAS NO ONE THERE."

# GOAL AND PLAN

What is it about man that separates him from the rest of creation?

*YOU are a special object of God's love!* You are made in His image, created in finite miniature likeness to God. When Christ designed the flaring stars, He no doubt used some sort of plan. His *physical forces* (the laws of science) are steady and behave consistently. It is not difficult to make a blueprint of forces that may be diagrammed and precisely directed. In the animal kingdom, He likewise locked into their beings a series of  programmed impulses we call *instinct*. These guidance systems are similar in many ways to His material creation controls; they may be blueprinted and tabulated because they are sure and predictable.

*But you are different!* You were made to be a tiny outflow of God's own infinite Being; twice-born, to be part of God's *own family*. God has placed one awesome gift in your control that gives you the opportunity to succeed or fail the ultimate test of life — the power of *creative choice*. Are you delivered from sin by His transforming power and cleansing blood? Then the great God invites you to share His *very own life* and offers you the challenge of living as He does — intelligent choice for the highest good of the created Universe.

What an amazing privilege — to be *wholly free* to choose! The Lord God gives you this in trust for your own destiny and perhaps that of others. You are free — free to serve Him out of love, or free to reject His goodness and mercy. God will not *help* you unless you ask Him to, and He will not *stop* you unless it is absolutely necessary. This life is your time of testing. God will only intervene if selfish choices begin to threaten the over-all highest good of His Kingdom. And because of this gift of freedom, your destiny *cannot* be blueprinted!

*You will not find the word "blueprint" in the Bible, nor the word "plan."* Scripture gives no hint that God maps out

267

precisely each path you *will* choose, nor that He plans out what you actually *do*. To do that would be to take your freedom of choice, and God guards that for man. Each choice you make is an *act of creation*, introducing brand-new factors into the Universe. God has chosen to give you freedom, and works *for* or *against* your choices to accomplish His over-all purpose. Christianity is unique in that the Lord God is *actively involved NOW* with man, and that man is not a mere product of blind chance or a fatalistic Universe. The God of the Bible is a Living, moving God Who has not set up history and stepped out of the picture. He *cares* about man and *loves* him. He steps into history at every turn and demonstrates His power to all who dare follow His challenges.

*God's will for your life is a GOAL, not a blueprint.* His one *ultimate* goal, or purpose, is for you to be conformed to the image of His Son, the Lord Jesus (Romans 8:29). A goal is your point of aim, the star that fixes your direction and your destiny. Every Christian that follows His law of love is *locked into a pattern* that will transform his or her life into God's own image. Based on this goal is every *sub-purpose* and lesser goal for all history and for each of His children. Some of these lesser goals are designed expressly for *your* life, that you might fulfil a happy place of service in His Kingdom. They give progressively higher levels of trust, and the next goal is revealed only when the present goal is completed. They will always fit the *earthly goals* the Lord Jesus accomplished during His earthly visit — to "seek and save that which is lost," to "destroy the works of the devil" and to finish the Father's work (Luke 19:10; 1 John 3:8; John 6:36-40; 17:4).

## DAY-BY-DAY DISCOVERY

God hasn't left us without instruction! The *Bible* is His work Manual — but isn't a Celestial "rule-book". It contains not POINTS but PRINCIPLES. *All Bible laws* are *"guide-*

lines" for man's highest good. Using these as foundation-stones, we build a life for the Lord from His day-to-day guidance.

What is the difference between plans and goals?

*Guidance is a life-long process.* God will reveal goals, help you reach them, then set new, higher ones. God's *goals* never change. His over-all strategy (prophetic, historic spans of time in which He revives certain truths) in the control of His *sovereign power* cannot be affected by *our* choices. But plans ARE dependent on our choices, and must change as often as choices do. On a football field, the *goal* is unchanging, but each side must change PLANS to reach that goal as fast and as swiftly as the opposition changes its tactics. It is for this reason that God will not give you a detailed diary of your life ahead. He wants you to make a DAY-BY-DAY DISCOVERY of His revealed will, and *that* daily discovery is guidance.

*God's will for your life* is thus a continued discovery of the *most effective* present PLAN to eventually reach (through a series of sub-stages) His *ultimate goal.* The *plan* will vary with time, circumstances and choices; but God will always work *with* you, daily wanting to point out the best course. Should you fail to consult Him on one of these choices, *all is not lost!* An opportunity may pass that can never be recalled, or "locusts" may eat good years that belong to God. But the moment self-dependence is confessed and His pardon obtained, He can make even *failure* abound to His glory! He does not *plan* your sin; but once forgiven, your fall can be even turned to an asset — perhaps to help some other with the same problem. In this way, "all things work together for good to them that LOVE GOD . . . called according to His Purpose" (Romans 8:28).

---

## MIND OF A SERVANT

As long as we work with God's *goal* for our lives, there will be exciting discoveries in seeing how choices we make and situations God arranges around them abound to His glory. We have *freedom* because we know we are on God's side and nothing is too hard for the Lord.

Only when we make *selfish* choices does conflict come. We choose not for God, but for self. Our purpose conflicts with His. All the related Universe clashes against our selfishness. Gone is our sense of purpose, freedom and inner harmony. How can we stay with God's purpose?

His privileges of *sonship* depend to some extent on our attitude of *servant*-ship. Service is a password to discipleship. The Son of God Himself became a servant. True power and authority is found only in being a "servant of many." As we yield OUR wills and rights to God, He will grant us His power and authority. But not until we have the "mind of a servant"!

---

## DISPOSING OF WHAT YOU "DESERVE"

---

### 1. *DISCIPLES ARE LOVE-SLAVES* —

A *Christian* is a person who has been delivered from the service of *sin* and become a *love-slave of Jesus*. We are all slaves of the power we have chosen to obey; that power is either God in *Christ,* or *selfishness.* No man is a true Christian who has not made the Lord Jesus LORD of *all known areas* of his life. Deliberate withholding of obedience to God and refusal to surrender known rights are signs of a phony Christianity. If Jesus is not truly our *Lord,* then *we* are not really *Christians* (Romans 10:9).

Slavery to *sin* is marked by *fear of punishment* and *hope of reward,* as well as *guilt* and *emptiness.* Slavery to Jesus Christ is marked by *LOVE* — unselfish choices for the highest good of God and His creation. It is the sign of the true Christian. He loves Christ, and he loves others; and he does what his Master asks him to do. Early Christians all called themselves "servants" (Greek *doulos* — *slave*) of Christ. *You* are a love-slave of Christ or a bond-slave of sin! (Romans 6:12-22; Philippians 1:1; James 1:1; 2 Peter 1:1; 1 Corinthians 7:21-24).

## 2. SLAVES HAVE NO RIGHTS OF THEIR OWN —

Describe in your own words the attitude of a true servant.

When a man becomes a *slave* he ceases to have *any say* in his life, as long as he remains a slave. He has been *bought with a price* and belongs absolutely to his master. All that a slave has, and is, lies under the control of his new owner. He is not free until *death* from the control of his lord. He is called to serve and go on serving regardless of praise or blame, weariness or sickness, thanks or disgrace. Likewise, when sin rules our lives, we are the slave of sin. It absolutely rules our every action. The only way out of this is *death,* and that is the sting of sin that burns in its final wages.

The Lord Jesus offers a new kind of service and an *alternate way* of death to escape from the slavery of sin. Christ challenges us to *die* to *our old way of life,* allow Him to bury our selfish past and live as *His* love-slave. As long as we are under His control we will be paid His wages and not the wages of sin. But if He is to be Boss, He must be *absolute* Boss. This involves our total surrender of ALL our rights to Him. Until this happens, He is *not* our real Master and Lord (Matthew 10:24-39; Philippians 2:5-8; 3:7-8).

Are YOU continually worried? angry? wanting more no matter how much you have already? Then you have not learned the lesson of the love-slave. A slave cannot hold anger at being asked to do something for his Lord. He has no rights of his own. He is not worried about his life, because all he has and owns is in the care and keeping of the one he belongs to. He owns nothing; he has no power, possessions or personal rights. The love-slave of God has counted as loss what other men call gain. His motto — "If the Lord is glorified — the servant is satisfied." Everything he has and is belongs to his Master; and YOU?

## 3. TRUE FREEDOM IS LOVE-SLAVERY TO CHRIST —

There is certainly NO freedom in sin! Sin is a hard taskmaster that pays its slaves in the coin of a cemetery. We are *made to be directed* by some power or control. We can *choose* that power — *selfishness* or the *Saviour.* Christian freedom is a new kind of control where we are free to do anything we like *because* we choose the things that are best for everyone, and the things that do not enslave to selfishness.

271

Thought:
Only a slave
for Christ
can know
true
freedom.

It is impossible to let both powers control our life at the same time (Matthew 6:24; 7:16-23; James 3:11-13). We are slave to one OR the other—right now! We cannot be a *mixture* of bad and good. Our hearts are fixed on pleasing *Christ* or pleasing *ourselves.* If we do not really belong to Him, His laws will seem tiresome, His demands will seem extreme and we will resent and rebel against His commands. But once we have given Him our love and become His slaves, we enter the path to true freedom and God opens the door to sonship in His family. God is a loving Master! He is not harsh, or unfair or overbearing. His yoke is easy and His burden is light (Matthew 11:29; 19:29; Luke 17:10; 22:24-27; 9:23-25; 1 Corinthians 7:23b).

---

## DISCIPLES ARE LEARNERS

*All disciples are learners.* It is possible that you did not understand what becoming a Christian really was when you *first* gave your life to God. You acted on all the light you had, and God met you graciously in His love. But there is one basic lesson you *must* learn to be a true disciple — the lesson of *MEEKNESS.*

You must know *now* that the Lord Jesus wants *ALL* of you, and He is not going to stop dealing with you until He has it! He is very easy to *please,* but hard to *satisfy.* If you are still troubled by fits of *temper* or *worry,* you have not learned what it means to be a love-slave. To conquer you must learn MEEKNESS.

(Related table shown on page PH-9)

---

## MEEKNESS ISN'T WEAKNESS

*God never used a man until he first learnt MEEKNESS.* "MEEK" often conjures up a picture of a watery-eyed mouse-type people. Nothing could be further from the truth! The Lord Jesus was meek. A stallion is "free" — but wild and untamed. It lives for its own pleasure. It makes its own laws and runs with the herd. One day a new master captures it. He

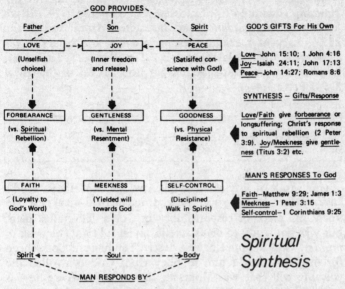

GOD PROVIDES

Father — Son — Spirit

| LOVE | → | JOY | ← | PEACE |

(Unselfish choices) — (Inner freedom and release) — (Satisfied conscience with God)

**GOD'S GIFTS For His Own**

Love—John 15:10; 1 John 4:16
Joy—Isaiah 24:11; John 17:13
Peace—John 14:27; Romans 8:6

| FORBEARANCE | GENTLENESS | GOODNESS |

(vs. Spiritual Rebellion) — (vs. Mental Resentment) — (vs. Physical Resistance)

**SYNTHESIS — Gifts/Response**

Love/Faith give forbearance or longsuffering; Christ's response to spiritual rebellion (2 Peter 3:9). Joy/Meekness give gentleness (Titus 3:2) etc.

| FAITH | MEEKNESS | SELF-CONTROL |

(Loyalty to God's Word) — (Yielded will towards God) — (Disciplined Walk in Spirit)

**MAN'S RESPONSES To God**

Faith—Matthew 9:29; James 1:3
Meekness—1 Peter 3:15
Self-control—1 Corinthians 9:25

Spirit ← — — — — Soul — — — → Body

MAN RESPONDS BY

*Spiritual Synthesis*

**(Related table from 'Disciples Are Learners' — page PH-8).**

What is the difference between meekness and weakness?

begins to break down its proud, stubborn will. This takes time and love, but one day the horse is "broken in." It has lost none of its power or energy.

But once-wasted force is now under control and can be directed into useful outlets. The horse is under the will of its master. It is MEEK — dynamite under control! MEEKNESS ISN'T WEAKNESS.

*Meekness is basically a YIELDED WILL towards God.* As diagrammed it is the *key response* of man to the claims of Christ. When we truly surrender to God, our lives should show the fruit of the Holy Spirit (Galatians 5:22-23). Our *human response* to God's shared *love, joy* and *peace* will be marked by *faith, MEEKNESS* and *self-control.* God never used a man until his life showed development of these three human responses. They are the foundations of human spiritual development in Christ, and *meekness is the key.* This determines the EXTENT of our faith and self-control; the more our wills are yielded, the greater our faith and discipline. These three responses combine with love, joy and peace to give Christian actions in reply to the three basic areas of human rebellion against God and His people.

273

What is the
difference
between holy
anger
and sinful
anger?

*Meekness is VITAL!* Without it there can be *no* true discipleship (Psalm 149:4; Colossians 3:12; James 1:21). It is a key to getting *guidance* and instruction from God (Psalm 25:9). Lack of meekness results in *worry* and failure to *get along with others* (Galatians 6:1; 2 Timothy 2:25; Titus 3:2). Without it we cannot inherit what God has for us (Matthew 5:5; 1 Peter 3:4).

---

## ANGER — THE WRONG FLAME

One result of unyielded will is *ANGER*. Moses was "God's angry man." In his youth he had not learned meekness. He knew his place of responsibility in God's deliverance plan, but was not ready to be used. His unyielded rights blew up in *murder*. God let him flee to a desert. Tending stubborn sheep for 40 years taught him to obey God! God controlled the volcanic will that was Moses to such a point where he was called "meek above every other man on the fact of the earth" (Numbers 12:3). Very rarely did he lose his temper again.

There is a *holy anger* in Scripture. *God* gets angry, and God does not sin. Holy anger is a righteous wrath for the *rights of God*. It is *sin* to feel anger from personal resentment and damaged pride, marked by resentment and destructive, unloving choices. But holy anger is a *right reaction* to wrong done against *others, especially God*. It is always marked by some constructive action taken to end the wrong that created the anger, and includes feeling sorry for the one who caused it, choosing a way to help him wherever possible, so he does not do the same thing again. Holy anger will be as *stern* as the *depth of love* we have for God. The Lord Jesus had it, and a Christian who does not have it is not really following in His steps. It is a Bible *command* that we "be angry, and sin not" (Ephesians 4:26, Mark 3:5; Luke 17:1-2).

But *selfish anger is SIN*. It ruins *PERSONALLY* by fanning the flames of bitterness, envy and jealousy. (Ephesians 4:30-32; Proverbs 16:32; 19:11). It damages the body *PHYSICALLY* by filling the system with tension, causing heart-attacks, ulcers and other physical ailments. It ruins our fellowship with others *SOCIALLY*, blasting friendships, family relations and testimony (Proverbs 21:19;

274

25:24). The Bible warns against selfish anger in no uncertain terms. Christians are instructed not to befriend or be seen with an angry man (Proverbs 22:24). The person who is selfishly angry at his brother is in danger of *judgment*. God classes anger as a terrible sin.

What is the "hidden blessing" for us in irritation?

## THOSE "NERVE-GRATERS"

*IRRITATION* often sparks selfish anger. An *irritant* is something frustrating you have no control over. Each day will bring us irritation. It is not *this* that is sin, but *our failure to respond correctly* to it. It could come from *circumstances, people* or even *ourselves.* Each trial, cause for complaint, and irritation, is actually a *test* of consecration. If you react in *love,* these obstacles can be STEPPING-STONES to power with God. React to them *selfishly* and they will be BARRIERS instead. We must learn how to handle irritations in Christ.

1. *"THEM!"* — People you bump into daily are big irritants sometimes. They do little things that "nark" you, or behave in a manner that "rubs you the wrong way." They don't arrive on time, don't do what they are supposed to — people are BIG irritants!

2. *"IT!"* — The place where you live or work can "get at" you. It's inconvenient, missing something it should have, or has got something it shouldn't have. The "roof leaks," the "thing outside" makes too much noise — you wish you were somewhere else.

3. *"ME!"* — *WE* are the MOST frustrating people we know! Some personal deficiency, defect or failure to live up to set standards, all combine to irritate. The acid of dissatisfaction with self churns us up inside and comes out in the way we live.

When did you last lose your temper and how many of the rules did you break in the process?

## WHEN RAGE RUSHES UP

1. *DON'T — EXPLODE.* Getting mad enough to "blow up" like an over-heated pressure cooker is both useless and dangerous. If you ARE in the right, you don't need to lose your temper; if you are wrong, you can't afford to!

2. *DON'T — EXPLAIN.* Trying to justify or defend yourself if you are angry with someone only makes it worse. Throw up a wall to protect your "rights," and you block the chance to conquer anger.

3. *DON'T — EXCUSE.* Shifting the blame on to the one you feel was the cause of your anger IRRITATES HIM! Result — two problems instead of one; two angry men instead of one.

4. *DON'T — ENCLOSE* it. "Anger rests in the bosom of fools." To hold anger inside, silently fuming is not the way to get rid of it. It will only make it worse. "Don't let the sun go down on your wrath" warns the Scripture. Don't hold on to anger.

## WHAT DO YOU DO WITH ANGER?

1. *EXAMINE* the irritation causing anger. God allowed it to happen to test your meekness. Take care of this, and it will help you grow in spiritual maturity. Therefore, THANK God for the source of irritation! It is trying your spirituality for its reality.

2. *EXPOSE* your sin. *Ask yourself* — "What selfish attitude has this irritation uncovered? Has some bad quality come to light not befitting for a son of God?" Irritation is like a flame playing on a sample of gold. Under intense heat, impurities come to the surface never before recognized. God, the Master Goldsmith, keeps playing on the flame until His gold is refined. When the gold is pure — He can see HIS FACE in it. A "scum-skimming" process of confession and asking forgive-

276

ness will quickly bring you to maturity, if you will learn to recognize God's hand in trials instead of fighting them.

What must be the first responsibility in recon-structing the damage brought on by a lost temper?

Unless you deal with the "scum," as God brings it to the surface, you will never *see the same problems in others.* There is an important principle for you to recognize in this, that could be summed up in Peter's words to the lame man, "SUCH AS I HAVE — give I unto thee!" (Acts 3:6). Do you want to help others into a better place with God? Then you can lead them no further than you have gone yourself. They will carbon copy your spirituality. Are you disgusted at the way someone has behaved that you have spent time with? Then check your own life for seeds of the same sin. YOU CAN'T GIVE IT IF YOU HAVEN'T GOT IT!

3. *EMPTY OUT* bad attitudes by recognition, repentance and receiving forgiveness. Then ask, "What *godly* attitude should I have had then? What is the response my Father would ask of me instead? In such a situation, what would the *Lord Jesus* do?" Never stop in the negative. Remember — in the mathematics of God and men, the cross is a PLUS SIGN! Seek the face of God and the Word of God for the *right* qualities to fill the empty gap — patience, peace, self-control, love, joy, etc.

When you treat trials *this* way, they can actually *HELP* instead of hinder. You have given yourself to God to be His disciple. Then don't protest at the training! Don't ask for sugar and then object to he stirring up. You have asked God to make you the best kind of Christian you can be — then He has much work to do. You are like a rough block of stone that needs to be chipped, chiselled and sanded. Every cut at the old shape will hurt! But God will do it gently so you can bear it. The more you *spare* yourself from these, the less will be your usefulness to Christ.

*This* is what is meant by "rejoicing in tribulation." Each trial, cause for complaint and irritation, gives you another chance to prove your consecration to Christ. If your motives are for the *glory of God,* OBSTACLES ARE STEPPING-STONES; if *not,* they are BARRIERS. Active faith clings to God in the face of discouragement. You will never see the Lily of the Valley until you are *in* the Valley; you will never see the Bright and Morning Star until you are in *darkness.* Don't consider trials and temptations as "intruders" —

277

What is the
root cause of
worry?

welcome them as friends! God is testing the "tensile strength" of your faith — He tries it to the breaking point, but never beyond. Each time a *test* gets tougher, so does your *faith*. God wants you to keep on trusting so when the heat goes on — you've got a smile and you can say — "I'm still believing, Lord!"

## VICTORY OVER WORRY

*WORRY* is the other destructive force stemming from unyielded rights. Occasions for worry are also *opportunities* for you to discover the faithfulness of the Father. There are *six basic essentials for living.* When one of these rights are threatened, self-love (self-preservation) signals danger to the personality. It is expected that a man who is trying to run his *own* life will worry. He has no Heavenly Father's promise of provision, and must take full responsibility for insuring and meeting all these needs himself. He assumes a responsibility that is not rightfully his, and *this* produces worry. These six needs are —

1. *ACCEPTANCE* — A sense of belonging, being thought well of, feeling loved and cared for by someone.

2. *ACCOMPLISHMENT* — a longing to do something worthwhile, leave a mark in history or society, make the most of time, talents and opportunity.

3. *PROVISION* — Having food, housing, clothes and money to meet needs, pay bills, rent and taxes.

4. *POSSESSIONS* — Having things we can call our own — goods, possessions or belongings we can use in the business of living.

5. *SAFETY* — To be guarded against illness, incapacity or disability; being in good health, protected from hurt, danger or disaster.

6. *SECURITY* — Assurance of the future, whatever "tomorrow" may bring; a sense of guidance, sure direction as we venture into the unknown.

## FREE AS A SLAVE!

How can an unsurrendered heart be harmful not only to the individual but to others as well?

*The following steps* can be used to *surrender rights* to get rid of worry or anger. If you will carefully and prayerfully follow these now with your cherished right, you will be free!

1. *FIND your right.* What happened or has taken place that made you angry or worried? What actually *caused* your feelings? *Write it out* if it will help you. Discover your right.

2. *WRITE DOWN* your right on a slip of paper. Perhaps it was the right to do what you want with your own *time, money* or *things:* the right to *dress* or act the way you always wanted to; the right to be *thought well of* by someone you like a lot who has shown no interest in you; the right to a certain *sport, friend,* etc.

3. *Build a little fire,* either outside somewhere where you can be alone with God or in the secret place of your *heart.* Use this fire as an "altar" where you can *"offer up" in prayer* this right to the Lord (Genesis 22:1-18). This will be your secret sacrifice, known only to yourself and God. From this moment on, it will be *HIS* right, not yours.

4. *EXPECT God to take His right!* Let Him test your sincerity. If the right has been truly given to Him, it is now HIS (as it *should* have been in the *first* place). It is no longer yours to worry about or get angry over. You may only *ask* Him if you can *"borrow"* it for a time, and if He says "No" you should not mind. You are only His *love-slave;* and because you are a slave, you will know the freedom of joy that comes from serving the most attentive Master in the world! *Your motto now* — "If the *Lord* is *glorified,* the *servant* is *satisfied!*"

"THE MAN WITH THE SECRET OF EVEN LIVING DOESN'T MIND BEING CALLED ODD."

279

What is the
problem
with a
person trying
to receive a
knowledge
of God's
specific will if
he's not
willing to
listen to the
Lord in His
general will
as found in
Scripture?

## CONDITIONS OF GUIDANCE

*No man has ever been guided daily* until he has been willing to fulfil these essential conditions for knowing God's will. Check your life against these before you ask for guidance:

1. *A desire to know and do ALL the revealed will of God.* Don't *ASK* for guidance unless you are prepared to *ACT* on it! God is always willing to make His purpose known. If you "cannot" find an answer, it may well be that you have some *secret reservation* in your heart. God will not show you His will for you to merely *consider* doing it. Unless you are prepared to TRUST His wisdom and love and DO what He shows you, *don't ask Him.* Many saying they can't get God's guidance really mean they wish He would show them an *easier* way. God promises to show us *only* if we are ready to *act* on His revelation (Hosea 6:3a; Matthew 7:21; John 7:17; Hebrews 11:26).

That is why you must learn the *love-slave* lesson. God promises to guide the MEEK, or those with *yielded wills.* He will not guide those who want to run their own lives (Matthew 10:24, 37-39; Philippians 2:5-8; 3:7-8; 1 Corinthians 7:23b; Psalm 25:9).

2. *A willingness to be counted a fool.* Doing God's will often conflicts with a surrounding selfish world. Usually His will fits perfectly with sanctified reason and intelligence. Some Christians hide *non-involvement* behind a pretended fear of "uncertain guidance" . . . a lack of *witness initiative* under cover of "not knowing God's will." We need not always expect a voice from the sky when the path of service is clear. God gave us *common sense* and He expects us to use it. God's will is usually an *area* of *general direction* in which He leaves us relatively free to work for Him (Proverbs 3:23; 4:5-13; 6:20-22; 10:9; 11:3; Matthew 25:11-27).

Christians, in their hunger for God to speak to them in everything, often forget this. There is a tendency to equate amount of *"direct"* guidance with evident *depth of spirituality.* God often teaches us reliance in the big and little

280

things of life by honoring requests for "direction" in thrilling little answers that build faith. We should never grow out of referring problems and decisions to His wise counsel. We more often go astray in the little things where we tend to take matters into our own hands.

Describe the various methods of God's guidance and which He has used most often to guide you.

*Never forget,* however, that God created you a *man* and not a *robot.* He gave you free will and intelligence with the check of conscience. Don't make the mistake of thinking that the closer you grow to Him the more you will be specifically *directed* in all you do. Only PUPPETS are totally dependent on the pull of a string for every move they make. Christians are often afraid to use initiative in case they "get out of God's will". God's will is an AREA of *general direction* in which He leaves us free to work for Him. We must paint the lines of guidance with a ROAD-MARKER, not a drafting pencil!

This is where Christian guidance is so very *personal.* It is possible for us to tell the Lord what *we* want to do for Him, and for God to give it to us! Sometimes God will let us *choose ourselves* between two possibilities; sometimes He *asks us* to take a choice. He is a Father, Who wants to teach us *responsibility,* and guides by INSTRUCTION. If you have a clear picture of His general guide-lines from Scripture, you do not always have to ask for special guidance. He guides us ON THE MOVE for Him (Acts 16:6-7). He only asks that we be instantaneously open to His redirection and checks as we act.

"God's method in answering almost any prayer is the head-on, straight forward approach. It calls for courage as well as faith. It's the 'march-into-the-Red-Sea-and-it-divides' method, or the 'march-up-to-the-walls-and-they-fall-down' technique. It calls for *courage* as well as *faith.* He will take any promises or pledges we make to Him at their face value . . . He has a way of calling our bluff" (Peter Marshall - *Praying Is A Dangerous Business).*

However, sometimes the logical *"right"* way is not *at all* what we would "expect." Some directions cut *right across* all limited human knowledge of the "best" thing, even *contradicting* it! This is direction, from *intuition,* as our spirits connect in faith to the super-rationality of the Holy Spirit, Who has promised to guide us into all Truth (John 16:13).It is sensing *in spirit* what is the desire of God. *Young* believers usually begin being guided directly by their intuition and conscience, and accomplishing much for God, until they learn more about His ways in His Word by *study* knowledge. Just as there is a danger of Biblically-groundless guidance, so there is also the opposite danger; that our *minds* will be developed at the expense of the *intuitive sensitivity* of *conscience*. This will quickly kill the freshness of our Christian lives, the excitement of being prompted by the Spirit of God and being sensitive to His inner Voice.

We must *cultivate* this sensitivity; it is well worth it. It is a hot-line to His heart; it is the safeguard against being "puffed up" in the mind (1 Corinthians 8:1; 13:4; Colossians 2:18) and becoming proud in the flesh. It will keep us dependent on Christ's direction, so we will not lose our *"first"* love in our love of His *Word.* The Holy Spirit can teach us to "turn on" to His promptings if we learn to OBEY this inner voice. NEVER act on a doubtful impression; it is *sin* to do so (Romans 14:5). Inward checks of the spirit usually signal *wrong,* in either action or timing. We will feel awed, scared even, when God asks us to do some big thing for Him; but we should *never* feel worried or afraid and insecure. We need to

develop our conscience until it is sensitive as air, and keep our spirit free from excitement, oppression or defilement, by guarding our hearts from *pride, extreme emotions* and *depression*. We will quickly pick up His special "call signs" in practice, if we will begin with a *clean heart* and a *clear conscience*. Such obedience to intuition may be counted madness in the eyes of the world, but you will be *God's* fool, and you will see His power (Matthew 11:25; Proverbs 11:5; 3:5-6; Psalm 25:4-5; Isaiah 11:2; John 10:3; Galatians 5:18; Acts 26:24; Mark 3:21; 1 Corinthians 3:18-20; 2 Corinthians 5:13).

3. *A clean conscience from the past.* Guidance will always be hindered or misunderstood if there are still things in your life that God has urged you to get right. How *can* He show you more if you have disobeyed in the little things? (Luke 16:10). Every time you kneel to pray, the finger of His Spirit will point *back* to your clear duty to get that thing cleaned

up and put right. A clear conscience is absolutely *essential* to distinguishing between the voice of God and the voice of the Enemy. *Unconfessed sin* is a prime reason why many do not know God's will. It is the "pure in heart" who see Him (Matthew 5:8; James 3:13-18; Matthew 5:23-24).

By what standard must all inner, subjective guidance be judged?

4. *Regular time in prayer and the Word of God. God's Book* is the whole basis of guidance. It contains principles and guidelines to almost every avenue of service. God's *WILL* is expressly revealed in His *WORD*. Bible study shows us what God expects in daily living, and most Scriptural principles of action can be directly applied to every problem situation in life. *NO guidance* will ever break the fence of *Scriptural precept.* Freedom in following the Lord Jesus always stays on the tracks of right and moral responsibility. The Bible is the broad base on which we must build daily guidance (Proverbs 6:23).

*PRAYER* teaches us BY EXPERIENCE what God's Voice sounds like. Many people don't have a clue as to what God's direction is because they simply never spend *long enough* with Him to recognize what He is like! It is not enough to know ABOUT the Lord, that is well and good; but it will never get you into His Presence. It is not sufficient to know OF Him either; you must KNOW *HIM.* This is the secret of wisdom in life: KNOWING JESUS (Job 28:12-28; Proverbs 8:1-21; 1 Chronicles 28:9). If you want to hear from *God* more often, how about letting *Him* hear from YOU more? If you want God to talk to you, you had better spend time talking to HIM (James 1:5).

"IF WE HAD MORE GUIDED MEN, WE WOULDN'T NEED GUIDED MISSILES."

How does a
person
familiarize
himself with
the speaking
voice of God?

---

**METHODS**

---

### 1. *VOICE OF GOD* (Audible)

God has sometimes spoken in a *voice* that could be heard by people. This happened to a number of people in the Bible. Study the examples of *Samuel* as a boy (1 Samuel 3:1-10), *Moses* (out of the burning bush) (Exodus 3:4-6) and to the *people* on Mount Sinai (Exodus 19:19; Hebrews 12:18-19), to *Aaron* and *Miriam* (Numbers 12:5-8), *Elijah* (1 Kings 19:9-13), the *Lord Jesus* and a watching crowd (John 12:27-30), and *Saul* with his band of men (Acts 9:1-7). *Peter Marshall*, "a man called Peter," heard God's voice saving him from death in a Scottish fog, and as a result entered the ministry; *Sundar Singh* of India had a similar experience.

*TESTS FOR GOD'S VOICE:* Although God rarely guides vocally, He speaks with —

(a) *A familiar, "unspooky"* voice, that may sound almost like someone we know and love. (Not to be confused with Satanic imitation of *dead* relatives and friends.) No tension, harshness or strangeness; it is sure and kind, never "scary." Little Samuel thought three times *God's* voice was *Eli's* when it woke him up (1 Samuel 3:4-5; John 10:14, 16, 27-28).

(b) Love, kindness, gentleness in His words. It is the voice of the *Good Shepherd* Who gives His life for the sheep. Never disturbs our spiritual peace even when rebuking; the voice of God is warm and secure; *never confusing* so a man is hindered from thinking.

(c) A voice that causes *rejoicing; spiritual uplift* (John 3:29-30). *Never demanding* or imperative; *never* urges sudden action without time to intelligently weigh issues at stake;

284

*never* asks unthinking obedience. The clamorous "commentary" urging a person into second-by-second decisions without ceasing is to be identified as the *Enemy*.

(d) Voice seems to come from *"within"* the spirit many times; moving from the center of our beings into the conscious mind, in a casual, matter-of-fact sort of way.

## 2. VISIONS AND DREAMS

God has often spoken to people this way to get across an idea that is difficult to describe in any other way. A vision differs only one basic way from a dream; the *vision* can occur when the person is wide awake and not sleeping. The dream or vision is implanted or inspired by the *Holy Spirit* and can be explained only by Him.

Nearly *all* the prophets of Scripture were given dreams and visions to instruct them, among whom were *Isaiah* with his awesome vision of the Lord (Isaiah 6:1-8), *Ezekiel,* who saw the strange, science-fiction type scene near Chebar (Ezekiel 1:1-28) and *Daniel,* with his famous re-screening of Nebuchadnezzar's lost dream (Daniel 2:1-19) and interpretation (Daniel 2:22-47). A vision at mid-day sent *Peter* to the Gentile world to preach (Acts 10:9-16). *Joseph* was warned and protected by two dreams at Jesus' birth (Matthew 1:20; 2:12-13). God has *promised* visions to young men in the last days (Joel 2:28; Acts 2:17).

*TESTS FOR GOD-GIVEN DREAMS AND VISIONS;* Using the following as a rough guide:

(a) Very *realistic,* like an *actual scene* of life. A sense of *import, value* fills it.
(b) Usually *short,* not rambly or confused; *clearly defined* in purpose, sequence.
(c) Definite impression made for certain *action* left in mind on awakening.

What is the difference between a dream and a vision? What prophetic significance do we find about them in the Scriptures pertaining to the last days?

Why must
all occult
connections
be thoroughly
renounced
and repented
of in the life
of a
Christian
before a
dream or
vision could
be considered
as a viable
possibility for
guidance?

(d) **Person awakens** feeling *closer to Christ*, spiritually *refreshed* or challenged.

(e) Leaves person *awakened to God's claims* (Acts 26:19; 10:19; 16:10).

(f) *Visions:* Easily distinguished from physical world on which it is superimposed.

(g) *Visions: NEVER* given in *mentally NON-ACTIVE* conditions (e.g. disorientating effects of drugs, hypnotic or other self-induced trances, high-energy music, yoga or other Eastern disciplines, transcendental meditation or occult, spiritist conditions).

(h) *Never* recurring suggestions for *occult* powers or secrets; not *sensually arousing* to attitudes of immorality, hatred or fear; never *depressing, deadening* or *confusing.*

Many men of God have had vivid spiritual dreams, like *John Newton,* the famous hymn-writer, and *Dr. A.J. Gordon,* the beloved Baptist minister of Boston. Others like *Charles G. Finney* saw a *vision* of Christ at their conversion; some like *D.L. Moody,* a vision of Heaven and the new world of God on their death-beds. If you want to develop your spiritual sensitivity to the dream to open it as another channel through which the Lord can teach you, follow these suggestions:

(a) Be *serious* with Him, and *expect Him* to speak to you in His own time this way.

(b) Learn the discipline of *silence* during your day, to cultivate your spirit.

(c) Learn how to fall asleep with your mind *filled with thoughts of God. Prayer* and *praise, Bible-reading* just before bed will help you to relax in His love.

(d) If you have a dream that you believe comes from God, *WRITE IT OUT* the instant you wake up. *Do not delay.* Write it out in as much *detail* as you can.

(e) *Think deeply* about what you dreamed, asking the *Holy Spirit* to guide your imagination. Often your dream is symbolic, and can give you deep insights.

(f) If you like, *discuss* your dream with a spiritual, considerate friend. Some comment they give may be the very key that unlocks the whole thing for you.

(g) The importance of the dream in guidance is *threefold:* Firstly, our whole beings are *relaxed* in sleep, and not occupied with secular concerns; Secondly, God by His Spirit can have *direct access* to our spiritual natures with our entire inner being's attention focussed on what He is showing us; Thirdly, He can show us things in symbols that we would otherwise never see, as the mind during sleep can *lucidly see* simple things, placing them in proper context, analyzing, evaluating and marvelling at them. God can *preview* our decisions for us by the dream, so we know what to do when we wake up (1 Kings 3:5-15).

Do a study of angelic visitation in the Bible noting the similarities and differences in each case.

### 3. VISITATION (*Angelic* messenger, or *appearance* of Christ)

*Angels* often appeared to men of God in the Bible. In the past they sometimes brought messages from God to His servants. At times *God Himself* appeared in a physical form, a manifestation of the Word of God, the Son, second Person in the Godhead. He is referred to as the *"Angel Of The Lord"* in His dealings with men in this way. The Bible reveals that God has many angelic beings that serve Him in various ways (Genesis 3:24; Ezekiel 28:14-15; Isaiah 6:1-3; Revelation 4:6-9; 5:6-14; Psalm 103:20-21; 148:2-5; 84:1).

Study their earthly visits with *Abraham* (Genesis 18:1-33 one of these three "men" is a *Logophanes* — the "Angel of the Lord"), *Lot* (Genesis 19:1-16), *Moses* (Exodus 33:19-23), *Joshua* (Joshua 5:13-15), the *children of Israel* (Judges 2:1-5), *Jacob* (Genesis 32:24-30), *Manoah* (Judges 13:2 30), *David* (2 Samuel 24:16), *Elijah* (1 Kings 19:7), *Zacharias* (Luke 1:11-20), *Mary* (Luke 1:26-35), the *shepherds* (Luke 2:8-12), *Philip* (Acts 8:26), *Peter* (Acts 12:7), *Paul* (Acts 27:23). The holy angels have special *powers and abilities,* man command-posts throughout God's Kingdom in service to Him, and were to help *protect* and *prepare* man for his wonderful future in Christ (Psalm 34:7; 35:5-6; 2 Kings 6:15-17; Isaiah 63:9; Matthew 26:53; Hebrews 1:14). They apparently can *still visit Earth,* moving among people in human form (Hebrews 13:2).

### TESTS FOR A VISITOR FROM GOD:

It is important to remember *two things* about angels;

How would ignoring the advice of other Christians be evidence of pride in the life?

FIRST, they NEVER receive *any* WORSHIP (Colossians 2:18; Revelation 19:10; 22:9; 1 Corinthians 6:3) and second; since the ascension of Christ and the coming of the Holy Spirit, they NEVER impart *Divine revelation,* which is now the exclusive ministry of the Holy Spirit and the Word of God (John 14:16-17, 26). Angelic ministry *can* protect, deliver or supply a servant of God, but never TEACH him. They always glorify and DEIFY the Lord Jesus; they never act outside of the express will of God, revealed in His Word; they are detailed to basically meet *material needs* Any supernatural visitor avoiding these precepts is to be recognized as *Satanic.*

1. *GODLY MEN AND WOMEN (Advice* of experienced Christians)

Guidance is often clarified by discussion with Christians who are known for their close walk with God; we call it *counseling.* Such guidance should NEVER be used for the sole evidence of any important decision; Scripture gives a serious warning about listening to men without *first* seeking God's face (1 Kings 13:11-22; 1 Chronicles 13:1-12). *Study* Proverbs 15:22; 11:14; 12:15; 13:10; 20:18; 24:6; 27:9; Acts 6:1-5; 15:1-31; 1 Thessalonians 2:11-13).

*TESTS FOR GODLY GUIDANCE:*

(a) "To the law and testimony" (Isaiah 8:20). Must ALWAYS be in *Scriptural precepts!*

(b) NEVER contramands *previous* command of God; NEVER breaks God's laws.

(c) Confirms *already-established* conviction of heart given by the Spirit of God.

(d) Leaves heart with *peace, joy* or *spiritual conviction, never* depression, despair.

(e) TIME will substantiate their verdict; will "come to pass" (Deuteronomy 18:18-22).

(f) Follows basic in *"Tests Of New Knowledge"* (TS-31); *non-condemning* (JN-  ).

288

(g) BEWARE of people offering guidance with constant preface of "God told me," "God showed me," "I have a witness," often a sign of *pride* or *deceiving* spirits.

(h) WATCH OUT for the *half-truth*; deception usually begins with something that is partly right, or one side of the truth, that is followed on your acceptance by a *lie*.

What is the divinely appointed purpose of the gifts of the Holy Spirit?

## 2. GIFTS OF THE HOLY SPIRIT (*Special directions* from the *Spirit of God*)

Scripture records various supernatural manifestations of the Holy Spirit, where God carries out *through human vessels* some work normally above human ability or wisdom. They are to show that God is *really with* His people (1 Corinthians 12:12-14, 27; John 14:12-14; Mark 16:15-18), *edify* the Church (1 Corinthians 14:3; 12,26; Ephesians 4:11-13) or to *deliver* God's servants in times of crisis. Study the following Bible passages relating these (Romans 1:11; 12:6; 1 Corinthians 12:1-12; 12:27-31; 14:12,26-30; Ephesians 4:8-14; 1 Timothy 1:6).

God has guided here basically by the *word of knowledge* "fragment of Divine knowledge"(Genesis 18:17,19; 1 Samuel 9:19; 16:7; 1 Kings 19:18; 2 Kings 6:12; John 4:16-18, 29,39; Acts 9:11-12; 10:5-6; 16:9); the *word of wisdom* (Divine reasoning behind revelation) (Genesis 12:1-2; 41:33-36; Exodus 31:1-4; Deuteronomy 34:9; 2 Samuel 5:23-24; 1 Kings 3:11-12, 28; Matthew 10:18-19; 22:15-33; Acts 16:1-11) and the *gift of prophecy* (in the *Old Testament*, generally a *fore*telling, in the *New Testament*, a *forth*-telling; *neither* to be confused with *occult fortune-telling* (Numbers 27:21; Deuteronomy 33:8; 1 Samuel 28:6; 30:7-8; 22:13; Ezekiel 2:1-2; Acts 11:27-30; 16:9-10; 20:23; 21:10-13). *Notice this:* In NO CASE are such directions to assume priority over the *Written Word* of God, and in EACH case must be *tested* by it; such directions from God ALWAYS involve the ratifying *consent* of the individual; none are "fates."

### TESTS FOR SPIRITUAL GIFTS

*Spiritual gifts* are available to every Spirit-filled Christian (1 Corinthians 12:7). They are NOT the way *we* can use God, but the way *God* can use us. Each is a facet of God's great

What
outward
results come
from a
properly
employed
gift of the
Spirit?

love and power, reflected through the clean glass of human personality. Although only *God* can decide which are the most useful for us in our ministries and needs, we *are* told to "covet earnestly" those that God has in mind as best (1 Corinthians 12:31). We are NEVER to tell God,"Speak to me *in a voice,*" "Guide me in *THIS* way," etc.! We are to ask for *His guidance,* and anything outside of the Word of God and the Spirit's witness is HIS affair. God usually gifts the *humble* (1 Corinthians 1:26-30), the *dedicated* servant of Christ, who is showing the FRUIT of the Holy Spirit, demonstrating to God that he can be trusted; and those who have asked for prayer at the hands of other Christians (1 Timothy 4:14; 2 Timothy 1:6).

Spiritual gifts operating in the life of clean Christians are marked by these signs:

1. *Natural expression,* in the context of the ordinary human personality; not "weird."
2. Never marked by "wild-fire" excitement, screaming, harshness or bitterness.
3. Function in a spirit of *worship,* praise, love, humility and meekness of heart.
4. Though unpremeditated, recipient is ALWAYS in *control* of operation (1 Corinthians 14:26-33).
5. *Mental faculties clear;* thinking, speaking sound, not dull or confused (2 Timothy 1:7, 13).
6. WATCH expressions through a condemning, judging spirit, *without* spiritual love or fruit.


3. *GOD'S SERVANTS IN THE MINISTRY: (Ministry of preaching and teaching)*

When men of God spend time getting a message from the Lord for others, there is opportunity to learn much of God's ways and words from their anointed preaching. *Take notes* on each such message; keep a notebook for your own study from these; perhaps the very direction you most need was given before; and you have forgotten it! Study: Isaiah 46:10-11; Exodus 4:10-12; John 3:27; Acts 20:27; Romans 10:14; 1 Corinthians 2:1; 1 Peter 4:11. All such messages may be tested by either of the previous two sets of tests and checks.

## 4. PERSONAL: *(Individual direct guidance)*

What are the attributes of the voice of the Holy Spirit?

A. *WORD of God (The Holy Scriptures,* the *foundation* of all guidance)

(1) *Regular Bible reading* — The "jig-saw" principle. You fill in a portion of a "puzzle" each time you read a section of the Bible. A key piece fitted in suddenly reveals a whole picture.

(2) *Open-page method* — definitely not to be abused!

Ask God in faith to guide your fingers to the right Scripture for your need. Open the Bible, trusting Him to speak to you from it.

(3) *Mental suggestion* of a chapter, verse or book — In prayer God will sometimes bring to mind one of these. Turn to the place and begin to read until God speaks to you.

(4) *Recalled memory verse* — Often God has brought to mind a verse of Scripture in time of temptation or difficulty that brings clear instruction. Establish a memorization program (Psalm 119:9-11, 15-16, 33-35, 65-68, 97-105; Proverbs 2:1-20; 3:1-6; 4:1-13; 2 Timothy 3:14-17).

B. *WITNESS of the Holy Spirit* (An *Inner Voice* known by all true children of God)

The Holy Spirit is able to *check* you inside as to whether something is of God or not. You must *NEVER* act on a doubtful impression, *especially* if it is accompanied by *haste*. God *leads* not *pushes!* Rush urgings are usually of the Enemy. There is never a feeling of *worry* or *fear* with the Voice of the Good Shepherd. His Voice is gentle, familiar-sounding, loving and leaves you with a sense of *spiritual uplift* and *rejoicing,* never fright (2 Timothy 1:7; John 10:3-5; 10:14, 16, 27-28; 3:29-30). Try spiritual impressions by the Word of God whenever you feel a sense of uneasiness or fear (Romans 8:9, 14; John 6:36; 14:17; 1 John 4:1-3, 13; 2:27; Colossians 1:9-10).

*TESTING THE SOURCE OF A "WITNESS" OR TEXT:* Only Biblical if they do *not:*

Can you think of a time in your life when God's answer to you was neither yes nor no, but wait?

1. Weaken *reliance* on *God Himself,* or the power of *self-decision* and volition.

2. *"Puff up"* (*"You* are being specially guided by God") or *crush* down into despair.

3. Create an *increasing compulsion* or web or error from the "guidance" verse or suggestion; Satan specializes in the out-of-context suggestion to ensnare a seeker.

4. Suggest *absurd* or *foolish* things, governing *food, dress, sex* or *manner of acting.*

5. Create a *slavish fear* of *unwillingness to act* lest you "fail to do God's will." In Scripture, men were guided WHILE GOING (John 4:3-4; Acts 8:4; 15:36; 16:6-7). When you do not *need* specific guidance, stay inside *Bible* precepts and ACT for God.

C. *WAITING on God (Listening to Him* in prayer and getting to know His Voice)

God has *three answers* in guidance: (1) *"Yes,"* (2) *"No"* and (3) *"Wait."* We cannot go *demanding* to God, and sometimes there must be delays. Our lives are bound up with others, and *God* must wait until they are ready often before giving *us* the go-ahead. This is the *most difficult* of all answers, but the most necessary. Here is the test of a love-slave (Psalm 62:1, 5; 33:20; 37:9; 25:5; 27:14; 40:1; 130:5; 37:7; Proverbs 20:22; 27:8; Isaiah 30:18; 8:17; 40:31; 49:23; Hosea 12:6; 1 Chronicles 28:9).

*The following method of guidance* combines most guidance principles into *three basic steps:*

1. *DIE to your own desires.* Take your own desires to God in prayer and "place them" to one side for the Lord to  crucify. *Pray* — "Lord Jesus, I take my *own* desires and put them — here; *I will to die in* my own mind to these things I most want to do. I want to wait for *Your* desire."

2. *RESIST the devil* by taking your stand in the Name of the Lord Jesus. Each child of God has a place of *power with Christ* the Head of the Church in heavenly places (Ephesians 1:17-23; 2:1-7). Standing in *His* authority,

drive back the Enemy's voice by quoting to him IN *FAITH* an appropriate Scripture. Like a sword-thrust, it will force him into retreat (James 4:7; 1 John 3:8b; 1 Peter 5:6-9). "Satan, in the Name of Jesus I *resist* your suggestions *as it is written* . . ." Do it clearly, simply and trusting that the power of Christ will back up your stand against him.

3. *There is now no voice left but the Voice of God.* By faith take the *mind of Christ* (1 Corinthians 2:16). Ask God if He will now be pleased to show you. Any *IMMEDIATE,* clear answer must be the Voice of God; take the *first,* definite impression. DO what He tells you to do. If there is *confusion,* it will come from *unbelief* by not taking the first impression. If nothing comes immediately — thank God for His answer of "Wait" and *praise* Him instead.

Describe the "process of elimination" whereby we can rest assured that the voice we are following is the Lord's.

---

## GROWING UP WITH GOD

---

There are *three basic stages* in growth from a child to an adult. They are summed up in the following chart to help you understand God's *timing* for the specific guidance areas of marriage and vocation in your life.

| AGE | CHARACTERISTICS |
|---|---|
| | CHILD — (BASICS) |
| To 6 years | ABILITIES — Learns to walk, talk, play, etc. |
| 6 — 12 | ACCUMULATION — Learns to read, write, spell. |
| | |
| | TEENAGER — (BUILDING) |
| 13 — 15 | ORGANIZATION — Builds physically, mentally. |
| 16 — 19 | ORIENTATION — Relates knowledge to world around. |
| | |
| | ADULT — (BELONGING) |
| 20 — 24 | EXPANSION — Mental maturity; adds advanced knowledge. |
| 25 — 29 | EXPERIENCE — Opportunity to add practice to theory. |
| | |
| 30 — on | TOTAL HARMONY — Personality, leadership, social harmony all fully tied together |

What kind of common-sense decisions should be a part of finding God's will for your vocation?

Since a *man's* best *learning* years lie between *20-24*, this is the best time to concentrate on a career. The years he can spare *before* marriage between 25-29 will be of extra value in giving him some practical experience in the field he has chosen. If God has led a *girl* into marriage; however, it is better for her to marry in the *earlier* years, since her career will be her husband and children. Experience has proved the most successful marriages in Western cultures are formed when the couple has at least left their teenage years; for a man, the best age is between *24-26;* for a woman, between *23-25.*

## GOD'S WORK FOR YOUR LIFE

The two *most important choices* you will ever make in life next to becoming a Christian are your *job* and your *marriage.* Most young people need guidance in both these fields. If you have just given your life to God, and are young, it is up to you to ask Him what He wants you to do in these fields. When our heart, or ultimate choice in life changes from serving ourselves to serving God, all decisions based on the old way of  living are subject to change. Sometimes we will have to *change* our careers, sometimes we will have to *give them up.* Use the following principles to help you find God's vocation for you:

1. *Follow your interests and abilities.* Find out what you do *well* and what you don't. Very often God gifts us in our early years with talents we can use for Him in later life.

2. *Have many interests.* Seek to be educated across the cultures, in science, in arts and in the humanities. Widen your field of hobbies, sports, past-times and talents. Learn to use as many things as possible and *keep learning.* God gives a good selection to use!

3. *Read about the things you like to do,* often and widely. Read *biographies,* and spend time early laying your hands on everything you can about the field you like most.

4. Get some *practical experience* early; take a part-time job, or talk to others about it.

5. *Be open to change*, but ask God: "Father, I like this particular work; I am interested, and feel I could do well in it. I will study it carefully and develop my talents in it for Your glory, but will you confirm to me the wisdom of this choice as I do? I say before You that if there is something else You want of me, I will happily do that, and give up this."

What kind of conditions would dictate the necessity of changing jobs upon becoming a Christian?

Should you *change* your *present* vocation if you have just been saved? Use these guides:

1. *Follow the path of maximum usefulness to God.* You have *many* possible callings; *one* is best under God at one time; observe the one that is most effective, and do that for Him.

2. *Remain in your calling* unless *specifically* directed otherwise (1 Corinthians 7:20-24). *No* job is to be thought "secular" if done to the Lord. Each can be a mission-field for the Lord; God uses all such occupations to invade society with His "salt," retarding its corruption.

3. *Surrender your job* if it is your god or breaks the law of love in any way. If it is *doubtful* it is *wrong* for you. All careers are expendable in the service of the Lord Jesus. Until you have done this from your heart, and are willing to be happy in anything, you are *not* in God's will. Though some Christians can keep their jobs (Acts 18:3) others must not (19:27).

4. *MINISTRY* is an ordinary part of your vocation, and not something special. However, if God is calling you into "full-time" ministry, meaning trusting God to supply your needs through the work of the Gospel alone, you will recognize His call in two major ways: (1) an *INCREASE in ministry* to a point where you cannot effectively handle two jobs at once and (2) an *all-consuming interest* in the work of preaching the Gospel. At such times, you can say, "Father, I cannot do both these jobs at once. I am willing to trust you to meet all my needs if You want to call me into this work "full-time." Then, if your ministry "dries up" simply go *back* to your ordinary job and serve God there. This can be a flexible balance.

"BE A SHOUTING CHRISTIAN — BUT NO LOUDER THAN YOU LIVE IT."

## GOD'S PARTNER FOR YOUR LIFE

Generally, take *no serious thought* of marriage until you are at least in your *twenties*. Give the *first fruits* of your life to God, and take the early years to develop both your career and ministry. If God has marriage in mind for you, He will open the door at the right time. You should concentrate on getting your *own* life prepared for His work and His choice. Most marriages fail because of some form of *pre-marital sex*  (from kids getting too deeply involved in dating, by seriously dating too young) and by *too-early marriages* (usually for the same reason). When you are ready for marriage, *emotionally*, *physically* and *spiritually* and feel God wants you to marry, look for: (1) *Born-again Christians* — the unsaved have different standards — *NO* DATING here; (2) Friends with *similar likings* and interests, and similar *callings* from the Lord; (3) *Similar spiritual levels*; true companionship is built in the Spirit of God; and it is key that the one you marry will be able to share your discoveries with God without boredom or lack of understanding. Look at his Dad or her Mom to help you see through romance to intelligent love! Think too of bills, house-cleaning, dishes, etc. And SEEK GOD VERY CAREFULLY before you choose!

## TESTS FOR TRUE LOVE

Do you *REALLY love* your boyfirend or girlfriend? Test out your date-life against this "John-Three-Sixteen" exam and see if you are REALLY "in love" with your friend:

*"For GOD . . ."*

All true loving is done FOR GOD. We do not know what it *means* to love until we can unselfishly choose the highest good for God and everyone else. Christian love takes place within the context of Christian witness and fellowship. Our love is to be holy, set apart for God's sacred usage. The Christian is in sympathy with God; the power that energizes Him, energizes them; and the love God has is holy. Love never breaks God's laws; it is *against sin* in all forms and of all kinds. Love hates selfishness everywhere, at all times. Honestly now: are you dating your friend FOR GOD'S GLORY?

What is the difference between biblical love and emotional romance?

### "... *SO* loved ..."

Real love is *special*. It can feel more deeply than any other kind of love, but it is *not* just a feeling; it is tremblingly alive to all the joys and pain of the world around it; but it is not just a sensitive compassion. Love is far *more* than feeling; it is also intelligent. No one who loves with God's love ever "falls" into it; that is *romance,* and while romantic feelings are beautiful and exciting, they are *not enough* to hold a marriage together.The love of God is primarily a WISE CHOICE for the highest happiness of the one loved. Love is an *action of the will;* love is something you *DO;* but it is *sure* and *careful.* A girl must promise the Lord that she will bring her boyfriends *to God* for His approval, and NOT use her feelings to justify her actions. A guy must be sure that his primary motive in dating a girl is to bring her *closer to Jesus.* Feelings are strong in the young, but you must understand that feelings can come from ANY person who is interesting to you or attractive, who shows some interest and affection for you. *Enjoy* the feelings; but do not let your heart run ahead of your mind and will. Love takes its time; it thinks before it commits itself. If you trust your feelings you may be hurt very deeply. Trust *God.*

### "... the WORLD ..."

Love wants to include *everybody* in its happiness; love has a *great heart.* If you are in God's love, you will want the whole world to share it. Do you love with this love? You can tell counterfeit affection; it is selfish; it wants to keep *to* itself. True love does not try to control other's lives exclusively; it is not envious or worried when the one loved spends time with others. It leaves the one it loves free to make their own choices. True love cares for *all* creatures and does not willingly inflict pain. It is not partial to only a select few; it is color-blind. Do you mind *sharing* your love with others; do you want to tell the world about the one you love? If you are envious, you do not love with God's love. If you cannot *witness* or *pray* with your date, you don't love them.

" . . . that He GAVE . . ."

True love always wants to *give gifts.* Love works out ways to make the other happy all the time. It would help *everyone*

the same way if it could; but it does whatever it can. Love, from its very nature will *deny itself* to promote a greater good whenever it is wise to do this. You can *give* without loving, but you cannot *love* without giving! Love is first concerned with' God's will, then *others'* needs; it only *then* thinks of its own. Love

does not *use* the other person as a tool for personal pleasure or popularity.

" . . . His ONLY-begotten Son . . ."

There is always a *cost* to true love. Love cost God His Son; love cost Jesus His life. Love means the willingness to *give up everything* for the one loved. When love prevails, things are chosen for their *true values,* and not just for some personal gain. Love counts the cost, but does not keep on counting it. Now, how much do you love *God?* Do you love enough to say goodbye to someone who has grown in your affections if this relationship begins to interfere with God's will for you? Do you have that unreserved trust in God that leads you to say in happy surrender, "Your will be done, Father"? Until you have learned absolute surrender to God, you will be a stranger to true unselfish love.

Because love always involves a whole person, and marriage is a mental-spiritual-physical blending of two lives, when two people love each other in God's way and God's time, there will be a *mutual surrender* to each other. And this is the problem with "free love," it isn't *love;* and it isn't *free!* If love means a total sharing, how can you give *everything* to the one you *really* love if you have already given away part of yourself to someone else? Purity is not replaceable, except through the forgiveness of God, and there will always be scars. When you spend, through sex, a part of your innermost being on someone you are not really committed to in marriage, you are not free to *keep* it for someone you really care about. And when you do not have everything of yourself to give, your love cannot be full and total.

What are the advantages for a single person in the ministry?

### "... that WHOSOEVER BELIEVES in Him ...'"

Love involves *absolute trust.* To love fully and deeply you must trust *yourself* and trust the other person wholly. Love has *faith* in the loved one's character and integrity. Love hardly notices when others do it wrong; love is able to live with another person's failures and weaknesses because love knows the other person for what they really *are,* and is willing to *be* known for its own true character. Love does not seek to *impress,* or *pretend.* "When you love someone, you will be loyal to them no matter what the cost; you will always believe in them, always expect the best of them, and always stand your ground in defending them" (1 Corinthians 13:7 — Living Letters). Love holds on when hurt or misunderstood; it still remains even when it is not returned. Do you have this kind of love for your friend?

And now, will you trust wholly *in God* that He will bring the right one at the right time for you? God loves YOU! He *cares* about your happiness. Will you give Him that unreserved trust so you will be perfectly happy with whatever God does?

In *Paul's day,* some young men who had been greatly used of God wrote, asking if they were being fair to their sweethearts by putting off marriage so they could give their full time and attention to God's work. Paul replied in effect that since the chance for Christian work and witness was limited that we were to live as loose to our world and families as possible because of the eternal value of God's work. Since married people could not shirk their home responsibilities.(1 Timothy 5:8) they would be tied up with important duties in their families, and these are much more limiting than the unmarried realize. They become a distraction to some of God's work, but they are not to be neglected.

299

*Avoid marriage* — at least while you are *young*. For some there will be the high calling of a permanently *unmarried* life; there are some kinds of Christian service which are open in special degree to the single worker. The disciple of Jesus may choose to forego his or her right to marriage in order to give more time to the work. This voluntary vow should result from the desire to wholly give himself or herself to ministry  to and for the Lord, and a special sense of *God's guidance* in the matter. If God calls, He will give the needed grace. To be married is His gift to *most*, but to be *not* married is His gift to some. Marriage is good, but if not marrying is equally possible for you, then; and *only* then, is celibacy better. Paul had good practical reasons why he could wish every Christian had the gift God gave him — of being contentedly and happily single (1 Corinthians 7:1-2, 6-9, 17; Matthew 19:10-12).

"Blessed are they which do HUNGER and THIRST after RIGHTEOUSNESS; for they shall be filled" (Matthew 5:6).

# SIMON THE ZEALOT
## (WHO FOLLOWED WITH FIRE)

"The Kingdom of Heaven suffereth violence; and the violent take it by force."

Matthew 11:12

What would Jesus' choosing a man like Simon indicate as to the spirit we are to possess for Christ?

**PHASE:** 5 .. *Building "Go" into the Gospel*
**SECTION:** 9 .. *"S" For Seeking and Finding the Invisible God*
**MATERIAL:** .. *Master Keys To Combat Lukewarmness and Laziness*

Cunning and desperate, he has hidden in caves, crossed rivers and climbed mountains. His enemy is uneasy. The little band to which he belongs will fight to the last. Already the world felt the impact of these Zealots. Rome mobilizes legions but this intense guerilla warfare cannot be checked. The enemy can no longer freely travel its conquered roads. With burning passion, *Simon the Zealot* believed his cause was just and  would rather die for right that would one day triumph than live under wrong.

*Zealot* — *a word of fire. Zealot* — a man who burned with intensity born of devotion to a cause. And *Simon* — Jesus chose YOU for His army!

---

## HATEFUL HALF-WAY

---

"I know your works that you are neither cold *nor* hot; I wish you were one or the other! But since you are merely lukewarm, I will vomit you out of My mouth!" (Revelation 3:15-16).

*These are the words of Jesus to the majority of professing Christians today.*

*Something tragic has happened to our generation.* There are thousands of churches. Members are added yearly. Evangelistic campaigns are conducted regularly, and many decisions are recorded. Business goes on as usual in the hands of pastors, teachers and travelling evangelists. Missionaries, still itinerate, showing slides and raising funds. Christian organizations proliferate. Churches regularly contribute to social causes. Everything seems smooth, well-oiled and highly functional. And God is *sick of it!*

302

What is *really* happening? The church has never been such a *minority*. The secular world has laughed it off completely as a "black number" in a modern world. Historians call this the *"post*-Christian era." Revitalized religions from the East have invaded Western culture with a vengeance, collecting hundreds of thousands of adherents. No one but a struggling few *seriously* believe that spiritual awakening can come again to the nations. The darkness of occultism has captured the interest of the young who once walked forwards in camps and conventions to spend their lives for God in missions. The hundreds of "decisions" made annually seem to have little effect in society. Youth alternately *mock* the church, *curse* it or *cry* over it. And *God* cries!

What are the contributing factors to the present low state of spirituality in certain segments of the church today?

*One hundred years ago, revival swept America.* Thousands of souls entered the Kingdom of God under the searching sermons of a humble servant of Christ, Charles G. Finney. It has been estimated that over *half a million* were converted to God as a direct result of his ministry, and that by conservative count over *80%* remained true to Christ to the day of their death without backsliding or falling by the wayside. *Social reforms* swept the land like cleansing fire. Bars, saloons, dance-halls and theatres closed down for good. Strangers entering towns invaded by God's Spirit were struck down in the streets with conviction. Hearts that had never been stirred were broken by the Word of God, melted like wax in the furnace of the Holy One's visitation. God moved across the land like a storm, and men bowed and surrendered like wheat before the wind.

*The years have passed.* Century 21 is almost here; yet we have never seen a voice raised strong enough to *stir the church* and *shake the world.* A wave of watery *churchianity,* militant *proselytism* and unintelligent *evangelicalism* seem to be the only forms of apparent "conversion" confronting a generation hungry for reality. The church world is fast drifting into an "easy-believism" salvation Christ *would not recognize.* Lest He be grieved Who bought the Church with His blood, men who profess salvation must examine anew God's own conditions and signs of true conversion.

We can go *forward* or *backward,* but we *cannot* stand still. We can go forward in faith, experimenting with every new tool of technology and media we can get our hands on. We

Why is the
"status-quo"
mentality so
deadly to the
Christian
Church?

can go *forward* to meet the challenge of the most sophisticated, cultured, worldly-wise, un-impressible civilization of
all time that is rocked with the largest problems, heartbreaks
and degradations of history; we can and *must* go forward to
communicate. But it is time we went *backward* too; back to
the *Bible,* back to the *early church;* back to their *message* and
back to their *God.* It is *high time* we came back to God. We
know it. The world knows it. And *God* — God COMMANDS
it.

## WHAT HINDERS GOD?

The early church evangalized *entire cities* at a time. There
were so many conversions that pagan religions began to die
out. For every *hundred* Christians that died in the jaws of
beasts or as living torches lighting Rome's ghastly arena, *three
hundred spectators* gave their lives to the martyrs' Christ. *All
Asia Minor* heard the Gospel in just *two years* (Acts 19:10)
*without* the benefit of radio, television specials or witnessing
films. The church did more in *that* generation than our present one could do in a thousand years. What in the *world* is
wrong with us?

*WE* hinder God. We have been so busy collecting *quantities*
of converts that we have forgotten that Jesus *never* worked
with crowds. He called only a *few.* He was primarily interested in *quality.* Thousands of others listened and *left*
when He did (John 6:66). His was no easy road! He put up
standards so high that it cost a man his *life* to follow. But
those who paid the price shook their world and turned it
upside down (Acts 17:6). God is *not interested* in people
who will only go half-way with Him. The *lukewarm must go*
before anything happens. Multitudes have gone to Hell
already because of the hypocrisy and rampart selfishness in
"churchy" lives. God would rather have a man profess
atheism and *live* it than a man profess Christianity and not
live it. We have seen quite enough of the people who have
made "Jesus Saviour, but not Lord" who are "saved although
unsurrendered," who are "following Christ," but still serving
themselves. The *world* has had enough of religious professors
who call licence "grace," holiness "extremism," sin "weakness" — and who offer *this* hypocrisy as *Bible salvation!*

Because so few understand the nature of *true* conversion, they often reject their own *counterfeit* experience assuming that God has failed and the Christian life is not real. So many believe they are Christians when in fact they are *not*. This manual contains two of Finney's searching messages on "Counterfeit Conversion," the "People-Pleasers" (JZ- ), an adaptation of the message on *"Religion of Public Opinion"* and this sermon on *"Legal Religion."* Both have been condensed, simplified and paraphrased to adopt them to oday's vocabulary. They may shock and shake you; they were *made* to! Few men have preached messages so relevant as this; if your own faith is real, it will stand this examination. If not you will have time to do something about it before you meet God (2 Corinthians 13:5; John 5:39).

What is the difference between self-love and selfishness?

1. *The natural state of all men before true conversion is wholly selfish.*

*Selfishness* is *supremely seeking one's own good because* it is his own. There is a difference between *selfishness* and self-

*love.* Self-LOVE is simply the *inbuilt desire for happiness* and *dread of misery.* This is *natural,* and *essential.* It is *not* sin. But *selfishness* is the desire of happiness and dread of misery *above all other's rights,* including *God's.* He who is selfish places his own care above any interests of greater value, such as the glory of God and the highest good of the universe. And every unconverted man knows that all other such men *are* selfish. He conducts all his dealings with others on this basis. *Scripture* calls selfishness as *SIN*, and pictures it as a *wrong choice of life,* or purpose, a wrong *ultimate motive* of the heart(1 Kings 11:9-11; 15:3; 2 Chronicles 12:14; Psalm 28:3; 66:18; 78:37; 95:10; Jeremiah 17:9-10; Ezekiel 14:2-3; 18:30-32; Matthew 5:27-30; 9:4; 13:15; Mark 3:5; 7:18-23; Luke 21:34; Acts 8:21 (18:24); Romans 2:4-6; Hebrews 3:15-17).

2. *A man who lives in a converted state is not supremely selfish, but loving, or benevolent.*

A true child of God *does not live to please himself.* Benevolence (good-willing) is *unselfishly choosing the good of*

305

**What are the evidences of a true biblical conversion?**

*others.* This is *God's* state of mind. God IS love (1 John 4:16,8). He unselfishly chooses the highest good of His universe. This love, or benevolence, forms the *whole* of His character. *Everything God does* is an expression of His love; it sums up His every action and is the motive behind His every choice. God is purely and unselfishly loving. He does not make His creatures happy just to promote His own joy, but because He *loves* their happiness and chooses this for its own sake. He does feel happy Himself in bringing them joy, but He does not do it to gratify Himself. And this love is *holiness.* It is the *only basic law* God requires of men (Matthew 22:36-40; Mark 12:28-34; Luke 10:25-28; Romans 13:8-10; Galatians 5:14; 1 Timothy 1:5; James 2:8-10).

*A true child of God is in this way like God.* This does not mean that no one is truly converted until they are purely and perfectly loving as God is; but that their *prevailing choice of life,* and *supreme purpose,* is benevolent. They sincerely seek the good of others for its *own sake,* not just to make themselves happy or escape punishment. Just as certainly as the converted man yields *obedience* to God's law — "You shall love the Lord your God with all your heart and soul and strength, and your neighbour as yourself" — just as certainly as he is *like God,* he is *benevolent,* and a *true Christian* (1 John 4:7; 1 Peter 1:16; Jude 21; Romans 13:10; 1 John 5:3; John 15:9-14; 17:14-26; 1 John 4:16-17).

3. *True conversion is an ultimate change from a state of supreme selfishness to benevolence.*

It is a change in the *HEART,* or *ultimate purpose* of life, not a mere change in the *way of living.* A man may change

his *outward actions,* and yet live for the same *purpose.* It is the intent, or design of his actions, that give them character, and not just the means used to carry out that intent or purpose. *Conversion* is a *change* in the *whole life end,* from serving self to serving God and others. The true Chrisitan chooses as *his* goal the glory of God and the good of His Kingdom. He chooses this goal for its *own* sake, because he sees it as the greatest good, above even his own individual happiness at times. He is not *indifferent* to his own happiness, but he prefers God's glory because it is the greater good. He chooses others happiness according to their real importance as far as he is able to value it. He no longer lives for *himself*; he begins to live in love for God and others. This change is total and ultimate, involving the whole personality (Matthew 6:22-24; 7:17-20; 12:33-35; John 3:19-21; Romans 6:16-18; 2 Corinthians 5:17; Titus 1:15; James 3:10-11).

What are the two basic attitudes out of which submission can spring?

## HOPE AND FEAR — OR LOVE?

There are only *two basic principles* of Divine or human government — *fear* and *confidence*. All obedience springs from one of these two. In one case people obey from hope of reward (for themselves) or fear of punishment (to themselves); this type of fear-obedience is the essence of the *selfish man's* life. The other class obey from *love* and *confidence* in the one in authority. Consider two children. One obeys his Dad  because he trusts him. He has faith which works by love. The other yields only an outward obedience from hope or fear, because he does not trust him. So are the lives of the *true saint* and the *counterfeit*. The true saint has confidence or faith in God that leads him to obey and wholly submit himself into His hands. The counterfeit, like the devil, has only a *partial* faith and partial submission. He believes and trembles (James 2:19). So a person may believe that Christ came to save sinners, and on *that* ground may submit to be saved for his own safety, *without* submitting to be *led* and *ruled* by Him. His submission is made only on the selfish condition that *he* will be happier. It is never with that unreserved trust in God's character and love that leads His true child to say — "Thy will be done." The counterfeit's faith is the *religion of fear*. It is the religion of *law,* and not of *love.* It is totally selfish, and totally non-Christian.

You can tell a man or woman in the religion of fear. Some of their characteristics are:

307

What are the
evidences
of the
counterfeit
convert in
relationship
to prayer
and Bible
study?

1. *They serve God like taking medicine.*

The counterfeit convert obeys God, not because he *loves* Him, but because he hopes to get something *good out of it for himself.* The true child of God delights in doing God's will. When Christ and the Gospel is loved for their own sake, there is no weariness or struggle in serving. His commandments are not grievous (1 John 5:3; Matthew 11:30; 23:4; Luke 11:46). The man in the religion of fear reads the Bible and prays because he knows he *should;* it would not do to say you are a Christian and not read the Bible! But they do not *enjoy* it; they never go to prayer meetings unless it is absolutely necessary, or unless it will be of some benefit for them. When they *do* go, they are cold, dull, listless and lifeless, and glad when it is over. Their only enjoyment in religion is chiefly one of *anticipation;* they hope they will be happy in the next world, but never enjoy the service of God in *this* one. The true child of God *already* enjoys His peace; heaven has begun already in his soul. He has eternal life *now,* not merely the *prospect* of it. He has the very feelings of heaven in his life; he anticipates joys higher in *degree* only, not in different *kind,* in heaven itself. He is not waiting until he dies to taste the thrill of eternal life (John 1:12; Revelation 3:20; John 11:25-26; 14:23-27; 15:3-11; Romans 5:1; 14:17; 15:13; 8:1-17; Mark 12:28-34; 1 John 3:2).

2. *They do what they have to, not what they really want to.*

The counterfeit convert is moved by his *convictions,* not his *affection.* His "faith" is the religion of fear. He is *driven* by *warnings,* not *drawn* by the *love of God* (John 10:3-5; 2 Timothy 1:7; John 10:14, 16, 27-28; 3:29-30). He regards the law of God for fear that God will pass him by if he does not, but he does not *LOVE* to do what God requires in His law. He is filled with the *spirit of fear,* lest he make the wrong move or do the wrong thing. God is not a loving and compassionate heavenly *Father* to him, but a stern, exacting taskmaster (1 Peter 2:7; Hebrews 10:7).

He is more or less *strict* in religion according to what he knows to be right, but does not have a *heart* to do it; the more he knows, the more miserable he becomes (Matthew 23:23). Here is a key difference. The true saint *PREFERS* obedience; the counterfeit *PURPOSES* or intends it, but usually *fails* to do so. He knows he should, like Paul before his conversion (Romans 7) but fails, because his heart is not in it (Ezekiel 33:31-32; Matthew 21:28-31; Luke 6:45-46).

3. *A counterfeit convert has a basic motivation of fear, not love.*

Why does the true convert not have to continually reinforce his faith with hopes of heaven?

He is not only afraid of *hell* but of *punishment, judgment* and *disgrace* in men's eyes. He still *lives* for *himself, thinks* of himself and seeks his *own* happiness and safety supremely. These fears keep him *outwardly* moral. He keeps up a kind of obedience that is formal, heartless, loveless and completely worthless (Matthew 15:1-20; 23:4, 13-33; Galatians 4:3-12; 5:4-6).

His happiness in religion is only his *hope* of *heaven* or *reward.* Most of his joys are those of anticipation, because he is not really happy doing right and loving God here and now. This is not his purpose, but the *way* he has chosen to try to get his *own* happiness. When his hope of heaven is strengthened, he enjoys religion a great deal. But the true saint is happy serving God *anywhere* in *anything.* He is not interested in saving his *own* life because he has *lost* it (Mark 8:34-35; Luke 9:23-24; 12:24-26; 14:26). He would even be happy in *hell* IF he could do God's will there; for he would still be doing the things in which his happiness consists (Exodus 32:30-32; Mark 8:35; 10:45; Romans 9:3). If the duties of faith are not *joy* to you, and your happiness rests on the strength of your hopes, you have no *true* faith — it is all selfishness (Philippians 2:21; 2 Timothy 3:2a, 5). This does not mean that true saints do not *enjoy* their hopes — but it is no great thing with them. They think very little about them. Their thoughts are taken up with God and saving others (Matthew 25:31-46; 1 Corinthians 10:23-33; Romans 14:5-8; Philipians 3:3-14).

4. *They are more afraid of punishment than sin.*

The counterfeit keeps *on* sinning because he does not really hate SIN — only *punishment* for it. The true child of God is more afraid of *sin* than *punishment.* He does not ask — "If I do this, what will happen to me?," but feels, like *Joseph* — "How can I do this wicked thing and sin against

309

God?" (Genesis 39:7-9; Ezekiel 8:12; Job 31:33-34; Romans 2:16-29; 2 Timothy 2:19). The counterfeit keeps committing the same sin by convincing himself that God will forgive him eventually, and they can always repent of it *afterwards*.

Because the counterfeit lives in known sin, he likes to hear sermons on the security of the believer, on God's grace and mercy, on His longsuffering, His only trouble is that he does not realise the majority of these scriptures do *not* apply to him, because he is *not saved at all!* Proof positive of this is his *love of sin* more than *God;* he likes to be soothed along in it, not shocked *out* of it, *comforted,* not *challenged, assured,* not *examined.* His conscience bothers him so much already that he cannot stand sermons that throw further light on his true state (John 3:19-20; 9:39-41; 12:44-48; Matthew 13:40-43).

His *greatest blessings* come out of hearing sermons on *saints who sinned.* He fondly imagines God exposes such tragic failures to set *precedents* for those who would follow His Son! Instead of such stories *breaking their hearts.,* that men of God should fall so *low;* instead of accepting this as a message to watch and pray — to keep under the body lest they should become a castaway — they actually *enjoy* it! They see *themselves* in the saint's sin; they feel strengthened, not shocked, *glad* and not *grieved.* If their own souls can be temporarily assured, they care very little what happens to the rest of the world. They like sermons that give them a licence to go on in sin. They prefer ministers who can preach with conviction on *abstractions.* Listen to them pray, and they basically pray for their *own salvation* (Luke 18:9-14; John 9:31-34).

### 5. *They have a spirit of GET instead of GIVE.*

True Christians *enjoy* giving and helping others more than being helped by others because they love. Their hearts are set on the highest good, and their deepest, sheerest joy is to be able to do it (Matthew 20:28; Mark 12:42-44; Luke 3:11; 2 Corinthians 12:9-13; Hebrews 12:2). *Counterfeit* converts are always looking for ways to get from others whatever they can. Especially is this true in daily *business.* If selfishness rules our conduct there with men, as sure as God rules we are selfish before Him. A man in the religion of fear finds it *hard* to give anything of HIS to God. He may have to, to keep his reputation; but it bothers him no end (Luke 6:30-35; 16:11-16; Matthew 25:41-45; 1 John 3:16-17). The counterfeit never enjoys *self-denial*. If a man sets his heart on anything, he enjoys everything he saves for it and the more he saves from *other* things to give to this, the more he is pleased. The phony finds it hard to give to Christian work; it is easy to

What does the counterfeit fear above all else?

see that his *heart* is not in it. It gives him a pain in the neck to give to God. He cannot understand the joy of unselfish giving, to advance God's kingdom, because it drains resources from his own little world where he rules as king (Deuteronomy 15:7-11; Matthew 10:9; 13:44-46; 19:29-30; Luke 12:13-34; 16:19-25; 18:18-30).

6. *Their prayers and cares for others are born out of fear for themselves.*

The counterfeit is chiefly afraid of hell *himself,* and when he is strongly convicted he is afraid that others may go there too. The *true* saint prays for the sinner because he has a sense of the *evil* of sin which sinners commit; the counterfeit because he has a fear of the terrors of hell. The phony prays for a sinner's *safety;* the Christian prays for safety *from sin.* Christians feel compassion for the sinner, but *grieved anger* on God's behalf for the sinner's rebellion. The man in the religion of fear feels more sorry for the sinner than for God because he *shares his sin* and *sympathizes with him.* A counterfeit can never understand how God could allow a loved one to go to hell. They feel more for the "loved one" than for the God whose heart the rebellious "loved one" has *broken.* Christ's words commanding supreme love of His followers over all other earthly loves have no meaning to them. They do not supremely love Him; they love *themselves* and everything connected with their own happiness (Matthew 6:33; 22:36-40; 10:37-39; Luke 14:25-26).

It is not extravagant to say that the religion I have described appears to be that of a very *large majority* in the church. To say the least, it is to be feared that a *majority* of professing Christians are of this description. To say this is neither unloving nor censorious.

311

Why is sin, as a *manner of life*, always referred to in the past tense in the New Testament?

This religion is *radically defective*. There is *nothing* of true Christianity in it. It differs from Christianity as much as the *Pharisees* differed from *Christ* — as much as the Gospel faith differs from legal religion — as much as the *faith of love* differs from the *religion of fear*. Now, let me ask you — to which of these two classes do you belong? Is Christ the center of your life, or are you trying to fit Him in for your own happiness?

If you have *failed* this test, go *back to Judas* and *really* give your life to God! If you pass, then you may consider the following three rules for keeping the glow in your Christian life. Follow these three simple principles and you will stay "on fire" to witness for the Lord.

---

## THREE KEYS FOR KEEPING THE GLOW

---

1. *We must be CLEAN* — Continually turn away from all obvious sinful and harmful indulgences, confessing and being forgiven and cleansed from every sin. Sin as a *manner of life* is always referred to in the *past* tense in the Christian (1  Corinthians 6:11; Titus 3:3). The true child of God must take up his cross *daily* and follow Jesus (Luke 9:23) and be able to say with Paul — "I am dying daily" (1 Corinthians 15:31). There is no true salvation without repentance from all known sin at the point of conversion, but sin has a subtle way of working itself into our hearts again unless great care is taken; and Satan paints a pretty picture of the past. It is often so easy to go back because we have Christ's "treasure in earthen vessels." Such a state of retreat brings defeat in which effective witness is impossible. God directs us to "cleanse ourselves from all filthiness of the flesh and spirit, perfecting holiness in the fear of God" (2 Corinthians 7:1). We have His promise — "If any man sin, we have an advocate with the Father, Jesus Christ the righteous" (1 John 2:1) and "If we confess our sins, He is faithful and just to forgive us our sins, and to cleanse us from all unrighteousness" (1 John

1:9). Without this daily cleansing, witness will be worthless. Is it not highly embarrassing to say the least, to plead with a sinner to give up his sin when we are holding on to some as well? Salvation is salvation FROM (not *in*) sin, and we have better show it in our lives.

For the Christian, what is the subtle danger of wasted time?

2. *We must be UNCHOKED* — We cannot afford to waste time. The sin of *wasted time* has trapped more Christian people than any other sin today. Satan knows no sold-out young man or woman of God would ever deliberately do some gross sin. Knowing this, he works the quiet way — he persuades them to waste a little time on the pretence of *relaxation* or legitimate entertainment. You cannot tell a vision with too much television; the harmonies of heaven are too often drowned out by the hard rock of the casual transistor radio; many a soul has gone to hell as a Christian read his comics; many a young man or woman has gone down the moral drain with too much time on their hands! Every Christian must dare to *discard* all questionable and unprofitable activities for the warfare of soul-winning! "No man that warreth entangleth himself with the affairs of this life, that he may please Him who has chosen him to be a soldier" (2 Timothy 2:4). Many things do not *seem* sinful in themselves, but we may find ourselves so hung up in them that time is crowded out for Christ. This is what Jesus meant by the parable of the sower — "The *cares* of this world, and the deceitfulness of riches; and the *lusts of other things entering in* choke the word; and it becomes unfruitful" (Mark 4:19).

The *use* we make of our lives in Christ is largely up to *us*. There are all kinds of vessels in a large house — gold, silver, wood and clay. If we are willing to purge (thrust out, clean out) *ourselves* from what is unworthy or unclean, we shall be vessels unto *honor*, set apart, meet—highly useful for the master's use and prepared unto every good work (2 Timothy 2:21). We must *cut off* every excess weight, put *crash priority* on the things that count most and conserve the cream of our time and energy for that special task Jesus has set us.

3. *We must be CHRIST-DEPENDENT* — *Jesus* is our power, our strength, our wisdom. Salvation is an impossible thing — but with God all things are possible! Jesus said — "Without *Me*, you can do *nothing*" (John 15:5). Where can

What is the
great
distinction
between
love and
legalism?

you get the wisdom necessary to lead souls out of darkness into light? In Him is hid all the treasures of wisdom and knowledge (Colossians 2:3). Hebrews 12:1-2 sums up the secret of spiritual victory: "Let us lay aside every weight (be *unchoked*) and the sin which doth so easily beset us (be *clean*), especially from that particular form of sin you find the strongest temptation to) and let us run (steadfastly, determinedly, doggedly keep ON running) the race lying before us   LOOKING UNTO JESUS, the Author and Finisher of our faith!" This is simple to *say*, very difficult to *learn*, but astonishing in power. *Jesus Himself* is the secret of power over sin; Jesus *Himself* — His love — His Presence — His power! You can't fight sin in your own strength. The more you struggle with it, the *greater* its power grows over you. But you may look to Jesus and experience instant deliverance! *No definition of power over sin will work for you until you learn to extract power from your Saviour.* LOOKING UNTO JESUS!

---

## OBEYING THE COMMANDER

*OBEYING GOD IS NOT:*

  *TRAGIC — "I HAVE to!"*

What does it mean to "be perfect" as our Father in heaven? Many sad saints are *grimly determined* to be holy.

Jesus said, "Be of good cheer!" (John 16:33). The commandments of God are not grievous! (1 John 5:3). God never intended you to always keep the RULES in mind. This is both impossible and unnecessary. Moral law is the rule of action to will the highest good of God in every situation, but in PRACTICE, goodness is usually *spontaneous*. Your GOAL is the GOOD OF GOD and His Universe, NOT the law that defines it! The first is love — the second, *legalism*. Loving God is a *"want to,"* not a *"have to."* You can't LOVE God because He commands you to — God doesn't expect a love from a sense of duty or obedience, but obedience and duty *out of* love. GOD HIMSELF is our goal, NOT the rules for getting to Him.

*MAGIC* — *"I* am supernaturally made *ABLE* to."

*Holiness is not a miracle* in the sense of something out of the usual, strange, beyond reason or natural laws. Holiness is God's expected standard for the human race. It is amazing to discover that God still cares for us despite our sin, but this is only miraculous in the sense of "I wonder *why?*" Holiness is a CHOICE — living for God because you WILL to do so. God calls you in love — you respond. He doesn't "wave a wand" and you "grow a halo!" No "black root of sin" needs weeding from your heart before you are able to obey the Lord. Holiness is simply *obeying the light you have* from a *right intention* of heart. God expects you to do what He knows you CAN do. Obey, and He reveals more of His love and light, tuning your love out of the world to Himself.

God's perfection is not *freedom from mistake.* Fully obeying God is NOT inability to sin — there is no virtue in "not being able to" sin. Our judgment will never be infallible; we do not know as God knows, all the facts. Man is free — able to sin or love God. Not *CHOOSING* to sin is different from not being *able* to sin. He asks only that we live up to the light we have from a right heart-motive.

*OBEYING GOD DOESN'T MEAN YOU MUST BE:*

1. *EXCLUDED*

God has no plan for hermits. The Lord Jesus didn't ask us to be IN the world and OF the world (*live* sinner), OF the world, but not IN the world (*dead* sinner) or even OUT of the world and not of the world (a DEAD Christian). He asked us to be *IN* the world, but not *OF* the world!

2. *EXHAUSTED*

God doesn't ask the same *knowledge* or *faith* of us we could have had if we hadn't been lazy or messed up our past so much. The love law doesn't require that we love Him as much as we COULD have if we had spent more time with

Ask some of your friends to give you their definition of holiness and see if any of them agree with the definition as found on this page.

315

Describe
what it
means to
have your
mind
"stayed on
Jesus."

Him. Faith is an act of will based on obedience to our grasp of Truth. As we know God more, our faith is greater. He only asks your whole trust and confidence in what YOU KNOW of Truth *NOW*. You can't believe what you don't know! God asks us to use all the strength, knowledge and faith we have NOW *to the extent it is needed* for His glory. He asks no more or less than we have to give.

*God doesn't always have to be DIRECTLY in your thoughts.* Your mind is a tool. When it is needed for daily work, you don't lose spirituality because at the time you are not thinking of the Lord! You can concentrate on geometry, not Jesus, and *still* be holy. God only asks that SUPREME PREFERENCE be given Him when He needs your attention. Revival excitement must be SHORT or people will become insane. We cannot think constantly of two things at once.

### 3. EXCITED

Revival Christianity is NOT excitement. It is *Christians obeying God.* God doesn't ask us to use ALL our powers of

will, thought and feeling equally for everything. Holiness is not using to the utmost EVERYTHING you have *all* the time, but using ALL THAT IS NEEDED *WHEN* it is needed. This varies with our health, fitness, business needing to be done and circumstances. "All your heart, mind, soul and strength" means FULL CONSECRATION to the TASK IN HAND. Life alters its demands. God expects you to respond as fully and wholly as the job in hand requires.

God doesn't take away *natural feelings*. Even HE gets angry when men abuse His beautiful world. Loving God is loving DESPITE injury and hurt. It is CHOICE TO WILL GOOD despite feelings of being wronged.

*Perfect love* will bring perfect *peace*, but this is NOT always quietness of mind. Bible peace is a *satisfied conscience* and a *lack of agitation* or *worry*. The Lord Jesus was always at peace, but He was NOT always *calm*. He wept, was very angry at times, felt deep agony at Gethsemane and Calvary.

316

He was NOT always happy; (Finney said "A very happy Christian is not usually a very useful one.") – but He WAS always *holy*. You too, may carry in your heart sorrow for a suffering world. But obeying God will keep you in perfect peace (Isaiah 26:3; 32:17; John 16:33; Philippians 4:7).

Can you think of any appetite that is currently exercising more control over you than you know it should?

## POWER WITH GOD

There is nothing more "tastefully" connected with the sense world than *FOOD* and man's enjoyment of it. Yet APPETITE felled *Adam* in the garden, and desire for food tempted *Jesus* in the desert! *Esau's* sin was nothing more than allowing appetite to overrule his reason, and for a bowl of beans he sold his birthright. Esau had not learned physical control. Food is one of the strongest desires, and can be a most  deceptively deadly enemy of power with God. When body appetites rule reason, when there is a lack of self-control, man becomes earthly and sensual, effectively boosting physical drive to a point where spirit rule is impossible.

Food is *not* the most basic essential in life. The greatest bodily need is *AIR*. The second is not food, but *water*. Third is not food, but *sleep!* Food comes *fourth,* but in thousands of Christians lives it seems to be put first. Too much food clogs the system. To over-eat is a *sin of waste* and a *sin against the body,* shortening the physical life and dulling the spiritual. If you are not its *master,* YOU are its *slave!*

*Little is said about FASTING today.* Yet there are 55 references in the Bible about fasts and fasting, and it was considered in the early church as one of the pillars of the faith. All men greatly used of God in scripture held strict control of their diets.

*Elijah, Moses* and *John the Baptist* lived on scanty rations and all fasted long periods. *Jesus* Himself fasted forty days before His miracle ministry began. He was reproached by His

Why has
fasting
become an
almost
forgotten
practice
today?

His disciples for not eating. The apostle *Paul* said he was "in fastings often" (2 Corinthians 11:27), beginning his ministry with a three-day fast. Jesus said when He was taken away "THEN shall they (His disciples) fast"! (Luke 5:35). *The love of eating destroys self-control.* It is a last-days sign (Matthew 24:38; Luke 21:34) — before God destroyed Noah's world, people were "EATING AND DRINKING, marrying and giving in marriage" — *over-stressing* basic physical drives.

Now eating is not *in itself* SIN! But *too much* of, and the wrong *kind of* food, is harmful. Medically, improper eating habits are the *greatest single cause* of sickness, ill-health and early death. Man is the shortest lived earth creature (comparatively speaking). If he lived eight times his normal growth period as animals do, his average age would be 192! Man eats too much and too many wrong things.

"The *appetite for food* is perhaps more frequently than any other the cause for back-sliding and powerlessness in the church today. God's command is 'whether you *eat* or *drink*, of whatsoever you do, do all to the glory of God." Christians forget this and eat and drink to please *themselves.* They consult their appetites instead of the laws of life and health. More persons are snared by their tables than the church is aware of. A great many people who avoid alcohol altogether will drink tea and coffee that in both quality and quantity violate every law of life and health. Show me a gluttonous professor, and I will show you a *backslider*" (*Charles Finney*).

---

## DRUNK ON FOOD?

---

Those who have not learned discipleship may laugh to justify their love for food. The fact remains that ALMOST EVERY GREAT MAN OF GOD and every great *move* of God was born on the wings of FASTING AND PRAYER. History is starred with men who fasted — Luther, Spurgeon, Wesley, Whitefield, Booth and Finney.

*Why does the Bible regard gluttony as such a serious sin?* In some cases *death* was the penalty of a lust for food!

(Numbers 11; Deuteronomy 21:20-21). A glutton is a rebel from the cross of sacrifice.

"They are enemies of the cross of Christ — whose end is destruction, whose *god is their belly,* and whose glory is their shame; who mind earthly things" (Philippians 3:18-19). Over-eating seriously injures the body. It opens the door to illness. It makes a man lethargic, lazy, apathetic. You can be made *drunk* on food! Excess sweets and starches are converted in the body to *alcohol.* This dulls the senses, dopes the body and grieves the Holy Spirit. Too much meaty food also fires the senses, stimulating sexual lust and greed.

What are the physical benefits of fasting?

---

## WHAT FASTING IS

1. *Fasting is a VOLUNTARY MISSING* of a *life need* — food, drink, rest, sleep, fellowship with others, etc. It is a sacrifice for physical or spiritual benefit. It is not *necessarily* absence of food.

2. *Fasting is profitable two ways.* PHYSICALLY, it rests and cleans the system, sharpening the mind and the feelings. SPIRITUALLY when coupled with prayer and Bible reading it builds devotion and faith in God.

3. *In a long food fast,* body poisons stored by wrong health habits are "burned away." Clogging wastes are taken from the system, cleaning the "temple of the Holy Spirit."

4. Fasting may be practiced *DAILY* by restricting food intake, or by a complete sacrifice of meals for a certain period. Little harm, and much good would result from missing a meal or two.

"YOU ARE NOT REALLY THE SALT OF THE EARTH
IF YOU DO NOT MAKE PEOPLE THIRSTY."

319

## WHAT FASTING IS NOT

1. *Fasting is NOT STARVATION. HUNGER* and *APPETITE* are two different things. Appetite is simply a *habit craving* for food. It is not true hunger. When a few meals are missed, stomach "pains" are the demand of appetite for satisfaction. HUNGER doesn't begin until *all waste tissue* is used up by the body. This takes WEEKS, not a few hours!

2. *Fasting is not spiritual merit in itself.* It is a *tool,* which when used intelligently is a key to power. But fasting brings no spiritual benefit if it is misused or boasted of to others. Fasting is a SCIENCE, with definite physical and spiritual rules that must not be broken (Matthew 6:16).

3. *Fasts are not impossibly difficult things.* Most of the discomfort of even a long fast is over in a few days. Provided the natural laws of the body are not broken, it is of greatest possible benefit to the Christian life.

Study this *four-stage graph* before you decide to take a long fast. You will see *two curves,* one beginning later than the first. The *height* of the graph is the amount of effort needed to stay on the fast; the *length of days* varies between individuals, but will serve as a rough guide for your own experience. A *long* fast *begins* when you pass the first two hard curves:

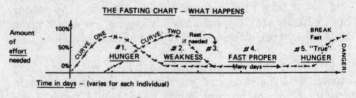

THE FASTING CHART — WHAT HAPPENS

"WE WOULDN'T BE PUT OUT SO EASILY
IF THE FIRE HAD A STRONGER HOLD."

320

In *STAGE ONE,* intense *appetite* pains grow for a few days. These stay until *stage TWO* where body *weakness* is also felt, owing to the "burning up" of waste material in the system. Don't give up here! You are *not* Dying! Any head-aches, slight fever and bad breath are caused by oxidising wastes in the system. It is ESSENTIAL to *DRINK MUCH WATER* — at least SIX GLASSES A DAY. This softens waste and helps the body to eliminate it through natural channels. In a long fast, bowels and kidneys, skin and breath all release more waste than usual. This is the toughest part of the fast. You may need sleep for longer periods here, and might even have to go to bed for a day or so.

What are the spiritual benefits to a prolonged fast?

*Washing the face* removes poisons from the skin (Matthew 6:17). Frequent bathing is needed. The *breath* becomes very bad-smelling as the lungs throw off poison. This can be countered to some extent by putting a menthol crystal (available from a pharmacist) on the tongue. The breath clears within two weeks and becomes fresh and clean.

*After this period of weakness* (DON'T WORK DURING A FAST!) comes *stage FOUR* — a time of *physical fitness* and great well-being. The body is clean, the spirit world becomes real and seeking God's blessings can begin. Satan will do everything in his power to *prevent you* from reaching stage four. You will sense his reality during this period so earnestly seek the Lord. *The Bible will become a new book.* From now on until HUNGER RETURNS *(stage five)* you are wonderfully free to touch God. Only when *hunger comes back* must the FAST BE BROKEN, for now STARVATION IS BEGINNING. Continuing on after this can result in bodily destruction and death. It takes *as much* willpower to *break* a long fast slowly as to *begin* it.

---

## RULES FOR THE LONG FAST

---

1. *DON'T WORK HARD!* JESUS SAID *"Pray* and fast!" Harm has been done to those who have carried out long fasts and hard manual labour at the same time. The body may need long *rest periods* to make up for the lack of energy intake during the fast.

Can you think of times in your own life when fasting could be especially helpful?

2. *Don't fast where you will inconvenience others.* It is best to take a vacation for any lengthy fast and be alone. This avoids social embarrassment.

3. *Begin with small fasts.* Miss a meal or two, then try longer periods. The battle not to eat is both physical and mental; you may have to try several times for success. ALWAYS SPEND THE *SAME TIME BREAKING* A FAST AS YOU DID *TAKING* IT. This applies especially to the longer fast. "Break" a fast slowly with fruit juices (not milk), then, non-milky soups, etc., until you gradually resume normal diet. Sudden large meals after long fasts can cause violent stomach cramps and great harm, if not death. So be careful and sensible. If you over-eat in breaking a fast, *immediately resume fasting.*

4. *DRINK PLENTY OF WATER.* The importance of this cannot be overestimated. If you don't, you will poison yourself with your own body wastes. You can survive only about three days without water. A food and water fast is a rare "desperation" fast, and must last no longer than three days. Water helps remove hunger pains to some extent. For long fasts, use warm, distilled water.

Some scriptures on fasting: Ezra 8:21-23; Isaiah 58; Daniel 6:18; Jonah 3:5; 2 Chronicles 20:3; Judges 20:26; Joel 1:14; Nehemiah 1:4; Luke 4:1-2; Matthew 6:16; Mark 9:29: 1 Corinthians 7:5; 2 Corinthians 6:4,5).

## BENEFITS OF FASTING

1. It is a most effective tool for helping *reduce over strong physical desires.* A fast diminishes all natural desires to a low level, helping you bring these under control.

2. It can be used in *times of special temptation* when the soul must cast itself on God for deliverance, or for carrying out *difficult* but important tasks (Acts 1:3; 14:23).

322

**3.** For making *decisive, critical choices.* When we cannot find the mind of God, a fast can put us in a place of spiritual sensitivity. Fasting and prayer coupled with reading God's *Word* boosts faith sky-high, and can put us in a place of extraordinary mental clarity and perception, or for *mighty acts* with God (Matthew 17:20-21).

**4.** In *crisis times or sickness,* your body knows what to do — fast. It automatically shuts down on appetite, helping rest us. At such times, eating is actually a *hinderance.* Fasting and prayer can carry the believer *close to God* for healing restoration.

### KEEPING AFLAME

*There are ways to keep the heart set on seeking God.* We need to be drawn closer to Christ. Anything that brings before us spiritual light, that casts us on Him is legitimate fuel for devotions. We BECOME WHAT WE THINK ABOUT. Thoughts shape our lives. To feed the mind with things of God will keep us aflame.

**1.** *Read BIOGRAPHIES of God's great men.* Try to read at least one book a month. These dead still speak. Time proves a man's work Dwell on the lives of those who had power with God and prevailed. Look for the secrets of THEIR Christian walk. What did these men have that *you* can develop?

**2.** *Take NOTES on anointed messages from servants of God.* Every sermon or teaching of truth that stirs and draws you closer to the Lord becomes a PART of your LIFE. Careful, full notes will recall their atmosphere, spirit and feeling as well as the teaching itself. FILE these neatly in loose-leaf folders, retyping if possible for clarity and readability.

**3.** *Spend as much time as possible with men who are used of God.* The essence of fellowship is the presence of the Holy Spirit making Christ real between believers. To be in the presence of such who exalt the Lord Jesus in their lives, is to sense something of the heart of God. Jesus called the disciples first of all to BE WITH HIM. The magic of His own

How many biographies of great Christians have you read within the last two years?

How can
continual
contact with
the "work-
aday"
world take
the edge off
our
spirituality?

strong spiritual communion with the Father inspired the
disciples to greater heights of faith and love (Mark 3:14;
Hebrews 10:25; 1 John 5:7; Acts 2:42; Galatians 2:9).

4. *GUARD YOUR TONGUE.* Don't be light minded and
sin with your lips. God has promised to endue the believer's
word with *power.* Loose use of the tongue takes away the
touch of God. Too much talk signals the sin of *foolishness*
(Proverbs 10:19). The Lord Jesus never wasted a word. Even
His longest messages are master pieces of condensed power.
We are told we will be *judged* for every idle word we speak.
Only God can tame a man's tongue. It is the expression of
what we are. Let your words be few, and you will not waste
the convicting channel of the Holy Spirit (Ecclesiastes 5:1-7;
Proverbs 13:3; James 1:26; Matthew 5:37; 12:36-37).

5. *Go to the "Desert Bible School."* This is simply a place
of loneliness. Moses, Paul, Elijah and Jesus learnt lessons of
power with God there. Too many words, too much mixing
with people takes the edge off spirituality. Great eagles fly
alone — great men of God walk alone. Solitude is the test of
our facing reality. That which we are willing to face on our
own, without the insistent clamour of a busy life, is that
which is real. Don't be busy DOING — you can't BE! Love is
sweetened by stillness. The deepest rivers of God run silently
(Exodus 3:1; Psalm 91:1; Proverbs 18:1; Song of Solomon
2:4; Matthew 6:18; Luke 1:80; Galatians 1:15-18).

---

## PRAYER — HOT-LINE TO GOD

---

### WHY PRAY?

*God knows everything knowable.* He knows your need and
that of all His children. Why do we need to pray? Does
prayer bring help because we must beg and beseech God to
act? Isn't He willing to do that which needs doing? Will God
only work as He hears from our own lips what He already
knows?

PRAYER is *AWARENESS OF GOD.* To pray is to see as
GOD sees. Prayer is a focused intent, so the whole heart is

324

fixed and centred on the Lord. Prayer is God-consciousness. As we pray we become aware of need, of failure. We see as God sees. We begin to realize spirit realities. We FEEL as GOD feels.

Prayer puts us in a place where we can understand and work with God. It is not to get God in touch with US, but to get US in touch with *Him!*

What are the four different kinds of prayer? Is your prayer life balanced with each?

*Where do you pray TO?* God is everywhere at once. He is before us, above us, beneath, behind and within us all at the same time. *AWARENESS,* not distance, separates us from touching Him. He has given us prayer to put us into contact with Him. Prayer-times are GROWTH times — you cannot afford to skip them or your spirit will be stunted. Cut them short and many hours of Christian work will be wasted.

When we pray with *NEEDS* in mind, it is *SUPPLICATION* a *dependent* awareness of God. *INTERCESSION* is awareness of God with *another's* need on our hearts. To WAIT on God — a powerful, silent form of prayer — is a *reverent* awareness of His Presence. The prayer of PRAISE is a joyful, *worshipping* awareness of the Lover of our souls (1 Timothy 4:4; Jeremiah 33:3; Hebrews 4:16; Psalm 62:5; 9:1-2; Isaiah 40:31).

Prayer connects a *circuit of power;* where God Himself is the Source of energy; we are the transmission wires; the object of prayer the thing to be energized; and prayer is the switch. Prayer, co-operating with faith actually *calls into being* the circumstances and material realities we need for the service of God. PRAY — prayer is as mighty as God is! You can pray that secret sins will be brought to light so we will have a common love in the church today as brothers and sisters in Christ. Can you pray for a brother to be freed of "splinters" with a power-pole poking out of the eye of YOUR will? (Matthew 7:4). Can you pray for a friend without catching divine concern that the Lord's will shall overrule and that men might see Jesus in him?

Prayer that *UNITES* to *IGNITE* is real prayer. Before the world is changed, WE must be changed! Prayer teaches and

325

transforms developing in our "negative" lives a picture of Jesus. Prayer has no rival in teaching us God-dependence. Only by awareness of Him will we grow LIKE Him. When the Lord Jesus prayed on the mountain with Peter, James and John, HE changed (Luke 9:28-29). He shone like light in whiteness. This simple object lesson in the supernatural taught the disciples what prayer *really does*. It TRANS-FIGURES those who use it. It makes them the "light of the world."

Why would it be easy to slip into a selfish prayer habit over an unsaved loved one?

---

## IMPROVING YOUR PRAYER-LIFE

*It's too easy to get SELFISH in prayer.* Why do YOU pray? Is it to prove you belong to God? Is it just idle curiosity to see what He can do? Then he cannot honor it.

Is it to *GLORIFY HIS NAME?* Then PRAY! God will surely hear and answer. We must put His glory *FIRST* in prayer or we shall have no results.

"There are a great many things often said in favor of the cause of *missions*, which are in the character of appealing to *wrong motives*. How often we are told of heathen who are IN DANGER of going to hell and how little is said of the GUILT of six hundred millions engaged and banded together as *rebels against God* or of the dishonor and contempt poured upon God our Maker by such a world of outlaws."

"*Parents* often pray very earnestly for their children because they wish God to save them, and they almost think hard of God if He does not. I knew a woman very anxious for her son's conversion, and she used to pray for him with agony. He still remained impenitent, until at length she became convicted that her prayers and agonies had been nothing but the fond yearnings of *parental feeling* and were not dictated at all  by a just view of her son's character as a wicked and wilful rebel against God. There was never *any* impression made, until she was made to take a strong ground against him as a rebel and look on him as deserving to be sent to hell. And *then* he was converted. She was never before influenced by the right motive in prayer, desiring his salvation with a supreme regard for the glory of God" *(C.G. Finney)*.

There is no limit to what God can do with you *as long as you don't touch His glory.* Many seekers miss God's answer because they want to be the stars of the show. They want men to say "There goes . . .! They are in touch with God!" The Father shares anything with His children — *except* His glory. "I am the Lord — that is MY Name — My glory will I give to no man."

Thought: If you pray for the conversion of thousands on the foreign field, are you willing to be the one to bring them the message?

## WHO SHOULD WE PRAY FOR?

We cannot pray for God to "save sinners" without being involved *ourselves.* NOWHERE does God tell us to ask Him to save the lost; He *is* doing all He can at this very moment. If He could change a rebel will to freely serve Him, He would! But He cannot force a man to love Him. He knocks, pleads, strives and waits, but can do no more through prayer if we are not willing to be part of the answer to that prayer.

The *Lord Jesus,* faced with a vast, seemingly unreachable field of people said "You pray that the Lord of the Harvest will SEND OUT *laborers* into His harvest field" (Matthew 9:36-38).

*QUESTION:* Who will be the FIRST one to hear God's call if YOU pray like this?

## THE WILL AND THE WAY

Ever wondered why God doesn't seem to answer some prayers? Check your prayer-times for these answer blockers:

What is the
difference
between the
attitude of
prayer and
the action of
prayer?

1. *The WICKED prayer* — Goes beyond God's commandments and promises and asks something plainly forbidden in Scripture (James 4:3).

2. *The UNFORGIVING prayer* — Denies the very grounds of prayer — that we OURSELVES have been forgiven! Nursed grudges kill a prayer time.

3. *The CLUELESS prayer* — Find out all you can, so you can pray with understanding. Paul wanted his safe-guard taken from him (2 Corinthians 12:7-9).

4. *The SELFISH prayer* — Our own interests in view, not God's glory (Ezekiel 14:3).

5. *The SELF-RIGHTEOUS prayer* — Secretly comparing ourselves more favorably than others. This kind of foolishness bounces off the ceiling (Luke 18:10-14).

6. *The DOUBTING prayer* — *Faithless:* doesn't really believe a promise; and the *WORDY prayer* — *Falseness:* makes a pretty speech to impress others listening, are also prayers that don't go through Heaven's switchboard.

---

## WHY SEEK HIS FACE?

---

Why can't we just *"expect"* God to work, if prayer is awareness? Why can't we just forget saying words and look for Him to work? At times in the Christian life such an expectant attitude does take the place of "words" to God. This is how we can "pray always" (Luke 18:1; Ephesians 6:18) — always be in an ATTITUDE of prayer.

But it is also too easy to rush past *our* responsibilities when we want to see God work. He will not be a *"push-button"* God — He is a Person, royal beyond all earthly rank — He is not "demanded of" and will not let us use *prayer* as a push-button. God asks nothing less than our total dependence on Him. Without Him we can do *nothing* (John 15:5). A habit of asking teaches us dependence and the PERSONAL element in God's concern. If we are desperate enough to lay bare our hearts before Him and show that we mean business by applying ourselves to prayer, He cannot fail to demonstrate His power (Luke 18:1-7; John 15:7; 1 Peter 3:12; 1 John 5:14).

What are some of the phony "masks" that can be worn during our prayer times?

---

## AS EASY AS BREATHING

---

In her book *"Prayer — Conversing With God,"* Rosalind Rinker makes an exciting study of the *naturalness* of prayer. She defines it as a TALK between you and God. "Prayer is a *conversation* between two people who love each other." To revolutionize your prayer life:

1. *DON'T PRETEND.* Be *honest* with yourself before God. Pray what you really *think.* Don't excuse sin, by convincing yourself it was a moment of weakness. Don't pretend you are brave or happy if you feel lonely or sad. When you get honest in your prayer-life you will discover power with God.

2. *BE NATURAL.* Don't speak in an unnatural way. As well as being LORD and Master, God is also your Father and Friend. Do you have a close word of affection for your earthly Dad? Have you ever used it for your Heavenly Father? Never be too "spiritual" to be affectionate.

3. *Don't talk TOO MUCH!* What would YOU think of a friend who telephoned, poured out a large list of wants, added a quick word of thanks for past favors and hung up before you could say a word? Some prayers are like that! Give God time to speak to you. Wait patiently in His Presence before you begin to talk. Cultivate His consciousness. Talking too much shows no belief that God wants to speak. A conversation has two sides. Prayer isn't a lecture.

4. *Pray SPECIFICALLY.* What's the use of asking the Lord to "bless the world and all the people in it"? How would you know if He did? If you want to see definite ANSWERS why not pray for specific things? "You have not because you ask not" (James 4:3). When you find a promise, when your motives are for God's glory, ask in faith! Make a request for that which you CAN BELIEVE God will answer. He will do

What specific guidelines can you think of that would make for a more effective group prayer meeting?

"exceeding abundantly above all that we ask and think according to the power that worketh in us." Faith in a prayer answering God makes a prayer-loving Christian.

5. *PRAY ALWAYS.* Sound impossible? This means always be in a prayer-*attitude* . . . awareness of God. If you don't feel like praying — you NEED to! Praying-always men are rarely surprised at miracles because they live in the consciousness of God. Prayers don't have to always be *long* — Peter's three-worder brought fast results (Mark 14:30; Luke 18:1; Ephesians 6:18).

6. *ON YOUR NOSE OR YOUR TOES? Position* in prayer isn't important, but should reflect the state of your heart. You don't have to close your eyes! (John 11:41; Matthew 14:19). This helps shut out distractions; but with practice you pray at a desk, on a field, on a field; walking along the road or even driving a car! When you are talking to someone and need quick guidance, such prayer is essential (Nehemiah 2:4).

7. *GROUP prayer is different.* You talk over the common problems with each other and the Lord. If you are meeting for prayer, set a chair "for the Lord," and pray around it. True to His promise "where two or three are gathered together in My name there am I . . ." — *You will sense His presence.* Such a setting can make group prayer mean more than a set of "speeches" to each other with closed eyes! In *private* prayer, God may lay some prayer burden on a heart. This should be brought to the Lord as a group; all should pray as led until you feel God has undertaken for the work. In general, no prayer here should be much longer than a minute.

TO TRY:

A GROUP PRAYER ON ONE SUBJECT WHERE NO PERSON PRAYS ANY LONGER ON THAT SUBJECT THAN ONE MINUTE.

"Then he called for a light
. . . came trembling and said
'Sirs, what must I do to be
saved?' And they said 'Believe
on the Lord Jesus Christ and
thou shalt be saved and thy
house.' . . . And the Lord
added daily . . . such as should
be saved" (Acts 16:29-31;2:47).

# ANDREW

## (WHO INTRODUCED TO JESUS)

"Philip cometh and telleth
Andrew; and Andrew . . .
Jesus."

John 12:22

What
prerequisites
must be met
before one
can be a
truly biblical
witness for
Jesus?

PHASE:        6 .. *Into All The World*
SECTION:    10 .. *"H" For The "How-To" Of Personal Witness*
MATERIAL:      .. *Letting Your Lights Shine*

*Andrew was an introducer.* Whenever someone wanted to meet the Lord, they seemed to go to *Andrew;* and then *Andrew* introduced them to Jesus. *Andrew* didn't have all the answers to the problems brought to him. But he DID know the One Who was the Answer! He simply introduced men to the Lord Jesus — confident that whatever the need, Christ could meet it. We too, must learn to be introducers — meeting need by bringing the needy to Jesus.

"The church is looking for better *methods;* God is looking for better *men,"* (E.M. Bounds).

To be a witness for someone is to share their life with another; to stand in their place and as best you know how, be for others what that person is really like and what they do.

You do not have to learn to be a witness. You already *ARE* a witness! You are a witness to *whatever* or *whoever* is foremost in your life. You are telling the world right now what god you *really* belong to. You cannot live life without showing the world your real interests. Your words and your life are tied inseparably together; you will always convey to others around you what you really love and live for most. Your words will either prove this, or call you a liar. Anyone who watches you closely, follows you around for a day can tell if you really mean what you claim with your lips.

*Every day you are witnessing.* What are YOU witnessing to? Your witness is the total package of your attitudes, character and actions. It does not lie. No careful observer is fooled. What are you witnessing to? Whatever your god is, you will show the most interest in. If it is anything else but Jesus, your closest friends already know. It will be the thing you like to talk most about, read most about, center your life around, love and live for. Say — could you get to heaven on the testimony of your next-door neighbor?

If you call yourself a Christian, you have already *been* witnessing — for or against Him. If you have claimed to belong to Him, but your *life* does not back up your *words,* men and women have rejected Christ and the Gospel because of you. That is why Jesus said, "He that is not for Me is against Me; and he that gathers not with Me scatters abroad."

What must be the right motive behind any and all evangelical movements?

I know of no *Bible* plan that will enable you to present Christ to others without your OWN life being Christ-like. True Christianity IS Christ! You can present another philosophy or religion without its founder by a "canned" plan, and change a few words to sell *soap* just as effectively with it; but you cannot present *Christ* to another until you properly Represent Him and His love. If you would be His witness, you must really *KNOW* Him to *show* Him.

The world is *filled* with movements for evangelism and methods of witness today. Some work inside structured churches, some work outside; some are planned and highly organized; others arise loosely and spontaneously to minister to needs. But THESE ARE ALL WRONG and have NO RIGHT TO EXIST — *unless* they are staffed and supplied with men and women and young people who have the *right motives!* God is looking for people who want to see Him glorified above everything else, and who want to stop people from hurting Him by their selfishness and sin. Much of our evangelism today fails right here; people do not serve God from the right motives.

---

### MOTIVE

---

The Lord Jesus viewed the winning of *one soul* as worth more than the whole world. He spent much of His time talking with ONE person at a time about their relationship to God. True soul-winning is impossible without concerned, *personal contact.* Jesus put the life and the love of His Father on exhibition to the world. This is true witness. When the world is lost and running from God, He must go looking for men to convince them of His love and concern despite their sin. He wants to do this by living His life through and in, men and women who will yield to His direction, and this more-

Why is the "don't-look-at-me-only-Jesus" mentality inexcusable for the Christian?

than-human team seeks out lost sinners to bring them the message of reconciliation and forgiveness.

To be Christ-like in attitude means to be real — absolutely real. God hates phonies. If you have any other reason for wanting to witness to others apart from a genuine concern and love for them and for God, forget about trying to "witness." You will only do more harm than good. LOVE is the only acceptable motive for the witness — an honestly unselfish concern for the highest good of God and His wayward creation. It involves a level of concern that made even Christ cry (Matthew 9:36). Love is not primarily something you feel; it is something you DO, and is directly measured in unselfish sacrifice.

Witnessing like Jesus means Christ-likeness in *CONDUCT*. The world is full of selfish people, who only *think* basically of themselves, *care* only for themselves and *live* only for themselves. God's *new* people are to be totally different — they are to *live* like *Jesus*. It will do you no good to say, "I'm full of sin and iniquity — look only to Jesus!" to the sinner. He has every right to say — "But I can't *see* Jesus. I can only see *you*. And if He hasn't helped you, what makes you think He can change me?"

The Lord Jesus said, "As long as I am *in* the world, I am the light of the world." He is no longer in the world but "He  is risen" and left us as His witnesses. "As My Father has sent Me, so send I you" (John 20:21). "You shall be My witnesses únto the uttermost part of the earth" (Acts 1:8 ASV). To be effective witnesses for Jesus we must live above the world's standards and values, so that unbelievers will take notice and ask us what the secret of our lives is. We must live our lives so that with Paul we can say — "Those things, which you have both *learned* and *received*, and *seen* in me do, and the God of peace shall be with you" (Philippians 4:9). Men must be able to be "followers of us and the Lord" at the same time (1 Thessalonians 1:6). Think of the victory over sin Paul daily experienced when he could say — "Wherefore I beseech you, be ye followers of *me*" (1 Corinthians 4:16).

334

This was no boast; it was simply the statement of a holy life founded upon the witness of the Holy Spirit as the source of his strength — "Be ye followers of me, *even as I also am of Christ*" (1 Corinthians 11:1).

What are the things that can block the spontaneous witness for Christ in our lives?

God's blue-print of Christian witness for youth is outlined in *1 Timothy 4:12.* There is no real reason why a young person cannot be as effective for God as an older adult, provided there is a basic *understanding* of what is involved and a *consistent* life. We are to be examples by *word* (what we *say* — speech), *conversation* (what we *do* — actions), *charity (why* we do it — motives), *spirit (where* we do it — led and directed by), *faith (when* we do it — obedience to the word of God), *purity (how* we do it — a clean channel through which Christ can operate). God is mobilizing youth in this last generation for the mightiest awakening history has ever seen.

Witnessing like Jesus means *consistency* — the ability to be the same all the time. To be like Jesus, we must keep being changed by the indwelling Holy Spirit in a humble walk of faith. We are to "keep *ourselves* in the love of God" and this is a daily matter. Christianity is not a set of rules, but a fellowship with a living, loving Person. It is "Christ in you, the hope of glory" (Colossians 1:27). In this life of grace and faith, we are to be marked by the sign that "sin shall not have dominion over you" (Romans 6:14). Christianity *is* Christ; resurrected, real, bringing to the new-living heart, peace and power (2 Corinthians 3:18).

*Four elements* interact to bring a man to a new birth. No man is *ever* saved without God investing a good deal of persuasion in his life. Keep in mind these four elements that make up a part of any conversion experience:

### 1. *God is SPIRIT (The Holy Spirit)*

The work that Jesus did when He witnessed is done today by the *Holy Spirit.* His job is to *convict of sin* (John 16:7-13) by guiding the sinner's thoughts back over his miserable past to reveal his true lost state before God. He knows everything about the sinner you are talking to, and by direct *intuition* can give you the right words to say that will hit him at the core of his selfishness. The Holy Spirit works through the

What are the
dangers of a
truthful
witness
without the
compassion
of the Holy
Spirit?

*Truth,* giving it vividness, authority and terrible clarity.
Under His power, the Word of God burns and cuts like a
blade of fire.

Men do not naturally WANT *to obey God* because their
selfishness has too strong a hold in their lives (Jeremiah
13:23). According to the Bible, sinners are *deceitful, self-
satisfied; proud* and *stubborn.* They *resist God, reject truth*
and, although guided by Satan, are *unconscious* of bondage
(Titus 3:3; Revelation 3:17;
Romans 1:30; 7:7; 1 Timothy 6:4;
2 Timothy 4:4; Acts 7:51; John
8:33,44). Before the message of
salvation makes any sense to the
sinner, he must be *awakened.* He
must *see* that he is in big trouble
and that nothing he can do or say
for himself can excuse his guilt. He

must see with full force that as a self-centered REBEL he has
become an ENEMY of God (Romans 5:10). But you must
learn how to work *with the Holy Spirit* in speaking about this
to the person you are trying to win. Truth without His
compassion and grief will only further *harden* the sinner's
heart. The Holy Spirit is pictured in Scripture as playing an
*active part* in man's salvation, both in *directing* the pattern of
witness and making *real* the truth presented. He can pour in a
blaze of "hail and love" together, so that the rebel may give
up his sin, surrender his will to God and be saved. He
restrains and pleads with men to totally renounce all rebellion (Genesis 6:3; Proverbs 1:24; Isaiah 1:8; Ezekiel
33:11; John 4:23-24; 16:7-11; Acts 7:51; 2 Corinthians
3:5-6; Ephesians 3:5-6; Revelation 3:20).

### 2. God is HOLY (The Truth)

*A sinner lives in a pretend world.* He convinces himself
that what he does is right, knowing all the time he is *wrong.*
He *wants* to be self-deceived. His pride keeps him dishonest
whenever he realizes afresh that he needs to surrender to
God. He keeps his conscience appeased by comparing himself
with the rest of the selfish world around him, who can give
no example of the reality he is running from. Without a
standard of truth and holiness he can manage for a while;
unless God can get across his path someone who WILL

demonstrate the truth. Before, he had used *"no example"* as an excuse; now he may be forced to using *words* as an escape from God instead. Faced with a living demonstration of God's love for him, his own guilt becomes painfully real.

What is the Holy Spirit's role in the conversion of the lost?

The sinner becomes aware of God's holiness in *direct proportion* to how much YOU are filled with God's Spirit. This is why it is so vitally important to know the "enduement of power" and to spend *time* in God's Presence to obtain the *spirit of prayer.* A sinner must SENSE God's reality *in you.* A key avenue of this communication is a Christian's *eyes;* they can become like a spiritual X-ray, exposing in tender fire, the innermost intent and thoughts of his heart (Mark 3:5; Luke 6:10; 22:61; Acts 3:4). The Lord Jesus Himself must be seen in your face! If through this witness, the sinner can bring himself to be *honest,* and look past you to the Christ you represent, that *very look,* will bring him life (John 6:40).

## 3. *God is LOVE (The Witness)*

Truth first shows the UGLINESS of sin in contrast to *God's goodness.* When we deal with secular men, we must spend far more time showing them their true *guilt* before God than was needed a century ago. Man no longer think their guilt feelings are a symptom of any *real* wrong; they are trying to live without absolutes. Thus, man must know the BAD news about himself and his relationship with God before the "Good News" makes any sense to him. We need Divine wisdom here, to "open their eyes, and to turn them from darkness to light" (Acts 26:18).

"To *WHOM* does the Holy Ghost say *'Believe'* . . . ?" (Acts 16:31). Now, MARK — NOT to *all sinners* indiscriminately. Here is a grand mistake in the teaching of this age; that these words are wrested from their explanatory connection and held up independently of all the conditions which must ever, and did ever in the mind and practice of the Apostles accompany them . . . How *can* an unawakened, unconvicted, unrepentant sinner "believe"? As soon might *Satan* believe. It is an utter impossibility. It is useless and as unphilosophical as it is unscriptural to preach "only believe" to such characters, and Christians have not done their duty and have not discharged their responsibility to these souls when they have

What is the
foremost
task of the
Christian
when sharing
Christ
with the
unconverted?

told them that Jesus died for them and that they are to believe in Him. Oh dear no! They have a much harder work to do, and that is to *open their eyes* to a sense of the danger, and make them by the power of the Spirit *realize* the dreadful truth . . . The eye of the soul must be opened to such a realization of sin and such an apprehension of its consequences as shall lead to an earnest desire to be saved from it" (*Saving Faith* — Catherine Booth).

*God's great means of conviction* is the *LAW*, used by His Spirit to drive sinners out of their excuses and into the love of Jesus. Yet the law has no power *in itself* to change the sinner to make him love God. Only the truth of God's concern and love contrasted with his own selfishness can subdue his proud will and break his heart. The sinner must realize that the *Lord Jesus is his Friend*, and will *welcome* him the moment he is willing to turn his back on sin and give himself up to God. Unless he senses this Divine concern, he will only go on into *deeper* rebellion and despair. This demonstrated concern is YOUR task. How can he see that *God* cares? By YOUR care. How can he know that God loves him? By  YOUR love! For this reason, you must *never argue* or give any impression you are "looking down" on him. This does not mean you will *excuse* his sin or talk about it as if *he* had nothing to do with it; that he was helpless and not guilty. Don't treat sin as some unavoidable weakness. You certainly cannot show love by making it easier to be saved than GOD HIMSELF has required of the sinner — TOTAL honesty, COMPLETE repentance and an *entire consecration of heart* to God. DO show your love by earnest concern, solemn presentation of the truth and the yearning of your heart that He might be "saved and come to the knowledge of the truth" (1 Timothy 2:4). *Expose* his sin and show him the *insanity* of living in it. Hedge up his way completely from excuses so he must cry out to Christ for help. *Your own grasp* of the grief of God over man's sin and the greatness of the sacrifices made by Him to deliver man from its bondage will produce in your expression the sweetness and compassion of God. You are not merely a "tool" in God's hands in witness; you are to play an *ACTIVE part* in helping persuade men on Christ's behalf to be reconciled to God. The Bible shows that the *witness* is actively involved with God in turning men from death to life (Jonah 3:2-4; Matthew 3:2; 28:19; Luke 14:23; John 15:16; Acts 26:18, 28; Romans 11:14; 1 Corinthians 9:19-23; James 5:19-20).

What is the "great ally" of the Christian as he shares Christ with the non-Christian?

### 4. *God is LIGHT (The Sinner)*

The sinner's mind admits reality, but he does not want to *FACE* it. HE *ALWAYS KNOWS* RIGHT. NEVER forget this when you witness. The sole reason for his sin is a *deliberate choice* for self-pleasing *against* his own reason and conscience. You have a *powerful ally* in the conscience of the one you talk to. It says "Amen" to every truth the Holy Spirit makes real from your lips. The sinner is forced, in spite of himself, to *inwardly* at least, admit the truth. What is the SINGLE thing that God requires of the sinner FIRST OF ALL? How would you counsel someone who said that they "could" not believe, or repent, or forsake some particular sin? Once you have grasped the all-important witnessing principle of the SELF-DECEIT of the human heart the answer is plain. God requires ONLY *honesty* towards Him! Let a man but bare his heart honestly before God, and lay out before Him all the excuses, problems, doubts or difficulties, and conviction of sin, faith and salvation will follow in short order. Your whole task is to get the sinner to be HONEST *before* and *towards* God. When he is, the light of the glorious Gospel will shine into his heart. It is then up to him to repent and of his own free will turn in response to your message from the Lord. Thus, the *sinner* has a part to play in his OWN salvation — the free choice out of awakened love for God (Isaiah 55:7; Ezekiel 14:6; 18:30-32; Acts 17:30-31; 2:38; 3:19; 20:21; Luke 13:3,5; Ephesians 5:14; 1 Peter 1:22).

## WHEN THE MASTER WITNESSED

*What was the plan of Christ* in witnessing? How did *He* set about to win people? When the Lord Jesus was on earth, He did not *use* a "plan." He had rather an UNDERSTANDING of salvation, and was thus *able to adapt* to every person who

Why must a Christian have a thorough understanding of the biblical doctrine of sin before he can witness effectively?

came to Him and meet them where they were. A proper and thorough understanding of the basic facts of sin, responsibility, grace, love, repentance and faith in Christ are ESSENTIAL to proper witness. If you are not clear or convinced on these great truths of the Word of God, your witness will be weak and largely ineffective.

*Go BACK to "JUDAS" and RE-READ the whole chapter* before you read any further. Fix in your heart what true conversion is.

## ESSENTIAL FACTS FOR THE CARELESS SINNER

In witnessing to a truly secular man or woman, you must get across to them their *true guilt* before God. You understand by now the true nature of salvation; keep in mind these facts as you witness to the careless sinner:

1. *All happiness* depends on each moral creature *living unselfishly.*

2. Man was made to be governed *morally,* and not by *force.* For this reason he needs a Governor who can *direct* him into the choices that will be most wise, and bring the highest happiness to the Universe of which he is a part.

3. *GOD* has the right to be the Governor and Director of our lives.

His right does *not* come from the fact that He *made* us, or even that He *loves* us best. His right rests in the fact that we *NEED* guidance, direction and ultimate authority and God is the *only* one Who is best qualified for the task. His qualifications rest on the fact that —

(a) He is *everywhere present* to observe all actions of the Universe.

(b) He *knows every fact* in existence fully and perfectly, having *perfect wisdom.*

340

(c) He has at His disposal *endless power* and energies to help and direct men or enforce right.

(d) He is the only example of *perfect justice* and *completely unselfish conduct* in the Universe.

Why is God's wrath against sin a true demonstration of His love?

These qualifications both oblige *Him* to *rule* us, and oblige *us* to obey *Him*. To refuse to do so is both *unintelligent*, dangerous to the Universe, destructive of the happiness of others and deserving of punishment. *Selfishness* is thus the *essence* of sin. *All men know* it is wrong in itself. Selfishness denies God's right to be God, ignores the happiness of others except as it contributes to the sinner's own happiness and left unchecked would ultimately destroy the Universe. Because selfishness is an *infinite* evil, God had to assign an *infinitely* great *penalty* for committing it. This penalty is *endless death,* much like the death sentence in human government, but on an eternal scale. If a man insists on breaking God's guidelines for happiness, God must curb his rebellion by *sentencing* the sinner for the highest good of the Universe. It cuts off the sinner forever from the Universe he has refused to live intelligently in, and brings him an endless agony *equal in measure* to the *guilt* he has incurred. This terrible sentence of judgment and death *grieves* God; but He may not wisely suspend it without harming the Universe, unless a *substitute* is found for the penalty that will still satisfy justice and the rebellious sinner will meet certain conditions of pardon.

## FOR THE CONVICTED —

God, in loving wisdom and infinite kindness, *found* a way to restore a man caught in the web of selfishness! He has contacted Man in two amazing ways:

1. *By INDIRECTLY* passing on His offer of *pardon* and *conditions* of it through men He found who were willing to seek Him, find Him and love Him. The *basics* of this message is in a unique collection of books called the *Bible*. It describes *why* God made man, *what* He had intended for him, and what has happened through *sin.* The most astonishing part of its message is that despite man's rebellion, refusal to seek his Maker, persistence in selfishness and deliberate rejection of God's appeals to live rightly, God *still loves man* and is not bitter towards His wayward creation. God is but terribly *grieved,* and longs to restore him.

341

2. *By DIRECTLY* meeting men in person. The most amazing of all these contacts occured about 2,000 years ago, splitting history in half; God *Himself* became like His creature man, and lived among us for 33 years to show His care and concern for our race. God came in human flesh as *Jesus Christ.* He was *born* uniquely, *lived* incomparably, *died* prophetically and *rose again* from the dead triumphantly. His earthly mission was *three-fold:* (1) To show us what our *Maker* was really like; (2) To show us how *we* were supposed to live; (3) To *die* an agonizing death out of love for us, as a *substitute* for the penalty of our sin.

*Now God can offer forgiveness, full pardon and restoration* to His family on two conditions —

1. *REPENTANCE* — That the sinner is willing to *forsake* his previous selfish way of life, whatever the cost to his plans, his pride or public image in the world.

2. *FAITH* — That he is willing (from that point on) to trust Jesus Christ as His own personal Substitute for the penalty of sin, to *love* and to *obey Him* as his Lord and Master forever.

This surrender is one of the *heart* (his ultimate choice) and centers around *ONE PARTICULAR POINT* of obedience. This is usually the ONE THING the sinner is *most unwilling* to do for God. When *this* is yielded, a transforming climax from selfishness to love occurs, which the Bible calls being "born again."

In general, you may give the sinner *ANY direction,* and tell him ANYTHING that includes a change from selfishness to surrender out of love to the Lord Jesus. The Holy Spirit strives to search out the excuses and hiding-places of the sinner's heart in witness, to pull them out of their hiding-places and draw them to submit their hearts to God. Their objections and difficulties are as different as men are different; as you witness, God will direct you to find out these errors and the places where the Holy Spirit is pressing on their consciences, press the same places and thus lead him to the Lord.

GO BACK TO "JUDAS" AND RE-READ THE WHOLE CHAPTER

There are many "soul-winning plans" and "salvation outlines" for Christian workers today. Beware of those which have a —

What are the dangers of a pre-planned salvation approach?

1. *"Pat" approach.* If an outline is memorized and used on a sinner that involves psychological "traps" to cut out any of his excuses, he could resist or resent these while being forced by the pre-planned words to continue with the conversation. Although many have been effective, such "pat" approaches have two dangerous weaknesses: (a) It implies complete *reliance* on the "plan" and no option for the Holy Spirit's own *specialized* witness; it can thus easily become *mechanical*; (b) It does not allow enough *scope* to search the sinner to the roots of his selfishness; a "decision" may be made to relieve the psychological pressure of the "traps" without a *true* change of heart. The QUALITY of convert is dependent on the *CLARITY* of his understanding and commitment to the Truth of God. Any plan that minimizes *either* the *guilt of sin,* man's *responsibility* and need for *total surrender* to God or our own *dependence* on the leading and empowering of the *Holy Spirit* is dangerous and can produce converts that are at best weak and sickly in faith, filled with doubts and failures.

2. *False presentation of the true nature of salvation.* Unscriptural ideas of man's nature and guilt, and his required action in conversion will sow seeds of destruction that will bear fruit in rapidly *back-sliding* "converts." It is better for a person NOT to hear, than to hear INCORRECTLY, get a false hope and go to Hell. Jesus said — "By their fruits you shall know them." We cannot always blame a falling away of converts to the "wayside and the weeds" (Mark 4:1-20). We must always ask ourselves: "Have I done MY job to *prepare the ground?* And am I sowing GOD'S seed?"

*Not all men can be given the same directions.* A general "pill" cannot cure all ills. It is the Holy Spirit's task to "custom" the witness to the situation at hand. This means that for *every person* there will be a *different message,* although each will follow a general PATTERN of instruction, with God the Holy Spirit outlining and underscoring certain points that will most cut home into the sinner's heart. What you *say* to sinners may vary; but whatever is said, you should *NOT* give him any directions that (a) are INCOMPLETE and

How will
witnessing
differ if you
have only a
few minutes
with a
person as
opposed to a
situation
where
repeated
opportunities
will come up
with the
same
individual?

leave him without a clear picture of what God *requires* him to do; he should be fully ready to *die* and meet God the moment after he follows your instructions; (b) nor any instructions that do not include a *complete* and *total* change of HEART, in turning *FROM* SIN *TO* CHRIST out of *LOVE*. *In general you may give the sinner ANY direction, and tell him anything that will include a change from supreme selfishness to surrender to Christ as Lord and King* as well as Saviour from sin. The *Holy Spirit* will help you search out the excuses and hiding-places of the sinners' deceitful heart, to pull them out of their darkness and draw them to submit their hearts to God. Find the man's *main* "God"; if it is not Jesus Christ, challenge him to *forsake* it and give his heart to the One Who made him, loves him and cares for him.

In most witness, *daily contacts with others* will create the chance for a personal word. As you show the fruit of the

Spirit and live the life of Jesus "Christ in you," His Spirit will draw those who need help across your path. *ASK God for this;* your task is to be alert to *see* them and be ready to help them.

Don't try to *"scheme"* how you will lead talk around to spiritual things. *Honestly, sincerely* be concerned about THEM. LISTEN! Find out their real problems and needs. If you try to keep in mind some "canned" plan or presentation, they will sense that you have "something on your mind" that isn't related to what they are saying — i.e. they may think you don't *really* care about *them* at all. If you listen carefully, God will show you their *point of need,* and also what needs to be surrendered for salvation.

The *best way* of bringing their attention to Jesus when the opportunity occurs is to *raise a question at a point of interest.* This was *Christ's* way of witness. He either *created* a situation that made the other person ask a question, or directly *asked* one Himself. These were always loving, geared to the sinner's basic need and never offensive. It was a question that could *not* be answered with a "Yes" or a "No" and created interest for further ones. He answered *these* in the same way, encouraging the sinner to open up his

344

problem, face his sin and give Him their trust. Here are some that have been used with effect by others —

(a) Have you ever seriously considered Christ's claims on your life?

(b) Are you interested in spiritual things?

(c) Have you ever thought about becoming a real Christian?

(d) If someone was to ask you, "What is a true Christian," what would you answer?

(e) Have you ever personally discovered Jesus Christ, or are you still in the process?

(f) Do you think it is possible to know for sure before you die that you are going to Heaven?

(g) How did you personally give your life to Christ? (For sinner posing as a Christian).

(h) Some day when you stand before God, what reason are you going to give Him as to why He should let you into His Kingdom?

Can you remember a time of personal witness when a well-thought-through question could have helped you clarify the claims of Christ to a non-Christian?

---

## DEALING WITH FEAR IN WITNESS

---

*FEAR* in witness is created by 3 basic factors: (1) inadequate *training* or *preparation;* (2) *Self-consciousness* from insufficient *prayer* or concern for the other person; (3) Not knowing what *might* happen when the truth is presented. A vast load lifts off the mind when you realize there are only 5 *basic attitudes* a sinner can adopt when witness occurs:

1. *Indifference —*

The worst attitude! *Prayer, care,* a loving but firm *warning* from the Word of God, coupled with an invitation to further consideration, are your only tools here.

2. *Curiosity —*

A sign of an awakened hunger for reality or further consideration. Present as simply as possible *God's claims on the life.* Use love, smile at yourself now and then, but be in firm and concerned earnest. Ask *questions* to make sure they understand what you say.

Why should "quick" decisions for Jesus be under suspicion?

### 3. *Hesitancy* —

Often a sign of sin being exposed. If questions come here, use them to center back on their personal responsibility to God, answering them as briefly as possible. If you feel they are only some kind of excuse, show them you understand it is just an excuse and that in giving it they are not sincere. For example: "How do you *know* God isn't just imagination?" "You are giving the same kind of excuse as I did when I lived for myself . . . I knew God was real all the time, but I didn't want to live for Him and I found it more convenient to deny His reality than to answer His claims on my life."

"Yes, but He might only be real to you; He's not real to *me!*"

"Of *course* He is not real to you; He never *will* be as long as you keep on serving and living for yourself; you only find He is real when you quit living in sin and honestly face His call . . ." etc.

### 4. *Acceptance* —

If real, usually a sign that the person has *already been dealt with* by the Lord for some time beforehand. Check first very carefully that they *fully understand* what they are doing (*NO* witness to those on drug or alcohol highs, unless *specifically* directed!) and make sure they have *counted the cost* of total surrender to Jesus. SUSPECT "quick" decisions made without question and without signs of struggle, surrender or resultant change after prayer.

### 5. *Rejection* —

When the truth is fairly and fully faced, the cost counted but finally rejected, they should first *fully understand* what they are doing to God's offer of mercy and love and what they are *choosing for ever* as their final destiny. Show your *grief* and *concern* that they have thus chosen. Sometimes a final clarification has brought home the terrible finality of rejecting Christ and His Gospel, and the soul has at last surrendered.

TO REMEMBER:
DISCOVER A NEED; PRESENT CHRIST AS THE ANSWER.

## COMMUNICATION WITH THE CARELESS

Why is it unwise to witness to people when they are agitated or busy?

*Most people don't care about Christ. When you do witness, don't go when they are:*

1. *Busy.* The sinner will not think your message is as urgent as his own work in hand. Wait until he is relaxed and ready to listen before you begin to witness.

2. *Drunk.* If you can smell alcoholic breath on the person you want to witness to, they are usually too drunk to be fully responsible. Men under the influence of alcohol talk readily about God, but such talk is rarely sincere and decisions made under drink rarely last. If you need to talk with him, get him sober first, or wait for another chance when he is not drinking. The same applies to a person on "drug high."

3. *Excited.* It takes a far GREATER excitement on your part to turn a man's thoughts to God when he is excited or angry. If you spark man's natural enmity against God while he is angry, it may turn into open violence. Don't provoke wrath — speak softly when you witness (Proverbs 15:1; 1 Peter 3:15).

*DO GO:*

1. *In God's timing.* He often changes situations through prayer, creating a need or sensitivity to His Spirit. You may be strongly directed to speak to a sinner at a certain time. This can be God's time to talk. Go immediately, as soon as God opens the way to witness. God has His times and seasons for men when they are most strongly influenced for truth.

2. *Early.* Don't put off witnessing, hoping for better times. It's ALWAYS a "bad" time to witness! Look for a chance to talk, and if none comes, MAKE ONE. Fix an appointment to

347

Why is it important that we *never* leave the impression with a person that he should repent "later"?

see him, and he will know it is important. Then *follow it up* until he yields to God or you are sure nothing more can be done.

3. *Alone.* People *hide* their true feelings about God when they are in a group. Pride can stop them from being honest and they strongly resist what they normally would yield to if alone. Get them away from the group, and you will see their true state.

## WHEN YOU TALK WITH THE CARELESS:

### A. DON'T:

1. *Be HARD* — Show that you *love him* and want him to have the best for time and eternity. If you are pushy and bossy, you will offend.

2. *Be HARSH* — There is no need to be abrupt, rude or coarse. Give the right impression about the Christ you love and represent (1 Peter 3:8-9).

3. *APOLOGIZE* — If he blames Christians or churches, *don't* agree or he will feel you are siding with him against God. Tell him he doesn't have to answer for *them,* but for *himself* and what about HIS sins? (And NEVER apologize for your *own* life! If you *have* to, you shouldn't be witnessing!).

### B. DO:

1. *Be SHORT* — Don't "spin out" what you have to say. Get his attention to the *point* as soon as you can, say a few essentials and press them home. Bring him to a choice and if possible get him to repent and yield to the Lord THEN. Try not to leave the idea he could repent "later." God expects them to repent NOW, while the SPIRIT strives; although he *may* need time many times for the Spirit to work.

2. *Be SWEET* — If you lose your temper, you lose your witness. If you are snubbed or laughed at, guard your spirit from flaring anger.

3. *Be SERIOUS* — Don't be *light* in attitude or speech. You are dealing in eternal issues. Could you be light-hearted if you are *really* convinced this man's destiny will be heaven or hell? *He* may try to "laugh it off." Sober sincerity and earnestness will convince more than words that what you say is truth.

How could a light or frivolous attitude hinder the work of the Holy Spirit in a witnessing situation?

4. *Be PATIENT* — *Stick with them* if they have real difficulty in understanding. *Repeat* what you say and *illustrate* it. If you know a question is an excuse, make him *see* it IS as excuse and that he isn't sincere in making it. Don't argue *against* it, but *make him feel he is SINNING to plead it,* enlisting his conscience on your side.

5. *Be PLAIN* — Don't hide anything you know about his character or relationship to God that will prick his pride. Open it all out, not to wound or offend, but because he *must see* where his problem is. Only a worthless surgeon covers rotting tissue that needs cutting out to save the patient. Don't hide the truth. It may hurt, but be plain or you won't help.

6. *Be PARTICULAR* — Don't talk about sin *abstractly.* Make him feel you mean *him.* Don't be afraid of underlining particular sins you know him guilty of, in case you "hurt his feelings." Hell will be far worse! Plainly but kindly, so as not to offend, face him with these, to prick his conscience and prove the fact of his rebellion.

7. *STICK TO THE POINT* — Don't wander around the main issues or get "side-tracked." Don't yield to "smoke-screens" and talk about *excuses* he makes, as this does more harm than good.

8. *Aim at his CONSCIENCE* — Your greatest internal ally in dealing with the sinner is his conscience. It is hard to stir feelings or convince the darkened reason in personal work. But impress on him the effect of past failures in his life and that of others, and the Holy Spirit will ram truth home with a pile-driving impact. The use of the Word of God and the response of conscience go hand in hand.

When the truth comes home in power to the heart of the sinner, prepare for "barriers" of defence. They usually take one or a combination of these four basic forms —

Why is the smoke screen of the religious sinner the hardest to tear down?

1. *MENTAL* — *Argument. Don't* argue back! Answer by *raising a further question* like — "What evidence do you have for that?" or by *further defining* what you have just said. Answer with *FACTS*, don't raise your voice, get angry or sarcastic or ridicule him. If you know he is making an *excuse*, smile and *point out* that. Stick to the basic points, keep pressing them home and don't get *side-tracked* by his "smoke-screens."

2. *PHYSICAL* — *Attack.* You may be *physically assaulted* in your witness for Christ. This is rare in countries with Christian backgrounds if your witness is not offensive or belligerent, but it may happen. In this case, you are under direct command to "resist *not*" evil (Matthew 5:38-48; 10:34-39; Romans 12:2; Titus 3:2; Colossians 3:13; Ephesians 4:2). You may not be able to control your *feelings* of hurt  or anger if this happens, but you can cry out inside to Christ to help you make the right *choice* and not hit back. This is showing true love.

3. *SOCIAL* — *Avoiding* you. One of the most common barriers. Let your witness strike home, and the sinner will try to steer clear of you. Don't "trail" them around if this is happening; just "happen" to be there at key times. It is not really *you* they are trying to hide from, it is *GOD*. They may avoid your *words* and *eyes,* but you might be able to get across to them that they *cannot* avoid your *love* and *prayers* (John 3:16-21; 12:44-48).

4. *SPIRITUAL* — *"Assuring"* you that they are *already* saved; they belong to a "good church"; they have their "own religion," thank you very much! You can clarify the religious sinner's stand before Christ by *asking them* about the events leading up to the time of their conversion and *what* took place. Point out the *essential difference* between a true Christian and a religiously selfish person. Missing in the *latter* will of course be a *true devotion* to *Jesus Christ* and the Christian *love* that marks the unselfish life. This is the hardest kind of barrier to crack because often the front is strikingly *similar* to true faith.

## BLOWING UP "BARRIERS"

Think of other replies *besides* the ones given on this page that could help you overcome the "feel" excuses of the sinner.

*Sinners take all roads to escape truth when presented with the Gospel.* Provided they are not objecting to your *presentation* (a poor attitude), excuses come from the sinners' committal to selfishness. If they can make you think they are not *able* to do what God asks (and you believe it!) you will never witness with power and confidence.

MEN *ARE* ABLE TO OBEY GOD. They know truth once presented in the Holy Spirit's power. Never forget this. They are rebels, not "weak" or "unable." Love is honest and holy, not sentimental. Leave them *no excuse* for not giving in to God. Should they reject His claims, once having seen truth they should know this very rejection will send them to Hell. *Probe each excuse and you will discover a rebel.* Clear grasp of truth in God's power puts mighty conviction on the sinner, but his excuses must be torn away or his rebel heart will hide beneath his "refuge of lies."

Sinners invariably make *excuses* to cover their rebel hearts. You must tear away these excuses or they will hide from reality behind their "refuge of lies". Use the following:

*"FEEL"* excuses —

1. *"I don't feel like accepting Christ right now."*

A. "Feelings follow right *choice.* God wants you to CHOOSE, not try to feel."

2. *"I don't feel ready to do it just yet."*

A. "You don't *have* to feel ready to come to God. You can't feel *any* better or *more* ready until you do what God *asks* of you — *give Him your heart.* Every breath you draw, every heartbeat without doing the thing God REQUIRES you to do only make you a greater rebel in the sight of God and further diminishes your chances for mercy."

351

How can a Christian convince an awakened sinner that he has not committed the unpardonable sin?

*"THINK"* excuses –

*"I don't think I can . . .* (repent, believe, forgive, confess, etc.)"

*Ask* – "Do you *WANT* to?" If they will *choose* to, without much feeling or clear understanding as to the "How" of God's control, get them to *pray* right then and there. *Ask them to pray* – "Lord, I would surrender, but I don't think I can . . ." If they will only ask *honestly*, God will meet them in powerful conviction and provide all necessary power for deliverance.

*"WILL"* excuses –

1. *"I'm willing to give my life to Christ, but I can't!"*

A. "What do you mean you *'can't'?* If you will truly choose, God will do the rest for you. He can solve every problem, forgive any sin, help you face any situation. There is nothing stopping you from giving your life to God but your own *will"* (2 Corinthians 8:12).

A2. Find out if they think they are *unpardonable.* If they feel the weight of sin, they might think they have been *too bad* to forgive. When the "unpardonable sin" (final rejection of the Holy Spirit's work) has been committed, all desire to choose for Christ *vanishes.* The very fact they are *under conviction* proves this has not happened (Isaiah 55:6-9).

A3. Make sure they are not bound by *Satanic powers.* Ask them if they have ever worked with ouija boards, spiritism or Satanic powers. You might have to make *specific prayer* to release their minds from the bondage of the Devil (2 Corinthians 4:2-4; James 4:7; 1 John 4:4).

## SHOOK-UP SINNERS

*Something has made an awakened sinner think about God.* They might NOT be convicted of sin! Sickness, death in the family, some disappointment or near-tragedy can waken men to God's claims. They are ready to listen with attention and seriousness. Don't lose time if you meet one. *Pour light in on their minds.* Don't be afraid to show him how it justly condemns him. Let God use Truth to reveal their sin and need of a Saviour. Once someone is awakened, the work of years can be done in minutes. Bring them *at once* to the point of decision. If you miss your chance, you may miss it forever. You dare not shrug off your responsibility or be silent if God has you ready for an awakened sinner.

How does the awakened sinner differ from other non-Christians? Why must we adjust our witness accordingly?

---

## CONVICTED – BUT NOT CONVERTED

There is always some *reason* for a convicted sinner not yielding to God. You must find it, bring it out and *deal* with it. Many times they *know* what it is, but try to hide it from you. Other times they are self-deceived and will not see the reason. *Ask* these questions:

(a) Have you done *something wrong* you are not willing to make *right?*

(b) Is there something you are *not willing* to *give* to God?

(c) Is there an *idol* in your life you are not willing to *forsake* for Christ?

(d) Has someone *hurt you* that you are not willing to *forgive?*

(e) Did you do something in the past you don't want to *confess?*

(f) Are you *prejudiced* against some person? (Christian with a poor witness?)

(g) Are you waiting for *God* to do something before *you* will?

(h) Do you think you have committed the *unpardonable sin?*

(i) Have you been playing with *spiritual powers* outside of Jesus Christ?

Meet *hesitation, confusion* or *silence* on any of these, and you can probe deeper. Usually it is just *ONE POINT* God strives with the sinner to yield. The moment he gives in, JUST because God asks him to — *true conversion* begins. Sinners often ask — "Will I have to *give up . . .?*" (some pet sin or idol). Tell him plainly — *"Yes."* It is probably the *only thing* they have to give up becuase it is their *god*. Don't yield an *inch* to make it easier. Give him all the promises of Christ for provision and power; but if God is dealing with them on one point, don't compromise or pass it by, or they will get a false hope and a sham experience. Jesus didn't give in with the rich young ruler although He loved him. If the young man had been allowed to keep the god of his possessions, he would have felt relieved, called himself a true disciple, joined the church and STILL gone to Hell. Don't try to make it *easier* than *God* has.

Here is a simple outline of steps in salvation which can be used in counseling. Emphasize the particular sections that the sinner needs to clearly understand. Work with the Holy Spirit to find these, and ask after each: "Are you willing to do this?"

*SALVATION* is God's plan to restore man to a holy, happy relationship with Him. All problems of sin, doubt, failure and lack of victory or God's power can be conquered by the following steps —

### 1. RETHINK —

Stop running away from the Voice of God and look at your life. We do not naturally *want* to obey God; only if we let the Holy Spirit show us our sin as GOD sees it will we realize just how bad we have been. To do this, you MUST be TOTALLY HONEST!
Don't *pretend.*
Don't "play down" your sin.
Stop making *excuses!*
*Admit it* from your *heart;* "God, I am all wrong!"
If necessary, get paper and pencil and WRITE DOWN the things that have come between you and God, and stopped you from serving Him as you ought.

### 2. REPENT —

Turn your back on your old way of life. Be WILLING to *lose* any habit, any plan, any friend that you have been living

354

your life for instead of God. This is not easy, but Jesus said if we wanted to follow Him, we must first *count the cost* (Luke 14:25-33). Salvation is like a real marriage. Two people promise themselves to each other, pledge their love to each other before a watching world and give up all their old dates. This is what God wants you to do to know His love.

### 3. RENOUNCE —

Give up all *RIGHTS* to your own life. If you are going to be a part of God's world — changing family, you cannot be your *own* boss any longer. You must *DIE* to your own plans, dreams and ambitions and be willing to do whatever God wants you to do. He knows EXACTLY what will make you most happy. It may hurt to surrender everything at first, but God knows best and will *never* ask you to do anything that you will regret in the end. A true Christian has nothing of his own; time, talents, money, possessions, friends, career and future — all must be surrendered for his King's service wherever and whenever He wants them.

### 4. REPLAN —

Be prepared to make many *changes* in your life! The very moment you make this heart-choice for God, the old "you" will die, and a new person inside you will begin to live. If the Holy Spirit is speaking to you about getting something right with someone, you must be *willing* to do it, for God to help you. Wherever you need to confess wrong, or restore or repay something to someone, the Lord Jesus will give you the courage and the words to say. Becoming a Christian implies the WILLINGNESS, as far as humanly possible, to *right all known wrong* (Proverbs 28:13). If you have written out a list of things that have come between you and God, ask NOW His forgiveness for those against Him; plan to make right all others with people you know you have wronged, and feel guilty about. The circle of *confession* must fit the circle of *committal* of sin. Those against *God,* confess *only* to Him; those against one person, to *that person alone;* those against a *group,* to the *group.*

### 5. RECEIVE —

The Lord Jesus Christ by FAITH (a loyalty of love to the Word of God) to *rule in your heart as King.* He must be your

Jesus said that a man could not serve two masters. What does this mean and how must this truth be employed in our witnessing?

355

Why must
great care be
taken in our
words with a
new convert?

absolute *"Boss"* from now on! This act of faith is neither an "idea" or a mere "feeling" but an ACT, a CHOICE of your WILL, made *intelligently* and *carefully*. Give Him your doubts, your weakness and your loneliness. Your heart will never have peace, your doubts will never clear up and you will never die to the world until you trust, surrender and BELIEVE from your heart! *Be totally honest with Him.* Receive Christ into your life as your Lord and Master to live for Him from this moment on, forever (Romans 10:9-10).

## WHAT TO TELL YOUNG CHRISTIANS

*What instructions do you give those whom you lead to the Lord?* Help them through to Christ by suggesting that which they should tell the Lord — (a *typical prayer outline:* "Lord Jesus, please forgive me for my sin. I admit to you honestly today that all my life I've lived for myself. I want to give up all rights to my life right now, and ask you to forgive my sin and make me one of your children. Be my 'Boss' from this moment forewards in everything I say and do. Thank you Lord — Amen.") Then leave them a couple of suggestions for going on with the Lord Jesus. *Whatever you do:*

*DON'T TELL HIM:*

(a) *"Now you are saved!"*

Why *not?* For *several reasons,* it is better not to say this because:

1. *You* don't keep the Book of Life, *God* does. He knows if a prayer was a heart-cry or not, and whether new life has begun. You don't. You have no right to tell him what God alone can assure him of.

2. *Better they find out their salvation for themselves.* Faith is strengthened by testing, not propping. If it IS real, it will stand life's hard honesty.

3. *If YOU tell him*, it is *your* word he relies on. You will find he could be YOUR convert, not God's. And YOU will have to keep him instead of the Lord. Letting *God* grant assurance will soon prove if his stand was an experiment or an experience.

What can be said to *encourage* a new convert?

(b) *"How do you 'feel'?"*

The Christian life is a choice of the will. Choose God's way and feeling will follow. But don't give the impression that FEELINGS are a total salvation guide or he will lose assurance with a headache! Teach him his *duty*; feelings or not.

(c) *TOO MUCH!*

Keep *some* instruction for another time. If you give him too much at once, he will not remember it, get confused and feel a failure, before he begins. Babies don't start learning for some months the more complex truths of life. Neither do *spiritual* babies. A few things at a time!

*DO ASK HIM:*

1. *"Did you REALLY MEAN what you asked God?"*

This will help you discover *doubt.* If he still doubts, there is still DUTY to be done. *Doubt almost always shows an incomplete heart consecration.* Something has not been yielded. See if he has held anything back in such a case. Don't be afraid to *dig deeply* here. Unless a *first* work is deep and thorough, the resulting Christian life will be less fruitful, useful and blessed. Give him clear, strong and firm directions. Tell him it is *sin* to have *reason* to doubt, and sin to doubt *without* reason (Romans 14:23). If you leave them uncertain, they will at best be sickly, shaky Christians (1 John 5:11-13).

2. *"Would you like to thank God for what you just did?"*

This is an *acid test of reality.* If he can honestly thank God for his salvation, you can be reasonably sure it is genuine.

*TEACH HIM TO:*

1. *Expect to enjoy God's love and favor.*

357

Why should
our advice to
new Christians
always be
geared
around
choice rather
than
feelings?

This won't mean he will always be excited, nor always directly thinking of God, but his heart should be *at peace* and enjoying the blessing of Christ. Give the idea it "won't matter" if he loses the sense of God's love and favor and, when through *your* fault he backslides from God, you shouldn't be surprised. Sin *should* cause doubt and worry in the Christian, so he will tearfully go back to God to confess his wrong. The only real evidence of salvation is to OBEY GOD FROM THE HEART (Luke 6:43-49).

2. *Get in with other Christians who love Christ whole-heartedly.*

Don't put him in with backslidden hypocrites or he will take his standards from them. If, however, he doesn't *want* to be with God's people, there is something wrong with his salvation (1 John 1:7).

3. *Renounce ownership of all he has — time, talents, money and possessions.*

Unless he has truly done this to the best of his present knowledge he is *not* a Christian. They should not be left to think *anything* still belongs to them. Nothing is their own any more — property, influence, body or soul. All belongs to *God.* They have chosen to be not their own but God's servants, to be ruled and directed at His pleasure.

They have no right to use anything as if it were theirs; to spend one minute or one cent outside the Lordship of Jesus Christ (1 Corinthians 6:19-20).

---

## SIGNS OF SALVATION

---

*True Christians will show definite signs of a real experience with God* that has resulted in a genuine conversion to Christ. The following are EVIDENCES — *(not* PROOF!) that a person has passed "from death to life." The first group are

*EXTERNAL* — ones that you, the *counsellor*, can recognize. The second are *INTERNAL*, and those which the new Christian should look for in his *own* life.

*OUTWARD:*

1. *DESIRE FOR SCRIPTURE* — A true Christian wants to read the Bible to find out what God expects of him. Scripture is spiritual "food." "Man shall not live by bread alone, but by every word that proceeds out of the mouth of God" (Job 23:12; Jeremiah 15:16; Deuteronomy 6:5-7; Matthew 4:4; Romans 10:17; 15:4; 1 Peter 2:2).

In your new convert's life? Yes [ ]   No [ ]

2. *DIFFERENCE OF STANDARD* — *A radical change in habit,* action and purpose. A New Christian wants to be *different* in word, thought and deed. It may take time for the inward change to show outwardly in some things, but never condemn a new convert for what he *is* until you find out first what he wants to *be!* "Therefore if any man be in Christ, he is a new creature; old things are passed away; all things are become new" (2 Corinthians 5:17; Galatians 6:15-16; Ephesians 4:20-24; Philippians 3:7; 1 John 3:1-3).

In your new convert's life? Yes [ ]   No [ ]

3. *DIFFERENCE OF SELF* — A child of God begins to tighten the rein on old habits of self-indulgence. A sterner eye is given to areas of life (such as food and drink, changing both the quality and the quantity). Harmful stimulants, late nights (and late mornings), extravagant dressing and living begin to be dealt with by the Cross. "Every man that hath this hope in him, purifies himself, even as He is pure" (1 John 3:3; Luke 3:11; Matthew 16:24; 1 Corinthians 10:13; Galatians 5:22-23).

In your new convert's life? Yes [ ]   No [ ]

4. *DESPISED BY THE WORLD* — A new Christian will experience *trouble* from those who know him well, who don't understand his new life, or from "dead" Christians who have backslidden in heart and whose lukewarmness the new convert will show up. "Yes — all that live godly lives in Christ Jesus shall suffer persecution" (John 15:18-21; Acts 5:40-41; Romans 8:18; 12:20-21; 2 Timothy 2:12; 3:12; Philippians 1:28-29; 1 Peter 2:20-21).

In your new convert's life? Yes [ ]   No [ ]

5. *SEEKS OTHER CHRISTIANS* — A *hunger for fellowship* and a real *love* for true children of God is a sure sign of the new birth. "By this shall all men know that you are my disciples — if you have love one toward another" (John 13:35; Acts 2:42; Romans 15:5-6; Ephesians 3:17-19; Hebrews 10:25; 1 Peter 1:22; 1 John 1:2,7; 3:14; 7:7-13).

**In your new convert's life? Yes [ ]  No [ ]**


6. *SERVES THE LORD* — Looks for ways and means to please the Lord Jesus — begins to witness for Him, and wants to win souls. "For me to live is Christ and to die is gain" (Psalm 107:2; Philippians 1:21; Matthew 10:32; 25:29; John 14:12; 1 Peter 3:15).

**In your new convert's life? Yes [ ]  No [ ]**


7. *STICKS TO THE TASK* — *Keeps pushing forward for the Lord* despite failure or setbacks — a determination to stay true to God. " . . . This one thing I do — forgetting those things which are behind, and reaching forward for the things before, I press towards the mark . . ." (Philippians 3:13-14; 1 John 1:4; Romans 6:1-14; 2 Peter 1:10; John 5:37, 39; Psalm 37:23-24).

**In your new convert's life? Yes [ ]  No [ ]**


*INWARD:*

1. *ASSURANCE OF GOD'S LOVE* — This clears away doubt, makes the Christian active for the Lord, decided in his faith and holy in his life. "All that the Father gives Me shall come to me; and the one that comes to Me I will certainly never cast out" (John 6:37; 5:24; 16:27-33; Acts 13:39, Romans 15:13; 8:38-39; 1 John 1:12; 3:20; 4:18; 5:12-13).

**In your own spiritual life? Yes [ ]  No [ ]**

2. *ALL-SUSTAINING PEACE* — This peace upholds and undergirds the believer through all trials and tribulations. A *freedom from fear* no matter how dangerous, difficult or deadly a situation may be. "The peace of God which passes all understanding, shall guard your hearts and minds through Jesus Christ" (Philippians 4:7; Luke 12:32; John 14:1-2, 27; 2 Timothy 1:7; 2 Corinthians 5:1,8; Isaiah 32:17; 41:10; Psalm 23:4).

**In your own spiritual life? Yes [ ]  No [ ]**

3. *AWAKENED CONSCIENCE* — Greater awareness of thoughts, words or deeds which do not please the Lord. A  respect for the power of sin; a fear of the Lord and a keeping of His commandments. "We know that we are of God and the whole world lies in wickedness" (1 John 5:19; 1 Corinthians 2:14; Romans 12:2; John 14:15,21; Proverbs 19:23; Jeremiah 32:40; 1 Timothy 1:5; James 1:12; Hebrews 13:8; Revelation 3:5; 1 Peter 1:13-16; 2:9).

In your own spiritual life? Yes [ ]    No [ ]

4. *SEARCH FOR TRUTH* — A genuine desire for reality and solid foundations on which to build the new life both in the Word of God and from other spiritual Christians. "For everyone that does evil hates the light . . . but he that does truth comes to the light, that his deeds may be made manifest that they are wrought in God" (John 3:20-21; 5:39; 8:12,31; Matthew 7:21; :Acts 17:11; 1 Corinthians 2:9-16).

In your own spiritual life? Yes [ ]    No [ ]

5. *SPIRIT WITNESS* — The Holy Spirit provides the indescribable consciousness of *acceptance* with God on the merit of the Lord Jesus. "For as many as are led by the Spirit of God, they are the sons of God" (Romans 8:14; 8:9; John 14:17; 1 John 4:13; 5:10 ).

In your own spiritual life? Yes [ ]    No [ ]

6. *SONSHIP AWARENESS* — When God is truly Father, the child of God has a warm sense of *parental affection* and care from the Lord. "And because you are sons, God has sent forth the Spirit of His Son into your hearts crying — 'Dear Father' " (Galatians 4:6; Romans 8:28-29; 8:15-17; John 1:12; 16:26-27; 17:5-6; 21-26; 2 Corinthians 6:16-18; Ephesians 2:18; 1 John 3:1-2).

In your own spiritual life? Yes [ ]    No [ ]

7. *SOCIAL CONCERN* — An interest in the *needs of others*, with desire to promote righteousness, do good "studying and devising ways and means to convert, sanctify and reform mankind." "But whosoever has this world's goods and sees his brother in need and closes his heart against him,

how does the love of God abide in him?" (1 John 3:17; 3:16-24; 1 Peter 2:2; 2 Corinthians 9:6-7; 9:6, 8; John 9:4-5; Proverbs 11:25).

---

## RECOGNIZING REJECTION OF GOD

---

*Those who have deliberately grieved away God's Spirit* by continual   rebellion against Truth are in terrible danger of being *forever lost.* There are, again, some *evidences* (NOT *proof*) that a man has been forsaken of God, and further attempts at witness may be futile:

1. *RICH AND PROSPEROUS IN SIN* (over a long period) — A person who profits greatly from the fruit of sin is in danger of sacrificing eternal rights and riches for material wealth. "I was envious . . . when I saw the prosperity of the wicked . . . until I went into the sanctuary of God — then I saw their end" (Psalm 49; 73:3-19; Jeremiah 5:27-29; Luke 12:15-21).

2. *RUNS FROM TRUTH* — Makes a HABIT of avoiding places and people connected with salvation — stays away from Church, the Bible and soul-winning Christians. If a fatal disease is spreading, the ones *sure* to die are those who ignore the remedy. "As I live, saith the Lord God — I have no pleasure in the death of the wicked . . . turn ye, turn ye from your evil ways; for why will you die, oh house of Israel?" (Ezekiel 33:11; John 5:39-40; 8:24; 9:41).

3. *REBELS INSTEAD OF REPENTS* under chastisement — in trouble allowed to make the soul cast itself on God, the reprobate instead becomes more and more bitter against Him. "Why should ye be stricken any more? You will revolt more and more" (Isaiah 1:5; Psalm 94:12; Proverbs 3:11; Revelation 3: 19).

4. *AGES IN SIN*—Most people are saved *under the age of 25.* The older a person gets in rebellion against God, the less likely

362

 it is that they will repent. Those who set their hearts to make their mark in the world then "coldly calculate to give their lives to God later" are trying to take advantage of God's forbearance. They try to give the jaded remnant of a Devil-serving life to God. It will not work. "My Spirit will not always strive with man; for that he is flesh" (Genesis 6:3; Ecclesiastes 12:1; Romans 2:4-10).

5. *ABSENCE OF CHASTISEMENT* — When a person has *NO* trouble he is *IN* trouble! Satan never seems much to bother with the person who has no interest in the things of God. He will keep him for "later." "Despise not the chastening of the Lord; for whom he loves, he chastises" (Hebrews 12:5-8; Proverbs 3:11; Psalm 94:12; Revelation 3:19).

6. *ACCEPTS DAMNING HERESY* — God sends "strong delusions" that they might believe a lie, because "they obey not the Truth, but have *pleasure* in unrighteousness." The more certain their damnation is, the more certainly they believe it. "Beware how you trifle with truth. How often have sinners argued in favor of a lie too long for the sake of argument, until they have come to believe their own lie and are lost forever" (2 Peter 2:1-3; Romans 1:28-32).

> Am I sure I am a Christian?  Yes (Thank God)          [  ]
> No (Go back to "Judas") [  ]

There are a number of good tracts on the market today that bring out enough emphasis on personal responsibility to be effective in a careless society. Some of these are *"Let's Talk Sense," "Chicken," "Trapped"* and *"Afterglow"* by David Wilkerson, available from Teen Challenge, 444 Clinton Avenue, Brooklyn, New York 11238, *"Becoming a Christian,"* John Stott (I.V.F. Press, 130 North Wells, Chicago, Illinois, 60606), *"Here's How," "All Or Nothing," "Destined for Greatness," "How Much For The Man"* and others from Life Messengers, Box 1967, Seattle, Washington, 98111. Ask also about the *"Youth Aflame"* series of salvation tracts, including the *"Counterfeit Conversion"* series of three, *"These Are The Facts"* and the cartooned outreach series.

"Blessed are ye, when men shall revile you and persecute you, and shall say all manner of evil against you falsely, for My sake . . . Rejoice . . . for great is your reward" (Matthew 5:11-12).

# JAMES ZEBEDEE

## (WHO WON HIS CROWN)

"Jesus said . . . 'Ye shall indeed drink of My cup' . . . and Herod killed James, the brother of John with the sword."

Matthew 20:23; Acts 12:2

PHASE:        6 .. *Into All The World*
SECTION:     11 .. *"I" For Identification With Christ*
MATERIAL:      .. *Separation From The World and Sacrifice*

*James Zebedee,* one of the "Sons of Thunder," was one of the little band of disciples to "fall asleep" in Christ. Each disciple had counted the cost of following the Stranger Who had captured their hearts. They knew what it would mean to testify of the Living Christ to a God-rejecting world.

Too much a friend of God to love the world that crucified his Saviour, *James* paid the ultimate price of discipleship and sealed his faith in blood. One by one, all disciples but John, followed him to death by violence, and with the exception of *Judas,* to a martyr's crown. You too may be called to make the supreme sacrifice. Your Lord and master has to be crucified to conquer, And YOU? Can you follow in His footsteps,  Whose path to victory was marked by drops of His own blood? You were called for this purpose — "Christ suffered for you, leaving an example for you to follow in His steps."

---

## LIFE BY DEATH

It is an unchanging principle of God that *life* must first come from *DEATH.* The seed falls into the ground and dies — from that broken shell springs the grain of new life. The lamb is slain, but the sprinkled blood signifies new life for the penitent. "If any man shall lose his life for My sake and the Gospel's, the same shall save it," said the Lord Jesus (Matthew 16:25; Mark 8:35). It is strange, but true, that we cannot wholly live until we first truly die.

*Our eyes dim, our hair greys — we grow old.* President to pauper, Asian to Zealander, all must die. Death is the one final certainty of life, the common denominator of all mankind. We travel to a common end. Men are often foolish about death. They dress up a body as if it were alive, talk about bereavement as if it were a "sad parting."

But death is *NOT* the "sad end" for a *Christian!* There IS real pain of parting when loved ones who shared so much of our lives go — but it is sorrow for OURSELVES. We miss them; their smile, the odd emptiness now they are not with us; such things touch gentle strings of sadness. But it is grief that only *WE* feel. Those with no hope beyond the grave have reason to be "of all men most miserable" (1 Corinthians 15:19). But for the disciple, death is robbed of its bitter sting. Life will not finish in ruin, but reunion; the grave is not the end, but the beginning of a new life to come with Christ (1 Corinthians 15:20-22).

How does crucifixion graphically illustrate the demands of discipleship?

## CRUCIFIXION — A NEW KIND OF DYING

*All over the ministry of the Lord Jesus hung the calm shadow of the cross.* It was always in His mind. He knew that the beautiful story of men brought back from sin must begin in ugliness. If a grain of wheat was to live, it must first fall into the ground and die. If any man would follow Him, that man must take his place on a personal cross. *What did He mean — "take up your cross"?*

*The Roman crucifixion* was probably the most terrible form of death in history. The man hanging on the cross, pegged there by iron spokes driven into his flesh, experienced almost all that was horrible and ghastly. He felt dizzy, feverish, ill. Cramp gripped him continually. The mental shock of nakedness before a jeering crowd stabbed with shame. Raging thirst and an agonized dragging up of the chest to draw breath combined with the dull sickness of *blood loss.* Such was the awful agony of the cross.

*Besides all this,* the Son of God bore in His body the sin of the world. No human mind can ever understand the stark horror the Holy One must have experienced as He felt for the first time the heartbreaking shock of sin. He visualized it all at once, and the burden *broke His heart.* He took our penalty. He became our great Substitute. He bore judgment we deserved. He died in OUR place. That was the cross for Christ.

*When the Lord Jesus said,* "Take up YOUR cross," did He mean THIS? Were we to die in the same way? Tradition tells us that Peter did — upside down by request, feeling himself to be unworthy to be crucified that same way as his Master. But Christ was thinking much more than our following Him

to some physical Calvary. It is the TRUTH of a cross we are to take up, not a wooden one. The Cross is a place of *death* — to all our rights, ambitions, reputation and defences. *Calvary is a defenceless position.* Jesus did not defend Himself, answer back or demand His rights. He was spit on, reviled and finally crucified. The royal law of love required that it was expedient that one man should die for the people. (John 12:50). The love that wills the highest good of God and His Universe puts even a man's *own* salvation on the altar if such an act could bring greater glory to God (Exodus 32:1-32; Romans 9:3). It is on the *truth* of the cross that we die to all *self-pleasing.* Dead men cannot fight fleshly battles. A man who has been crucified is dead, utterly dead to everything the world can offer to selfish choice.

"The cross is a *symbol of death.* It ends a human being, violently and abruptly. If you picked up a cross in Roman times and started down the road, you had already said goodbye to your friends. You were not coming back. The cross slew all of a man. It slew him *completely;* it slew him *for good.* It struck hard; it struck cruelly, and when it had done its work, the victim was no more."

*The Lord was saying in effect to His disciples* — "I won't stop you from following. But don't expect to be disciples just by looking at or listening to Me. Before the victory, I must pay a great price, run a grave risk and make a great choice. For each who would walk with Me, there must also be a *counting of the cost.* The price for each of you will be different. But until you make *your* choice and pay *your* price, there can be no question of discipleship. My disciples must fight out in their own lives the battle I fought in Mine — and WIN it!"

# DEFEAT OF SIN

*How shall we defeat sin? Salvation is a three-fold thing:*

## 1. PAST —

God says — "Your sins and your iniquities will I remember
no more. As far as the east is from the west, I will put them
from Me" (Psalm 103:12). When we come in repentance and
faith to the Lord Jesus Christ, He forgives us in love and
starts us off on a road to new life with clean clothes on our
soul. Beginning in God's eyes "just (as) if I'd" never sinned,
we are set free from the claims of the broken law of God as
far as its penalty and condemnation are concerned (Romans
6:17-23; 7:1-6; Galatians 2:16-20; 3:9-14, 22-26). God
*JUSTIFIES* us by *faith. "Legal" justification* is the process of
being declared not guilty. Man cannot plead that he is
innocent, nor bring forward any *excuse* that he had any right
to sin. The *law* is our *accuser* once we have broken it. If it
can be proved that the law was broken by a man ONCE, he is
just as guilty as the man who has broken it a hundred times.
No man except Christ has perfectly kept the law of God.
Broken, it *condemns* us. *We* are the *accused*. Once we admit
the wrong, we have to either give an excuse that is both
*TRUE* and *sufficient* reason to let us off or pay the penalty
of the broken law. Any excuse that is really a *lie,* especially if
it reflects on the court or government pressing the charges
can only aggravate a man's offense. We have shown in past
chapters that man is UTTERLY without excuse (Romans
3:19-20; 11:32; Galatians 3:22).

God justifies us, not by LAW (which, having been broken,
can only *condemn* us), but by *FAITH* — pardoning and
accepting us AS IF we were actually righteous. God treats us
as if we had NEVER sinned, releasing us from the penalty of
the law, restoring us into the right place with God in his
family and giving us rights of His very own children. God
forgives our PAST sins BY our act of repentance from sin and
our *trust* in the Lord Jesus for freedom.

*Christ perfectly obeyed God the Father's holy law.* He owed no suffering to the law for Himself, as He did not break it. He could therefore suffer for us, and to allow God to freely forgive men, substitue HIS death for the infliction of the penalty of the law on us. His Divine substitution made our pardon possible (Isaiah 53:5-6,11; Matthew 26:28; Hebrews 9:12; 1 Peter 2:24).

## 2. POWER —

As we abide in Christ, temptation is beaten. God has forgiven ALL our past sin and from the claims of the broken law of God. Now, for the Christian, the Bible is filled with promises of the mighty *KEEPING* power of God's love. We no longer need to be slaves to selfishness and sin (Romans 6:11-22; 8:1-4). *God's standard for us* is to, "Be perfect, even as your Father which is in heaven is perfect" (Matthew 5:48). This per-  fection is NOT freedom from mistake or some new magic "inability" to sin. It is *not* being perfect in wisdom, or knowledge or in physical being. It is also not to be confused with God's own *IN*FINITE perfection. It simply means to *live up to all the light we have out of love to Him* Who saved us and has called us with a holy calling. It is to live a life of freedom and victory, HABITUALLY overcoming temptation through the grace of Christ. If a five-month old baby is doing all a five-month old baby should be doing, that baby is perfect FOR HIS AGE; as he learns more and grows more, provided *he does all he would be expected to do* for someone of his age, intelligence and abilities, he is *perfect.* God does not ask you to be wise as some other Christian, nor have as much faith as another, but simply do all the Lord Jesus asks you to do HOW He wants you to and WHEN He wants you to. *This* is being "perfect" in God's eyes.

*To accomplish this state of continual victory.* God has made many provisions for us. He is the "Author *and* Finisher of your faith" (Hebrews 12:2). If He BEGAN it in your life, you can be sure He will FINISH it! He has set different *offices* and *ministries* in the Church, to bring men and women into a place of perfect power over sin in Christ

370

(Ephesians 4:15-19). God has taken a pledge to deliver you from all unbearable *temptation,* listing all His might and power in your favor as long as you seek to serve Him (James 1:12; 1 Corinthians 10:13; 2 Peter 2:9; Hebrews 2:18). When the Lord Jesus is received by faith to reign as King in your heart, He reveals to your soul all of His love and grace and strength that is necessary to keep you safe and secure near to God's heart and side. We do not have to be afraid of being torn away from the arms of Him Who loves us and Who has promised to be an eternal, faithful Friend. "They shall NEVER perish, neither shall any man pluck them out of My hand" (John 10:28; 3:15-17; 17:11; Luke 21:18; 1 Peter 1:5). He is abundantly able to "make you perfect, stablish, strengthen and settle you" (1 Peter 5:10) make you "perfect in every good work, to do His will, working in you that which is well-pleasing in His sight through Christ Jesus,to Whom be glory for ever and ever" (Hebrews 13:20-21). These, and many others are given by God as "exceeding great and precious promises, that by these you might be partakers of the Divine Nature having escaped the corruption that is in the world" (2 Peter 1:2-11).

What is the difference between the body Jesus will give us at the resurrection and the body we possess now?

## 3. PRESENCE —

We live in a terrible world. All around us are evidences of sin and the results of man's rebellion against His loving Creator. Our own inherited physical depravity is a constant source of temptation. As long as we are still in this world, we shall never be completely free from the presence of sin. All of us live in a sinful environment, full of weakness, fragility and death (Job 14:1-6; 15:14; John 3:6; 2 Corinthians 4:7-16).

However, the Christian can look forward to the day when the Lord will give us all *new, depravity-free bodies* with all sensibilities restored to perfect balance, completely free from pain, defect, disease and death. "It is sown in corruption, it is raised in incorruption; sown in dishonor, raised in glory; sown in weakness, raised in power; sown in a natural body, raised in a spiritual body" (1 Corinthians 15:35-55; 2 Corinthians 5:1-8; Philippians 3:8-15, 20-21). These new bodies could well be able to travel vast distances in a moment

What is the
simplest
definition of
sin that you
can give?

of time, explore the secrets of God's amazing Universe, never need medicine or a doctor's care or ever suffer pain (Revelation 21:1-4; 22:1-6; 1 Thessalonians 4:13-18; Hebrews 1:5-8; 11:36-40; 1 John 3:1-3). Should the Lord return before we see death, we shall be "caught up together" with the resurrected new bodies of the dead to "meet the Lord in the air — so shall we ever be with the Lord." The world is *on the brink of an invasion from space;* the rightful King and Ruler is coming back to His rebel planet (1 Thessalonians 4:16-17).

*Sin is a "me first attitude" of heart;* a supreme choice to gratify self. The ONLY answer to give you *power over sin* is to keep *LOOKING to JESUS* (Hebrews 12:2). You will never learn to have power over sin until you learn to extract power from your Saviour. Whenever we sin, it is because of our ignorance of Christ; when some temptation overcomes us it is only because we do not know and grasp the particular relation of Christ to our souls that would meet our need. The more *clearly* you have seen your own *sin* in the light of the *law* for conviction; and the more *vividly* you have seen the *Lord Jesus* with the eyes of faith at (or following) your conversion to Him, the more stable and victorious will be your Christian life. *You need to see* the Lord — high and lifted up (Isaiah 6:1-8; John 3:14-15; 12:32). Such a look will humble the soul, purify the heart and break the power of temptation.

---

### DEALING WITH SELF

---

Why do we so often listen to *temptation* rather than to the Voice of *God's Spirit?*

The *soul* is like a *radio control station.* In this "tuner" your WILL is the operator. Whatever impressions you choose to "dial" you can "amplify" and "record" (remember and experience) in your soul. The tug of the *outside* world must be balanced against the guidance of God in the *spiritual* world. We are all used to living externally. Our appetites are enormously developed in relation to the things of time and sense; to spiritual truths and objects we are naturally dead as rock. We have not learned to live by the *"frequencies of faith"* and listen to the Voice of God. Can you see what God the Father wants His children to do?

He wants you to "TUNE OUT" your concentration on the *sense* world more; the world you are *used* to obeying and learn to "plug in" to HIM. He needs your *spirit* developed to such a point where you can, if need be, follow a different set of directions from those pressing on your senses in a blinded world. To change the illustration, *becoming a Christian is like learning to drive on the other side of the road.* You must be careful for a while until you learn to think and act BY HABIT in this new way. It will take *time* and *discipline* to develop the right habit patterns. BEWARE of the CRISIS! In times of stress and sudden temptation, you may be tempted to return to the old way of life, especially if bad memory patterns have been deeply rooted in your mind. But *"God is faithful.* Who will not suffer you to be tempted above that which you are able; but will with the temptation also make a way to escape, that you may be able to bear it" (1 Corinthians 10:13).

*The more we think about sin,* the more *powerful* grows its hold on us. When we look to the Law, it can only hold out the scale of justice and judgment. The motives of the Law IN THEMSELVES can never *stop* a man from sin, and it is silly to think the same motives (of hope or fear) can RECLAIM the sinner. These legal motives not only *lose* part of their influence once the law is *broken,* but can actually produce in the selfish heart the exact OPPOSITE influence. Every convicted sinner seeing the standard of the holy Law of God (without the love of God expressed in the Gospel) only hardens his heart more in rebellion and raises the barrier of his pride. The *Devil* is the most infamous example of this; he has seen the law with all its justice, has once known the blessings of living by it, but only hardens his heart in greater rebellion against God in a returnless distance from obedience. No self-righteous efforts of making yourself "better" to conform to the standard will work, since they are all made with legal motives from selfish reasons. The very *fear of failure* or *hope of gain to self* by avoiding the law's penalty will divert your attention from God and faith, destroying the very love you need to bring you deliverance.

It is thus never *good to constantly check motives,* worrying about being pure or whether you are actually doing

What are the environmental factors we face that can become occasions to sin?

373

What is the
difference
between the
earth as a
created
sphere and
that which
we refer to as
"the world"?

what God asks. Even *praying over* sin for too long a period may fool you into further bondage because deep thinking about IT makes it seem irresistable. Such is the deceitfulness of sin (Hebrews 3:12-13).

*God has made full provision* for beating the three great enemies of our souls; the *world* (1 John 5:4-5), the *flesh* (Galatians 5:16-25) and the *Devil* (Ephesians 3:14-19). But these are all accomplished by TRUSTING in the Lord Jesus Christ, never by "willing" our way past selfishness by legal determination. As long as we wrestle with sin ourselves, we will lose every time. Temptation is *unavoidable,* but NOT *unbearable.* God allows it to strengthen your reliance on Him. Your response to temptation must be to *throw yourself ON CHRIST.* The amount of *reliance* you have on Him in moments of trial measure the "breaking-point" of your trust (1 Peter 1:5-9; 4:12-16). A man with great trust under temptation is far more precious than gold in God's eyes.

*Temptation from the world is effectively dealt with by the cross.* The "world" is not the *earth* God gave man, but rather the total world-SYSTEM that is ruled by Satan, filled with evil and hatred towards God and His children. It is headed for judgment and the wrath of God (Galatians 1:4; John 7:7; 14:30; 16:8; Ephesians 2:2; 2 Corinthians 4:4; James 1:27). God has called us out of it, so we are to stop following it, stay unspotted from it and stand by God in righteous anger against it (1 Corinthians 7:31; Galatians 6:14; Colossians 2:8; Romans 12:2; 1 John 5:5). *Worldliness* is not a THING — it is a *heart-attitude* that shows a still-selfish, Devil-serving life. The CROSS is the divine means of deliverance from the world. A dead man cannot follow the crowd; he cannot break God's laws, let his mind feed on filth or allow his hands or lips to do wickedness. He is DEAD to the world, with all its attractions and pleasures. If we are truly God's children, we have died to the world and its bubble pleasures; we live instead *to* and *for* Him.

Many times (and perhaps *too many* times) Christians blame their trials on the *Devil.* You are probably *not* important enough yet to merit personal daily visits from the prince of darkness! Much trial is allowed by the Lord to teach you the right responses to situations, or to check any self-dependence you may be developing. *Demonic trial* is always accompanied by definite signs of fear or uneasiness, and sometimes follows times of physical weakness OR elation. Your close trust in the Mighty One will keep you safe and put Satan or any of his demonic forces on the run (Proverbs 18:10; 1 John 3:8; Colossians 2:15; Luke 10:17-20; Mark 16:17-18). Satan is a DEFEATED enemy. Jesus has no fear of Satan because He is Master and all Hell recognizes it (Mark 1:23-27; 3:22-27; 5:1-20; 6:7; Colossians 2:15). If we are Christians, then we are IN CHRIST and have no need to fear the Devil (Galatians 2:20; Colossians 1:17; 3:4; 1 Corinthians 1:30; Ephesians 1:17-23).

If there is one word that can describe the character of Satan, what would that word be and how was that character acquired?

---

## DANGER FOR SATAN!

---

*Satan, arch-enemy of man and GOD,* is a powerful, dangerous foe. He has been in "business" for thousands of years and knows every trick in the book to trap men into sin. The Bible describes him as coming in the guise of an "angel of light" or walking the earth as a "raging lion" (2 Corinthians 11:14; 1 Peter 5:8). He hates you with the very hatred of Hell. He will always come with his two daggers of *doubt* and *pride.* The Devil is *wholly selfish* and will always accuse others of being so. He accused God to Adam and Eve of being selfish (Genesis 3:1-5) and Job, the righteous man who was perfect before the eyes of God (Job 1:1; 6-12). He will try to turn your eyes on to the world, cast doubt on the goodness, faithfulness and promises of God, and try to drive in wedges of fear, depression or discouragement to shake your trust in Christ.

*Dealing with Enemy depression* involves *three steps:* (1) *Resist the Enemy* in the Name of the Lord Jesus (James 4:7). Do it *firmly* and *in faith* that God will honor your obedience to His Word. (2) Use the weapon of *praise;* sing a psalm or hymn or song of Christian victory (Philippians 4:4). (3) Begin to *intercede in prayer* for others, and *thank and praise* God for what He is doing through them (Philippians

4:6). Satan will pull off the pressure immediately if he sees it only makes you praise and pray! Satan does not know *how* you *will* react, but he hopes it will be the *wrong* way. Fool him for a change. Do the *unexpected* thing *for God,* and depression from Enemy attack will lift. The "peace of God" will march round and round your mind.

FEAR is simply *LACK OF FAITH* in God. Get hold of some *Bible promises.* Read them out *loud* if necessary (1 Samuel 12:24; Psalm 27:1; 118:6; 23:4; 3:5; Isaiah 35:4; 59:19; Romans 8:15; 1 John 4:18; Luke 12:32). Now this is *God's Word.* He *means* what He says. If you have placed your life in His hands, He will keep you. FEAR is an enemy. Nothing that uses this tool of the Devil is Christian. The "fear of the Lord" is NOT related; it is simply to "hate evil" and involves an *awe* and *reverence* for God (Proverbs 8:15; 1:7; 19:23; Job 28:28; Psalm 2:11; 19:9; 34:11; 111:10;112:1). It is NOT fright or horror. "In the fear of the Lord is STRONG CONFIDENCE" (Proverbs 14:26). If you have been afraid, confess your unbelief as SIN (Romans 14:23). Then obey the Word of God with full trust in the protection of the Lord Jesus. Use *prayer* and *praise* also.

Sometimes, his *demonic spirits* invade the spirits of those who live in the grip of sin, taking the place reserved for the Holy Spirit in the control center of the heart. This is called in the Bible "demon possession," and the world is filled with many of these very real powers of darkness who seek to destroy men (Matthew 15:22; 17:15; 9:32-33; 12:22; Mark 5:1-13; 9:14-29; Luke 6:18; Acts 8:7; 16:16). The sinner, bound for Hell, is in terrible danger, made far more deadly by the searing effect of sin on the conscience.

Where there has been *any form* of occult involvement, there MUST be a complete confession of this *as sin* to Christ, and a *total renunciation.* Until this occurs, NO freedom from Satanic attack can be expected. Use these steps to victory: (1) Make a *confession of faith in Christ* ALOUD; if difficult, call upon the power of the blood of Christ to break Satan's hold. (2) Confess *AS SIN* all occult involvement, *specifying BY NAME* each form of participation, e.g. "Father, I confess that I have broken your laws by consulting a fortune-teller, by using an ouija board, by following a horoscope. I confess

these as sin and ask for Your forgiveness in Jesus' name." (3) *Renounce Satan,* and command him to depart with all his forces and works. This must be a firm COMMAND of faith, *not* a request. It is to be spoken in Jesus' Name. It must be firmly made, finally committed and done OUT LOUD. (4) *Prayer* made for specific deliverance. Satan is commanded to loose the victim and free him.

What affect does a holy life have upon satanic forces of darkness?

In spite of his power, the Christian does NOT have to be afraid of him. Satan is called subtle and cunning in the Scriptures, but never wise, because when he first sinned he did the most stupid and foolish thing that had ever been done in the Universe. The Christian, walking in the light of God and in the power of the Holy Spirit, is free from the grip of these terrible forces. The wicked one *cannot* touch him (1 John 2:14; 5:18). A holy life makes Satan himself afraid. The Son of God was "manifested to destroy the works of the Devil" (1 John 3:8). The true Christian need never fear Satan or his demons because "perfect love casts out all fear" and "greater is He that is in you than he that is in the world" (1 John 4:18; 4:4; Isaiah 35:4; Joshua 1:5-9; Psalm 27:1).

## CLEANING UP RELATIONS

*Why have friends?*

Everywhere the Lord Jesus went, He was popular. Men sensed His loving concern for them; the Pharisees scathingly called Him a revealing name — a *"friend* of publicans and sinners" (Matthew 11:19). He shows His love for all — tiny tots, little children, young and old (Mark 10:13-16; 2:15; 12:37). All who followed Him were captured by the radiance of His Presence.

Christians are NEVER promised *popularity,* but people long for friendship. Whenever God met a responding human heart, He demonstrated His love; if instead, there was only

377

In what sense is a Christian to keep himself "unspotted from the world"?

further hardness and opposition, that same rejected love was recorded to one day judge the rebel (John 12:44-48). Jesus could love the sinner and not lower His standard; His counsel condemned the self-righteous and proud but comforted the sinner conscious of his need. God's love is not a FEELING, but firstly a CHOICE — to unselfishly will the highest good of another. A *feeling* of affection or happiness and delight in the person loved may follow this choice as a trailer follows a turning car. God's commandment is "love one another" in all relationships.

*This will mean showing ourselves friendly to all men we meet.* Harsh demands and argument have *no place* in the life of a follower of the Son of God. Make every effort to win the respect and admiration of those you meet for the glory of God by demonstrating His love. A man with *no* friends is not usually a true disciple of Christ. *A real Christian is intensely loveable.* Without this love in action from the outworking power of the Holy Spirit in your life, all "Christian" actions are a terrible travesty of a child of God.

If *YOU* have few friends, is it because of:

1. *SHYNESS?* Some Christians are *afraid to be themselves.* Conscious of some real or imaginary personal deficiency, they hide from others. Recognize self-consciousness for what it really is — PRIDE! Be willing to be known for what you are. Others too, have had limitations, but these have not hindered their witness. Never use shyness as an excuse for not being friendly. Ask God for holy boldness to look your world in the eye.

2. *A RUN FROM REALITY?* Some think that to keep yourself "unspotted from the world" means to keep away from sinners! There is no holiness in such hiding from the task God has given us to "Go into all the world and preach" (Mark 16:15). He is no soldier who has not tried his weapons in the fight; he is no saint who has not felt the darts of temptation strike the shield of his faith (Ephesians 6:10-16). *True faith is tested by trial and action;* to hide from sinners is to miss your purpose as a witness to His love.

**3.** *SILENT WITNESS?* Some sinners have the impression that Christ is boxed up in a church or cathedral and Christians are strange types who endure the misery of religion in the hope of life after death. Perhaps you don't do anything *wrong* before the eyes of the world around you — but what *DO* you do? Confession of Christ is done by MOUTH!

When was the last time you made a conscientious effort to make a new friend?

---

FRIENDS . . .

---

*How do you go about being friendly?*

**1.** *Forget about yourself.* Put the needs of the world and the glory of God FIRST in your life and you will find your happiness and friendship coming naturally out of this unselfish love. Never lose touch with the world of the sinner; talk often with them to try to find out their knowledge of God and needs, so that you may meet them through Christ. If you will be NATURAL in your friendship, Christ will be SUPERNATURAL through you.

**2.** *LEARN their NAMES when you meet them.* Remember them! To help you do this, use it as many times as you can in your first conversation with the person as soon as you are introduced and WRITE IT DOWN shortly afterwards. This is very important. Don't forget.

**3.** *Always show GENUINE INTEREST in their problems and troubles.* There is a danger in witness that can only be removed by much prayer and concern; that of treating PEOPLE as OBJECTS. They may interpret your thoughts of, "How can I witness to this one?" as something on your mind that is MORE IMPORTANT than the problem they have opened their hearts to share with you. In such a case it would not be too surprising if they suddenly seem to "close up" on you and cease to communicate. REALLY care.

**4.** *Make OPPORTUNITIES for friendship.* Don't be guilty of just saying "Hello" to a small circle of Christian friends. If you see new arrivals at school, work or on outings who seem to be out of place, feeling strange or embarrassed, YOU be the one to make them welcome. Talk *naturally* — be

Why can't a person be a crowd-pleaser and a God-pleaser at the same time?

*genuinely interested* in what they are doing. Talk about THEM and when the opportunity naturally arises out of your conversation bring in the beauty of your Saviour. A man who would have friends must first show himself friendly (Proverbs 17:17; 18:24; 19:6; Matthew 11:19; John 15:13-14).

---

### . . . OR FIENDS!

---

What about those old "friends" who stay around to tempt you or drag you down?

*All friendships made for selfish reasons* before your conversion must go on the altar of sacrifice with all other things that belonged to your past life. All future *friendships* as well as those you keep from the past must be made or kept with the motive of WILLING their highest good in relation to their standing with God. Jesus said, "Strive to enter into the strait gate; for wide is the gate, and broad is the way that leads to destruction, and MANY there be that go in that way; but strait is the gate and narrow is the way that leads to life; and FEW there be that find it" (Matthew 7:13-14; Luke 13:24). *The way of the crowd is usually the WRONG way.* If you would keep God's standards and favor, you had better face it — you are *not* going to keep many friends. The only ones left will be those you will have through eternity — those willing to totally sell out their lives to God.

If you are going to serve Christ, you will have to give up the "in" crowd. You are NOT a true Christian if you put pleasing people above Christ.

Many profess conversion or religion, when on a *close* look it will be seen that their *leading object*, prized beyond anything else, is the *good opinion of the crowd*. Sooner than lose this, they would *deny* their religious stand. Their whole "faith" is based on this. You can see by a close look at their lives that they will do *nothing* to lose this good opinion of men. They will not face the hatred, scorn, ridicule and unpopularity from unbelievers that *must* come if they really gave themselves up to root sin out of the world.

*How can you tell a people-pleaser?* If a man professes to love God and put *Him* first, yet makes the praise of *men* his idol, how can you tell? Test your *own* character by these signs if you hope you do not belong in this class of counterfeit converts . . .

What are the dangers of judging our performance by the success or failures of others?

1. *They do what Paul says* — "measure themselves among themselves . . . (2 Corinthians 10:12) and for this reason do *not* find *true* faith.

There are a vast many people who, instead of making *Jesus Christ* their standard and the *Bible* their rule of life, obviously aim at no such thing. The great question they ask is — "Do I do *as much* in religion and be *as good as others* in the crowd or church around me?" Their aim is to keep up a respectable *religious front* for others. Instead of seriously asking for themselves what the Lord and His Word requires,  they look simply at the common run of professing church people and copy *them.* They do that which is outwardly *respectable,* not primarily that which is *right* (Psalm 36:1-2; Proverbs 12:15; 16:2; 30:12; Ecclesiastes 11:9; Judges 17:6; Matthew 6:1-7; 16-18).

2. A people-pleaser *never bothers to raise the standards of right* around him.

They are not bothered that the general standard of piety is so *low* in the church that a visiting early church Christian would have to *backslide* to be in fellowship! People-pleasers like the "present" standard. because they have conformed their religious reputation around it. If the *real* friend of God and man tries to wake up the church and raise the tone of faith, he seems critical and meddling to the people-pleasers (Matthew 25; Mark 6:1-3; Acts 5; Jeremiah 14:10-14).

When *Jesus* denounced the church leaders of His day, they said "He has a *devil!*" He dared say that unless a man's righteousness exceeded *theirs* they would not make it (Matthew 5:20). A large part of today's church people have the same *attitude* as the scribes and pharisees, and the same

381

Usually, a people-pleaser will stand with the crowd when a man is condemned and turn the *other* way when he is honored. When does this normal course of action not hold true?

*destiny.* Every effort to open their eyes to make them see they are living lives so low, so wordly, so *phony* that God is grieved terribly, only excites ill-will from them. They forget how *Jesus* said His strongest *words of judgment* to those who had a reputation of being the most pious people of His day. It was their *hypocritical spirit* that roused His soul. He *saw through* their fake fronts of piety, called them hypocrites and thundered over their heads the terrible words — "How can you escape the damnation of Hell!" No wonder there is excitement when the truth is told, when so *many* love the praise of men more than the praise of God. They do not seem to know that the lives of so many professing Christians are almost as different from God's standards as *light* is from *dark* (Leviticus 11:44; Psalm 24:3-4; Jeremiah 23:9-22; 26:10-15; Romans 6; 1 Thessalonians 4:3-7; Hebrews 12:14; 1 John 3:3-10; 5:18).

3. They often *oppose* men and measures and efforts to wake the church as long as they are *unpopular* but if they become *popular, fall in with them.*

The *opposite* is also true; if the work becomes *unpopular* they will turn *against* it (Matthew 3:7-10; Mark 6:14, 17, 20, 22, 26; Luke 13:23-27; John 6:60-66; 7:10-13; Acts 6:8-13). Let a man of God begin to wake up churches to *true* faith. While he is little known, the people-pleasers are not backward to speak against him. But let him go on and gain influence and they will profess to be his warmest friends (Luke 9:7-9; John 2:23-25).

This class of person *stands with the crowd* when it *condemns* a man, and turn the *other* way when he is *honored.* There is only *one* exception. That is, when they have become so far committed to the opposition that they cannot change without disgrace. And then they will be silent, until another chance comes up for letting out the smouldering fires that are burning within them (Matthew 22:15, 22, 24, 46; Luke 11:27-28; Acts 5:17-33).

They never aim at forming a *public sentiment in favor of godliness.* They always follow the crowd *as it is,* and feeling after the tide, go that way, shrinking back from everything that goes in the face of public sentiment (Jeremiah 42:16 cf. 43:1-7; Luke 14:25; John 9:18-25; Acts 24:24).

4. *People-pleasers separate God's requirements* strongly enforced by *public feeling* and those that are *not* — they do the first to please men and break the rest as it suits them.

Thought: Is the god you worship worthy of the ultimate choice you give it?

A people-pleaser is very careful to stay away from sins forbidden by public opinion, but does *other* things not frowned on that are *just as bad.* He will never miss public worship — oh no! — because he could never hold a reputation for religion if he did . . . but neglects other things *plainly required* in the Word of God. When someone HABITUALLY DISOBEYS *any known law of God,* the obedience he *seems* to have to other laws is not from a true love for God, but from *selfish* motives (Luke 16:10; 1 John 3:3-6; John 14:21). He does not, in fact, obey *ANY* command of God (James 2:10). Obedience to God implies an *obedient state of heart,* and therefore *nothing* is obedience that does not imply a supreme regard to God's authority.

Now, if a man's *heart* be right, whatever God requires he regards of more *importance* than anything else (Matthew 6:33; 22:36-40; 10:37-39). If he regards anything else of *greater* importance, *THAT* is HIS GOD. *Whatever we supremely regard* — *that* is our god; if it is *power,* or *riches, comfort* or *pleasure, honor or power,* that is the god of our hearts. If it is Jesus, that man is a true Christian; if it is *anything else,* whatever his reason, this is his true god; and all his religion is selfish. He is a *counterfeit convert* (Deuteronomy 6:5; Luke 16:10-15; Matthew 6:24; John 8:34-36).

How is it with *you,* friend? Do you habitually neglect *any* command of God because it is not sustained and enforced by  public opinion? If you profess to be a true Christian, you probably do not neglect anything strongly urged by *public sentiment.* But how is it with *others?* Do you habitually practice some things acceptable among men that you know to be contrary to the law of God? If you do, write down your name — "people-pleaser" (Luke 18:9-14).

5. They are apt to sin *away from home* when they would not if they were with others they know.

Many a man who is *outwardly* very religious and respectable *in his own community* drops his mask at a distance and begins to act like he has always lived *inside*. If he is fairly sure no one knows him there, he will *sin*. If he is a religious man in church, *away from* church company he is ready to "let his horns grow." The true Christian in love with God, *does not lead a double life.* The things that make him happy in church are the *same* things that make him happy a thousand miles from it (Jeremiah 23:24; Matthew 15:8; Titus 1:16; 2:7-15; James 2:9; 1 John 2:3-6,23).

A people-pleaser also often indulges in *secret sin.* I am now speaking of something by which you may know *yourselves.* If you allow yourself ANY sin secretly, when you know how to get out of it; but you can "get along" without any human being *knowing* it, know that GOD sees it, and He has already written down *your* name, *hypocrite!* You are more afraid of *disgrace* in the eyes of men than disgrace in the eyes of *God.* If you love God as you claim to, and were tempted to do such a thing, you as a true Christian would react like *Joseph* — "How can I do this wicked thing and sin against GOD?" (Genesis 39:7-9; Ezekiel 8:12; Job 31:33-34; Romans 2:16-29; 2 Timothy 2:19).

*They may not secretly sin,* but secretly neglect *duties* that if known would bring them shame. Things like Bible study and secret prayer for instance. They will appear very pious at church, but in the privacy of their own rooms, live *different lives.* How is it with *you?* Do you habitually and secretly omit some things, knowing *how* and *why* you should do them, and yet are careful to perform all your public duties? Need it be *said* that you "love the praise of men more than the praise of God?"

6. *People-pleasers* dread the thought of being called *"fanatical."*

They miss a *first principle of Scripture* — That ALL THE WORLD is wrong! The world's feelings are all against God, and every one who intends to serve God must from the start oppose its opinions. It is true and always *has* been, that "they that will live godly in Christ Jesus shall suffer persecutions." They shall be called "fanatical," "extreme," and the like. They have always been, and always *will* be, as long as the world is wrong (Matthew 5:11-12; John 15:18-25; Acts 14:22; 21:27-31; 26:24-29). But people-pleasers never go

How will a people-pleaser manifest himself in the area of dress and fashion?

further than people's opinions. They say they "must" do this to influence such men. Right against this is the purpose of God's true children. Their leading aim is to reverse the world's order and turn the world upside down, to bring all men to obey God and all the opinions of men to conform to the Word of God (Acts 2:37-40; 17:6; Luke 12:49; Matthew 3:1-3; 4:16-17; John 8:44-50; 12:37-43).

7. They are very intent on making friends on *both sides* of the line.

They always make *compromises and concessions to the crowd*. They try to take both sides. It has always been so for centuries, that men could make a good show of religion without ever being labelled as "holy." The standard is still so low that a great mass of churches still try not to be set down as *"reprobates"* on one hand or *"fanatics"* on the other. They are "fashionable Christians!" Their style of religion is fashionable and popular and they generally follow the world's fashions in dress and custom. No matter what *GOD* requires, they are carefully determined not to offend His enemies. If they are ever faced with a *choice* between displeasing their crowd or God, they will offend *God* (Proverbs 4:14; Exodus 23:2; Matthew 14:1-10; 21:23-27; Luke 12:51-53; John 15:14; Romans 12:2; James 4:4).

8. They will do more to gain the *applause of men* than the *applause of Heaven*.

They are more anxious to know what *men* think about them than about *what* God thinks. If such a one is a minister preaching a sermon, or a singer giving a song, they fish for compliments, more interested to know what men thought of it than what God thought of it. If an elder or church member prays or speaks in a meeting, he is thinking, *if* he is a people-pleaser, how he sound to those who listen (Matthew 15:7-8; 23:14; Jude 16; James 2:1-4). If he makes anything like a failure, the disgrace of men cuts him ten times more than the

When a person is reluctant to speak out for God, what is this an evidence of?

thought that he has let God down or hindered others (1 Corinthians 7:23; Ephesians 6:6; Colossians 3:22-23).

*Females* of this kind are vastly more concerned in church how they *look in the eyes of men* than how they look in God's eyes. You can see at a glance what this religion is, the moment it is held up to view. No one is at loss to say what *that* man or woman's name is - it is *hypocrite*. They go into God's house with hearts as dark as midnight, while everything on the outside is respectable and decent (1 Samuel 16:7; Matthew 23:5-7; 23:28; 1 Peter 3:3; 2 Corinthians 5:12).

9. They are often *ashamed* to *do what they should;* so *much* ashamed they *will not do it!*

When a person is so much ashamed, it is plain that his *reputation* is his God. How many people-pleasers do you know *now?* They are ashamed to acknowledge Jesus Christ, ashamed to reprove sin in high and low places, ashamed to speak out when Christianity is assailed! If they *really* loved God, how *could* they be? If a man really loved a girl, would *he* be ashamed to defend her if she was slandered? If a man's children were abused, would he be ashamed to stand up for them? *Not if he loved them* (Joel 2:26-27; Jeremiah 17:13; Mark 8:38; Romans 1:16; 9:33; 10:11; 2 Timothy 1:12; Philippians 1:20; Hebrews 2:11; 1 John 2:28). The people-pleaser does not really love GOD; he loves *himself* and his *reputation among others.* When among church people he is very bold for the truth and makes a great show of his faith. But put him among Christ's enemies, where it would be a *reproach* to be called a Christian; put him to trial and he will *sell Christ out* like Judas or deny Him before His enemies (Matthew 10:32-33; 26:47-50; Mark 4:16-17; Luke 9:26; 12:9; John 1:20; 9:22; 12:42; Acts 3:13).

There is a great deal more *apparent* piety in the church than *true* piety. There are many things which sinners suppose are good which are abominable in the eyes of God. It is easy for people to take credit for people-pleasing lives and make themselves believe they are models of *piety,* when in fact they are only examples of *hypocrisy.*

But for the love of reputation and fear of disgrace, how many *in the church* would break out in open apostasy? All

386

that holds them back from open sin is *public opinion, fear of disgrace* and *desire to gain credit for virtue.* When a person is good from a *regard to God's authority,* whether public sentiment favor or frown upon it — that is *true* faith (John 8:28-29; Acts 5:40-42). If otherwise, they have their reward. They do it for the sake of gaining credit in the eyes of men, and they gain it. But if they expect any favor in the hands of *God* they will assuredly be disappointed (Ezekiel 14:6-8; John 7:3-7). Who will agree to take the *Bible* for your rule and *Jesus Christ* for your pattern, doing what is *right* in all cases, whatever man may say or think? If you are not willing to take this stand, you are a stranger to the grace of God. A people-pleaser is by *no means* His child. If you are not resolved upon doing what is right, *public sentiment or not,* you love the praise of men more than the praise of God.

What is the basic sin of the people-pleaser?

*Friend, I have been honest with you.* If I did not really love you or care, I would not have risked your censure. I have told it like it is. If you mean to be a Christian you must give yourself *wholly up to Christ.* You cannot float along to Heaven on the waves of public sentiment. I will not pretend you *can* when *God* says you *cannot* (Luke 14:25-27; 1 Thessalonians 2:3-6).

The Lord Jesus said — "Whosoever will be ashamed of Me and of My words in this adulterous and sinful generation, of

him also shall the Son of Man be ashamed when He comes in the Glory of His Father and with the Holy angels . . . Whosoever shall *confess* Me before man, *him* shall the Son of Man also confess before the angels of God; but he that *denies* Me before man shall be *denied* before the angels of God."

Did Jesus *mean* it? (Mark 8:38; Luke 12:8-9).

"Wherefore come out from among them, and be a separate people . . . and I will receive you saith the Lord . . . and will be a Father to you, and you shall be My sons and daughters" (2 Corinthians 6:17-18). And now, *will you do it?* Who is on the Lord's side? Who is willing to say — "we will no longer follow a multitude to do evil, but are determined to do the will of God in all things no matter *what* the world thinks or says about us"? (John 12:24-26).

What kind of
tests can you
use to check
the validity of
your present
friendships?

*"Search the Scriptures;* for in them you *think* you have eternal life; and they are they which testify of Me . . . I RECEIVE *NOT* HONOR FROM *MEN* . . . how CAN you believe, hwich receive honor one of another, and seek not the honor that comes from GOD ONLY?" (John 5:39, 41, 44).

---

## BREAKING OFF FROM BAD FRIENDS

---

*Why do YOU keep the friends you have?*

Being honest about your present "pals" will save you from crowd compromise. Honestly ask yourself about these questions:

*I KEEP MY FRIEND —*

1. *To GIVE — or to GET?*

Give [ ]          Get [ ]

Are you pals for what you can do FOR him or her; or for what they can do or give to YOU? Be honest with yourself.

2. *To SHARE — or to be SELFISH?*

Share [ ]          Selfish [ ]

Is your friendship with this person two-way or one-way? Is it an EXCHANGE of mutual helpfulness with you giving unselfishly that which builds up and helps your friend — or is it just a TAKING pleasure FROM him or her on your part?

3. *Because they HELP — or do they HINDER?*

Help [ ]          Hinder [ ]

Was your companionship made IN CHRIST so both of you could be drawn closer to Him; or does your friendship drag down your God-set standards and purity?

*Many people keep "patrons" as a mirror to their own pride.* Hungry for some selfish admiration, recognition or esteem, they build others around them who feed their own self-opinions. They convince themselves that there are "friendships" — but ALL their love is really for *themselves,* mirrored in those they spend time with. They see in the

388

approval of others a means to feed selfish pride. We must be brutally honest with ourselves when it comes to our friendships. Think now; are any of YOUR friendships made like this? Are your friends just a "mirror"? Sincerely, honestly go over every friend you have. Have you kept patrons for pride?

Thought: No one in the entire universe has been brokenhearted as many times as God has.

*Are you afraid of losing any of your friends?* Could you be willing to stand *alone* for the Lord should it be necessary — if ALL your companions turned aside from God to follow the crowd down the "broad way"? If you are not, you are not yet fully identified with Christ. Such a test of a severed friendship may try your devotion to the Master. If a friendship was made for a *selfish* reason, when or if it is threatened you will be worried or angry. If it is CUT, you will not be grieved so much as *offended* and perhaps bitter. On the other hand, a friendship made *in Christ* may be broken in sorrow, or hurt, but there is never frustration or barriers thrown up on YOUR side to restoring your friend. How does *GOD* feel when He loses friends? To *Ezekiel* were given words of unspeakable grief — "I am *broken* with their whorish heart which has departed from Me" (Ezekiel 6:9). The *Lord Jesus* was a Man of sorrows and acquainted with grief; He brought men blessings and was regarded with rejection by all but a few. The unutterable sorrow He felt as He saw the awful fate men forged for themselves taxed His compassion and sympathies to the limit, and broke His heart (Hebrews 5:7; John 1:11; 5:40; Luke 19:41-42; Matthew 23:37; 9:36). God's grief over the rebel is a *factual sorrow,* not some imaginary picture of an unfeeling God's nature. His heart is torn with pity and sorrow over those who have turned their backs on His love. The Holy Spirit can be "grieved" like a mother who has lost her child (Ephesians 4:30).

See the apostle *Paul* with tears in his eyes pleading with the men who would not surrender to his Lord! (Acts 20:19, 31). His letters were often damp with tears as his heart yearned over the wayward and the rebel (Philippians 3:18; 2 Corinthians 2:4). Read the story of *Abraham* and his son Isaac to get the feeling of real identification with God's purposes. Think of the unutterable sorrow and grief the old man felt as he took out his only little son to kill him! Here was the strongest bond of friendship threatened; yet he was not bitter or rebellious against his Lord for the commanded separation — only an agonized trust that the Lord knew best; and the Judge of all the earth would do right (Genesis 22:1-17). Will *you* be willing to sacrifice even the dearest friend you have should the royal law of love require it? "They that sow in tears shall reap in joy; he that goes forth weeping, bearing precious seed, will doubtless come again rejoicing, bringing his sheeves with him" (Psalm 126:6; 30:5; Revelation 7:17).

---

## ON BEING CRUCIFIED

*No man can crucify himself.* He can but take his place on the cross and let another nail him there. A cross is etched in the heart of discipleship. If you put your hand in God's for His highest, be ready for the print of a nail! A cross always wins by killing the man. It silences all opposition, not by compromise, treaty, friendship or surrender, but by *death.* You have asked to be like Him. Then you must stand with Him and identify with Him. Only scarred lives can save.

*God will arrange circumstances to discipline the soul,* focusing on our lives the things that most affect us. All areas of life come under His silent, searching light. Nothing is forgotten or missed. In love and infinite tenderness, God will allow all you can bear, to crucify the rebel you used to be so he can awaken you into the new life of the man or woman He wants you to be. *George Mueller* was asked for the secret of his saintly life. He replied:

*"There was a day when I died, utterly died to George Mueller;* to his opinions, preferences, tastes and will; died to the world, its approval or censure; died to the approval or blame of even my brethren and friends. Since then I have studied to show myself approved only unto God.

We often do not recognize hindrances and unyielded areas of our lives that are trouble spots for enemy concentration. God sees them all and will deal with them as far as we will let Him and as much as we can bear it. He cleans out selfishness in two ways:

How do our circumstances test our spiritual progress?

## 1. RE-ARRANGES CIRCUMSTANCES to discipline the soul.

You always considered yourself *"meek"* until you bumped into someone you couldn't stand. You believed you were *unselfish* until envy stirred in your heart over a brother's good fortune. You thought you *loved others* until someone tested your sacrifice and you were found wanting. You prayed for LOVE, and God sent you an "unlovely." You prayed for *patience* and God delivered to your door someone who tried your nerves to the limit. You prayed for FAITH and God kicked out all the "props" and left you in darkness!

*QUESTION: Did you recognize HIS HAND?*

We are convinced that we are "good enough as we are," but GOD is *harder to convince.* What He has begun to form in our lives is far too precious to Him to be imperfect! You are "quite clever"? He will deal with you until you learn not to trust self-dependently in your own wisdom. Do you base your assurance of His love on your feelings? He will send in days of darkness and barrenness until you know the "valley of the shadows" is really only the shadow of His Presence. You pray, "Not my will, but Thine be done"? He will confront you with a difficult choice and you may find it is really *"Not Thy* will, but MINE be done!" You may fight and struggle for a while, but when at last you give in — one more area will die to self-control and live from that time on only for the glory of God.

*The cross always cuts us where we hurt most.* Nails of circumstances, thorns of trial and the lash of testing spare neither feelings or our carefully guarded reputations. Are you a disciple IN TRUTH? Then the Holy Spirit has a *right* to deal with you as He sees fit for your own good and happiness. You know that if it is the God Who loves you Who commands it, it will be the best thing Infinite Wisdom can plan and carry out with your co-operation. Don't *fight* it

Describe the
process that
the Holy Spirit
uses to
conform us to
the image of
Christ.

then — but JOIN it, and rejoice in it (James 1:2-4; 1 Peter 3:8-17; 4).

## 2. REVEALS CHRIST — In all His relationship to the spirit

Endurance (I'm still believing, Lord!") is FAITH tried almost to the breaking-point. As a balance to arranging *circumstances* as an external discipline, the Holy Spirit can shine a little glory into the spirit when the going seems too tough. It can be a word, an action or a new little glimpse of truth; but it is always there, a diamond in the dirt of trial to keep the disciple in love with his Lord and on the right path when he feels like fainting.

*The Holy Spirit's main task is to take the things of Christ* and *reveal them* to the disciple in his every need. He makes them LIVING REALITIES, not just words or ideas ABOUT the Lord Jesus. The living Presence of the King of Kings making a daily demonstration of His love and kindness wed the soul to heaven. We have lost sight of the Lord Jesus in many of His important relationships to us. We have known Him as a pardoning, justifying Saviour; but as an indwelling and glorious King in the heart, with all His majesty and greatness, power and beauty He has been but little known.

*The conditions of seeing Christ* with the eyes of faith are *submission* and simple *obedience* to the will of God as it is revealed (John 14:21-23). As we will to do *His* will, He will reveal more and more of Himself to us, filling our hearts with the rapture of His Presence. Whatever temptation comes across our pathway, we will not follow its gay lure, but instead cast ourselves on the Lord Jesus Who is abundantly able to satisfy the need from His own treasures of love (Philippians 3:8; 4:19; Ephesians 1:3-23).

*When we are lonely,* we will see Him as the great Friend. When we are misunderstood, He will be to us our Counsellor; when we are afraid, the Prince of Peace (Isaiah 9:6; Song of Solomon 5:16). In discouragement He will be for us the Companion of the grey roads; in our shame, He is our great High Priest, Who ever lives to make intercession for us. The Lord Jesus becomes all things to all men that will bring them closer to the goal of the Father, that they might be ONE in love and moral beauty through eternity. Inward touches of the revelation of the Holy Spirit are spirit wine — given to gladden the heart of each disciple on the journey up the mountains of His Kingdom.

What are some of the sure results of genuine identification with Jesus?

---

## HOW TO KILL YOUR ENEMIES

*If you truly identify with Christ, you will make enemies.* A man who lives a life of surrender to God in a rebel world is the odd man out. His very life is a condemnation of the selfishness of society around him. It is for this reason that the Lord Jesus very clearly warned His disciples of the dangers in following Him.

What man cannot *understand,* they will seek to *destroy.* It was so with the fine young man Stephen, who stood up before the religious rulers of his day and testified to the rights of Christ on the life of the outwardly religious but inwardly selfish. They were cut to he heart and rushed on him, gnashing at him like animals (Acts 7:51-54). It was so with Peter and James and John, with Paul and Silas and with the long line of saints and prophets that followed God cost what it may down through the centuries; a *friend of God* is an *enemy of the world.*

If you are going to make enemies because of your un-questioning love and obedience to the Son of God, it is perhaps necessary to add a few words on *getting rid of them...*

Go OUT OF YOUR WAY to do them good!

*Render good for evil* (1 Thessalonians 5:15; 1 Peter 3:9). Do all you can to help him. If he hates, *love* him back just as strongly. If he criticizes, praise his good points to others; when he slanders your name, look for something nice you can say about him. If he is thirsty, give him drink; if he is hungry, feed him. If he strikes you, turn your cheek. Fight only for Christ your King, never for yourself. He is the One you should stand up for, explain or justify to another, never yourself.

Describe God's "secret weapon" and how it works.

*When misunderstood,* wait on the Lord until you share His strength. God is the Judge — God is YOUR judge! Let *Him* do the fighting; let Him do the vindicating. Trust Him for the open answers or the silences. His methods are more economical. *Adam's race makes an enemy —* "the way to get rid of him is to hate him out of range or influence, slander him out of position or if all else fails, and you can get away with it — kill him!" *Result:* Either two enemies (you *and* him) even more hateful than before, or one less person in the world that was bad, but could have been made useful.

*God's new men* have a *secret weapon* that kills the enemy with *kindness.* They try to return good for evil and love for hatred. In the very least, there is left only *one* enemy, whose enmity and hatred exists only in his *own* heart, and not in *yours;* if however, the weapon of the "new man" succeeds, the old enemy is destroyed — a FRIEND takes his place! Result: Two friends, both working for the glory of God and useful for His Universe.

To do this, of course, is always the *hardest* thing. Which is easier to do when hit — hit back or forgive? The former. Which commands the most respect in the long run? The latter. And which is God's command? You guessed it!

"Dearly beloved, *avenge not yourselves;* but rather *give place* to wrath; for it is written: 'Vengeance is Mine; I will repay' said the Lord. Therefore, if your enemy hunger, feed him; if he thirst, give him drink; for in so doing you shall heap coals of fire on his head. Be not overcome with evil; but overcome evil with good (Romans 12:21; Titus 3:2; Colossians 3:13; Ephesians 4:2; Matthew 5:43-45).

394

"And I will pray the Father, and He shall give you Another Comforter . . . for He dwelleth with you and shall be in you . . . Be FILLED WITH the SPIRIT" (John 14:16; Ephesians 5:18).

# PETER

## (WHO FAILED, THEN FLAMED)

"Ye shall receive power after that the Holy Ghost is come upon you . . ."

Acts 1:8

What were
some of the
Peter's old
character
traits that
were
transformed
at Pentecost?

PHASE:       7 .. *Enablement Of Witness*
SECTION:    12 .. *"P" For The Power Of God*
MATERIAL:       .. *Director Of Operations*

None ever fell so far, yet climbed so high, as *Simon* called *Peter.* Self-confident, rash, rough and rugged, the Big Fisherman pictures many Christians today; willing to fight the world, but cowards from the cross; daring to walk the water, but failing to walk with God! *Simon* met force with force; he failed. *Simon* cursed and denied Christ. The love of the Lord Jesus broke the old *Simon* for ever after the Resurrection, and he  became a new man. The command of a new Director enabled and empowered him to be forever, *"Peter."* The bruised reed became a building block, and God used this "stone on fire" to help shape a world. Are you an old *Simon* — or a new *Peter*?

---

## CHECK-POINT

*You are now at the beginning of a miracle.* If you have honestly and faithfully dealt with those areas of your life, needing surrender to the control of the Lord Jesus Christ, something is about to happen.

If you have hidden from honesty, passed over that which was hard on the old selfish life and refused to face Truth, you have missed your miracle.

*This is a check-point.* Have you done what God has shown you? If not, GO BACK and do your duty. Unless you are ready to wholly obey your Captain, you are not ready to fight in His army. But if you are — *expect a miracle!*

## MEET THE DIRECTOR

How do we know from the Scriptures that the Holy Spirit is a person rather than a mere "force"?

The most mysterious figure in the Godhead is the Divine Director of operations, the *Holy Spirit.*

It is He Who moves men's hearts through the corridors of history even as He moved on the face of the waters at the beginning of the world. He empowered Moses and Elijah, John the Baptist and Paul as they high-pointed history for God. It was He Who overshadowed the lovely young virgin Mary and conceived in her the Holy Son of God. When the Lord Jesus began His ministry and was baptized in the river Jordan, the heavens opened and the Holy Spirit descended on Him in the form of a dove. It was the Spirit that drove Him into the wilderness; the Spirit that communicated His Father's power and truth to a needy world, (Genesis 1:2; Numbers 11:17, 25-29; Judges 13:25; 2 Kings 2:9, 15; Luke 1:26-35; Mark 1:10-12).

The Lord Jesus breathed on the disciples and they received the Holy Spirit to witness of Christ's resurrection life to the world. Gathered in an upper room, 120 disciples continued in prayer until the mighty flood of the Holy Spirit totally captivated and filled them with power from on high.

In the Old Testament, much is made of the work of God the *Father;* in the Gospels we see the work of God the *Son;* but from the Resurrection through to today's generation, it is the task of the *Holy Spirit* to direct the Church through the Word of God. The Bible shows us that the Holy Spirit is distinct from the Father and the Son, but Himself God. He is a Divine Person with intelligence, feeling and will. The *Father* is the *source* from which Divine work begins; the *Son,* the *medium* through which it is performed; the *Holy Spirit* is the *Executive* by which it is carried into effect. He acts to personally teach, lead, guide and glorify Christ in the lives of disciples (Isaiah 11:2; Matthew 28:19; John 14:26; 15:26; 16:13-14; Acts 8:29, 39; 10:19; 13:2; 16:7; 15:28; Romans 8:9; 1 Corinthians 12:11; 2 Corinthians 13:14; Galatians 4:6).

397

What kind of theological agreement has there been among men who have been greatly used by God down through the history of the Church?

Most of the work of the Holy Spirit must remain unrevealed in its fullness until the Church and the plan of redemption is complete. But — *no Christian life is complete* without the command and strength of this Director! Unless He controls and empowers, there can never be let loose on the world the atomic power of true discipleship.

---

## ALL AGREE — POWER NEEDED!

---

Even a cursory reading of revival history is convincing; among all God's servants that have deeply affected their generations there is a *harmony of deeper experience* with Him. Terms used to describe this power have been as different as their denominations, conversion experiences and educations; but the *experience itself* has always been essentially the same. As there is practical agreement among evangelical Christians with regard to the way of salvation, so there is a practical agreement among those who believe in a deeper Christian experience than conversion. In a court of law, testimonials are rejected if all testifying give the same evidence in the same words and manner; it would prove there had been collusion among the witnesses. However, if each witness uses his own words and way of presentation, yet their testimony agrees in essential facts, the evidence is convincing. *And the evidence of history is this:* no man or woman has ever been used of God until they had first discovered the secret of *power with God.*

Christians have called this experience by many different names. Men like *D.L. Moody, R.A. Torrey, C.G. Finney, William Booth, Andrew Murray, George Whitfield, A.B. Simpson* and others have called it *"the baptism of the Holy Spirit,"* others, like *G. Campbell Morgan. Robert Murray McCheyne, Praying Hyde* and *C.H. Spurgeon* have preferred *"the filling with the Holy Spirit."* Some have called it *"empowering,"* others *"the anointing of God,"* but the question is *not,* "Can you *name* it?" but — "Do you *HAVE* it?"

398

*Billy Graham,* in his message *"How to be Filled with the Spirit"* put it this way:

What is the difference between the Holy Spirit's indwelling and His anointing?

"The very fact that we believe *one* thing and some of us another does not do away with the fact that GOD says — "Be *filled* with the Spirit." *I believe that is the greatest need of the church of Jesus Christ today.* Everywhere I go, I find God's people lack something; God's people are hungry for something. Many of us say that our Christian experience is not all that we expected; we have oft recurring defeat in our lives, and as a result across the country from coast to coast there are hundreds of Chrisitan people hungry for something we do not have . . . I am persuaded that our desperate need tonight is not a new organization or a new movement — nor a new method. We have enough of these. *I believe the greatest need tonight is that men and women who profess the Name of Jesus Christ be filled with the Spirit!* We are trying to do the work of God without supernatural power. It cannot be done! When God told us to go and preach the Gospel to "every creature" and to evangelize the world, He provided *supernatural power* for us. That power is given to us by the Holy Spirit. It is more powerful than atomic power . . . it is more potent than any explosive made by man. Do you know anything of the power of the Holy Spirit?" (Greater L.A. Crusade, 1949).

This enduement of power is *NOT* the receiving of the Holy Spirit in *salvation.* When a man is truly born again, his conversion is dependent on, and effected by, the Holy Spirit in response to his repentance and committal to Christ (John 3:5-6; 7:37-39; 14:16-17; 20:21-22; Romans 5:5; 8:9-16; 1 Corinthians 2:10-12;3:16; 6:19; 12:3; 2 Corinthians 1:21-22; 5:5; 6:16; Galatians 3:2; 4:6; 5:25; Ephesians 1:13-14; 2 Timothy 1:14; 1 John 2:27; 3:24; 4:13). But this conversion TO Christ is not to be confused with a *consecration* to the great work of world evangelism and the *enduement of power* to carry out this task.

*In CONVERSION,* the soul is *drawn* by the Holy Spirit (Proverbs 1:23; John 16:7-11), God's own Agency in salvation. The Bible reveals that the Holy Spirit, Himself God, is a Divine *Person* Who carries out the executive work of the Godhead (Isaiah 11:2; Matthew 28:19; John 14:26; 15:26; Acts 8:29, 39; 10:19; 13:2; 16:7; 15:28; Romans 8:9; 1

Corinthians 12:11; 2 Corinthians 13:14). This conversion experience is a personal transaction between the soul and the Lord Jesus relating to its own *salvation*. To accomplish this, the Holy Spirit first *convicts* of sin — (Genesis 6:3; Psalm 51:12-13; Micah 3:8; Zechariah 12:10; John 16:8-11; Acts 2:37) then points the convicted sinner to *Jesus* magnifying Him and making His sacrificial death real to the penitent. In salvation, the soul yields up its doubts, rebellion, self-righteousness and its pride; it accepts Christ as Lord and Saviour, trusts Him and supremely loves Him. The sinner's pride is humbled; his selfish purpose of life is finished; he is cleansed and all his guilty past is forgiven. The Holy Spirit *enters his life* (Romans 8:9, 11; 1 Corinthians 3:16; Ephesians 3:17; 2 Timothy 1:14; James 4:5) there to abide in settled union (John 14:17; 1 John 2:27; 3:24) and *baptizes him into the Body of Christ,* the Church (1 Corinthians 12:13).

The disciples had *already* been saved before the day of Pentecost (Luke 10:20; John 15:3; 15-16; 17:6-9). The resurrected Christ had breathed *(emphusao — breathing of impartation)* on them (John 20:20-22), and said *"Receive ye* — (2nd Aorist Imperative — when spoken by one in authority, command is obeyed *immediately)* — the Holy Ghost." They had already utterly renounced any idea of living for themselves and devoted their lives to the reaching of a world. The Lord Jesus had commissioned them to "make disciples of all nations" (Matthew 28:19, marg.). But they still lacked the promised *power* to fulfil their task! The Lord's last promise to them was — "You shall receive POWER after that the Holy Ghost is come upon you . . . and you shall be witnesses unto Me . . . " (Acts 1:8). They were told to *wait* until they were endued with power "from on high" before commencing their work (Luke 24:29). They had met the Lord; they knew Him as Saviour; but they did *not* have the power of the Holy Spirit to do His work (cf. *Samaritan Christians:* Acts 8:14-17; believed and were baptized already, but not empowered; *Paul;* Acts 9:17 ["brother"]).

*R.A. Torrey,* world-renowned evangelist and Bible teacher of the last century, explained it this way —

"The baptism of the Holy Spirit is a definite experience of which one may and *ought* to know whether he has received it

400

or not . . . the baptism of the Holy Spirit is an operation of the Holy Spirit *distinct from*, *subsequent* and *additional to* His *regenerating* work. In regeneration, there is an impartation of life, and the one who receives it is *saved*; in the baptism of the Holy Spirit there is an impartation of *power*, and the one who receives it is fitted for service" *(What the Bible Teaches)*.

Describe the Spirit's work in the enduement of power.

The word *"baptism"* used by Torrey here is a *symbolic term* in scripture that signifies (1) complete *exposure* and *cleansing* from all sin and (2) an *overwhelming sense of God's presence and power* to energize for Christian service. By following the example of the Lord Jesus in water baptism, many Christians understand this symbol in the *first* sense (Romans 6:3-11; 1 Corinthians 12:13; Ephesians 2:1-7; Colossians 2:10-12), but have never known it experimentally in the *second* sense — *a clothing of energy* for Christian service. Without this sense of covering, surrounding and energizing of the Holy Spirit, Christian work and witness is fruitless, joyless and practically impossible.

*The church has two great needs;* two discoveries it must make afresh if we are going to make an impact on our generation. We must realize with burning conviction that the vision and commission for world evangelism is NOT just reserved for faithful ministers and pastors, missionaries and evangelists, but *is given to EACH OF CHRIST'S disciples* as his or her LIFE-WORK. All of us are responsible for the souls of men and women who pass into eternity all around us. Whatever our vocation, whatever our calling, "whether we preach or pray, or write or print, trade or travel, labor with our hands, keep house or state," our whole lives and every influence must tell of and for the Lord Jesus Christ and His Kingdom.

*The second great conviction* that must burn itself into our hearts is the *absolute necessity* of the enduement of power for every disciple to carry out this task. Much is said today of our dependence on the Holy Spirit by many people; but oh, how little is this dependence realized! Without the promised power of the Holy Spirit in operation, no man or woman who seeks to work for Christ can ever be truly effective. We cannot do a work of God in the wisdom and strength of man. It is neither hard, unloving, unjust or unscriptural to say with men of God, both past and present, that "The lack of the fullness of the Holy Spirit, the absence of power from on high should be deemed a *disqualification* for any man who would speak as the oracles of God." We must accept the service in which Christ offers to use us. We have the same promise as the early disciples; in spirit, we have the same task before us.

CHECK: AM I REALLY FILLED WITH THE SPIRIT OF GOD?

---

## GOD'S DANGER MEN

*Being under God's total control is to live a dangerous life.* If you are daily led and empowered by the Holy Spirit you will experience:

*HOLY MADNESS* — A famous lecturer once said, "Our real choice today is between *holy* and *unholy* madness. It is  possible to be mad without blessing, but it is impossible to get blessing without madness." It is possible to live our lives in holy or unholy madness. Both kinds will change the world. No generation has ever been moved by mediocrity. Men who change history are always nonconformists. They come to protest; to prod for and probe out the things that hinder in history. They are never comfortable to have around; but such men live as mountains above the valleys, lift humanity out of the rut and make earth move in new orbits.

*The Book of Acts is a book of REVOLUTION* — men of boldness, daring and of almost incredible power with God. Wherever they went there was either revival or revolt. THIS was holy madness — a madness to the world but cool-headed, clear-eyed sanity with God! Paul before Festus and Agrippa was accused of such madness (Acts 26:24). When the Gadarean maniac was restored to his RIGHT mind — the men of Gadarea were afraid! The world has always been afraid of men in their right minds. *Sin* is a kind of insanity. When a man's life is holy, it is only natural that the world will accuse him of being a fool. Of even the Son of God Himself, it was said "He is beside Himself" (Mark 3:21). This is not wide-eyed fanaticism or uncontrolled extravagences. This "holy madness" — obeying God rather than men's opinions and feelings — can grip the heart of the simplest child of God. He may be called eccentric, illogical or even a fool. But he will be *God's fool,* and he will change the world (1 Corinthians 4:9-10).

Give specific examples from the book of Acts as to when the Holy Spirit came upon certain groups of believers and the results.

*HOLY SADNESS* — The greatest saints often endured deep sadness. The prophets and the apostles were distressed by the tragedy of a church and the world "walking hand in hand." A Spiritual Christian, although outwardly happy, may be wounded in spirit over people's rebellion against God.

The power of the Holy Spirit is given for HOLINESS, not primarily for happiness. God has no laughter without tears at present. The true man of God cannot help but sorrow over a powerless, carnal church and the hypocrisy of professed followers of the Lord.

Can you drink the cup of sorrow with Christ? Some of God's choicest jewels are crystalized tears. The greatest of all art, poetry and faith comes from conflict. He is no soldier who has no scars. Will you walk the path of grief with God?

*UNHOLY MADNESS* — Standing with God means *conflict* with the world, the flesh and the Devil. Make up your mind to be opposed by both a carnal church and the world if you would be used of God.

"Very likely the leading men in the church will oppose you. If you are above their state of feeling, church members will oppose you. If any man will live godly in Christ Jesus, he must expect persecution. Often elders and even the minister will oppose you if you are filled with the Spirit of God."

*"You must expect frequent and agonizing conflicts with Satan.* Satan has very little trouble with those "Christians" who are not spiritual, but lukewarm, slothful and worldly-minded. Such do not understand spiritual conflicts — the Devil lets them alone. They don't disturb him, nor he them.

In what ways was the Holy Spirit's presence with the Church of even greater practical benefit than the personal, physical presence of Jesus himself?

But spiritual Christians are doing him a vast injury and therefore he sets himself against them. Such Christians have terrible conflicts. They have temptations that they never thought of before, blasphemous thoughts, atheism, suggestions to do deeds of wickedness, to destroy their own lives and the like."

*"You will have greater conflicts with yourself* than you ever thought of. You will sometimes find your own corruptions making strange headway against the spirit" (Charles G. Finney — *Revival Lectures*).

## THE PURPOSE OF POWER

The 120 gathered expectantly in the Upper Room on the day of Pentecost knew *what* they were waiting for. This  energizing experience was to be an *overwhelming sense of God's Presence*. It was to mean even more to them in terms of intimate, loving communion with God than the *physical Presence* of Jesus had meant on earth. He had been WITH them; now by this anointing of the Holy Spirit, He would seem not only back *with* them, but welling up *inside* them and all *around* them! They were to be utterly flooded in the sense of His closeness and power. They had already been given *one* "power" — that of *legal right* or *authority,* to become the *sons of God* (John 1:12). Now they were to have *"dunamis"* (Greek) *power* — strength, might, energy, explosive *enabling power* — to act, think and LIVE like their Lord with the outpoured energy of Heaven! (Luke 24:49; Romans 15:13; 1 Corinthians 2:4; 1 Thessalonians 1:5).

In this *empowering,* the soul is introduced BY the *Lord Jesus* TO the *Holy Spirit.* The role of Christ and the Spirit are thus *reversed* from that of salvation. The Holy Spirit has introduced the soul to *Christ;* now Christ makes the indwelling Presence of His *Spirit* real to the believer. The climax of this energizing process is the flooding up of God's reality in the soul like a fountain, until the believer is utterly *immersed* in His power and love. Once initially understood and experienced, this is to be the *continuous experience* of each believer — deeper and deeper baptisms or fillings with the Holy Spirit as we look to Him in faith for delivering and transforming power (Acts 2:4; 4:8; 31; 6:3; 5:8; 7:55; 9:17; 11:24; 13:9; 13:52; Ephesians 3:19; 5:18; 1 John 1:4).

*SYMBOLS* and *emblems* of the Holy Spirit used in Scripture describe the *results* of a Spirit-filled life. *WATER* is an emblem (Exodus 17:6; John 7:38-39); it *cleanses, fertilizes* and *refreshes;* it is *abundant* and *freely given.* So the Holy Spirit cleanses, brings life, revives and refreshes the soul — He too, was fully and freely given when the risen Christ was glorified. FIRE is an emblem (Acts 2:3; Luke 3:16). Fire *purifies, illumines* and *searches.* The Holy Spirit accomplishes what we cannot do ourselves; He searches our hearts, illumines and purifies us. The *WIND* is a third emblem (John 3:8; Acts 2:2) — it is *independent, felt* in its effect, *powerful* and *reviving.* God the Holy Spirit is independent in His operation — He is not controlled by anyone! He moves with power, His presence is felt and how He revives the work of Christ when He comes to the drooping members of the church! The *DOVE* (John 1:32) teaches us the work of the Spirit in making us *gentle, innocent* and *loving;* the *VOICE* of the Spirit, His *teaching, guiding* and *warning* ministry; the *SEAL,* His work to *impress, secure* and *make us Christ's own.*

## RECEIVING POWER

The Holy Spirit is the *gift* of the Risen Christ. His anointing, filling, empowering work is a *baptism of love* that gives *power* to make *Jesus real* to *you* and *known* to *others.* The most impressive evidence of this power is the *ability to make the things of God real;* a man filled with the Spirit of God becomes deeply, intensely *believable.* The Holy Spirit works to impress the heart and seal the preached word of God with conviction. When an empowered man speaks or prays, his words strike fire. His words *stick* in the heart like darts of love. Now, how is it with *you,* beloved? Have you obeyed God's *command* to *be* filled with the Spirit? His gift is offered to *every* child of God who is willing to simply meet these conditions:

1. *HONESTY* — Do you really WANT God's power? God will not give His gifts for self-glory — (to make you a "great" man or woman or to "build up your church" etc.). He will *not* grant His power so that selfish pride may be exalted (Acts 8:18-24; James 4:3). He does not empower to *free from trouble,* to make you *happy* or even to make you *holy;* although, of course, these often follow a Spirit-filled life. He fills  only *for His glory,* and *that* must be your motive.

2. *CLEANLINESS* — Are you in *dead earnest* to be used of God? *William Booth,* founder of the Salvation Army and man of God said — "Before we go on our knees to receive the baptism of fire, let me beg of you to see to it that your souls are in harmony with the will and the purpose of the Holy Spirit. See to it that the channel of communication by which the Holy Spirit must be received is kept open. It is no use . . . praying, singing, or even *believing* if there still is something you are holding back or even refusing to do. *Out with it; give it no rest; give it up.* Destroy your idols and stoppages with an everlasting destruction. Let there be free communication between you and God. Let all go and *you shall be flooded before you rise from your knees* . . . the world shall feel the power of it, and God shall have all the glory" *(Salvation Soldiery).*

3. The *GIFT* of the Holy Spirit is neither *earned* nor *deserved.* He is not given on the basis of *"special attainment"* in holiness with God. The gift of the Holy Spirit is primarily for *POWER;* a man who receives this empowering has no *more* Christian character immediately *after* his experience than he had *before.* The fullness of the Spirit is a SOURCE of *help* to BUILD a Christian character, and is certainly *not* given BECAUSE of a high degree of consecration to Christ. Therefore, He is to be invited to energize *only on the basis of the clear promises of God,* and with the *condition* that all obvious sin is forsaken (Galatians 3:2). Scripture shows that God is *more than willing* to give the Holy Spirit to His

children, and *longs* to do so. You do not have to *beg* and *plead* with your heavenly Father to obtain this promised power; the very fact that He not only *promises* but *commands* us to be "filled with the Spirit" (Ephesians 5:18) is the highest possible evidence that we *can* receive it. For God to *command* is equivalent to a certainty that we *can* obtain, for He does not command unless we have power to obey. Once the dams of conscious hinderances are swept away, you may not even have to ask God to fill you. In fact, you will probably not be able to *keep Him* from doing so!

What can prevent people from receiving the Holy Spirit's power?

4. *OBEDIENCE* — When you have dealt with all obstacles, you must receive by *faith* from the hand of God. There is *nothing to be afraid of* in receiving God's power. The Lord Jesus said — "If you, being *evil* know how to give GOOD gifts to your children, HOW MUCH *MORE* shall your Father which is in heaven give the Holy Spirit to them that ask Him?" If you come as a little child in love to your Father, do you think He will give you something to *harm* or *frighten* you? (Luke 11:11-13). Don't you think you can *trust* GOD to keep you from excess and extravagance? The Holy Spirit's power is a LOVE-gift for *every* child of God. You need not be afraid to fully *open your life to His love.* If there is something you are not willing to have happen, some personal point of pride you hold, or some right you don't think God *need* ask you to surrender, be sure that VERY THING will be the reason why you still have no power with God or man. *Obedience* is better than sacrifice (1 Samuel 15:22).

---

HOW CAN WE KNOW?

---

*Experiences of every saint of God differ.* To some, this enduement comes as dew; to others as floods on dry ground. God has *His* own means of meeting your need; never seek to copy that of another. Get an experience from *man* and you will never be sure; get one from *God* and you will know what you have is real.

A God-empowered man becomes *INTENSE.* When a man or woman walks in the Spirit of God, they have power to *make Christ real* to others. The Truth becomes a two-edged

407

sword in their hands to bring others to the feet of the Son of God. There will be an *exalting of the Giver.* The Holy Spirit reveals the Lord Jesus to the soul. His love and goodness take on a new freshness and life. The Spirit-filled man is CHRIST-LIKE. *A.W. Tozer* has these words to the seeker —

"No one in the Scriptures or Christian biography was ever filled with the Spirit who did not *know* he had been, and nowhere was anyone filled who did not know *when.* And no one was ever filled *gradually"* (*Man — Dwelling-Place of God*). All disciples of the Lord are under responsibility to avail themselves of this holy energy. However they make this volcanic encounter, they can be sure of *one* thing; they will SEE and FEEL and KNOW the *difference* in their lives. Any "filling by faith" that does not include a *definite change* in power with God and man is rubbish. All the theological terms in the world cannot substitute for a barren heart.

*And now, will you do it?* Will you go to God, and *ask* Him? He has given you a measure of faith to lead you into this consecration. Do not grieve or resist Him; accept His commission and fully consecrate yourself with all you have to the reaching of men and women for God. Lay on the altar of God all you have and are. Persist in prayer and faith; let the sense of His love well up in your heart until He floods and fills you with praise. Do not be afraid; there is no more wonderful experience in the world for a Christian to meet His Lord like this! Speak to Him in whatever words He lays on your heart. He may come *quietly* as a river or mightily like a flood; but you shall KNOW and you will *never be the same again.* Go now, and seek Him; go NOW as a little child; let Him make your life a miracle!

---

## THE PLUS SIDE OF POWER

---

1. *PEACE* — Even in a storm of persecution, you will be at peace with God. Men may assault your character, your

reputation or even your life. But they will never be able to shake the "perfect peace that passes all understanding" (Philippians 4:7). With a conscience "void of offense towards God and man" (Acts 24:16), your life says clearly, "Through the grace of God, I have complete victory over sin." As long as you are the world's enemy, you are warmly assured of God's friendship. The Lord Jesus walks with you. God keeps you in the hollow of His hand. Your life is immortal until your work is finished. The Holy Spirit anoints your life and lips with the good gifts of God and the fruit of righteousness. If God be for us — who then can be against us? (Romans 8:31).

What are some of the scriptural evidences in the life of the believer that will testify to the Spirit's empowering presence?

2. *PURPOSE* — Life will no longer be a meaningless search. Consciousness of God's Presence and of His purposes dredges out past shallowness and His deep rivers run through your soul. You live no longer to please men, but your Father who sees in secret (Matthew 6:18). You are no longer worried when people speak against, slander or criticize you. Having NO reputation, you cannot LOSE it! Living NOW in *eternal* life, *death*  for you is no grim horror. For His sake, you gladly suffer all things — counting your life as an expendable coin for your King.

3. *POWER* — Above all, you become *useful* to God. Instead of barrenness, there is blessing. There is fruit and flowers instead of dry branches and dead leaves. The perfume of His Presence makes life a fragrance. The love of Christ radiates out from your heart to light a tinsel world with reality. Carnal church-goers sense you have reality whether they admit it or not. The Lord Jesus takes first place in your conversation. He becomes Number One in your affections.

---

## STAYING IN GOD'S FULLNESS

1. Keep up a *daily* devotion to God; search and surrender, re-search and surrender again. Dedication is a *life-long process*

How does
the Holy
Spirit
"balance out"
emotional
extremes?

(Hebrews 12:14; 2 Corinthians 7:1; 1 Thessalonians 3:13; Acts 4:31).

2. Acquire the habit of living by the *present* moment. Trust God *NOW*; do God's will *NOW*; do not offend God NOW. Do the NEXT thing He shows you (Philipians 4:6; Colossians 4:5).

3. *Avoid the extremes* of *gloom* and *levity.* Be cheerful, but not light; be sober, but not morose. Do everything in the Name of the Lord Jesus (Titus 2:12-13; 1 Corinthians 10:31).

4. *Cultivate the deepest humility* and *reverence* in your approaches and addresses to God. Never allow yourself to use light or irreverent expressions of Him or His great work, however joyful or ecstatic you may be. *Walk softly* before God (Genesis 17:1; Micah 6:8).

5. Acquire the habit of *constant vigilance* against sin. Absolutely refuse to comply with temptation under any circumstance or to any degree. In the strength of God you must say a firm "No" every time, or you may lose in an unguarded moment what has taken you years of toil and what you may never be able to regain (1 Thessalonians 5:6; James 4:7).

6. *Never dwell* on *one* subject excluding others just as important. Never let *one* topic become all-important, or God will be grieved. *Danger signs* are: deliberate aversion to experiences falling short of God's best; distrust in the faith of those who make no special efforts to be holy; no desire to listen to other Bible topics; lessening interest in labor that aims directly at conversion of souls, or feeling inept at this (Colossians 1:10).

7. *Avoid display,* affectation; do not seek to be conspicuous. Seek no prominence because of your learning, talents, piety, person or possessions. Let your testimony be artless, simple and honest; let it *exalt Jesus* and *humble you.* Cultivate a sense of unworthiness and gratefulness to God. Let your *dress* administer to comfort, convenience, decency and modesty. Stay out of the limelight (Colossians 4:6; James 4:10; 1 Peter 5:5).

8. *Avoid all evil speaking.* Never talk about the faults of an absent person. Do not dwell on persecution from others in thought, word or prayer, especially in public. Avoid a censorious, fault-finding spirit; you may *grieve,* but never *fret;* you may *sorrow* over the condition of things, but do not scold (James 4:11; Philippians 4:8; 1 Thessalonians 5:14).

What does it mean to be seated with Christ in the heavenly places?

## COME ALIVE IN CHRIST

*Salvation is wonderfully more than just freedom from sin!* In His great mercy, the Father makes US alive just as Jesus is alive from the dead. Astonishingly enough, in His eyes we are in the SAME spiritual place as Christ! We are "raised up with Him and made to sit in heavenly places." The Father lifted His only-begotten Son above a vast pyramid of powers; kings, rulers, dictators — men, demons and angels. Higher and higher He rose, above all things in earth and heaven. Nothing man can name in power was missed to be subjected to His authority. "He has put ALL things under His feet . . ." and WHY? (Ephesians 1:19-20).

This staggers the mind. God did *all this — FOR THE CHURCH!* We rose *with Him* in the Father's eyes. We share His place of authority. Next time trials press you don't look UP — look DOWN! To the glory of God, you are in His Body. You can share in His power and resurrection energy. You express His life on earth. No difficulty can be too great for the Christ in you. "All power is given to Me in heaven and in earth — and lo I am with YOU always, even to the end of the world" (Matthew 28:18,20).

*We are living in dark days, but we have had dark days before.* In each era, God has found men and women He could trust to carry His Word cost what it may. It is time Christians came to grips with the pressing needs of today! *Social reform* is an essential fruit of true conversion; where the sin of men grieves God and affects humanity made in His image, the child of God will do *all in his power* to change the situation. Something is *missing* from our brands of Christianity today; early discipleship was marked with a concerned compassion for the lost. The Lord Jesus spent the vast majority of His

What is the
fatal flaw of
secular,
social reform
movements?

public and private ministry in *meeting human need;* He healed the sick, fed the hungry and befriended the social outcast. The Christ of Scripture was interested in the *whole* man; He calls His followers to do as He did, and neither His concern nor His compassion has changed from the days when He first walked the earth. The cross has a way of level-ling barriers of race, class, color, position and power; NO man can truly call himself a follower of Christ unless he is concerned with meeting the need of his fellow-men and truly changing his world for the better (Isaiah 58:1-12; Jeremiah 7:2-7; Matthew 5:9, 13-16; 9:35-38; 25:31-46; Luke 9:11-17; Mark 12:31; 1 John 3:17).

To begin with *secondary* reform efforts is to ignore the *root* of the problem: human *sin* or *selfishness.* Man does not need *reform,* but complete *regeneration;* not a second start, but a second *birth;* not a change of *conditions,* but a change of *heart!* Until human selfishness is struck a death-blow, and each individual concerned stops living for *themselves,* all social reforms are doomed to failure. The problems of our generation are complex and certainly not *easy* to solve; but they have a *simple* solution. Man must come back to his Maker, put his life under His control and direction, and begin to live as he was made to live; for the highest good of God and all the Universe according to their real values.

*Social* revolution begins with *personal* revolution. No man can really change his world until first of all he *himself* is changed! History is charged with revolutions, but none have been more powerful or far-reaching than the *spiritual* revolu-tions God has thrust into time, by His men and women, filled and thrilled with the love of Christ. Into the darkness of the 12th-13th centuries, the pillar of fire moved to restore a perverted and unrecognizable faith. The *church* was a maze of ritual, ceremony and idolatry. *Immorality* was rife in the clergy; *war,* not *love,* was the new tool of conquest; into this midnight of Satan came the dramatic of God's clan, the prophetic people who dared and shocked and challenged and shook their centuries! The wind of God began to blow over the lands, and restoration began.

*Secular historians* have a habit of *minimizing* the impact and import of these spiritual revolutions, but careful students of history can see the awesome overseeing power of the Living God at work in the chronicles of time. It is simple fact that with every spiritual awakening, chains of ignorance, superstition and fear were struck off a generation, and the entire era experienced a leap forwards into progress, both in science and the humanities. It is a matter of historical record that men like Wycliffe, Luther, Wesley, Carey, Finney, Booth and many others, as the heralds of Christ's love and power to their generations, each did more directly, or indirectly, to help their fellow-men and society than all the contemporary *secular* efforts put together. The Gospel is *still* the power of God "unto salvation"; the *real* answer to the social problems of our age still lies in a *radical reformation* centered not in civic, political, social, educational or even *religious* restructuring, but in a personal life-transforming encounter with the Living Christ of Scripture!

Why does the non-Christian have the right to see something different in the life of the one who claims to be a follower of the Lamb?

*Men cannot see the real you.* We express ourselves by our faces, our words and our actions. No-one can see the Lord Jesus daily at work in the world but IN US! Don't say to a sinner — "Ignore my life. I am a poor example. Look to Jesus!" The sinner must *expect* to see Christ in your life. He has every right to say — "I can't see Jesus! I can only see YOU. And if He hasn't made your life different what makes you think that He can help me?"

*God expects you to walk in the Christian life.* After you learned to crawl as a baby, you tried to stand on your feet

and walk. The fact that you DID try showed that you were a normal, healthy child. You may have fallen often, but it didn't hurt for long; and you were helped up and coaxed on. Finally the time came for you to stand on your own feet and walk by yourself. This was a big moment in your life. Right then you began on the road to manhood.

*Today the church is filled with thousands of "spiritual babies".* We have confused the need for dependence on the Lord for immaturity through laziness and lack of victory and

What kind of
spiritual
activity will
characterize
the final
events prior
to the
personal
return of
Christ?

vision. These weak Christians still need to be spoon-fed or nursed with bottles after years of feeding at the family table (1 Corinthians 3:1; Hebrews 5:13).

How God is *grieved* over such twenty or thirty year old "children"! Never could a Father feel more pain than in trying to show love to a retarded son or daughter. We will, of course, always need help from others as we grow in the Lord. Each of us are given some special ability or calling by the Holy Spirit to develop and use as a part of Christ's team (Romans 12:3-13; 1 Corinthians 12:4-7; 4:11-16). We need each other to cheer and encourage. But we must also learn to stand up and walk for ourselves — to do all in our power to study to show ourselves approved to our King.

---

## FRIEND, TAKE THE TORCH — IT'S OVER TO YOU!

---

*We look in amazement at the Book of Acts.* What marvellous things these simple men did in God's power! What astonishing miracles, what thrilling tales of conversion, guidance and deliverance!

But that is now past. And never forget — that was the *BABYHOOD* of discipleship. God is coming back to an adult church. The *MAN is always greater than the child.* God is doing something with this last generation that has never been done before. The age of the Holy Spirit is also the final age of church history — climaxing in the second coming of Jesus Christ. It will usher in a flood of power never before seen on earth. Those who have learned to walk along with God may share in the miracle of God on stage in human history.

*Christ is seated today at the right hand of the Father.* He has finished His work in buying back your soul and mine. All power is in His hands for victory and conquest through the life of His body, the Church on earth. He commands, not a frightened, scattered little group of failures, but a powerful, aggressively militant Church. He is the "Director of Operations." Right now he is readying an army of dedicated soldiers of the cross to march into the world and call men to repentance.

414

*Time's final drama is about to take place.* We are on the verge of the greatest moments of history. God is about to invade, not in the silence of a Bethlehem stable, but in power and great glory. When the Author walks on stage, the play is over. The needle on the clock of Time ticks off the last few seconds to midnight.

Will *you* walk with your hand firm in the hand of God? Will you walk unafraid of the shadows?

*Will you light a dark world — with the torch of*

YOUTH AFLAME?

SO SEND I YOU!

**JUDE** *UNDERSTANDING & VISION*

*NON-CHRISTIAN or*

☐ *Unwillingness to change* ideas or practices.
☐ *Materialistic* spirit — preoccupied with things.
☐ *Over confidence* in the ability of fallen Man.
☐ *Crowd-conscious*, people-pleasing attitude OR
☐ *Callousness* as to the life and happiness of men.
☐ Trend towards living life like a mere *machine* OR
☐ Tendency to surrender *rationality* for *experience*.
☐ *Passivity* of mind, reason, conscience and judgment.
☐ *Double-thinking* and standards in all of life.
☐ Lack of real *purpose* and *meaning* for self and world.
☐ Increasing *despair*, deadness, sense of guilt.

*CHRISTIAN PHILOSOPHY*

☐ *Working philosophy* of life, both rational *and* meaningful.
☐ *Logically consistent* within accepted premises.
☐ *Creative*, full use of faculties of personality in discovery.
☐ *Vitality* of life, with spiritual power and *freshness*
   of thought.
☐ Growing *excitement* in all areas of discovery.
☐ Love of *God* and *man; self-acceptance* and trust.
☐ *Hatred and selfishness*, and active *opposition* to such.
☐ An *eagerness to learn* and *change* with this knowledge.

*NON-CHRISTIAN or*

☐ Life both basically *dishonest* and *selfish*.
☐ Tendency to *reject* any *authority* or obligation.
☐ *Unreasonableness* of thought and action; moral madness.
☐ *Partial* — prefers interests on basis of self-gratification.
☐ Unwillingness to be known in their *true* character.
☐ *Opposition to good*, unless for some self-interest.
☐ Trend towards *injustice* and *cruelty*, open *intemperance*.
☐ Love of *reputation*, self-gratification, power or position.
☐ *Fear* of exposure, criticism, failure and often *life* and death.

*CHRISTIAN EXPERIENCE*

☐ Desire for knowing God's *will* and His *word*.
☐ Difference in *standards* of speech, dress and action.
☐ *Self-discipline* of life for the highest good of all.
☐ *Care* and *concern* for the unfortunate and miserable.
☐ Basic *truthfulness* and *honesty* in *every* area of life.
☐ Serves God *openly* and consistently with gladness.
☐ Opposes *sin* in own life and others despite crowd reproach.
☐ *Patience* under trial, readiness to *forgive* and *help* others.
☐ Treats all according to their *true value* before God.

## IMPURE DATING/SEX LIFE

- ☐ Poor *concentration, apathy* and *dullness* in study.
- ☐ Extreme *shyness*, avoidance of Christian fellowship.
- ☐ Little *self-discipline;* shoddiness of clothes, appearance OR
- ☐ Extreme *finickiness*, exaggerated attention to minor details.
- ☐ *Philosophical bent;* prone to *argue*, especially over Scripture.
- ☐ *Overattention* to opposite sex; public lack of self-control.
- ☐ Emotional *instability; impetuous* and *inconsistent* in decisions.
- ☐ Destructive guilt channelled into *"good deeds," "religious work."*
- ☐ Personality breakdown; increasing *"deadness,"* loss of vitality.

## or PURE

- ☐ Actively *creative;* quick to use new ideas for Christ and man.
- ☐ Deep, consistent *insight* into Scripture; *quick* to grasp truth.
- ☐ Not argumentative in spiritual matters; response to *authority*.
- ☐ *Disciplined, forceful* life; becomes a spiritual *leader* or *inspirer*.
- ☐ Hatred and disgust for all forms of impurity, public and private.
- ☐ Intense *love* for Christ; *freedom* in showing love, affection to others.
- ☐ *Peacefulness* of spirit; channelled and controlled sexual energies.
- ☐ Vibrancy and *aliveness* of life; increasing magnetism of personality.
- ☐ A holy *boldness* for God; readiness to serve and speak for God.

*DIRTY or*

☐ *Abnormal* "spirituality" without real love for God in evidence.

☐ *Overtalkativeness;* quickness to *condemn* other's faults.

☐ Unkemptness *or* perfectionism; carelessness *or* over-concern.

☐ Inability to witness, through some hidden relectance or fear.

☐ Periods of depression *or* wild abandonment; *suicide* tendencies.

☐ Inability to look others clearly in the face; withdrawn personality.

☐ Tendency to *run away* from responsibility or obligation incurred.

☐ Inability to overcome *temptation;* continual yielding to sin.

☐ Loss of *joy,* confidence and faith in God. Doubt, skepticism grows.

*CLEAR CONSCIENCE*

☐ No fear ot meeting others, or talking freely with people.

☐ A *relaxed, joyful* Christianity; no hidden tensions or guilt.

☐ Control of the *speech;* a *readiness to forgive* and help others.

☐ *Concern* for others, and a genuine purpose to witness for God.

☐ *Transparency* of personality; a readiness to share.

☐ Ability to *face up to mistakes* or to sin, and get it right.

☐ Power to *resist* temptation; decreasing failure to obey God.

☐ Freedom of faith and joy; an *overflowing happiness* for others.

☐ Self-*trust* and self-*respect;* a true appreciation of man's possibilities.

*PRIDE or*

☐ Over-emphasis on *dress;* over-concern for *looks, hair-styles,* etc.

☐ *Fear* of meeting others; extreme *self-consciousness* or shyness.

☐ Extremes of *fashion* and customs; *"showing-off"* to draw attention.

☐ Craze for *"spirituality"* that is not relaxed and happy, but driven.

☐ Self-centered *conversation* that is self-*exalting* or self-*condemning.*

☐ Tendency to "name-drop" or to *undervalue* own work or achievement.

☐ Continual *contention* with others; *critical* spirit, *envy,* jealousy.

☐ Frustrated desire to be like someone *else;* internal "civil war."

*HUMILITY*

☐ Willingness to be known and evaluated for wnat you really *are.*

☐ A *self-forgetful* desire to please God and serve others.

☐ Consistent, joyful attention to the will of God *without complaint.*

☐ *Acceptance* of any physical deformity or deficiency that mars.

☐ Deliverance from tendency to blame *God* or *others* for above.

☐ Growing *deadness* to the praise of others, as well as their reproach.

☐ Ability to learn from others you respect without trying to *copy* them.

☐ Freedom from *internal turmoil, envy* or *secret sin;* self-acceptance.

☐ Ability to thank and praise God for your life AS IT IS *now,* minus "masks."

*UNBELIEF or*

☐ *Doubt, uncertainty* and indecision, often with secret *sin*.

☐ *Skepticism* over any light presented to the mind and heart.

☐ *Resistance to truth*, especially where it demands *action*.

☐ Little *honesty*, no real effort to discover God's will or word.

☐ Mind wears "colored glasses," sees only what it *wants* to.

☐ Increasing *intellectual pride; man-centred* philosophy.

☐ Spark of genuine zeal in discovery of truth begins to die out.

☐ Unwillingness to *revise* previous ideas in light of new knowledge.

*FAITH*

☐ A *stable*, dependent faith in God and His Word; *working* life philosophy.

☐ *Openness* to new ideas; an ardent love of truth for its *own* sake.

☐ *Honesty* in facing facts; ability to see *both sides* of an issue.

☐ Increasing desire to *know God* and *make Him known* to others.

☐ A sense of one's own *ignorance;* willingness to *expose it* to learn more.

☐ A mind duly influenced by evidence; to know and *do* the whole truth.

☐ A willingness to *practice* as fast as one *learns; change* belief or practice.

☐ Growing *humility*, increasing *zeal* and growing *Christlikeness*.

## JOHN

### BITTERNESS or FORGIVENESS

☐ *Hardening* features; *deep-set* eyes, tight jaw-line or lips.

☐ Little *concern* shown for others; very *sensitive* and "touchy."

☐ Very *possessive*, and with only a *few* friends; *fear* of losing them.

☐ Avoids meeting new people; resentment shows in little or no *gratitude*.

☐ Excessive *flattering* or *praise* for some; cutting *criticism* for others.

☐ *Grudges* against certain people; bad *friendships*; *stubborn* or sulky attitude.

☐ Unwillingness to *share* or help others; *defends* wrong — "What's wrong with ...?"

☐ *Mood extremes* of ecstacy or depression; thinks about committing *suicide*.

### LOVE, UNITY & FORGIVENESS

☐ True *concern* for others' welfare and happiness; ready *gratitude*.

☐ *Ease* in making new friends; a *happy, outgoing* spirit of welcome.

☐ Readiness to help the poor, the ignorant or the vile; compassion.

☐ *Insights* into the needs and difficulties of others; *creative* wholeness.

☐ Willingness to *obey authority* and *accept responsibility*; faithfulness.

☐ Readiness to *forgive* and *forget*; a spirit free from vindictiveness.

☐ No tendency to blame luck or God for misfortune caused by self.

☐ *Thankfulness* to God; willingness to repay *good* for evil.

**PHILIP**  *SURRENDERED WILL — MEEKNESS*

*UNYIELDED RIGHTS*

☐ Uncontrolled, ungoverned *temper;* fits of anger or rage; cursing.

☐ *Impatience* with others; *irritability;* flare-ups under pressure.

☐ *Family quarrels* and fights; tension and hostility towards others.

☐ Tendency to *murmur* and complain; *dissatisfied spirit;* restlessness.

☐ *Greed;* a miserly, stinting attitude; little willingness to sacrifice.

☐ Intense *worry* over acceptance, accomplishment, possessions or security.

☐ *Unyieldedness* towards God; stubborn attitude; swift to *retaliate* for wrong.

☐ *Physical tension*-ailments, like ulcers, heart-attacks and high blood-pressure.

*or  YIELDED*

☐ A sweet, *controlled temper,* with a *peaceful-spirit* under trial.

☐ Very slow to lose *patience,* even under intense provocation.

☐ *Harmony* with others, especially in family and business circles.

☐ *Forbearance* for others, with sincere seeking of their good.

☐ Dwindling temptation to dwell on, magnify, or speak of our troubles.

☐ Less temptation to *fret* or *resent* it when we are crossed or abused.

☐ Less *anxiety* about life, and growing ability to make light of our trials.

☐ Increasing reluctance to treat anyone as an enemy, or dwell on their faults.

## SIMON THE ZEALOT  *SPIRITUAL HUNGER*

*APATHY*

☐ No real *enjoyment* in devotional privileges of a Christian.

☐ Apathy, dullness, and growing *disinterest* in the *Word of God.*

☐ Loss of interest in both secret and public *prayer;* unconcern for the lost.

☐ Slackening interest in *evangelism, missions* and *spiritual awakening.*

☐ A wakefulness to the *world,* enjoying its music and pleasures.

☐ The dwindling of truly spiritual *conversation* or fellowship.

☐ A *self-indulgent* spirit; loosening standards, moral principles.

☐ No spirit of prayer; prayer only for self-interest exclusively.

☐ Growing *spiritual blindness* and loss of discernment.

*or INTENSITY*

☐ Rich and continual enjoyment in the service and worship of God.

☐ Increasing *deadness* to the world; a singing heart to God in praise.

☐ Spontaneous love and joy; *no formality* in religious experience.

☐ No book is more precious than the Bible, to read and memorize.

☐ The love of conversation that relates to *Christ* and living for Him.

☐ Growing desire to hate the things *God* hates, love the things *He* loves.

☐ A deep interest in the *newly saved,* with care and concern for them.

☐ Increasing harmony of all powers with the will and purpose of God.

☐ A longing for *extended times alone with God* in the secret place.

435

## ISOLATION

☐ A loss of *first love;* growing *shallowness, levity* and hollowness of experience.

☐ Fear to be involved in *personal work* with the sinner met in daily life or work.

☐ Growing addiction to *material comforts;* rationalizing away of responsibility.

☐ Ability to talk to others *about* witnessing without actually *doing* it yourself.

☐ Ability to manage "Christian" and secular activities so they squeeze *out* actual witness.

☐ Ability to *look* involved without actually *being* so; growing fear of challenge or exposure.

☐ Involvement in mechanical details without brokenhearted *prayer* for the lost and damned.

☐ Gradual replacement of *holy boldness* with *professional methods* that do not need God.

## or COMMUNICATION

☐ Genuine love and *concern* for others; a *daily* preparedness to speak for the Lord Jesus.

☐ A growing trust in *God;* a child-like *faith* in His wisdom, direction and power.

☐ An increasing depth of *power in prayer* for the salvation of the lost and heedless.

☐ A daily willingness to live *beyond* human capabilities and wisdom.

☐ A *deliberate involvement* with the stream of sinning humanity to reach them for God.

☐ An openness to being shaken out from comfortable refuges of excuses.

☐ *Abandonment* of every idea, method, programme or activity that relieves your trust in *Him.*

☐ A growing *wisdom* in the winning of souls to God; the mark of the favor of Heaven.

## CROWD-PLEASING

- ☐ *Fear* in witnessing; overconcern for what people may think.
- ☐ Hesitation in taking a stand for Christ; prevalent *fear of man*.
- ☐ Many *close friends* among the *unconverted*, without witness.
- ☐ Readiness to *compromise* Christian standards in a crowd.
- ☐ Unwillingness to sacrifice *reputation* for good of God or man.
- ☐ Increasing tendency to chafe and *complain* under pressure.
- ☐ Greater desire to please *men* than God; unable to reprove sin.

## or *CHRIST-HONORING*.

- ☐ Growing *deadness* to the flattery or censure of men. *Boldness* in witnessing; leadership among Christians.
- ☐ Growing jealousy for the *honor of God* and *purity of* His church.
- ☐ Willingness to put *principles* above *personalities* for Jesus' sake.
- ☐ Ability to firmly and effectively *reprove* sin wherever possible.
- ☐ Growing *calmness* under affliction, disappointment or bereavement.
- ☐ Increasing concern for the *rights* of God and all men.
- ☐ Full-hearted courage to stand for God even under heavy pressure.

*PARODY*

- [ ] *Doubts* about salvation; uncertainty as to really knowing God.
- [ ] *Narrowness* of faith; inability to believe that God can really do a work.
- [ ] Tendency to accuse those who are spiritual of *fleshly* or *satanic* behavior.
- [ ] Reputation among the carnal and impenitent as one of like mind.
- [ ] Sense of *unreality* in spiritual things; cold, dead, *formal* religion.
- [ ] Lack of *power*, fruitfulness and radiance in faith; personality *bondage*.
- [ ] Unconcern for the salvation of sinners and the cleanliness of the church.

*or POWER*

- [ ] *Brokenness* over the state of the church and the lostness of the world.
- [ ] Intense *opposition* by leaders in the church, or ministers that are carnal.
- [ ] Searching *pungency* and *urgency*, practicality and *power* in preaching.
- [ ] Frequent conflicts with *Satan;* intense conflicts with your *own* corruption.
- [ ] Ability to *believe God* for the humanly impossible; faith in miracles.
- [ ] Power to make Jesus *real* and *known* to self and *others;* believability.
- [ ] *Intensity* of *personality;* sense of the *communion,* love and joy of God.

When you find an area of failure, do not attempt to reform your *outer* conduct. Take your sin to God *as you are*, contrast what you *are* to what you know He wants you to *be* and let the Holy Spirit search you deeply. Let godly sorrow do its work. Repent at *once*, and then fully *yield yourself to God* and begin to live in His strength the way He wants you to. You must learn the secret of living the Christian life is *taking the Lord Jesus Christ* by *faith* in *whatever relation you need Him* — as your *wisdom*, your *truth*, your *forgiveness*, your *self-acceptance* or *humility*, your *purity* or *power*, your *righteousness* or *ruler*, your *King*.

```
┌─────────────────────────────────────────┐
│                                           │
│   SELECTED BIBLIOGRAPHY                    │
│                                           │
└─────────────────────────────────────────┘
```

*STRATEGY and STRUCTURE:*

*Master Plan Of Evangelism,* Robert Lyman Coleman, Revell.
*Thirteen Men Who Changed The World,* H.S. Vigeveno, Gospel Light.
*The Normal Christian Church Life,* Watchman Nee, Premium Literature Co., Box 18505, Indianapolis, Indiana.
*Youth's Exciting Possibilities,* LeRoy Dugan, Bethany Fellowship Press.


*JUDE:*

*Escape From Reason,* Francis Shaeffer, IVF Press.
*The God Who Is There,* Francis Shaeffer, IVF Press.
*Death In The City,* Francis Shaeffer, IVF Press.
*Tortured For Christ,* Richard Wurmbrand, Spire, N.Y.
*Honest Religion For Secular Man,* Leslie Newbigin, Westminster.
*Know Why You Believe,* Paul Little, IVF Press.
*It All Depends,* Fritz Ridenhour, Gospel Light.
*The Spiritual Man,* Watchman Nee, Premium Literature Co., Box 18505, Indianapolis, Indiana.
*What's The Difference?* Fritz Ridenhour, Gospel Light.
*Angels Of Light,* Hobart E. Freeman, Logos Intl.
*I Believe In Miracles,* Kathryn Kuhlman, Prentice Hall.
*God Can Do It Again,* Kathryn Kuhlman, Prentice Hall.


*JUDAS:*

*Mere Christianity,* C.S. Lewis, MacMillan.
*The Spiritual Man,* Watchman Nee, Premium Literature Co.
*What Is Man?* T. Austin Sparks, Premium Literature Co.
*The Moral Government Of God,* Gordon C. Olsen, Men For Missions, Chicago, Illinois.
*An Examination Of The Modern Gospel,* Men For Missions, Chicago, Illinois.
*The Origin Of Sin And Its Characteristics,* E.W. Cook, Men For Missions, Chicago, Illinois.

*True And False Conversion*, C.G. Finney, Men For Missions, Box 1297, Chicago, Illinois 60690.
*Systematic Theology*, C.G. Finney, Eerdemans, (Cl.).
*Finney's Lecture On Theology*, Bethany Fellowship Press, (Cl.).
*Life In The Son*, Robert Shank, Men For Missions, Chicago, Illinois, (Cl.).
*If Ye Continue*, Guy Duty, Bethany Fellowship Press, (Cl.).


## BARTHOLOMEW:

*Why Wait Until Marriage?* Evelyn Mills Duval, Assoc. Press.
*Love And The Facts Of Life*, Evelyn Mills Duval, Assoc. Press.
*Letters To Karen*, Philip W. Shedd, Spire, N.Y.
*Letters To Philip*, Philip W. Shedd, Spire, N.Y.
*I Loved A Young Man*, Walter Trobish, IVF.
*I Loved A Young Girl*, Walter Trobish, IVF.
*Sexual Happiness In Marriage*, Herbert J. Miles, Zondervan.
*Balancing Your Marriage*, Henry Brandt, Scripture Press.
*Divorce And Remarriage*, Guy Duty, Bethany Fellowship Press.


## MATTHEW:

*Lectures On Revivals Of Religion*, C.G. Finney, Moody Press.
*Psychocybernetics*, Maxwell Maltz, Zondervan.
*The Power Of Positive Thinking*, Norman Vincent Peale, Prentice Hall.


## JAMES THE LESS:

*Temperament And The Christian Life*, Ole Hallesby, Augsbury Publ.
*A Taste Of New Wine*, Keith Miller, Word Books, (Cl.).
*A Second Touch*, Keith Miller, Word Books, (Cl.).
*The Release Of The Spirit*, Watchman Nee, Premium Literature Co.
*The Christian's Secret Of A Happy Life*, Hannah Whitehall Smith, Spire, Fleming Revell.
*The Hearing Heart*, Hannah Hurnard, Churches' Ministry Among Jews, London.

*The Normal Christian Church Life*, Watchman Nee, Premium Literature Co.
*Missionary Methods — St. Paul's Or Ours?* Roland Allan, Men For Missions.
*Church Growth*, Donald McGavaran, Gospel Publishing House.


## THOMAS:

*Who Says?* Fritz Ridenhour, Gospel Light.
*Man Alive!* Michael Green, IVF Press.
*Who Moved The Stone?* Frank Morrisson, Faber, London.
*Miracles*, C.S. Lewis, MacMillan.
*Realities*, M. Basilea Schlink, Zondervan.
*Countdown*, G.B. Hardy, Moody Press.
*The Conquest Of Inner Space*, Lambert Dolphin, Good News Publ.
*Runaway World*, Michael Green, IVF Press.


## JOHN:

*Parents On Trial*, David Wilkerson, Hawthorn Books.
*How To Win Your Family To Christ*, Nat Olsen, Good News Publishers.
*God's Pattern For The Home*, Good News Publishers.
*Keys To Better Living For Parents*, Henry Brandt, Moody Bible Corres.
*Build A Happy Home With Discipline*, Henry Brandt, Scripture Press.
*The Attributes Of Love*, C.G. Finney, Men For Missions.
*God's Love For A Sinning World*, C.G. Finney, Kruegel Publ.


## PHILIP:

*God's Fool*, George N. Patterson, Faber, London.
*The Cross And The Switchblade*, David Wilkerson, Pyramid Books.
*God's Smuggler*, Brother Andrew, Spire Books.
*How To Win Over Worry*, John Haggai, Zondervan.
*Peace With God*, Billy Graham, Pocket Books.
*Dreams: The Dark Speech Of The Spirit*, Morton T. Kelsey, Doubleday.

## SIMON THE ZEALOT:

*True Discipleship*, Walterick Publ., Box 2216, Kansas City, Kansas.

*The Disciplined Life*, Richard Shelley Taylor, Beacon Hill Press.

*God's Chosen Fast*, Arthur Wallis, C.L.C.

*Three Kinds Of Professing Christians*, C.G. Finney, Men For Missions.

*Prayer, Conversing With God*, Rosalind Rinker, Zondervan.

*A Treasury Of Prayer*, Leonard Ravenhill, Bethany Fellowship.

*Revival Praying*, Leonard Ravenhill, Bethany Fellowship.

*Power Through Prayer*, E.M. Bounds.

*How To Pray*, R.A. Torrey, Moody Press.

*With Christ In The School Of Prayer*, Andrew Murray, Spire.

## ANDREW:

*Include Me Out*, Colin Morris, Epworth Press.

*How To Give Away Your Faith*, Paul Little, IVF Press.

*Tell It Like It Is*, Fritz Ridenhour, Gospel Light.

*What Shall This Man Do?* Watchman Nee, Premium Literature Co.

*The Three M's Of Witnessing*, Gordon C. Olsen, Bible Research Press, Chicago, Illinois.

*Personal Evangelism*, John R.W. Stott, IVF.

## JAMES ZEBEDEE:

*Man — The Dwelling-Place Of God*, A.W. Tozer, Christian Publ. Inc.

*Sanctification*, C.G. Finney, C.L.C.

*Springs In The Valley*, Mrs. Chas. E. Cowman, Zondervan.

*A Plain Account Of Christian Perfection*, John Wesley, Men For Missions.

*Christian Perfection*, Francoise Fenelon, Harper and Rowe.

*The Ultimate Intention*, Sure Foundation, Box 222, Mt. Vernon, Missouri.

*Victory Over Demonism Today*, Dr. Russel Meade, Christian Life Publ., Wheaton.

PETER:

Power From On High, C.G. Finney, C.L.C.
Deeper Experiences Of Famous Christians, G. Gichrist Lawson, Warner Press, (Cl,).
They Found The Secret, V. Raymond Edman, Zondervan.
The Enduement Of Power, Oswald Smith, Marshall, Morgan and Scott, (Cl.).
The Person And Work Of The Holy Spirit, R.A. Torrey, Zondervan.


BIOGRAPHY:

Through Gates Of Splendour, Betty Elliot, Harper and Rowe.
Shadow Of The Almighty, Betty Elliot, Harper and Rowe, (Cl.).
A Man Called Peter, Catherine Marshall, Spire.
The General Next To God, Richard Collier, Dutton, (Cl.).
Billy Graham, John Pollock, McGraw-Hill, (Cl.).
Charles G. Finney — Autobiography, Fleming Revell, (Cl.).
John Wesley, Basil Miller, Bethany Fellowship Press.
Sundar Sing, Cyril J. Davey, Moody Press.
Remarkable Incidents, C.G. Bevington, Newby Book Room, Niles, Michigan, (Cl.).
Portrait Of A Prophet, Clarence W. Hall, Salvation Army Depot, Chicago, Illinois, (Cl.).
David Brainherd, Jonathan Edwards, Moody Press.
Moody, John Pollock, MacMillan, (Cl.).


REVIVAL and REFORMATION:

Revivalism And Social Reform, Timothy L. Smith, Abingdon. (Cl.).
Lectures On Revivals Of Religion, C.G. Finney, Moody Giant, Revell.
In The Day Of Thy Power, Arthur Wallis, C.L.C. (Cl.).
Heart-Cry For Revival, Stephen Olford, Revell, (Cl.).
Why Revival Tarries, Leonard Ravenhill, Bethany Fellowship, (Cl.).

*DEVOTIONAL:*

*Streams In The Desert,* Mrs. Chas. E. Cowman, Zondervan, Michigan.
*John Doe, Disciple,* Peter Marshall, Revell, (Cl.).
*Mr. Jones Meet The Master,* Peter Marshall, Revell, (Cl.).
*My Utmost For His Highest,* Oswald Chambers, Dodd-Mead Co., (Cl.).